DIODORUS SICULUS, BOOKS 11–12.37.1

# DIODORUS SICULUS, BOOKS 11–12.37.1

## Greek History 480–431 B.C.— the Alternative Version

*Translated, with Introduction and Commentary, by Peter Green*

 UNIVERSITY OF TEXAS PRESS, AUSTIN

This book has been supported by an endowment dedicated to classics and the ancient world and funded by the Areté Foundation; the Gladys Krieble Delmas Foundation; the Dougherty Foundation; the James R. Dougherty, Jr. Foundation; the Rachael and Ben Vaughan Foundation; and the National Endowment for the Humanities. The endowment has also benefited from gifts by Mark and Jo Ann Finley, Lucy Shoe Meritt, the late Anne Byrd Nalle, and other individual donors.

First edition, 2006

Requests for permission to reproduce material from this work should be sent to Permissions, University of Texas Press, P.O. Box 7819, Austin, TX 78713-7819. www.utexas.edu/utpress/about/bpermission.html

Library of Congress Cataloging-in-Publication Data

Diodorus, Siculus.
   Diodorus Siculus, books 11–12.37.1 : Greek history 480–431 B.C., the alternative version / Diodorus, Siculus ; translated, with introduction and commentary by Peter Green.
      p.    cm.
   Includes bibliographical references and index.
   ISBN 0-292-70604-9 (hardcover : alk. paper) —
   ISBN 0-292-71277-4 (pbk. : alk. paper)
     1.   Greece—History—Athenian supremacy, 479–431 B.C.
I. Green, Peter, 1924–   II. Title.
   DF227.D56  2006
   938'.04—dc22
                                       2005014976

*To my students of the past four decades,*
*who asked so many of the right questions*

Though writing the lives of our predecessors presents difficulties to those who undertake it, the practice offers no small benefit to society at large; for by frankly delineating noble [and base] actions, it adorns the virtuous and diminishes the base, through the praise and censure appropriate to each. The praise, one might say, is a prize for virtue that costs nothing, while the censure is a punishment for vice that draws no blood. It is good for later generations to be reminded that whatever life a man chooses to live determines the way in which he will be remembered after his death, and thus to avoid the passion for setting up memorials in stone (which exist in one place only, and are liable to the sharp inroads of decay), and rather choose reason, allied with the virtues in general, which reach everywhere through word of mouth. Time, which withers all else, keeps these immortal, and indeed with increasing age renders them younger still. And clearly my words are true of such men, for though they existed long ago, they are recalled by all as though they were alive today.

D.S. IO, FR. I2

Il y a guère de mauvais témoins. Un récit très imparfait peut renfermer des renseignements utiles. . . . Un témoignage ne forme pas un tout indivisible qu'il faille déclarer véridique ou faux. Pour en faire la critique, il convient de la décomposer en ses éléments, qui seront éprouvés, l'un après l'autre.

MARC BLOCH

# CONTENTS

# PREFACE

My acquaintance with Diodorus goes back half a century, and involves a most improbable prophecy. While writing my first published book—an excruciatingly naïve account of my recent travels in Italy and Sicily—I found myself getting interested in that early Sicilian nationalist Ducetius. To find out more about him, I turned to Diodorus, as anyone must who studies the ancient history of Sicily. When my book appeared it was, to my considerable surprise, picked out by Harold Nicolson as the subject of a lead review in the London *Observer*. This, I very soon realized, was in order to let Nicolson play with it, as cat with mouse, and exercise his cultured irony at my expense. Still, column-inches, good or bad, measure publicity—something my publisher was quick to point out—so I couldn't really complain. The acme of damning with faint praise was reached by Nicolson in his final sentence, where, magnanimously, he assured his readers that one day this neophyte author would "write a commentary on Diodorus Siculus that would delight us all." Since I happened to remember—and so, I'm sure, did Nicolson—that Macaulay had described Diodorus as a "stupid, credulous, prosing old ass," I wasn't convinced that this was an unalloyed compliment. But it certainly stuck in my mind. In the fullness of time—and fifty years on can surely be so described— it looks as though Nicolson's improbable forecast may, at long last, be coming true. The commentary, at least, is materializing. How many people it delights will, of course, be quite another matter.

For a great deal of my career as a professional classicist, I—like so many of my colleagues—looked on Diodorus as a mere *pis aller* fallback, only as good as his source of the moment. While there is undoubtedly a certain amount of truth in this popular thumbnail evaluation, it is very far from the whole picture, as I discovered when I began to investigate him more closely, as a necessary preliminary to my projected commentary on Herodotos. What struck me first, and most powerfully, was the violent, contemptuous, and often seemingly near-hysterical academic chorus of dismissal, most pronounced among German, or Germanic-inspired, exponents of *Quellenforschung*. It struck me then, and still does, that any author capable of arousing such a degree of emotional vituperation in scholars has to be something more than a mere slavish copyist or mindless *Dummkopf*. So, indeed, it turned out. Diodorus also happens to be the only surviving continuous narrative source for Greek history between the Greco-Persian Wars and Alexander's Successors (*Diadochoi*): as a result, the academic world could, and did, claim to be faulting him, in effect, for not having adopted the historiographical principles of Thucydides, and for choosing instead to follow the (necessarily inferior) "vulgate tradition."

Again, there is some truth in this. Again, it is not the whole truth. As my research advanced, I began to realize that much of the hysteria was due to the need to preserve traditional rules and principles that enable textual critics or historians to make easy rule-of-thumb generic judgments. Too often for comfort, Diodorus' narrative disagrees with those of Herodotos or Thucydides: if these are *by definition* deemed superior, the awkward business of solving historical problems can be virtually shelved. A "mindless scribbler" (who must also, apparently, be a congenital liar) can be disregarded *whenever* his evidence conflicts with that of a blue-riband early source. This assumption that Diodorus' variants are always wrong must, of course—as I soon saw, and as the hostile tradition was well aware—be balanced against those many occasions on which the *Dummkopf* says what historians want to hear. The solution, in terms of *Quellenforschung*, turned out to be simple: when Diodorus gets anything right, the credit goes to his (conveniently nonsurviving) source, copied more or less verbatim, and, of course, without comprehension. As a recipe for saving historians trouble, this ranks with the cognate notion—also very popular in nineteenth-century Germany—of the uncontaminated manuscript tradition.

Unfortunately (as what follows should make amply clear), Diodorus, properly examined, turns out to be a rational, methodical, if somewhat unimaginative, minor historian, who planned on a large scale, and was quite capable of seeing major faults and inconsistencies provided he lived to correct them. This means that all the historical problems in his text that have for long been side-stepped on the grounds that his evidence is that of a virtual mental defective, and thus can always be disregarded when inconvenient, are back on the table for discussion. I hope I have always been alert to this problem. I first became really aware of it during the first few months of 1999. At the time, I was living in Athens, in a rather dingy Kolonaki apartment. Contrary to popular beliefs concerning the Athens climate, it rained almost every day. Kosovo was in full spate, and almost every Athenian I talked to, including many highly cultivated and cosmopolitan old friends, was rabidly, and often scarily, pro-Serb. (I sometimes got the distinct impression that they felt a little ethnic cleansing might be no bad thing.)

It was against this background that I began to translate Diodorus on the Persian Wars and the Pentekontaetia (Books 11–12.37), and then, as the rains eased off and a bedraggled spring emerged, on the reigns of Philip II and Alexander (Books 16–17). All the time I was acutely conscious, as was inevitable, of those characteristics in the "vulgate tradition" that earned the contempt of civilized scholars: the emphasis on ad hominem (or, even more often, ad feminam) motivation, the taste for scandal in high places, the heated rhetoric, the cynical belief that everyone had his price, that there was no crime or folly to which the ambitious would not stoop, the vigorous moral exhortations. After my day's work I would drop in to a local bar for a drink, where I found Athens television telling, *mutatis mutandis,* exactly the same kind of story with which I had been confronted in my translation.

This fortuitous, but highly instructive, coincidence made me face the fact that much of the rejection of the "vulgate tradition" stemmed directly from the robustly meliorist beliefs of nineteenth-century scholars, convinced that no civilized person, and a fortiori no civilized fifth-century Greek, "could possibly behave like that." Power indeed corrupts—Acton's old saw remains true in ways, and to a degree, that even he may well have never foreseen—and this is something that the historiography of the ancient world must never forget. Corruption can also, as several modern examples vividly demonstrate, have its luridly vulgar side. Those alleged ancient "myths" look uncomfortably plausible today. My judgments on events, during the Pentekontaetia in particular, have always, I hope, borne this in mind.

There are other built-in problems. The study of Greek history in the last couple of centuries has produced more than its share of ultra-conservative authoritarian dogmatists. For such figures Thucydides has always been a quasi-divine inspiration, "whose piercing eye," as Jenny Roberts dryly notes (*Athens on Trial* [Princeton, 1994], p. 296), "is still accorded a reverence long since withdrawn from his fellows." How could it be otherwise? Not a word about women, except the Periklean aside that they should shut up and stay home; a narrative exclusively devoted to warfare and politics; and ballooning abstract generalizations everywhere. Thucydides is the intellectual chauvinist's ideal: no wonder the few radical attacks on him have come mostly from women historians such as Mabel Lang, Jacqueline de Romilly, or Virginia Hunter. But there's also a flip side to this: hero-worship can get oppressive without a few dogs to kick around.

Hence, for ancient historians, the familiar displays of venomous contempt

for lesser luminaries such as Xenophon, Polybios, Quintus Curtius Rufus—
or, as we have seen, Diodorus Siculus. Xenophon, the country squire who
makes Socrates sound like an ordinary mortal, and whose pro-Spartan line
embarrasses Athenocentrics, is damned by historians for not being Thucydides, and by philosophers because he wasn't Plato. Polybios' Greek style is written off as *Kanzleisprache,* bureaucratese. Curtius has been dismissed as an am-
ateur, a "hasty and irresponsible rhetorician" (C. Edson) and, by Ronald Syme,
as "little better than a superior journalist" (Baynham 1998, 5 with refs.). Careful investigation reveals that few of these charges are in fact substantially true.
This raises the question of how far successive scholars have actually read the
authors they castigate, and how far they have simply taken over, unexamined,
the charges leveled by their predecessors. These, of course, are precisely the
charges they level at Diodorus. *Fabula de te narratur.*

Not all historians, particularly in recent years, have treated Diodorus in this
way, though his defenders have always formed a minority. This seems an appropriate point at which to acknowledge, with grateful thanks, the very substantial help I have had from earlier scholars in the process of readjustment
and rehabilitation, above all from the ground-breaking work of Catherine
Rubincam and Kenneth Sacks. Without their invaluable researches and advice, this work could hardly have been begun. To Professor Rubincam and to
John Marincola I am also indebted for a minutely detailed critical scrutiny of
my manuscript. Professor Marincola's own work constantly sharpened my critical judgment in the slippery—and now rapidly changing—field of Greek
historiography, and his generous evaluation of my original manuscript gave
me welcome encouragement when I most needed it.

Almost literally at the eleventh hour, my colleague Craig Gibson brought
to my attention Frances Pownall's remarkable new study *Lessons from the Past:
The Moral Use of History in Fourth-Century Prose* (2004), which confirmed, in
detail, the anti-democratic political agenda latent in moralizing tropes by historians such as Ephoros and Theopompos. Others, both living and dead, to
whom—not always through agreement—I am particularly indebted are:
D. Ambaglio, E. Badian, A. B. Bosworth, K. Brodersen, P. Burde, J. M. Camacho Rojo, F. Cássola, F. Chamoux, K. Clarke, M. Corsaro, R. Drews,
B. Eck, B. Farrington, E. Galvagno, J. Haillet, E. Lévy, R. Neubert, J. Palm,
M. Pavan, G. Perl, A. Pinzone, A. M. Prestianni Giallombardo, W. Spoerri,
C. Vial, and G. Zecchini. The extent of that debt will be apparent through-
out my commentary.

In addition, throughout the difficult gestation of this manuscript, I have
always been able to rely on the robust common sense and shrewd criticism of

my wife Carin, whose expertise in a quite different field of classics enabled her to bring to my findings the sharp insights of what might be described as a cognate outsider. Once again, too, and on this occasion more than usually, I am immensely grateful for the skill, speed, and resourcefulness shown by the staff of the Interlibrary Loan Department in the University of Iowa: Diodorus' trail is marked by a striking number of elusive, mostly early, foreign pamphlets and monographs, all of which—like so many rabbits from the conjuror's proverbial top-hat—they triumphantly produced for me. Bill Nelson, most accommodating of cartographers, produced all eight maps in this book exactly as I envisaged them, for which I find it difficult to thank him enough. Sherry Wert executed the copyediting of a difficult text with her usual thoroughness and good humor, and saved me from more embarrassing slips than I like to think about. Barbara Hird not only took on the making of a complex index at very short notice, but also, lynx-eyed, spotted another round of errors that all the rest of us had missed. Since then my ever-resourceful editor, Carolyn Cates Wylie, and the proofreader, Diane Mankedick, have gleaned a further small crop. While gratefully acknowledging the very great help that all five have given me, I must, of course, insist that any residual mistakes (and there will be some: no ship is wholly waterproof) are my sole responsibility.

My translation is based primarily upon Haillet's (2001) recension for Book 11, and on Vogel's 1890 Teubner text (despite Casevitz's caveats, 1972, xv) for Book 12. I have, however, made regular and eclectic use of Vogel's text and *apparatus criticus* throughout (as well as the text printed by Oldfather [1946], which is, with few but occasionally interesting exceptions, Vogel's); I have also consulted that of Casevitz for Book 12. There are two main families of MSS for Books 11–12: The first is headed by P (Patmiacus 50, tenth-eleventh century), in general the most reliable text, and its apograph S (Scorialis, fifteenth century); the second depends on M (Marcianus gr. 375, tenth century), from which there derives F (Laurentianus 70.12, fifteenth century). On the comparatively few occasions (cf. Haillet 2001, xxxvi) that textual problems occur, or that my readings diverge from those of Haillet and Vogel, the reader will find a note and discussion.

Finally, an apologetic word about the inconsistencies in my spelling of Greek proper names, where in recent years I have been moving steadily away from the old Latinized convention, which strikes me more and more as both inappropriate and not-so-subtly insulting. To be sure, we no longer replace Greek gods by their supposed Roman equivalents in translation (as Henry Cary was still doing as late as 1847 in his version of Herodotos: Jove for Zeus, Minerva for Athena, etc.); but otherwise our spelling still imposes a false Roman norm: terminations in -*um* rather than -*on*, Latin rather than Greek diphthongs (*ae* for *ai, oe* for *oi*), *k* replaced by *c,* and so on. I have done what I can to correct this; but there still remains for me, as for others, an irreducible quota of names to which, in their Latinized forms, we have become so acclimatized that to change them becomes virtually impossible. Thus I write Aeschylus, not Aischylos, Thucydides, not Thoukydides, Corinth, not Korinthos. I have also retained a higher percentage of Romanized forms when dealing with Romanized Sicily than elsewhere. Though there may be some basis for this, I do not flatter myself it is entirely logical. Here I must take refuge (while eschewing the grandiose assertion that follows it) in Walt Whitman's cheerful apophthegm: "Do I contradict myself? Very well then I contradict myself."

# ABBREVIATIONS

BOOKS AND JOURNALS

*AC*          *L'Antiquité classique*
*Act. Hist. Neerland.*   *Acta Historiae Neerlandicae*
*AE*          Ἀρχαιολογικὴ Ἐφημερίς
*AFLPer*      *Annali della Facoltà di lettere e filosofia, Università di Perugia*
*AIIN*        *Annali dell'Istituto Italiano di Numismatica*
*AJA*         *American Journal of Archaeology*
*AJAH*        *American Journal of Ancient History*
*AJPh*        *American Journal of Philology*
*ANRW*        *Aufstieg und Niedergang der römischen Welt*
*APF*         J. K. Davies, *Athenian Propertied Families, 600–300 B.C.* (Oxford, 1971)
*ASNP*        *Annali della Scuola Normale Superiore di Pisa, classe di lettere e filosofia*
*ATL*         B. D. Meritt, H. T. Wade-Gery, and M. F. McGregor, *The Athenian Tribute Lists*, vol. 1 (Cambridge, Mass., 1939), vol. 2 (Princeton, 1949), vol. 3 (Princeton, 1950), vol. 4 (Princeton, 1953)
*Atti Ist. Ven.*   *Atti del reale Istituto Veneto di scienze, lettere ed arti*

*BA*          R. J. A. Talbert, ed., *Barrington Atlas of the Greek and Roman World* (Princeton, 2000)
*BAGB*        *Bulletin de l'Association Guillaume Budé*
*BCH*         *Bulletin de correspondance hellénique*
*BMCR*        *Bryn Mawr Classical Reviews*

*CA*          *Classical Antiquity*
*CAH iv*      *Cambridge Ancient History*, 2d ed., vol. 4, *Persia, Greece and the Western Mediterranean c. 525–479 B.C.*, ed. J. Boardman et al. (Cambridge, 1988)

*CAH* v   *Cambridge Ancient History,* 2d ed., vol. 5, *The Fifth Century B.C.,*
ed. D. M. Lewis et al. (Cambridge, 1992)

*CAH* vi   *Cambridge Ancient History,* 2d ed., vol. 6, *The Fourth Century B.C.,*
ed. D. M. Lewis et al. (Cambridge, 1994)

*CAH* vii.2   *Cambridge Ancient History,* 2d ed., vol. 7, part 2, *The Rise of
Rome to 220 B.C.,* ed. F. W. Walbank et al. (Cambridge, 1989)

*CCC*   *Civiltà classica e cristiana*

*CE*   *Chronique d'Égypte*

*CHJ*   *Cambridge Historical Journal*

*CIL*   *Corpus Inscriptionum Latinorum* (Berlin, 1863–)

*CISA*   *Contributi dell'Istituto di Studia Antica dell'Università del Sacro
Cuore*

*CPh*   *Classical Philology*

*CQ*   *Classical Quarterly*


*DGRG*   *Dictionary of Greek and Roman Geography,* ed. W. Smith, 2 vols.
(London, 1856)

*DKP*   *Der Kleine Pauly,* 5 vols. (Munich, 1975)

*DNP*   *Der Neue Pauly,* 16 vols. (Stuttgart, 1996–2003)


Edelstein-Kidd   L. Edelstein and I. G. Kidd, *Posidonius,* vol. 1, *The Fragments,* 2d ed. (Cambridge, 1989)

*EFG*   *Estudios de filologia Griega*

EMC   Échos du monde classique/Classical News and Views


*FGrH*   F. Jacoby, *Die Fragmente der griechischen Historiker* (Berlin and
Leiden, 1923–)

*FlorIlib*   *Florentia Iliberritana*

fr. adesp.   fragmenta adespota


*G&R*   *Greece & Rome*

*GRByS*   *Greek Roman and Byzantine Studies*


*Hist.*   *Historia*

HMA   G. F. Hill, *Sources for Greek History between the Persian and the
Peloponnesian Wars,* rev. R. Meiggs and A. Andrewes (Oxford,
1951)

*HSCPh*   *Harvard Studies in Classical Philology*

hyp.   hypothesis


*IG*   *Inscriptiones Graecae* (Berlin, 1873–)

*JahrbCP*    *Jahrbücher für classische Philologie*
*JHS*        *Journal of Hellenic Studies*
*JNES*       *Journal of Near Eastern Studies*
*Journ. Field. Arch.*    *Journal of Field Archaeology*
*JRS*        *Journal of Roman Studies*

*Med. Ant.*    *Mediterraneo antico: Economie, società, culture*
*MGR*          *Miscellanea greca e romana*
Meiggs-Lewis    R. Meiggs and D. Lewis, *A Selection of Greek Historical Inscriptions to the End of the Fifth Century B.C.*, rev. ed. (Oxford, 1988)
*MH*           *Museum Helveticum*

*NC*           *Numismatic Chronicle*

*OCD*          *The Oxford Classical Dictionary*, 3d ed., ed. S. Hornblower and A. Spawforth (Oxford, 1996)
Ol.            Olympiad

*PA*           J. Kirchner, *Prosopographia Attica*, 2 vols. (Berlin, 1901–3)
*PAA*          Πρακτικὰ τῆς ἐν Ἀθήναις Ἀρχαιολογικῆς Ἑταιρείας
*PACA*         *Proceedings of the African Classical Association*
Page *SP3*     D. L. Page, *Select Papyri*, vol. 3, *Literary Papyri, Poetry* (London, 1942)
P.Oxy.         *Oxyrhynchus Papyri* (London, 1898–)
*PP*           *La parola del passato*

*QS*           *Quaderni storici*

*RE*           *Real-Encyclopädie d. klassischen Altertumswissenschaft*
*REG*          *Revue des études grecques*
*REL*          *Revue des études latines*
*Rend. Accad. Linc.*    *Rendiconti dell'Accademia nazionale dei Lincei (Classe di Scienze morali, storiche e filologiche)*
*Rend. Ist. Lomb.*    *Rendiconti (Istituto lombardo, Accademia di scienze e lettere, classe di lettere, scienze morali e storiche)*
*RFIC*         *Rivista di filologia e di istruzione classica*
*RhM*          *Rheinisches Museum für Philologie*

S-B            Supplement-Band
schol.         scholion, scholia

SCI          *Scripta Classica Israelica*
SO           *Symbolae Osloenses*

TAPA         *Transactions and Proceedings of the American Philological
             Association*

VDI          *Vestnik drevnei Istorii*

WJbA         *Würzburger Jahrbücher für die Altertumswissenschaft*

YClS         *Yale Classical Studies*

ZPE          *Zeitschrift für Papyrologie und Epigraphik*

## ANCIENT SOURCES

Ael.        Aelian [Claudius Aelianus], freedman, Second Sophistic writer,
            c. 160–c. 235 C.E.
            *VH   Varia historia*
Ael. Arist. Publius Aelius Aristides, Greek man of letters, 117–c. 185 C.E.
            *Panath.   Panathenaic Oration*
Aesch.      Aeschylus of Athens, Greek tragedian, c. 525/4–c. 456/5 B.C.E.
            *Eum.   Eumenides*
            *Pers.   Persians*
Aeschin.    Aeschines, Athenian orator, c. 397–c. 322 B.C.E.
Andoc.      Andocides, Athenian politician, c. 440–c. 390 B.C.E.
App.        Appian[os] of Alexandria, Greek historian, fl. 2d century C.E.
            *BC   Bella civilia*
Arist.      Aristotle of Stagira, Greek philosopher, 384–322 B.C.E.
            *Ath. Pol.   Athenaion politeia*
            *Poet.   Poetics*
            *Pol.   Politics*
            *Rhet.   Rhetoric*
Aristodem.  Aristodemos, Greek historian, ?4th century C.E.
Aristoph.   Aristophanes, Athenian comic playwright, c. 455–386 B.C.E.
            *Eccl.   Ecclesiazusae*
            *Kn.   Knights*
            *Lys.   Lysistrata*
Athen.      Athenaios of Naukratis, Greek essayist, fl. c. 200 C.E.
            *Deipnos.   Deipnosophistai*
Aul. Gell.  Aulus Gellius, Roman essayist, 2d century C.E.

Caes.    G. Iulius Caesar, Roman statesman and historian, 100–44 B.C.E.
         *BG*    *Bellum Gallicum*
Cic.     M. Tullius Cicero, orator and statesman, 106–43 B.C.E.
         *Ad Att.*       *Epistulae ad Atticum*
         *Ad fam.*       *Epistulae ad familiares*
         *De amic.*      *De amicitia*
         *De off.*       *De officiis*
         *Leg.*          *De legibus*
         *Leg. Man.*     *Pro lege Manilia*
         *2 Verr.*       *In Verrem* Actio Secunda
         *Phil.*         *Orationes Philippicae*
         *Rep.*          *De re publica*
         *Sen.*          *De senectute*
         *Tusc. disp.*   *Tusculanae disputationes*
Ctes.    Ctesias of Knidos, Greek doctor and historian at the court of
         Artaxerxes II, late 5th century B.C.E.

Dem.     Demosthenes, Athenian orator and statesman, 384–322 B.C.E.
Dio Cass.   Dio Cassius, Greek senator and historian of Rome, 164–
         c. 230 C.E.
D[iod]. S[ic].   Diodorus Siculus, of Agyrion, universal historian,
         1st century B.C.E.
Diog. Laert.   Diogenes Laertius, Greek biographer, ?3d century C.E.
Dion. Hal.   Dionysios of Halikarnassos, Greek critic and historian, late
         1st century B.C.E.
         *AR*              *Antiquitates Romanae*
         *Ep. ad Pomp.*    *Epistula ad Cn. Pompeium*

Eur.     Euripides, Greek tragedian, c. 485–407/6 B.C.E.
         *Suppl.*    *Suppliant Maidens*
Euseb.   Eusebius of Caesarea, bishop and polymath, c. 260–339 C.E.
         *Chron.*        *Chronica*
         *Praep. Ev.*    *Praeparatio evangelica*

Fast. Cap.    Fasti Consulares Capitolini
Front.   Sextus Iulius Frontinus, consul and governor of Britain, military
         writer, c. 40–103/4 C.E.
         *Strat.*    *Strategemata*

Harpokrat.   Valerius Harpokration, lexicographer, 2d century C.E.
Hdt.     Herodotos of Halikarnassos, Greek historian, c. 485–c. 420 B.C.E.

Hes.      Hesiod[os] of Askra in Boiotia, Greek epic/didactic poet, fl.
          c. 700 B.C.E.
          *WD   Works and Days*
Hesych.   Hesychius of Alexandria, lexicographer, ?5th century C.E.
Hor.      Q. Horatius Flaccus [Horace], Roman poet, 65–8 B.C.E.
          *Serm.   Sermones [Satires]*

Iambl.    Iamblichos, Greek fabulist, late 2d century C.E.
          *Vit. Pyth.   De vita Pythagorica*
Isokr.    Isokrates, Athenian speechwriter and rhetorician, 436–338 B.C.E.

Joseph.   Flavius Iosephus, Jewish historian, 37/8–c. 100 C.E.
          *AJ   Antiquitates Iudaicae*
Just.     Justin [M. Iunanianus Iustinus], Latin epitomator, 2d century
          C.E. or later

*Lex XII Tab.*   Laws of the Twelve Tables
Livy      T. Livius Patauinus, Roman historian, 59 B.C.E.–c. 17 C.E.
Lucian    Lucian [Loukianos] of Samosata, essayist and satirist,
          fl. 2d century C.E.
          *Hist. Conscr.   Quomodo historia conscribenda sit*
          *VH              Vera historia*
Lycurg.   Lycurgus [Lykourgos], Athenian statesman, c. 390–c. 325/4 B.C.E.
          *In Leocr.   In Leocratem*
Lys.      Lysias, Attic orator, ?459/8–c. 380 B.C.E.

Macrob.   Macrobius Ambrosius Theodosius, scholar and essayist,
          5th century C.E.
          *Sat.         Saturnalia*

*Marm. Par.   Marmor Parium (FGrH 239)*

Nep.      Cornelius Nepos, Roman biographer, c. 110–24 B.C.E.
          *Arist.    Aristides*
          *Cim.      Cimon*
          *Paus.     Pausanias*
          *Them.     Themistokles*
          *Timoth.   Timotheus*

Paus.     Pausanias of Magnesia-ad-Sipylum, travel-writer, fl. c. 150 C.E.
Philostr. L. Flavius Philostratos, Second Sophistic man of letters, 2d–
          3d century C.E.
          *VA   Vita Apollonii*

Phot.  Photios, Byzantine scholar and Patriarch of Constantinople,
c. 810–c. 893 C.E.
*Bibl.  Bibliotheca*
Pind.  Pindar[os] of Boiotia, Greek lyric poet, 518–?437 B.C.E.
*Ol.  Olympic Odes*
*Pyth.  Pythian Odes*
Plat.  Plato of Athens, philosopher, c. 429–347 B.C.E.
*Alcib. I  Alcibiades I*
*Gorg.  Gorgias*
*Menex.  Menexenos*
*Protag.  Protagoras*
*Rep.  Republic*
*Symp.  Symposium*
Pliny  Gaius Plinius Secundus [Pliny the Elder], polymath, 23/4–
79 C.E.
*NH  Natural History*
Plut.  Plutarch [Mestrios Ploutarchos] of Chaironeia, Greek biographer
and essayist, c. 50–c. 120 C.E.

| *Arist.* | *Aristides* |
|---|---|
| *Art.* | *Artoxerxes* |
| *Cim.* | *Cimon* |
| *De malign. Herod.* | *De malignitate Herodoti* |
| *Eum.* | *Eumenes* |
| *Mor.* | *Moralia* |
| *Nic.* | *Nicias* |
| *Pelop.* | *Pelopidas* |
| *Per.* | *Perikles* |
| *Pomp.* | *Pompeius* |
| *Sol.* | *Solon* |
| *Them.* | *Themistokles* |
| *Thes.* | *Theseus* |

Polyaen.  Polyaenus, Macedonian military writer, 2d century C.E.
Polyb.  Polybios, Greek historian, c. 200–c. 118 B.C.E.
Ps.-Xen.  Pseudo-Xenophon, anonymous pamphleteer popularly known as
the "Old Oligarch," 5th century B.C.E.

*Res Gest.  Res gestae divi Augusti*

Sall.  C. Sallustius Crispus, Roman historian, 86–34 B.C.E.
*Jug.  Iugurtha ( Jugurthine War)*
Steph. Byz.  Stephanos of Byzantion, Greek grammarian, 6th century C.E.

Stob.    Joannes Stobaios [John of Stobi], Greek anthologist, early
         5th century C.E.
Strab.   Strabo of Amaseia, Greek geographer, c. 64 B.C.E.–c. 20 C.E.
Suet.    Suetonius [C. Suetonius Tranquillus], Roman biographer and
         chief secretary to Hadrian, ?69–140 C.E.
         *Div. Iul.   Divus Iulius*

Tertull. Tertullian [Q. Septimius Florens Tertullianus], Latin churchman,
         c. 160–c. 240 C.E.
         *De anim.   De testimonio animae*
Theopomp.   Theopompos of Chios, Greek historian, 378/7–c. 310 B.C.E.
Thuc.    Thucydides son of Oloros, Athenian historian, c. 460–c. 403
         B.C.E.

Val. Max.   Valerius Maximus, Roman writer, 1st century C.E.
Varro    M. Terentius Varro, Roman scholar and antiquarian, 116–27
         B.C.E.
         *LL   De lingua Latina*
         *RR   De re rustica*
*Vit. Anon. Thuc.*   Anonymous *Life* of Thucydides
Vitruv.  Vitruvius Pollio, Augustine-era writer on architecture

Xen.     Xenophon s.o. Gryllos, Athenian general and writer, c. 430–
         c. 355 B.C.E.
         *Anab.      Anabasis*
         *Ath. Pol.  Athenaion politeia*
         *Cyr.       Cyropaedia*
         *Hell.      Hellenika*
         *Mem.       Memorabilia*

Zenob.   Zenobios, Greek Sophist, 2d century C.E.

DIODORUS SICULUS, BOOKS 11–12.37.1

# INTRODUCTION

Diodorus Siculus is known to few people today apart from ancient historians, and even they, for the most part, consult his text rather than read it. This may explain why the one fact virtually all classicists think they know about him—that he is a mere slavish copyist only as good as his source—has remained for so long unchallenged dogma. There can be few ancient authors who have elicited such scorn and opprobrium from the academic world. Wilamowitz dismissed Diodorus as a "miserable scribbler." Schwartz, in his article for Pauly-Wissowa, called the *Bibliotheke* a mere compilation, adding that "one could not describe his book as a work." For Wilhelm Soltau, Diodorus was "a man who inspires little confidence, a flat and foolish pen-pusher." A. D. Nock termed the introductory proem to the whole work, where Diodorus lays out his historiographical aims in detail, the work of "a small man with pretensions." Even today, a large majority of scholars concurs in finding this hapless author mechanically dependent on his sources (see, e.g., Jane Hornblower's 1981 monograph on Hieronymus of Cardia, and Bizière's 1975 edition of Book 19). An extreme example of this *de haut en bas* treatment of Diodorus as a copyist stupid to the point of mindlessness, dependent on one source at a time, never reading an available great original when an inferior derivative was to hand, is provided by Stylianou's recent (1998) commentary on Book 15. Here the object of his research is pilloried as "a mere epitomizer and an incompetent one at that," guilty of "empty and inept rhetoric," "slipshod methods," "incompetence, lack of care, and ignorance," endless muddles and blunders. A very English variant is that of Tarn, who observes, with supercilious disdain, "He was not a competent historian, but that he naturally did not recognize; he is rather stupid, but honestly in earnest; he writes what he *thinks* is history." [1]

---

[1] Wilamowitz: cited *per litt.* by the Egyptologist Heinrich Schäfer, *Von ägyptischer Kunst,* 3d ed. (Leipzig, 1930), 350–351: "V. Wilamowitz mir schrieb, '. . . er . . . überhaupt ein so miserabler Skribent ist.'" Schwartz 1903, col. 663: "D.'s Compilation—ein Werk

This is the ancient author who provides us with our only surviving connected narrative of events from the Persian Wars to Alexander's Successors, without whom our knowledge of ancient Sicilian history would be virtually nonexistent, and whose chronological system is mainly responsible for the solidity of the Athenian archon list. The contrast is piquant and revealing. An unprejudiced examination of Diodorus in fact tells us a good deal, not only about ancient history and historiography, but also about the habits and assumptions of modern historians.

### DIODORUS SICULUS: LIFE AND BACKGROUND

Who was Diodorus Siculus, and what did he think he was trying to accomplish? As so often in antiquity, virtually everything we know about this enigmatic universal historian derives from statements in his own work.[2] There are only two *external* references to Diodorus that I know of, and both raise more problems than they solve. First we have St. Jerome, who in his version of Eusebius' *Chronicle,* for the year 49 B.C.E., states that "Diodorus Siculus, the Greek historian, is [now] regarded as famous."[3] The other, equally brief, reference is in the *Suda,*[4] where we read that this Diodorus "lived in the time of Augustus Caesar and earlier"—which may well explain the surprisingly common assumption that Diodorus was an Augustan writer. In fact, as we shall see, his career took place entirely in the later years of the Republic, more particularly during the Second Triumvirate, and there are good reasons to suppose that he may well have been dead before, or very soon after, Octavian's victory at Actium in 31/0 B.C.E. This would appear to support Jerome's date of 49 as either his ἀκμή or the time of his first (partial, unrevised, and possibly pirated) publication; but there are serious problems here, too. Best, then, to start with what the *Bibliotheke* itself has to tell us.

---

kann man das Buch nicht nennen . . ."; Soltau 1889, 368, "Zwar ein wenig vertrauenerweckender Mann, ein schaler thörichter Scribent . . ."; A. D. Nock, *JRS* 49 (1959): 5 (= Nock, *Essays on Religion and the Ancient World* [Oxford, 1972], vol. 2, 860); Hornblower 1981, 28; Bizière 1975, ix; Stylianou 1998, 49, 139, 15, 137, 136, 138 (see also his review of Sacks, in *BMCR* 02.06.19); Tarn 1948, 2:63.

[2] Anti-Diodoran skeptics have taken this as sufficient reason not to believe any of them, apparently on the grounds that if he really was the *Dummkopf* they paint him to be, he must by definition also have been a chronic liar, an assertion the logic of which eludes me.

[3] See R. Helm, *Eusebius Werke: Siebenter Band: Die Chronik des Hieronymus,* 2d ed. (Berlin, 1956), 1:155: "Diodorus Siculus Graecae scriptor historiae clarus habetur."

[4] No. Δ 1152 Adler s.v. Διόδωρος: γέγονε δὲ ἐπὶ τῶν χρόνων Αὐγούστου Καίσαρος καὶ ἐπάνω. The Augustan assumption is encouraged by Sacks' odd belief (1990, 164) that here ἐπάνω, "earlier," means its opposite, "later," thus compounding the error.

Diodorus was born about 90 B.C.E., a native (1.4.4) of Agyrion, the modern Agíra, a hilltop town about midway between Enna and Centuripe.[5] Though patriotic enough to promote his birthplace by frequent allusions, he does not seem to have used it as part of his title as a historian: posterity knew him as *Siculus,* not as Ἀγυριναῖος or *Agyrinensis.* Indeed, he himself (apart from a miraculous medieval altar) was to be Agyrion's main claim to fame: a few years ago the town council erected a public statue of him, and in 1984 a Diodoran conference was held there.[6] It is possible (though by no means certain), as we shall see, that after a life spent mostly abroad—first traveling, then in Alexandria, and latterly in Rome—he returned to Agyrion and died there. One of the very few surviving inscriptions from the town is a grave-marker for "Diodoros son of Apollonios."[7] Coincidence? Probably: the name was all too common (it was, for example, also that of an immigrant gentleman from Melita [Malta] domiciled in Lilybaion[8]). It remains a striking coincidence nevertheless.

What does this elusive figure reveal about his personality? Rather more, in fact, than can be gleaned by checking the available indexes to his work—which tend to concentrate on public facts and conventional historical concepts—as opposed to actually reading him. It would be surprising, in a work on this scale, if something of the author's character did not emerge.[9] Conventionally religious, regarding history as primarily an instrument for moral improvement,[10] and fond of noting, in his moralistic way, how divine vengeance catches up with the impious, he is also fascinated by the oddities of myth, and criticizes historians for ignoring them. While his ostensible reason is the number of improving moral exempla they reveal, he gives the unmistakable impression (4.1.1–4) of relishing them for their own sake. Like John Aubrey or Sir Thomas Browne, he is an inveterate collector of exotic tidbits. He has a truly Herodotean taste for marvels (θαύματα, θαυμάσια): this of course does not stop him criticizing Herodotos for inaccuracy and over-

---

[5] On Diodorus' birthdate: Chamoux et al. 1993, viii with n. 3; Spoerri 1991, 317. For other references to his hometown (far more frequent than so insignificant a place would normally merit in a universal history), see 4.24, 80; 14.9, 78, 95–96; 16.82–83; 22.2, 3, 13.1. Cf. Chamoux et al. 1993, vii–ix; Oldfather 1946, vii–xi.

[6] See the proceedings, edited by E. Galvagno and C. Molé Ventura (1991).

[7] *IG* xiv 588, cited by Oldfather 1946, vii; Sacks 1990, 161–162 with n. 4; cf. Vidal-Naquet 1991, xii.

[8] Scramuzza 1937, 341–342 with n. 5.

[9] To make a not wholly inappropriate modern comparison, the ten volumes of Arnold Toynbee's *A Study of History* leave us perhaps rather more aware of Toynbee's idiosyncratic personality than we might have wished.

[10] Endlessly asserted: see, e.g., 1.1.2–5, 1.2.4–7, 4.1.2–3, 11.3.1–5, 18.59.5–6, etc.

credulity.[11] His digressions, too, are Herodotean, covering an astonishingly wide range of topics: the utopias of Iamboulos and Euhemeros, lawgivers such as Charondas or Zaleukos (discussed in the present volume), Akragantine luxury, Iphikrates' military inventions, the glories of Persepolis, Alexander's funeral bier, Indian suttee, the flooding of Rhodes, the myth of Lamia, and Dead Sea asphalt, to name but a few.[12] They constitute some of the most enjoyable and vivid episodes in his massive text.

Diodorus also reveals an all-pervasive and rather sour mistrust and dislike of women: as Casevitz says, his work "émane comme une défiance envers tout le sexe féminin."[13] Second marriages, he remarks, are cause for astonishment: better to trust yourself twice to the cruel sea than to a woman. He also gives, in great detail, accounts of two cases (studiously avoided by most modern scholars[14]) where in seeming women, after years of cohabitation, male sexual organs, painfully but triumphantly, finally burst forth.

His excuse for such anecdotes, richly replete with medical detail, is, he tells us, a desire to free the superstitious from regarding such phenomena as bad omens.[15] Here and elsewhere he shows a kind of simple Euhemerizing rationalism; he also inherited a highly Hellenistic concern with Tyche (Τύχη, fortune, Fate) as the dominant universal force (see, e.g., 17.38.5, 18.59.5–6).

The earliest date Diodorus offers us for his own activities is the 180th Olympiad, i.e., 60/59–57/6 B.C.E., during which, he says, he began his period of residence in Egypt.[16] Elsewhere (1.83.8–9) he describes, as an eyewitness, a scene in which a member of a Roman mission to Egypt accidentally killed a cat and, despite the general fear of Rome, was summarily lynched. This incident, he specifies, took place *before* Ptolemy XII Auletes was recognized as a "friend" by Rome. Now the recognition in question was achieved by the combined efforts of Caesar and Pompey in 59,[17] and the huge sum, 6,000 talents,

---

[11] Defense of θαυμάσια: 3.30.4; criticism of Herodotos: 1.37.4, 1.69.7, cf. 10.24.1; criticism of Timaios on similar grounds: 13.90.6–7.

[12] Utopias: 2.55ff., 6.1.1–10; Charondas: 12.11.2–19; Zaleukos: 12.20–21; Akragantine luxury: 13.81.3–84.6; Iphikrates: 15.44.1–4; Persepolis: 17.71.3–8; Alexander's funeral: 18.26.3–28.2; suttee: 19.34.1–6; the Rhodian flood: 19.45.1–8; Lamia: 20.41.3–6; Dead Sea asphalt: 19.98–99.

[13] Casevitz 1985, 123: an exhaustive and well-documented study.

[14] For a rare exception, see R. Garland, *The Eye of the Beholder: Deformity and Disability in the Graeco-Roman World* (Ithaca, N.Y., 1995), 130–132.

[15] Second marriages: 12.14.2; sex changes in women: 32.10.2–8, 11.1–4, 12.

[16] 1.44.1: τῆς ἑκατοστῆς καὶ ὀγδοηκοστῆς Ὀλυμπιάδος, καθ' ἣν ἡμεῖς μὲν παρεβάλομεν εἰς Αἴγυπτον.

[17] Suet. *Div. Iul.* 54.3.

they demanded in return would certainly have called for a mission to Alexandria, if only to ensure collection.[18] We can thus securely date Diodorus' arrival in Egypt to 60 B.C.E., and draw the almost certain conclusion that his residence in Alexandria was connected with the research on which he was engaged in preparation for the writing of his *Bibliotheke*.

There is one further controlling date for this Alexandrian period. Diodorus places the Macedonian conquest of Egypt in 331.[19] He also states unequivocally in Book 1 (1.44.4) that the latest dynasty, that of the Ptolemies, had then lasted for 276 years,[20] which gives us a date, *at the time of writing*, of 55 B.C.E. Diodorus was then clearly still in Egypt. Exactly how long he remained there—primarily in Alexandria, of which he shows eyewitness knowledge[21]—after 55 we cannot be certain. What we *do* know is that his arrival in Rome took place before 45, since he observed the Rostra outside the Senate House, and it was in 45 that Caesar had these removed.[22] There was a permanent Sicilian community in residence: whether he attached himself to it we do not know, but his solitary habits and distaste for rhetoricians make this unlikely.[23] He also tells us that he lived in Rome for a considerable time, mainly, he says, because he had easy access there to the abundant sources available,[24] in library or record office. He had what he describes as πολλὴ ἐμπειρία, "considerable experience," of the Latin language (1.4.4). It tends to be assumed that he spent the rest of his life in Rome, but this was not necessarily the case: when describing his business there, he uses the aorist (ἐχρησάμεθα, παρέσχετο) rather than the perfect, which would suggest past activities no longer continued.

[18] Cf. Oldfather 1946, viii. Not that Ptolemy got much beyond Rome's recognition in return for his outlay: in a year or so, after efforts at recouping his expenses by extortionate taxation, he was driven into exile by the Alexandrians (Dio Cass. 39.12.1–2, cf. Green 1993, 649–651) and had to pay a further 10,000 talents to get himself reinstated, forcibly, by Aulus Gabinius.

[19] 1.49.1: "When Aristophanes was archon in Athens," i.e., between July 331 and June 330. Other events date Alexander's arrival to the first half of this archontic year.

[20] ἐσχάτους δὲ Μακεδόνας ἄρξαι καὶ τοὺς ἀπὸ Μακεδόνων ἐξ ἔτη πρὸς τοῖς διακοσίοις καὶ ἑβδομήκοντα.

[21] 1.45.7 ad fin., 1.46.1–6 passim, 1.84.8–93, 1.95.6, 3.11.3.

[22] 12.26.1; cf. Casevitz 1972, xi n. 1; Rubincam 1987, 326–327.

[23] Cic. Ad Att. 2.1.15; cf. Scramuzza 1937, 342.

[24] 1.4.2–3, where he speaks of τῇ ἐν Ῥώμῃ χορηγίᾳ τῶν πρὸς τὴν ὑποκειμένην ὑπόθεσιν ἀνηκόντων, and explains that it is ταύτης τῆς πόλεως ὑπεροχή, Rome's supremacy, which ἑτοιμοτάτας καὶ πλείστας ἡμῶν ἀφορμὰς παρέσχετο παρεπιδημήσασιν ἐν αὐτῇ πλείω χρόνον.

The latest historical event to which he refers is the expropriation by Octavian of the Greek inhabitants of Tauromenion (modern Taormina) and their replacement by a Roman *colonia* (16.7.1). This event can be dated to 36 B.C.E.[25] Further, in his discussion of the various foreign rulers of Egypt, Diodorus stresses, as we have seen, that the "last of all" (ἐσχάτους) were the Macedonians. It is inconceivable that he could have written this had he been winding up his work later than 31/0, when, as the result of Actium, Antony and Cleopatra committed suicide and Octavian acquired Egypt, with all its remaining riches, as a Roman province.[26] This gives us a *terminus ante quem* of 35–31 B.C.E.

It also provides us with some very suggestive background material. Diodorus had grown up during Verres' notorious administration of Sicily (73–71), when heavy taxation and extortion played havoc with the economy of Agyrion. We know of various landowners who fled to Rome to seek redress from Verres' depredations: estates were ruined, personal property annexed.[27] Caesar, shortly before his death, gave Sicily at least the Latin franchise; Antony afterward (falsely, according to Cicero) claimed that Caesar's offer had been one of full Roman citizenship, and proceeded to push legislation through to this effect.[28] Though Octavian (again according to Cicero) rescinded all of Antony's enactments that same year (44), he almost certainly had to readmit them in 43 to secure Antony's then much-needed support. It was not until 36 that he gained full control over the island.[29] He then took vengeance on Tauromenion and other Sicilian cities for backing the popular Sextus Pompeius. He slapped an indemnity of 1,600 talents on the Sicilians, and took over large estates wholesale for himself and his supporters. The island lost its citizen rights (briefly held, and through the vicissitudes of civil war never fully implemented), and once more became subject to heavy taxation.[30] It also suffered worse depredations than even Verres had ever inflicted, including whole-

---

[25] App. *BC* 5.109ff.; cf. Oldfather 1946, ix–x; Scramuzza 1937, 345; Rubincam 1987, 327; Sacks 1990, 168 with n. 41.

[26] The substantial nature of Egypt's surviving treasures, despite continuous Ptolemaic depredations, can be judged by the fact that when Octavian's seizure of them became known, interest rates in Rome dropped from 12% to 4%. Green 1993, 673–674, 681–682.

[27] Cic. 2 *Verr.* 2.91–100; 3.18; 4.38–41, 80, 89.

[28] Diodorus treats the extension of Roman citizenship to Sicilians as an accepted fact, in contexts that suggest 44 as the date: 13.35.3, 16.70.6.

[29] Caesar's offer: Cic. *Ad Att.* 14.12.1 (22 April 44), cf. *Phil.* 13.5, 12.12; Scramuzza 1937, 343. Diodorus twice (13.35.3, 16.70.6) refers to Sicilian citizenship. Books 13 and 16 were in all likelihood drafted between 44 and 36.

[30] Cic. 2 *Verr.* 3.27.67 (Verres' depredations); Sacks 1990, 192–193, with refs. there cited.

sale confiscations and the forcible mass relocation of inhabitants.[31] Cities such as Tyndaris and Mylae, which had formed the center of Sextus' resistance, were turned over to Roman colonists.[32]

Agyrion lay at the very heart of the area that Octavian devastated. We have to ask ourselves whether, soon after 36, Diodorus may not have been, at the very least, among those many who lost their property—often, indeed, their lives—to Octavian's veterans and other colonists.[33] There are certainly more than adequate reasons here for him to be (as he shows himself in the *Bibliotheke*) admiring of Caesar, cool toward Octavian, less than sympathetic to contemporary Roman colonial practices, and a constant advocate[34] of humanity (φιλανθρωπία) and moderation (ἐπιείκεια) in the treatment of subordinate peoples by the powerful. There is also a very real possibility, as we shall see, based on the state of the work as we have it, that Diodorus died before his projected revisions to the *Bibliotheke* were complete.[35]

## THE *BIBLIOTHEKE* I: COMPOSITION, ANTECEDENTS, INFLUENCES

Diodorus claims (1.4.1) to have spent thirty years in all on his task, including travel in Europe and Asia for purposes of autopsy, since, as he says, it is not only run-of-the-mill historical writers who have fallen into error through ignorance of topography, but even some regarded as first-rate.[36] We have seen

---

[31] Dio Cass. 48.48.6, 49.11.5.

[32] *CIL* 10.7474–7476, 7478, 7480; Pliny *NH* 3.90; Dio Cass. 49.1–7.

[33] Hor. *Serm.* 2.6.55–56; *Res Gest.* 5.35; cf. Scramuzza 1937, 346.

[34] Sacks 1990, 79ff.

[35] Cf. Büdinger 1895, 182. Diodorus himself, ironically (1.3.2), noted this fate in other would-be historians, including his predecessor, and one of his main sources for the historical period, Ephoros (16.14.3).

The schema here presented is, of course, based very largely on what Diodorus tells us himself; and it is only fair to point out that almost every statement he makes concerning his life and the writing of his *Universal History* has been challenged by reputable scholars. Nevertheless, there is a strong likelihood that the general outline sketched above is at least approximately correct.

[36] 1.4.2: πολλὰ γὰρ παρὰ τὰς ἀγνοίας τῶν τόπων διήμαρτον οὐχ οἱ τυχόντες τῶν συγγραφέων, ἀλλά τινες καὶ τῶν τῇ δόξῃ πεπρωτευκότων. The truth of his claims has been challenged, mainly on the flimsy grounds that "almost every item . . . is a conventional proem topos," but also with the highly subjective assertion that "there is no evidence for first-hand knowledge of any country except Egypt" (Hornblower 1981, 25). If by ἐπήλθομεν πολλὴν τῆς Ἀσίας καὶ τῆς Εὐρώπης he means, primarily, Asia *Minor* and Italy, there is nothing especially incredible about the claim. Egypt he does not even mention in this context. The worst he seems guilty of here is putting a favorable spin on his real travels for

that he reached Alexandria in 60. It seems highly probable that his travel for research purposes came before then. If we allow five years for such travels, we have an overall period for the production of the *Bibliotheke* between the 60s and the 30s B.C.E., which would fit his own thirty-year estimate exactly.[37] Rubincam, followed by Sacks,[38] draws on the method of Dio Cassius (cf. Dio 72.23.5) to posit a working plan for Diodorus that involved his spending about half that period, say from 60 to 46, on research and planning, and only then beginning to write his final version. The main advantage of this theory, of course, is that references in the early books to Caesar's Gallic campaigns (e.g., at 3.38.2, 5.21.2, and 5.22.1) would all then be part of the original text rather than later insertions.

Against this we must set the very real possibility that when he was engaged on Books 1–6, the mythological and ethnographic section of his work, Diodorus may well still not have had a clear picture of the final shape of the *Bibliotheke's* historical narrative. It is also very possible that at least part of the first section was published in advance of the rest. Book 1 is entirely devoted to the myths, religious and social customs, and Pharaonic king-lists of Egypt. If we take Jerome's claim that by 49 Diodorus *clarus habetur* to mean that this was when he actually became well known as a historian (rather than the date being merely a mechanical calculation of his *floruit* at the age of forty), then it is tempting to identify the source of his fame as this survey of Egypt, in all likelihood completed by then. It is even possible that by 49 B.C.E. he had finished drafts of Books 2 and 3 as well, covering the mythical traditions of the rest of the non-Greek East: Assyria, India, Skythia, Arabia, Ethiopia, the African Amazons, Atlantis, and, for good measure, the earliest divine cosmogonies. As has long been recognized, these three books form a natural unit, with common themes and a non-annalistic structure. Further, the material they contained would be more readily available in the archives of the Alexandrian library than in any comparable Roman collection.

In his general proem (1.4.6), written last of all, Diodorus stresses that at this point, even though the *Bibliotheke* had been completed, it had not been fully revised, let alone published (a claim well supported by passages in Books 11–20 that have the air of a first draft, or even of working notes, rather than of a final text). Elsewhere, however (40.8), he complains that certain books (un-

---

the purpose of promoting his work. Professor Rubincam reminds me (*per litt.*) "that, given the conditions of ancient travel, it is highly likely that even a journey from Italy to Egypt might have involved passing through, and spending some time in, other places."

[37] Burton 1972, 43–44; Oldfather 1946, x–xi; Rubincam 1987, 324.

[38] Rubincam 1987, 324–326; Sacks 1990, 171–172; and, most recently, Eck 2003, ix–x.

specified) had, before he had corrected and revised them· to his satisfaction, been pirated and put into circulation—a practice against which he also inveighs, in general terms, in the proem (1.5.2). If Jerome is right in making 49 B.C.E. the date of his first prominence, then it would seem highly probable that what first gained him renown—even if in a way not of his choosing—was the pirated version of Book 1 (or, just possibly, of Books 1–3), which he would have lost no time in claiming as his own.[39] It is also reasonably certain that he would, in the traditional manner, give public readings of his books as he completed them, as well as circulate them among his friends for comment and criticism. During this process—which would have helped to build Diodorus' reputation in advance of the *Bibliotheke*'s more formal and final publication—corrections and insertions (including those to Caesar's campaigns) would naturally have been made.

The *Bibliotheke,* or "Library," sometimes referred to as the "Historical Library"[40]—a title that, it has often been remarked, suggests an appropriate modesty on its author's part as regards the originality of his contribution to learning[41]—was nevertheless conceived on a vast and ambitious scale. In forty (perhaps originally forty-two)[42] books, Diodorus aimed, as he tells us himself,[43] to deal with "events and legends prior to the Trojan War" (Books 1–6), "worldwide events (κοινὰς πράξεις) from the Trojan War until the death of Alexander" (Books 7–17), and subsequent narrative history down to the eve of "the war between Rome and the Celts," that is, Caesar's Gallic campaigns

---

[39] 1.4.6: ἡ μὲν ὑπόθεσις ἔχει τέλος, αἱ βίβλοι δὲ μέχρι τοῦ νῦν ἀνέκδοτοι τυγχάνουσιν οὖσαι. The possibility that Books 2–3 were issued, or pirated, early is supported by Diodorus' reference to Julius Caesar at 3.38.3–4 *without* mentioning his apotheosis, which he is careful to do in all subsequent references (e.g., 4.19.2, 5.21.2, 6.25.4, 32.27.1–3).

[40] Plin. *NH* praef. 25, talking about the fashion for fancy titles, tells us that "apud Graecos desiit nugari Diodorus et †βιβλιοθήκης† historiam suam inscripsit." (The genitive looks, as Hornblower [1981, 24 n. 24] says, nonsensical, and suggests "a curious misunderstanding" even in antiquity. But see Chamoux et al. 1993, cxxiv n. 131, for a possible syntactical justification.) The more explicit Βιβλιοθήκη Ἱστορική was probably a later elaboration: Hornblower 1981, 24 n. 24. Cf. H. Stephanus in Wesseling and Eyring 1793–1807, vi–vii.

[41] See, e.g., Farrington 1936, 5; Hornblower 1981, 24; Vidal-Naquet 1991, 2; Chamoux et al. 1993, xx–xxi. Sacks (1990, 77 with n. 107) suggests that Diodorus may have been recalling the great Alexandrian library (where he must have worked) and its literary-bibliographic tradition of the *pinax*, the *catalogue raisonné* of books on a unified topic, with an analytical description of the contents of each.

[42] Rubincam 1998b; and see Appendix A. Diodorus' originally designated terminal date was 46/5 rather than 60/59.

[43] 1.4.6–7, cf. Chamoux 1990, 244–245.

(Books 18–40). For the first six books, dealing with events prior to the Trojan War (1.5.1), he cannot, he says, date with accuracy (οὐ διοριζόμεθα βεβαίως), since he had no reliable chronological table from which to work.[44] But thereafter he correlates his narrative sequence annually with (a) the Athenian eponymous archons, (b) the quadrennial Olympic festivals (complete with a list of victors in the στάδιον, the 200-yard foot-race), and (c) the consular Fasti at Rome. His main guide here, he tells us, was Apollodoros of Athens (c. 180–c. 110 B.C.E.), whose *Chronicle* (Χρονικά), composed in iambic trimeters for ease of memorization (εὐμνημόνευτον), covered the period from 1184/3 to 110/9.[45]

Diodorus' chronological system borrows its "all-encompassing temporal framework"[46] of Olympiads and, within the Olympiads, of Athenian archon-years from Timaios (below, p. 18), and the conscious practice of interwoven synchronicities from Polybios (below, p. 21).[47] From the very start of the present volume (11.1.2), we are never allowed to forget the wider scene. Xerxes launches his expedition against Greece in the year "when Kalliades was archon in Athens," when "the Romans elected Spurius Cassius and Proculus Verginius Tricostus consuls," and when "the 75th Olympiad, in which Astylos of Syracuse won the *stadion,* was celebrated at Elis." Diodorus is well aware (20.43.7) of the problems—frequently stressed by modern historians—involved in the process of interweaving (συμπλοκή), with several simultaneous accounts in different regions being broken up year by year:

Here one might well criticize the practice of history, seeing that in life many various actions take place during the same period, but those who re-

---

[44] It was not that they did not exist: the Parian Marble (*FGrH* 239) of 264/3 provided firm dates for the most improbable mythical happenings (see below, note 62). Diodorus at least knew better than to trust such compilations.

[45] D.S. 1.5.1; Ps.-Skymnos §§25–32; cf. Pfeiffer 1968, 253–257. Apollodoros drew largely on the work of Eratosthenes. See also below, pp. 237–238. It is sometimes assumed that for the period after 110/09, Diodorus used the six-book *Chronological Table* compiled by Kastor of Rhodes (*FGrH* 250); but this is quite uncertain. As Spoerri says (*DKP* 3:152), "Fraglich ist, ob K. Diodors Quelle für die griech. und röm. Chronol. war." Cf. Schwartz 1903, col. 665; Cássola 1982, 828. Diodorus may indeed have taken up a position *against* Kastor (so Sacks 1990, 65–66), "whose chronology ignored certain accepted eastern mythologies and put Greek origins as far back as the barbarian."

[46] Clarke 1999b, 260. She also points out how Diodorus "extends the Thucydidean use of 'war-years' to cover not only the Peloponnesian War. . . . Each conflict has its own internal chronology, but Diodorus stresses the great spatial range of his narrative by applying similar chronological schemes to disparate wars."

[47] See Burde 1974, 102–110, esp. 108–109; Clarke 1999a, 114–116.

cord them are obliged to chop up their narrative and unnaturally allot separate time-sequences to simultaneous happenings; so that even though their treatment of the past embodies the truth, the written account, through lack of a comparable ability to reproduce events exactly, falls far short of a true presentation.[48]

As we shall see, at various points the process of συμπλοκή does indeed involve Diodorus in unintentional misrepresentation, often chronological, and misunderstandings (these last on the part of his chronographical sources at least as often as his own). His use of the Roman Fasti, or lists derived therefrom,[49] also involved him in a good deal of error, chiefly through a failure to take note of various nonconsular *interregna* when making his calculations of consular years, so that frequently—not least in Books 11–12—correct archonyears and Olympiads are juxtaposed to consular appointments that in fact belong some six or seven years earlier (those cited above for 480/79 should really be placed in 486).[50] Also, Athenian archons took office in July, Roman consuls in March, "thus requiring Diodorus to impose a seriously false synchronism every year."[51] Colleges are sometimes incomplete, names mangled.[52] The old theory, adhered to by scholars from Niebuhr and Mommsen to Schwartz, that Diodorus derived his consular evidence directly, and exclusively, from Fabius Pictor, has been replaced by a more plausible and flexible reading, which sees him as having utilized several later annalistic sources. For my present purposes, the general debate over his Roman chronography[53] is

---

[48] ταύτῃ δ᾽ ἄν τις καὶ τὴν ἱστορίαν καταμέμψαιτο, θεωρῶν ἐπὶ μὲν τοῦ βίου πολλὰς καὶ διαφόρους πράξεις συντελουμένας κατὰ τὸν αὐτὸν καιρόν, τοῖς δ᾽ ἀναγράφουσιν ἀναγκαῖον ὑπάρχον τὸ μεσολαβεῖν τὴν διήγησιν καὶ τοῖς ἅμα συντελουμένοις μερίζειν τοὺς χρόνους παρὰ φύσιν ὥστε τὴν μὲν ἀληθείᾳ τῶν πεπραγμένων τὸ πάθος ἔχειν, τὴν δ᾽ ἀναγραφὴν ἐστερημένην τῆς ὁμοίας ἐξουσίας μιμεῖσθαι μὲν τὰ γεγενημένα, πολὺ δὲ λείπεσθαι τῆς ἀληθοῦς διαθέσεως. Cf. Clarke 1999a, 120–121: "It is a real historiographical problem that a chronologically ordered narrative cannot truly represent contemporaneous events."

[49] As with his Greek material, a clear distinction should be made between his chronological and more strictly historical sources: Perl 1957, 123–126; Cássola 1982, 739–742.

[50] See below, Book 11, note 2.

[51] Clarke 1999a, 13. This, however, does not seriously affect the chronology of his Greek or, for the most part, his Sicilian narrative.

[52] The fault can be divided between Diodorus' sources, the manuscript tradition, and his own slips, though to apportion responsibility for each is, obviously, impossible.

[53] The key work is that of Perl (1957, esp. chs. 5 and 6, "Die Geschichtserzählung" and "Die Fastenquelle," 123–161). Spoerri 1991, 312–313 with n. 9, offers a useful summary. See also Stuart Jones, *CAH* vii.2, 321ff., and the shrewd assessment of Stylianou (1998, 27): "As

of secondary relevance only. More important is his inevitable tendency—examined in detail throughout the commentary that follows—to blur mid-summer distinctions between archon-years when narrating events through a campaigning season, and to write achronic introductions, or postscripts, covering an extended period, under the rubric of one specific year.

Fifteen of the *Bibliotheke*'s forty books (1–5, 11–20) survive virtually intact. They cover Diodorus' general introduction; the early history and myths of Egypt, Asia, India, Arabia, Ethiopia, Libya, and the Greeks; and Greek history from the Persian Wars through the fifth and fourth centuries. Ten of them run from 480 to 302/1, from Salamis to Ipsos, in an almost[54] unbroken sequence. For the remainder we have a large and varied collection of digests, excerpts, and other citations from a number of sources. The more important of these include Athenaios, Eusebius, George Syncellus, Photius (also in a *Bibliotheke*), the *Excerpta historica* of Constantine VII Porphyrogenitus, the *Suda,* the *Florilegium Vaticanum,* and the *Chiliades* of Joannes Tzetzes.[55]

For the reign of Philip II of Macedon, for the early period of Alexander's Successors, for Sicilian history of all periods, the *Bibliotheke* is our *only* surviving narrative source, and by far the earliest for Alexander's career. Without it, these periods would be all but irretrievable, and the chronological framework it provides—on which (despite its various built-in errors and disadvantages) we rely to a great extent for structuring ancient Greek history—virtually nonexistent. We would also (as regards the present work) know even less than we do about the Pentekontaetia, that elusive half-century between the Persian and Peloponnesian wars, and the brief, cryptic chapters on the same topic in Book 1 of Thucydides would be correspondingly more obscure.

We thus owe a very great deal to Diodorus and his *Bibliotheke,* something we would do well to remember when tempted to exercise our dismissive

---

it is fairly evident that all existing *fasti* have a common origin, the various differences between them, when not due to negligence or plain error, should be seen as the outcome of attempts to overcome certain difficulties of which the chief was the need to accommodate the lists to synchronisms known from Greek sources."

[54] There is one infuriating gap after 11.90.3 (covered in this volume: see Book 11, note 373) where the entire year 452/1 = Ol. 82.1 is missing in all surviving manuscripts; and another at 17.83.9, where a large part of the years 328/7 and 327/6 has likewise been lost, thus depriving Alexander historians of the campaign against Spitamenes, the murder of Kleitos, the *proskynesis* affair, the death of Kallisthenes, the Pages' Conspiracy, and Alexander's marriage to Roxane—all items vouched for by the surviving (later) contents list for Book 17.

[55] On these sources, see Wachsmuth 1895, 67–77; Walton 1957, vii–xxvii; and Chamoux et al. 1993, cxxiii–cxlix, where they are conveniently catalogued under the heading of "La Tradition Indirecte."

scholarly skepticism on him. Like Plutarch, but without the compensating factor of great literary and psychological skill, he frustrates (and thus irritates) modern historians—all desperately seeking to fill the gaps in a shaky record—by elevating *ethos* at the expense of *praxis*. But to fault him for not being either a second Thucydides or a post-Niebuhr analyst merely confuses the issue. Diodorus' universalist and morally uplifting objectives, together with his heavy, and inevitable, reliance on secondary sources, make him something like the Will Durant of the Greco-Roman world.[56] Such was, in effect, his declared purpose. He modestly hoped (1.5.2) "that throughout this narrative what is well-written may not incur envy, and that errors may get correction from more capable men."[57] His prayer has been more than fulfilled, though not quite in the way he anticipated. He never aspired to much more than wide-ranging inclusiveness (both chronological and geographical), and we should deal with him on that basis, rather than misdiagnosing him as an imbecile for his errors, and above all for his failure to answer all our questions in the way we would have liked.

What Diodorus set out to write was "universal history" (ἱστορίαι κοιναί or καθολικαί), a far from clear notion that, as Arnaldo Momigliano once remarked,[58] if "taken literally . . . verges on absurdity." After all, universal historians must "deal with the history of mankind from the earliest times, and in all parts of the world known to them."[59] Not surprisingly, as Diodorus points out (1.3.2–3), earlier historians had, for a variety of reasons, failed in the attempt, most often by omitting either the affairs of "barbarian nations" or (as in the case of Ephoros) "ancient legends, because of the difficulty in dealing with them." Here, mainly for moralizing purposes, he went directly against a well-established tradition by which Hellenic historians rejected the evidence of myth.[60] Certainly no one had attempted to encompass world events on such a scale right down to Diodorus' own day, "because of the mag-

---

[56] The attractiveness of the comparison may be judged by the fact that to my knowledge at least three people (Catherine Rubincam, Ernst Badian—who also drew a parallel with Arnold Toynbee—and myself) have, either in print or in conversation, arrived at it independently.

[57] 1.5.2: ἡμῖν δὲ παρ᾽ ὅλην τὴν ἱστορίαν τὰ μὲν γραφέντα καλῶς μὴ μετεχέτω φθόνου, τὰ δὲ ἀγνοηθέντα τυγχανέτω διορθώσεως ὑπὸ τῶν δυνατωτέρων.

[58] Momigliano 1984, 533; cf. Jal 1994, 57; Clarke 1999b, 252 ("A more preposterous aim could scarcely be imagined").

[59] Alonso-Núñez 1990, 173; Jal (1994, 57) defines universal history as "la relation des événements du passé, des faits relatifs à l'évolution de l'humanité, faits qui sont dignes ou jugés dignes de mémoire et qui concernent les hommes de tous les temps et de tous les pays."

[60] 4.1.1–4, 4.8.3; cf. Marincola 1997, 119–121.

nitude of the proposed undertaking." This, then, was the task he set himself, and on which he claimed to have spent thirty years of his life.

In some sense or other, the idea had been current in the Greek world ever since Herodotos' day: its evolution took place in a basically Mediterranean concept of the world, and was marked by a progressive expansion of explored boundaries, together with a considerably less adventurous foray into the further reaches of past time. The Trojan War, for Diodorus as for many,[61] was a convenient divider between human and legendary or heroic history; but the latter *was* still history,[62] and Diodorus' only complaint about it (1.5.1)— when explaining why here he abandons the annalistic structure followed in his later books—is, he says, the impossibility of establishing chronological markers for it with any degree of reliability. Moreover, in this historical continuum, the past is regularly evoked to illustrate and explain the present: Herakles founded Alesia (4.19.1–2), a great city that remained independent until Julius Caesar, like Herakles "declared a god on account of the greatness of his achievements,"[63] stormed it and made the Celts subject to the Romans. As Sacks reminds us, "a comparison with Heracles . . . was Diodorus' highest compliment."[64]

A number of factors had combined to create, by the second century B.C.E., a worldview that encouraged historians, as Polybios stressed,[65] to examine the past not only "piecemeal" ($\kappa\alpha\tau\grave{\alpha}$ $\mu\acute{\epsilon}\rho\sigma$), but also "overall" ($\kappa\alpha\theta\acute{o}\lambda\sigma$). Herodotos' survey of the provinces of the Achaimenid empire, as a background to the great conflict between Persia and Hellas, opened up the boundaries of Greek liminality, testing nationalist parochialism (and getting its author branded as a $\phi\iota\lambda\sigma\beta\acute{\alpha}\rho\beta\alpha\rho\sigma$).[66] Isokrates' Panhellenism reinforced this trend,

---

[61] See, e.g., 1.4.6, 5.1, 24.2; 3.52.2, 74.4; 11.37.6; 13.1.2; and elsewhere. Cf. Clarke 1999b, 257.

[62] As that third-century B.C.E. chronological table, the Parian Marble (*FGrH* 239) makes very clear: it starts with Kekrops, as first king of Athens (1581 B.C.E.), and includes such items as the quarrel between Poseidon and Ares over the Areopagos (1531) and the Amazons' attack on Athens (1256) en route to Peisistratos' tyranny (561/0), the battle of Marathon (490), and the death of Alexander (323). Cf. Green 1997, 38.

[63] $\tau\sigma\hat{\nu}$ $\delta\iota\grave{\alpha}$ $\tau\grave{o}$ $\mu\acute{\epsilon}\gamma\epsilon\theta\sigma$ $\tau\hat{\omega}\nu$ $\pi\rho\acute{\alpha}\xi\epsilon\omega\nu$ $\theta\epsilon\sigma\hat{\nu}$ $\pi\rho\sigma\sigma\alpha\gamma\sigma\rho\epsilon\upsilon\theta\acute{\epsilon}\nu\tau\sigma$. For the siege and capture of Alesia in 52, see Caes. *BG* 7.68ff.

[64] Sacks 1990, 179. And Caesar had gone Dionysos and Herakles one better in his invasion of Britain, something neither of them had undertaken: 5.21.2. For the veneration of Herakles in Diodorus' hometown of Agyrion, see 4.24.1–6 and the numismatic evidence cited by Sacks 1990, 179 n. 87.

[65] Polyb. 3.5.9, cf. 5.31.7, 39.8.3. See Clarke 1999a, 114ff.

[66] Plut. *Mor.* 857A.

emphasizing the unity of Greeks everywhere, though still in contrast to an Oriental Other.[67] It was under the influence of Panhellenism that Isokrates' student Ephoros—an important source for archaic and classical Greek history in the *Bibliotheke*—wrote what seems to have been the first real attempt at a "universal history," but omitting the mythical era, for which he understandably regarded the evidence as unsatisfactory,[68] and still, predictably enough, thinking in terms of Greeks versus Barbarians (the latter extended to include Carthage and Macedonia).[69]

Ephoros of Kyme (c. 405–330 B.C.E.) is on the list of the ten "canonical" historians of antiquity:[70] though this is no guarantee of his standards, it undoubtedly testifies to his popularity. He survives, unfortunately, only in fragments (of which there are, it is safe to say, considerably fewer than those hopefully attributed to him by Jacoby in *FGrH*). His *History,* as Diodorus tells us (4.1.3), began with the Return of the Herakleidai (i.e., the Dorian invasion), and he had brought it down as far as the siege of Perinthos by Philip of Macedon in 341/0 when he died. He also divided his work into books himself (earlier historians seem only to have been thus organized by Hellenistic scholars) and wrote an individual introduction or preface (προοίμιον) for each book

---

[67] See Green 1996a, 17–23. K. Bringmann (*Studien zu den politischen Ideen des Isokrates* [Göttingen, 1965], 109) observes that Isokrates "treated myth and history as a fund of παραδείγματα," and much the same could be said of Diodorus, who had clearly absorbed some useful Isokratean lessons—through Ephoros, it is generally assumed (see, e.g., Volquardsen 1868, 47ff.; Barber 1979, 184; and cf. Sacks 1990, 32 n. 36), but there is no reason why he should not have read Isokrates himself, just as he (arguably) also read both Herodotos and Thucydides: Neubert 1890, 22; Pavan 1961, 19–52; Lévy 2001, 333–341. Cf. below, pp. 24–31.

[68] *FGrH* 70 F 9: Harpokration cites him verbatim: περὶ δὲ τῶν παλαιῶν τοὺς οὕτω διεξιόντας ἀπιθανωτάτους εἶναι νομίζομεν, ὑπολαμβάνοντες οὔτε τὰς πράξεις ἁπάσας οὔτε τῶν λόγων τοὺς πλείστους εἰκὸς εἶναι μνημονεύεσθαι διὰ τοσούτων. It is possible, though far from certain, that he had Thucydides (e.g., at 1.20.1) in mind when writing this. Strabo (10.3.5 = *FGrH* 70 T 18) praises his handling of the foundation of cities, but he may well not have regarded such traditions as "mythical."

[69] D.S. 4.1.2–3; cf. Barber 1979, 22. Barber in general is now somewhat outdated. The fullest and most up-to-date treatment, that of Stylianou (1998, in particular 84–132), contains much valuable material, but is marred by its author's determination throughout to see Ephoros as the sole serious source in Books 11–16 for Diodorus as slavish copyist. In default of a monograph, the best modern assessment of Ephoros is probably still that of Schepens 1977, esp. 102ff. See now also Pownall 2004, ch. 4, 113–142.

[70] *FGrH* 70 T 34: the full list consists of: "Thucydides Herodotos Xenophon Philistos Theopompos Ephoros Anaximenes Kallisthenes Hellanikos Polybios." Diodorus mentions them all.

(16.76.5), possibly another first.[71] Like Herodotos, he stressed the value of autopsy, and thought Greeks had a shorter history than some of the Barbarians;[72] like Plato in the *Republic,* he blamed music for "the deceit and enchantment of mankind."[73] Like other conservative (and not-so-subtly anti-democratic) fourth-century historians, he aimed to show, by exempla (some from myth), prefatory rhetoric, digressions, speeches, and aphorisms, "how the collective moral behavior of a society leads to its remaining strong and free."[74] He still seems to have treated nations κατὰ μέρος rather than καθόλου, and to judge from his observations on the causes of the Peloponnesian War,[75] he had a taste for ad hominem political scandal (Perikles goes to war to deflect attention from his friends' prosecutions and his own questionable accounting) rather than Thucydidean theory.[76]

About a century later, Theopompos of Chios (?378/7–c. 320), writing in fifty-eight books a *Philippic History* centered (for sixteen of them) on Philip II of Macedon, but ranging widely over "the deeds of Greeks and Barbarians" (*FGrH* 115 F 25), introduced what Dionysios of Halikarnassos was later to describe as his ability "to scrutinize the invisible motives driving actions and their agents, together with their private emotions (for most people not easily discernible), and to lay bare all the secrets of seeming virtue and unrecognized vice."[77] This utilization of historical exempla for moral guidance was exactly

---

[71] Catherine Rubincam suggests to me, *per litt.,* that "the provision of a preface for each of his 30 books was surely an important part of the means by which Ephoros dictated that his book divisions would not be subject to editorial revision."

[72] Autopsy: cited by Polyb. 12.27.7. Brevity of Greek history: D.S. 1.9.5. Ephoros saw it as a succession of transient hegemonies: Pownall 2004, 131–132. On his analysis of the brief ascendancy of Thebes, lost (he argues) through lack of education (ἀγωγή) and culture (παιδεία), see Wickersham 1994, 124ff.

[73] ἐπ᾽ ἀπάτῃ καὶ γοητείᾳ παρεισῆχθαι τοῖς ἀνθρώποις: *FGrH* 70 F 8 = Polyb. 4.20.5 (cited by Athen. 14.626A).

[74] Pownall 2004, 141.

[75] *FGrH* 70 F 196 = D.S. 12.38–41.

[76] It is not so much that his evidence (derived in part from Aristophanes) is—as much modern history has taught us—per se implausible, as used to be thought, but rather that it leaves so much else out. Dover's point (1988, 45–52) that Ephoros and others not brought up in classical Athens failed to understand the nature of Old Comedy, and thus took Aristophanes' political satire over-literally, assumes a quite stunning degree of social and literary naïveté in these unfortunate non-Athenian outsiders.

[77] Dion. Hal. *Ep. ad Pomp.* 6 (p. 394 Usher): ἐξετάζειν καὶ τὰς ἀφανεῖς αἰτίας τῶν πράξεων καὶ τῶν πραξάντων αὐτὰς καὶ τὰ πάθη τῆς ψυχῆς, ἃ μὴ ῥᾴδια τοῖς πολλοῖς εἰδέναι, καὶ πάντα ἐκκαλύπτειν τὰ μυστήρια τῆς τε δοκούσης ἀρετῆς καὶ τῆς ἀγνοουμένης κακίας. Flower (1994, 169) claims that Dionysios calls this trait *original* to Theopompos, which if true would be very important; but in fact what he says is that no historian either

in line with most Greek ethical thinking (noted above in Ephoros) and was to prove immensely popular. Clearly influenced by the example of the Cynic diatribe, Theopompos attacked both peoples and individuals (politicians and rulers in particular) for greed, loose living, taking bribes, and excessive luxury, as well as for such military crimes as genocide or mass enslavement;[78] Dionysios of Halikarnassos remarks how often he "heaps blame on cities or generals for wicked resolutions and unjust actions."[79] His praise for virtue was less frequent, and contained a certain Spartan bias.[80] His violent rhetorical invective against the court life of Philip of Macedon and his associates (ἑταῖροι) was notorious in antiquity and is still often cited today.[81] Philip's own private life is held up to ridicule:[82] he is presented as a debauched and incontinent buffoon.[83] With Theopompos—whose private wealth seems to have freed him from the constraints of patronage[84]—moral judgments became a leading built-in objective of ancient historiography.

Theopompos' slightly younger contemporary Timaios (c. 350–c. 260), from Tauromenion in Sicily, is notable on several counts. He was not the earliest historian of the Greek West—that claim can more convincingly be made for his predecessor Philistos[85]—but he was certainly the most influential, and

---

before or since has done it "so precisely and effectively," οὕτως ἀκριβῶς ἐξείργασται καὶ δυνατῶς, not the same thing at all.

[78] See, e.g., *FGrH* 115 F 28, 31, 36, 49, 81, 85, 114, 124, 134, 233, 312, 323. The best assessment of Theopompos is now that by Pownall (2004, ch. 5, 143–175).

[79] Dion. Hal. *Ep. ad Pomp.* 6 (p. 396 Usher): ὀνειδίζῃ πόλεσιν ἤ στρατηγοῖς πονηρὰ βουλεύματα καὶ πράξεις ἀδίκους.

[80] See, e.g., *FGrH* 115 F 321 and 333, on Agesilaos and Lysander.

[81] *FGrH* 115 F 224–225a–b = Athen. 4.166F–167C, 6.260D–261A; Polyb. 8.19.13. Gambling, drinking, and in particular habitual and systematized sodomy were the main charges (ἀνδροφόνοι were changed into ἀνδροπόρνοι, killers into buggers, etc.).

[82] Evidence conveniently assembled by Flower (1994, 105); cf. Pownall 2004, 174.

[83] Yet even Theopompos had to admit Philip's skills as general and politician: "Never before," he proclaimed, in a justly famous phrase, "had Europe produced such a man as Philip son of Amyntas." Cited by Polybios (8.9.1–2): μηδέποτε τὴν Εὐρώπην ἐνηνοχέναι τοιοῦτον ἄνδρα παράπαν οἷον τὸν Ἀμύντου Φίλιππον. Of course, ἐνηνοχέναι could also mean "endured"; the ambiguity was surely deliberate. I am not persuaded by Flower in his attempt (1994, 116ff.) to demonstrate that Theopompos saw Philip as all of a piece throughout, a drunken clod who succeeded by a mixture of outrageous luck and unconscionable bribery. Theopompos was quite capable of distinguishing between public ability and private weakness (cf. Pownall 2004, 175): not a universally shared attribute, as critics of President Clinton so memorably demonstrated.

[84] Pownall 2004, 143; cf. Flower 1994, 11–25.

[85] Philistos of Syracuse (c. 430–356), colleague and friend of Dionysios I and II as well as author of a *History of Sicily* (Σικελικά) from the heroic age down to 363/2, seems to have

because of his thirty-eight-book *Sicilian History,* he remained "the standard authority on the history of the Greek West for nearly five centuries."[86] Like Herodotos, in his early books he devoted much space to the geographical and ethnic background of his subsequent narrative (*FGrH* 566 T 7). He was very alert to the steady rise of Rome as a Mediterranean power.[87] It is from his bitterest critic, Polybios (12.11.1–2), that we learn of the careful comparative research he carried out on various official lists, including those of the Olympian victors and of Athens' eponymous archons, to establish a general chronology. Work of this kind had been done before—Hellanikos had pioneered the use of victor-lists and the records of the priestesses at Argos, as well as (with some Atthidographers) dating by archon-years; Aristotle (or his students) supposedly published an *Olympionikai*[88]—but it was Timaios who systematized the use of Olympiads as a basis for dating historical events, and he may well also have established the first Olympic festival (776 B.C.E.) as a logical date for separating history from prehistory, λόγος from μῦθος. As Polybios conceded (12.10.4), Timaios' special and preeminent characteristic was "his display of precision over dates and records, and his special concern with this side of things."[89]

This, however, apart from his willingness to plunge into mythical times on the basis of probability, τὸ εἰκός, was about the only quality proper to a universal historian that Timaios' successors were prepared to grant him. They were not slow to attack him for other, less admirable fashions that he allegedly set: in particular, the way he appealed to a broad readership by saucing up his narrative with the rhetoric of Euripidean tragedy, and his pietistic trick of exploiting public superstition (δεισιδαιμονία) by using historical instances to emphasize the moral inevitability of divine retribution overtaking evildoers.[90] This was an old practice, used (as we have seen) by Theopompos, among oth-

---

imitated Thucydides in his methods, and to have had a similar weakness for authoritarianism in government (cf. Plut. *Dio* 36.3 = *FGrH* 556 T 23a; also T 15c (Quintilian), T 16 (Dion. Hal.), and T 17 (Cicero). Surviving fragments are few and mostly nugatory; but it is clear that later historians relied heavily on Philistos, and that the failure of his work to survive is a real loss.

[86] Pearson 1987, 271.

[87] According to Dion. Hal. *AR* 1.6.1, Timaios was the first Greek historian, apart from Hieronymos of Kardia, to discuss Roman history.

[88] Diog. Laert. 5.1.26; Jacoby 1949, 174ff.; Pearson 1987, 45–46.

[89] Polyb. 12.10.4: τὴν ἐν τοῖς χρόνοις καὶ τοῖς ἀναγραφαῖς ἐπίφασιν τῆς ἀκριβείας καὶ τὴν περὶ τοῦτο τὸ μέρος ἐπιμέλειαν.

[90] Polybios (12.24.5) describes him as being "chock-full of vulgar superstition and womanish miracle-lore": δεισιδαιμονίας ἀγεννοῦς καὶ τερατείας γυναικώδους ἐστὶ πλήρης.

ers; but it seems to have been Timaios who really launched it as a regular weapon in the Hellenistic historiographer's armory. Polybios also took him to fault for lack of autopsy and military experience, dependence on earlier written sources, and ignorance of geography, all regular (and inevitable) charges against universal historians.[91] More seriously, he asserted (12.25k) that Timaios' numerous inserted speeches were inept fictions, unrealistic and inappropriate platitudes, the work of a writer wholly ignorant of political *Realien*. Others joined in the chorus. Timaios' Sicilian patriotism skewed his objectivity. He was malicious, he was arrogant, he was ultra-critical.[92] But he was "commonly regarded as the most important historian between Ephorus and Polybios,"[93] and his influence, like that of the popular Alexander-historian Kleitarchos, was clearly far greater than his intrinsic worth: we ignore it at our peril.

It was, however, Alexander's Eastern conquests, and the literature that they inspired—not only the historical accounts, from Kallisthenes to Kleitarchos, but perhaps even more the travel literature, most notably Megasthenes' report on India—that really opened up the horizons of the old Mediterranean world in a radically new fashion. Herodotos had already challenged the poetic notion of Ocean as a great stream encircling the world.[94] Now Alexander (whose own faith in this myth had been rudely shattered by the daunting presence of the Ganges plain) had changed the face of the *oikoumene,* the known world, forever. Expanding knowledge had chased old travelers' tales to an ever-receding periphery. Historians such as Agatharchides of Knidos (c. 215–?140) renewed and extended the Herodotean interest in ethnography and liminal geography.[95] Mythic belief was reworked to fit new physical facts. The great Hellenistic kingdoms created by Alexander's Successors (*Diadochoi*) replaced the *polis,* the local city-state—already weakened by Macedonian power-politics and military conquest[96]—with the *megalopolis,* the huge international urban center. In reaction against these new trends, we find the universalist Stoic notion of the *kosmopolites,* or "citizen of the world"; a new moral version derived

[91] Polyb. 12.3–4 (geographical ignorance), 12.25f–g (lack of military experience), 12.25e (over-reliance on written sources), 12.27–28 (autopsy).

[92] He was punningly known (D.S. 5.1, Ister cited by Athen. 6.272B) as being ἐπιτί-μαιος, i.e., a fault-finder. Others referred to him (*Suda,* s.v.) as a "gossiping old woman" (γραοσυλλέκτρια).

[93] Pearson 1987, 1.

[94] Hdt. 2.23, 4.8, 4.36; cf. Romm 1992, 34–35; Green 1997, 38ff.

[95] S. M. Burstein, *Agatharchides on the Erythraean Sea* (London, 1989).

[96] Alonso-Núñez 1990, 177–179.

(perhaps by way of Theopompos' attacks on luxury, immorality, and atrocities)[97] from Cynic principles, of the old anti-tyrannical topoi against arrogant, unjust, and arbitrary rulers; and a hankering after off-the-map utopias such as those of Euhemeros and Iamboulos—factors that all left their mark on the evolution of universal history from the fourth century onward.[98]

The second great centralizing phenomenon in Hellenistic historiography was the rise of Rome to the status of a world power—by Diodorus' day, indeed, the only relevant world power for Mediterranean society as a whole. What had been blank spaces on the northern Atlantic map for Herodotos and his successors, beyond Gaul and Germany, or outside the Pillars of Herakles, were now being filled in.[99] What was more, they, like most of the Mediterranean, were being filled in under Rome's authoritarian aegis. By the mid-second century, Polybios could ask (1.1.5, cf. 3.4.1–5): "Who is so indifferent or indolent that he would not want to know how, and under what form of government, almost every part of the inhabited world ($oi\kappa o \upsilon \mu \acute{e} \nu \eta$) came under Rome's sole rule in less than fifty-three years, an unprecedented phenomenon?" It was to answer this question that he wrote his *Histories,* covering the period 220–146, the only Hellenistic historical work of which we possess a substantial part, and the first in which we can watch a universalist methodology being worked out, with Roman *imperium* as the unifying factor, in both geographical and chronological terms.[100]

Like Herodotos and (probably) Ephoros, Polybios saw the earth as a general stage on which world events were acted out. Though that world, as subdued by Rome, is limited in the *Histories* to "the Hellenistic kingdoms, Carthage and some barbarians in the West involved in the affairs of Greeks, Romans and Carthaginians,"[101] nevertheless Polybios was well aware of the peoples beyond those boundaries (3.37.1–38.3) and took care to make this clear. His universalism is wholly conditioned by Rome's steady expansion of

[97] Flower 1994, 169.

[98] Stoicism: Farrington 1936, 9ff.; Corsaro 1998, 421, 425; Green 1993, index s.v. "Stoics, Stoicism," sub-headings *kosmopolites,* macrocosm, microcosm, universalism. Theopompos' attacks on Philip: *FGrH* 115 F 27, 224–225; cf. Connor 1967, 133ff.; Shrimpton 1977, 123ff.; Murray 1946, 149ff.; Alonso-Núñez 1990, 177–179. Euhemeros and Iamboulos: Ferguson 1975, 122ff., 180ff.; Finley 1975, 184; Green 1993, 393–395; Manuel and Manuel 1979, index s.vv.

[99] Green 1997, 41–45; Romm 1992, 121–171.

[100] See Walbank 1972, 3, 67–68, and 1975 on $\sigma \upsilon \mu \pi \lambda o \kappa \acute{\eta}$; Sacks 1981, 96–121; Alonso-Núñez 1990, 183–190; Pavan 1987; Burde 1974, 25–34; Green 1993, 269ff.; P. S. Derow in *OCD,* s.v. "Polybios," 1209–1211.

[101] Alonso-Núñez 1990, 185.

conquest to supreme power. Before what he saw as the turning-point (*Ol.* 140, i.e., 220–217 B.C.E.), localism, he argues, still prevailed; but from then on "history emerges as an organic whole: the affairs of Italy and of Africa are interwoven (συμπλέκεσθαι)[102] with those of Asia and of Greece, and all things point in concert to a single end" (1.3.1). These interrelationships he sees as the key to a new universality in the historical process (cf. 5.33.4, 9.44.2). The spatial unity (surveyed annually from west to east, from Spain and Sicily by way of Greece to Asia and Egypt)[103] is set—perhaps using Timaios' system as model, approved with caveats by Polybios—against a firm chronology by Olympiads (with numbered years within each quadrennial period)[104] and a series of synchronisms, chiefly in *Ol.* 140.[105] A *soi-disant* Thucydidean rationalist, he nevertheless was not above availing himself of that useful fallback Tyche (τύχη)—Fate or Fortune semi-personalized, the random unpredictable factor in human affairs—to explain Rome's embarrassing triumph over the Greek world.[106]

With a nice sense of continuity, the great Stoic polymath Poseidonios of Apamea (c. 135–c. 51)—as Xenophon and Theopompos after Thucydides—began his (possibly unfinished) fifty-two-book *History* in 146, where Polybios left off, at the fall of Carthage and Corinth. We can trace fragments as far down as the mid-80s, after which the trail peters out.[107] Poseidonios' work embodies most of the major characteristics we have noted as fundamental to Hellenistic universal historiography. As a Stoic, he naturally accepted the idea of an overall unity governing mankind and the whole inhabited world (οἰκουμένη).[108] Indeed, he believed in the cosmos as a living, sentient entity, accepted the principle of universal *sympatheia,* and was convinced that Fate governed all human actions: unlike Polybios, he has no problems with Tyche.[109] It is not hard to see how such a nexus of assumptions could virtually identify Roman *imperium* with the cosmic order, microcosm with macrocosm, smoothing the way for a succession of emperors to be admitted to the heav-

---

[102] See Walbank 1975, 197–203, 210–212.

[103] Derow, in *OCD,* 1210.

[104] Errington 1967, 96–97.

[105] Walbank 1985, 289–312, esp. the table at 310–311.

[106] Green 1993, 53–55, 271–273, 284–285.

[107] Kidd 1988, 277–280. The last datable reference is to the enslavement of Chians by Mithridates, in 86: Athen. 7.266E–F, citing both Poseidonios and Nikolaos of Damascus.

[108] Burde 1974, 35: "Für . . . Poseidonios gab es als Stoiker natürlich keinen Zweifel an der engen Verbundenheit aller Menschen und der Einheit der Oikoumene." Cf. M. Pohlenz, *Die Stoa,* 3d ed. (Göttingen, 1964), 1:135ff.

[109] T14–26 Edelstein-Kidd; *FGrH* 87 F 109–110, 111b, 112; Laffranque 1964, ch. 4, 109ff.

enly pantheon.[110] The *orbis terrarum* and the *orbis Romanus* were steadily and inexorably merging. By Ovid's day, the idea had become a commonplace: *Romanae spatium est Urbis et orbis idem.*[111]

The *History* may not have ranged far into the past, but it was certainly wide-ranging in geographical terms, "covering the whole of the Mediterranean-centered world from Asia Minor to Spain, Egypt and Africa to Gaul and the northern peoples to Jutland."[112] It was also, of all the works noticed here, the most morally concentrated.[113] As Kidd shows, its aetiology, its *modus operandi,* its whole concept of historical explanation is that of a moral philosopher. For Poseidonios, though external factors may be contributory to motive (in the Thucydidean sense of πρόφασις), they are never the fundamental cause or motive itself, the αἰτία: this—in sharp contradistinction to the views of Polybios or Thucydides—is always the result of inner character, which may be national as well as personal.[114] The result is Poseidonios' marked interest in national ethnologies, which he then uses as both historical explanation of and moral judgment on the events of his narrative.

The judgments also walk an interesting social tightrope, since while Poseidonios (as might be expected) was "strongly biased in favor of the [Roman] *nobilitas,* and thus came out against the Gracchi, the *equites,* and, indeed, the 'independent' Greeks who had, so fatally for themselves, supported Mithridates,"[115] at the same time, as a good Romanized Stoic, he was preoccupied with the relationship between ruler and ruled, and in particular with the nature and moral status of slavery: indeed, it is Poseidonios who, in his *History,* narrated the accounts of the Sicilian and Italian slave wars[116] on which later sources primarily depend, with a visible "anxiety to prove that the atrocities committed by these slaves were not due to natural viciousness, but the result of justified discontent."[117] At the same time, the passage most often cited as proof of Poseidonios' moral rectitude, his diatribe against the Athenian

---

[110] Green 1993, 642–643.

[111] Ovid *Fasti* 2.683; cf. Jal 1994, §II, "Le Désir de globalité," 61–65.

[112] Kidd 1999, 25.

[113] See Kidd 1998, 38ff., for a thorough analysis.

[114] A good example is offered by the invasion of the Cimbri (F272 Edelstein-Kidd): the true explanation is not the floods that drove them out of Jutland, but "their own inherent piratical and nomadic character" (Kidd 1999, 26).

[115] Green 1993, 642 with refs.

[116] F51, 59, 60, 239, 250, 262, 265 Edelstein-Kidd; cf. Kidd 1999, 27.

[117] Wiedemann 1981, 200. His entire ch. 11 (198–223) conveniently collects all the testimonia for the slave wars in translation.

philosopher-tyrant Aristion in 88, during the Mithridatic War,[118] is chiefly
notable for its withering social contempt: Aristion is a *parvenu,* whose moral
and philosophical shortcomings are largely due to his lowly origins and consequent intellectual pretensions. The gap between such men's public conduct
and professed doctrine became a popular topos, as Juvenal's second satire
abundantly demonstrates. Slaves were one thing, jumped-up semi-educated
vulgarians who got too big for their lower-middle-class boots quite another.

## THE *BIBLIOTHEKE II:* AIMS, ACHIEVEMENTS, CRITICISM

These, then, were the main strands in the historiographical tradition on
which Diodorus could draw when formulating, and carrying out, his vast
project; and it is remarkable—though not really surprising—how many of
them duly show up, directly or indirectly, in the *Bibliotheke.* Diodorus is indeed, as Rudolf Neubert described him, "a child of his time,"[119] and his history, in Kenneth Sacks' words, "a document substantially reflecting the intellectual and political attitudes of the late Hellenistic period."[120] His early
geographical and ethnic survey (in particular its emphasis on Egypt), subsequently changing into historical narrative (not to mention the interest he displays in anecdotes, digressions, and θαύματα, marvels), reveals a close student
of Herodotos. From Ephoros he borrows the carefully planned division of the
*Bibliotheke* into books, each originally with its own preface (προοίμιον), a
weakness for ad hominem historiography, and a rather endearing streak of
local patriotism. His chronological system, combining Olympiads with the
Athenian archon-year, and relating both to the Roman Fasti, is adopted from
the work of Timaios and Polybios.

The strongest influence was also that closest to him in time. While his emphasis on history as a source of moral exempla and warnings may owe something to the παραδείγματα of Isokrates and Theopompos' anti-Macedonian
diatribes, its immediate inspiration was undoubtedly provided by the great
*History* of Poseidonios, published when Diodorus was already at work on his
own research, and by the general intellectual atmosphere of popular Stoicism
to which he was daily exposed in Rome. This is particularly true of his remarkable extended digressions on the utopias of Iamboulos (2.55.1–60.3) and
Euhemeros (5.42–46, 6.1.4–7) and his detailed account of the slave wars

---

[118]F253 Edelstein-Kidd = Athen. 5.211D–215B; cf. Kidd 1988, 863–887, 1998, 38–50.
[119]Neubert 1890, 10: "Diodor ist ein Kind seiner Zeit."
[120]Sacks 1990, 5.

(34/35.2.1–48, 8.1–11.1; 36.2.1, 2a, 2.6, 3.2–10.3), taken directly from Poseidonios' narrative.[121] Farrington argued[122] that Diodorus here looks back to a
period of pre-Romanized Stoicism with a radical concern for the rights of
man under slavery; but although, as a Sicilian, he took a special interest in the
slave wars, and undoubtedly (like Poseidonios) believed that unjustifiable ill
treatment lay at the root of the uprisings,[123] he also (again like Poseidonios)
believed in the old doctrine, revamped by Panaitios for the benefit of his Ro-
man patrons, that some men are slaves by nature ($\phi\acute{v}\sigma\epsilon\iota$ $\delta o\hat{v}\lambda o\iota$), and others
masters.[124] Treating slaves well was not a blueprint, then or later, for abolish-
ing slavery, and Diodorus shows himself a firm supporter of the social hierar-
chy.[125] This is exactly in line with Pownall's conclusion that the fourth-century
historians and their successors sought to promote aristocratic, conservative,
anti-democratic virtues by a constant appeal to higher moral criteria.[126]

When we search the *Bibliotheke* for its author's professions and methods,
we find a good deal of interesting material. The antecedent historical texts
to which he refers, including Herodotos, Thucydides, Xenophon, Ephoros,
Theopompos, Philistos, Timaios, Hieronymos of Kardia, and Polybios, form
an impressive list,[127] and the theory first popularized by Volquardsen[128] that

---

[121] See esp. F59, F250, F262 Edelstein-Kidd, with Kidd 1988, 293–295, and 1999, 129,
320–321, 336–337.

[122] Farrington 1936, 9–35: "Diodorus . . . seems to preserve for us echoes from the earlier Stoic period when its devotion was to the City of the World and not the City on the
Tiber" (35).

[123] See, e.g., 34/35.2.33, where he specifically chastises those who treat slaves badly, and
36.10.3, an admiring account of the slave-leader Satyros' end. This does not stop him, as a
local property-holder, from agonizing over the devastation of Sicily by the uprisings.

[124] For a remarkable instance of this belief in Poseidonios, see Athen. 6.263C–D (*FGrH*
87 F 8) = F60 Edelstein-Kidd. Kidd (1988, 297) is unjustifiably skeptical of its clear implications. On the whole problem, see Walbank 1985, 157–180, esp. 176–178 (= "Political
Morality and the Friends of Scipio," *JRS* 55 [1965]: 1–16, largely based on W. Capelle, *Klio*
25 [1932]: 86–113). The old doctrine was in essence that underwritten by Plato (e.g., *Rep.*
5.469B–C, *Laws* 766B, 778A), and Aristotle (*Pol.* 1252a26–1252b9, 1253b15–1255a3). Panaitios, as Walbank says (1985, 176), "gave the Romans what they were looking for."

[125] He endorses the manipulation of omens by higher authority to keep the lower orders quiet: 15.53.3–4; 20.11.3–4. He dislikes Sicily's populist despots: 19.1.1–5. He approves
the execution of aggressive demagogues: 15.57.4.

[126] Pownall 2004, 3–4, 176–182.

[127] See Chamoux et al. 1983, xxiii–xxv, for a convenient conspectus.

[128] Volquardsen 1868, ch. iv, 26–47. He writes (26): "Die Verwechslung der Erwäh-
nungen von Schriftstellern mit Quellenangaben verleitete zu der Annahme, daß Diodor
viele Werke benutzt, vielleicht sogar, daß er sie zu einem Ganzen verarbeitet habe"; cf. 5ff.
This assumption, on which he proceeds to pour scorn, is coming to be regarded, with rea-

he in fact read few of them, so that even his knowledge of a classic such as Herodotos was limited to references in Ephoros, is coming to be seen as, at the very least, a gross exaggeration.[129] Further, Diodorus at least talks like a serious historian. He gives due emphasis to selectivity (4.5.2) and proportion (4.5.4). He insists, where possible, upon autopsy (3.11.3) and close scrutiny of detail (4.46.5). Antecedent causes, topography, and social background are a necessary preliminary to narrative exposition, διήγησις (18.5.1). If he sets out to rationalize myth (3.52.1–3), he is in good company. He understands the artificiality of dividing up simultaneous groups of events to facilitate exposition (20.43.7; see also above, pp. 10–11). He regards it as essential to compare variant sources (2.32.1). He attacks lengthy speeches as a substitute for analysis (20.1–2.2). He recognizes the distortions that can be brought about by ethnic prejudice (3.34.6) and emphasizes that even the best scholars are not infallible. In an outburst that should win him sympathy from anyone else in the profession, he trashes those uncreative nigglers who spend all their time denigrating the work of others without producing anything themselves (26.1.1–3).

Diodorus has suffered, more than most ancient authors, from the effects on scholarship of nineteenth-century positivism.[130] Here was a (predominantly Germanic) world in which manuscripts enjoyed a tidy direct descent untroubled by lateral *contaminatio*, whereas late scissors-and-paste historians, similarly, obliged modern scholars by using one source almost exclusively for each historical period, and were so fundamentally stupid that all they could do was copy that source more or less verbatim, thus making its identification an easy matter. In 1911, Grenfell and Hunt pronounced: "Evidently Diodorus was a writer of very slight originality, and a future editor of Ephorus' fragments will be able to include most of Diodorus XI with confidence."[131] Ja-

---

son, as by no means as absurd as Volquardsen thought. See, e.g., Pavan 1961, 19–52; Sacks 1990, 51 n. 118; Lévy 2001, passim.

[129] Dionysios of Halikarnassos in his *Letter to Gnaeus Pompeius*, and Lucian later, a fortiori, in his essay "How History Should Be Written," make it clear that by Diodorus' day, Herodotos, Thucydides, and Xenophon were classics, and their texts readily available. The onus is on those who wish to prove that Diodorus had *not* read them, rather than that he had.

[130] Sacks 1990, 4: "The notion that Diodorus *is incapable of intruding into the text to any significant degree* has its roots in nineteenth-century scientific positivism" (emphasis mine).

[131] B. P. Grenfell and A. S. Hunt, *The Oxyrhynchus Papyri*, vol. 13 (London, 1911), 111, commentary on 1610 = *FGrH* 70 F 191. They predicted, accurately, that "the effect of 1610 on the criticism of other books of Diodorus" was "likely to be considerable" (something no one familiar with Stylianou's *Commentary* on Book 15 would be inclined to deny). What they failed to point out (see below) was that the identification of 1610 as the work of Ephoros depended on a circular argument.

coby and his successors took the hint, and we are still suffering from their enthusiasm. A corollary of this, of course, was that an *absence* of such direct copying from known and surviving texts (in particular those of Herodotos and Thucydides) had to mean that these authors were not used as sources, and indeed—despite their availability and reputation as standard classics—were probably not even read by the hapless *Dummkopf* of a compiler, whose knowledge of them had to be filtered through an inferior (and, conveniently, nonsurviving) secondary text, in Diodorus' case, of course, for the classical period, Ephoros.[132] It has only been very recently that this *simpliste* thesis has come under serious, and well-justified, attack.

Volquardsen's interpretation, presenting Diodorus as a mindless copyist, not only seriously skewed the historiographical evidence, but also, perhaps worse, tacitly invited subsequent scholars to sidestep difficult historical problems by ascribing them all to Diodoran stupidity, thus avoiding the need actually to explain them. A scapegoat that offered a yardstick for dealing with recalcitrant evidence, a tidy, manageable universe for the aspiring *Gelehrte,* and, perhaps best of all, the means of constantly reaffirming that *Gelehrte's* rigorous scholarly skepticism, was irresistible. The result has been a century and more of critical work for the most part devoted to *Quellenforschung,* the quest for Diodorus' putative sources. To what extent the effort was worthwhile remains an open question. In many cases there is no agreement on attribution: as Delfino Ambaglio recently remarked, when one passage of Diodorus can be claimed for five different sources, the suspicion arises that at least four-fifths of the industry is going nowhere.[133] Also, even the most critical scholars are not always proof against circular arguments. Sacks endorses the traditional identification of Ephoros as the author of P.Oxy. 1610 on the

---

[132] Volquardsen (1868) is the fundamental source for this basic argument (see in particular his ch. 5, "Verhältniss Diodors zu Herodot, Thukydides und Xenophon," 28–47, and ch. 6, "Die Art der Darstellung in den griechischen Geschichten der Büchern XI–XV Diodors," 47–51, as regards the period covered in the present work): later scholars, from Schwartz to Hornblower, have done little but repeat or develop Volquardsen's essential thesis. This can be summed up thus: (a) Diodorus made no use of the three major surviving historians, Herodotos, Thucydides, and Xenophon; (b) evidence supplied by his text—which he lacked the originality to provide himself—indicates one regular alternative source. Cf. Volquardsen's summation at 46–47. This source is then (ch. 7, 51ff.) firmly identified as Ephoros. Cf. Schwartz 1903, col. 679; S. Hornblower, in *CAH* vi, 8–10; and K. Meister's perfunctory entry for Diodorus in *DNP* 3 (1997), cols. 592–594.

[133] Ambaglio 1995, 9: "Di fronte all'attributazione di uno stesso passo a cinque fonti diverse . . . sembra difficilmente evitabile la conclusione che per un (probabile) pezzo di Quellenforschung buona ce ne quattro (sicuri) di cattiva."

grounds of close verbal similarity with D.S. 11.60.6 and 61.1.[134] But all this shows is that the papyrus fragment was very probably from Diodorus' source; the identification of that source is still made on the a priori assumption that for the entire classical period, Ephoros was virtually the only text on which Diodorus depended.

That Diodorus used Ephoros regularly is certain. He describes his *History* in detail (16.76.5, cf. 4.1.3, 16.14.3). He claims to have followed him as far as possible (κατὰ τὸ δυνατόν) in his practice of organizing the events of each book κατὰ τὸ γένος, that is, by nationality (5.1.4). He cites Ephoros on the antiquity of barbarian history (1.9.5), the myth of the Idaian Dactyls (5.64.4), the causes of the Peloponnesian War (12.41.1), a wartime temple dedication at Koroneia (13.41.2–3), the death of Alcibiades (14.11.1–4), and the assassination of Jason of Pherai (15.60.5). He uses him as a counter-authority to Timaios for estimates of troop numbers (13.54.5, 60.5, 80.5; 14.22.2, 54.5–6). Yet Diodorus does not refer to Ephoros either in his general preface or anywhere in the narrative covering the Persian Wars and the Pentekontaetia; and his one other mention of him (among a number of other historians, in an extended discussion of the sources of the Nile: 1.37.4, 39.7–13) is highly critical, ending with the dismissive comment: "But one would not on every occasion seek precise accuracy in Ephoros, seeing that in so many instances he fell short of the truth."[135] Ephoros is also criticized (1.9.5) for giving historical credence to mythical/prehistoric events. This is, on the face of it, an improbable choice, even for a reputed *Dummkopf*, as sole guide through the two most crucial centuries of Greek history, not least when, in the same context (1.37.4), he acknowledges the accuracy of Thucydides, whom we now know he was quite capable of rewriting in a highly un-Thucydidean style.[136] The old assumption

---

[134] Sacks 1990, 53 and n. 125, referring to *FGrH* 70 F 191. For refreshing and commonsensical skepticism, see Africa 1962, 86–89 (with the caveats of Reid [Rubincam] 1976, 357 n. 2), and Brown 1952, 343. Cf. Book 11, note 226.

[135] 1.39.13: ἀλλὰ γὰρ οὐκ ἄν τις παρ' Ἐφόρῳ ζητήσειεν ἐκ πάντος τρόπου τἀκριβές, ὁρῶν αὐτὸν ἐν πολλοῖς ὠλιγωρηκότα τῆς ἀληθείας. This statement does not disturb the skeptics one whit: for them, Diodorus remains a mental defective so dumb that he copied this criticism from his source (not, for once, Ephoros himself) without understanding its implications. See K. Meister, "Absurde Polemik bei Diodor," *Helikon* 13/14 (1973–74): 454–459, esp. 455; cf. Burton 1972, 21–22; Sacks 1990, 112 and n. 125. For a good discussion of Diodorus' casual and critical treatment of Ephoros as a source, see now Pownall 2004, 118.

[136] Lévy 2001, 333ff., on the relation between D.S. 12.62.6–7, 67.3–5, and Thuc. 4.12.3, 80. Comparing other passages in the two, Palm (1955, 62) had already concluded that "zwischen Thukydides und D.S. ist kein Platz für Ephoros," and Lévy (2001, 341) reaches

that Diodorus' prefaces are all merely Ephoran platitudes *réchauffé* has likewise come under hard, and well-justified, critical scrutiny.[137]

In this connection, researches like those of Palm and, particularly, Lévy
have done more than disrupt the old positivist notion of a mindless copyist
conveniently serving up, nearly verbatim, excerpts of one main source for each
period. They have also shown, when we can control both source and copy,
how effectively Diodorus eliminated all of, say, Thucydides' stylistic and psychological insights (while for the most part preserving his facts).[138] In other
words, the apparent absence of a track record in Diodorus' text for any particular source is not cogent evidence for his not having consulted or used it.

For the period with which I am primarily concerned—the Persian Wars
and the Pentekontaetia—Diodorus refers to Herodotos, Ephoros, and Thucydides, and it is a reasonable conclusion, as my commentary assumes, that
he had read them all.[139] In the case of Ephoros, we simply do not—*pace* the
tradition running from Volquardsen and Schwartz via Barber to Stylianou—
have enough of his text to judge either the extent to which Diodorus drew on
him or the precise effect on his judgment where he did. Were our knowledge
of Herodotos restricted to the comments of Dionysios of Halikarnassos, Plutarch's essay *De malignitate Herodoti* (*Mor.* 854E–874B), some ambiguous papyrus scraps, and thirty or forty *parti pris* quotations taken from the historian's
more whimsical asides, our conclusions would probably be about as reliable
as those commonly accepted regarding Ephoros—or, worse, Ctesias.[140] In
the circumstances, I am in complete agreement with Claude Vial, the editor
of Book 15 of the *Bibliotheke,* when she argues that Diodoran source-criticism

---

an identical conclusion: "Diodore reste très proche de Thucydide tant pour les faits rap-
portés que pour les termes employés. Il est donc inutile de supposer un intermédiaire, par
exemple Ephore, entre les deux auteurs."

[137] Sacks 1982, 434ff.; cf. Pownall 2004, 139.

[138] Lévy 2001, 341: "Mais Diodore ne comprend pas ou néglige ce qui fait l'originalité
de Thucydide, à savoir l'interprétation générale qui dépasse l'anecdote pour éclairer les relations sociales et les mentalités de Sparte. Si, à part quelques erreurs ou suppositions gra-
tuites, Diodore a bien conservé le recit des événements, il ne permet pas de retrouver les
conceptions de l'historien dont il s'est inspiré." See also Palm 1955.

[139] He also mentions Antiochos of Syracuse (*FGrH* 555), the fifth-century Western historian who slightly predated Thucydides, and whose book *On Italy* was chiefly concerned
with foundation legends. His *Sikelika,* in nine books, went down to the Congress of Gela
in 424, but again seems to have concentrated on colonial foundations: cf. Pearson 1987, 11–
18. For my present argument, Antiochos is not of great importance.

[140] When I wrote these words I was unaware that the idea had in fact been tried out: see
D. Lenfant 1999. I am grateful to Prof. Marincola for directing my attention to this remarkable, and disconcerting, article.

is far less important than the scrutiny of Diodorus' own text "as a source for the modern historian,"[141] and the present work accepts this as a guiding principle throughout.

Perhaps the most important result has been a systematic demolition of the myth that Diodorus himself was a virtual imbecile. Once we concede that he had, at the very least, a rational mind and some talent for historiographical synthesis, our whole approach to the various errors discernible in his text undergoes a fundamental change. We can no longer ascribe them all, contemptuously, to the vacillations of a mindless scribbler; they need to be explained on a rational basis. The possibility must be faced that Diodorus actually read the sources that he mentions, and perhaps others that he does not, and based his own narrative on a critical assessment of their findings.

We would, therefore, be ill advised to dismiss out of hand almost everything Diodorus tells us about his life and the composition of the *Bibliotheke* as a tissue of second-hand clichés borrowed from the writings of earlier historians.[142] We must also face the need to reassess many of the historical problems his text presents, hitherto conveniently shelved by a casual reference to his alleged intellectual incompetence. Of course, like all ancient historians, he made mistakes: in a forty-book project such as the *Bibliotheke,* granted the difficulty of cross-referencing in and between scrolls (something at which Diodorus was in fact better than most),[143] errors were bound to occur. Yet a

---

[141] Vial 1977, x, cf. xv: "Les recherches sur l'origine du texte de Diodore doivent céder le pas à l'étude de ce texte, considéré comme une source pour l'historien d'aujourd'hui." Cf. also Catherine Rubincam's sensible remarks (1998a, 512–513), arguing not for "a wholesale rejection of the methods and conclusions of traditional Diodoran scholarship focussed on *Quellenforschung,*" but rather for the recognition of (a) the limitations "in the case of an author whose text cannot be directly compared with surviving putative sources," (b) the inconsistent conclusions reached by different scholars working on various parts of the *Bibliotheke,* and (c) the consequent need to base research on the text as a whole. These conclusions, too, I would endorse.

[142] See, e.g., Hornblower 1981, 24–26. It is often pointed out, as proof of his unreliability, that Diodorus places Nineveh on the Euphrates rather than the Tigris: clearly, it is alleged, he never really traveled in Asia, and his claims to autopsy are fictional. But Diodorus himself in fact specifically acknowledges (2.2.2, 7.1–2) that he never visited Nineveh, trusting instead to the accounts of Ctesias and other travelers. (We can, if we like, fault his memory, since elsewhere—17.53.4, 55.3, by which time he may well have forgotten what he wrote in Book 2—he drew on a source that put Nineveh, correctly, by the Tigris.) He makes a similar admission concerning the Red Sea (3.38.1), and indeed sharply criticizes Ephoros for failing to use autopsy or to question travelers (1.39.9) regarding the annual inundation of the Nile.

[143] A valuable fact conclusively demonstrated by Rubincam in a series of well-documented articles (1987, 1989, 1998c).

number of those in the *Bibliotheke,* not least double accounts of identical or parallel episodes,[144] prove on closer inspection either amenable to rational analysis or of such a nature as to immediately strike the eye of an even moderately intelligent person on revision. So long as Diodorus was regarded as capable of lapses that would call a schoolchild's mental competence in question, such passages lacked proper attention, being accommodated, without further thought, as additional proofs of the scribbler's stupidity. But once we see him as a rational and reasonably diligent (if unimaginative) historian, this avenue of escape is shut off. When the historically explicable cases have been dealt with, the remainder only make sense if we assume that, for whatever reason (death being the most likely), Diodorus left his final revisions incomplete.[145]

What is more, his supposed "slavish dependence on his sources," [146] however exaggerated, can now be seen as an unexpected advantage in the light of Bosworth's exemplary demonstration that Diodorus and his like, whatever the rhetorical and moral flourishes they may have added, did not normally modify the *factual* tradition they inherited, much less "add bogus 'facts' out of their imagination." [147] Thus the historical testimony they present can, to a degree hitherto unaccepted, be taken as accurately representing that of their sources. As Bosworth does not fail to remind us, since those sources, *per contra,* the "contemporary historians who produced the first narratives of their age," were involved, often personally, in the events they chronicled, they were by no means immune to "partisan zeal and malice, and could include the most sensational exaggerations which were then accepted by subsequent his-

---

[144] For various instances and types of these, see, e.g., 13.34.1–3 = 13.36.1–5 (Athenian actions following the defeat in Sicily), 16.31.6 = 16.34.4–5 (Philip at Methone), 16.34.3 = 16.39.4 (battle of Orneae), and 12.19.1–2 = 13.33.2–3 (death of Diokles/Charondas).

[145] The virtual absence of such cruxes in the early books suggests (though of course cannot prove) how far the final overall revisions had proceeded. Diodorus makes it clear (40.8) that the pirated books (which I take to have been early ones) were still in rough draft. These he evidently lived to correct. When he states (1.4.6) that "the undertaking has reached its conclusion, though the books as yet remain unpublished" (ἡ μὲν ὑπόθεσις ἔχει τέλος, αἱ βίβλοι δὲ μέχρι τοῦ νῦν ἀνέκδοται τυγχάνουσιν οὖσαι), he is clearly describing the final achievement of a first draft, and allowing for corrections to come. Some passages in the surviving historical narrative of Books 11–20, indeed, could be still-unreconciled notes from alternative versions: see the discussions ad loc. (in the present volume) of the battle of Oinophyta (11.83.1) and Perikles in Akarnania (11.85.1–2, 88.1–2).

[146] Hornblower 1981, 28.

[147] Bosworth 2003, 194. The entire article is of the greatest historiographical significance. "The nature of the game was to operate with the material at one's disposal, identifying and criticizing falsehood and bias, combining details from several sources into a composite picture not paralleled in any single source, but not adding invention of one's own."

torians." He gives a nice fourth-century example: the *prima facie* improbable claim, reported by both Diodorus and Plutarch,[148] that none of the Silver Shields was less than sixty years old, which clearly goes back to Hieronymos of Kardia.

In dealing with the *Bibliotheke*'s account of the Persian wars and the Pentekontaetia, the historian's critical focus must, similarly, be concentrated above all on Herodotos, Thucydides, and whomever apart from these— Charon of Lampsakos? Ctesias? Hellanikos?[149]—Ephoros may have used. Here, of course, we come up against the ancient historian's endemic difficulty (to which *FGrH* is a standing monument) in its most frustrating form. Charon is little more than a name, Hellanikos subsists only in a handful of much-debated fragments, and the excerpts of Ctesias leave one wondering whether a physician at the court of Artaxerxes II could really have been such a tabloid-gossip addict throughout the unabridged twenty-three books of his *Persian History* that have failed to survive. Thus to evaluate the constantly present "vulgate tradition" drawn on by Diodorus, and its significant variations from Herodotos and Thucydides, becomes an intellectual charade: as Eliot said, "hints and guesses, hints followed by guesses." In the circumstances I have largely avoided trying to gauge the prejudices of works that have failed to survive,[150] finding it more profitable to concentrate instead on the inherent plausibility of the evidence as Diodorus assembles it.

The peculiar animus against Diodorus demonstrated by modern scholars stands in striking contrast to the high praise lavished on him from late antiquity to the eighteenth century. Pliny's *Natural History* (*praef.* 25) is one of the few surviving works by a Greek or Roman pagan author to mention him;[151] but this is not surprising, since such writers had full access to the sources on

---

[148] Bosworth 2003, 194; D.S. 19.41.2; Plut. *Eum.* 16.4; cf. Hornblower 1981, 192–193.

[149] Schepens (1977, 103) assembles and documents the possibilities. See pp. 39–47 below for a discussion of the (wholly inadequate) evidence, in particular that of Charon and Ctesias.

[150] Not all scholars have been so reticent: it was probably some of their more imaginative efforts that Housman had in mind when, in his introduction to his edition of Juvenal (1905, xxviii), he described *Quellenforschung* and *Ueberlieferungsgeschichte* as "those two lines of fiction."

[151] See also Athen. 12.541e–f (= D.S. 11.25). Zecchini (1987, 49–51 with n. 35) cites M. R. Dilts' edition of Aelian's *Varia historia* (Leipzig, 1974) for no less than twenty-three passages derived from Diodorus, while Sacks (1990, 162–163 with n. 10) demonstrates the likelihood of both Plutarch and Dio Cassius having drawn on the *Bibliotheke*. In any case, the traditional claim, most recently made by Hornblower (1981, 18), that Diodorus "is not cited by pagan authors, apart from Pliny," can no longer be sustained.

which he drew, and thus no need for a largely derivative digest.[152] It was, inevitably, Christian scholars and thinkers to whom the *Bibliotheke,* with its universalist schema, its useful chronology, and its constant trawling of the past for moral lessons, held an instant and irresistible appeal.[153] Fifteen of Diodorus' forty books survive today for precisely the same reason as do the countless volumes of Migne's *Patrologia;* and had it not been for the sacking of Constantinople by Western crusaders in the Fourth Crusade of 1204,[154] we might well have the *Bibliotheke* in its entirety.

Eusebius of Caesarea (c. 260–339 C.E.), whose lost *Chronicle* (preserved in Jerome's Latin version and an Armenian translation) set out—by correlating Biblical, Near Eastern, and Greco-Roman history into a single chronological sequence—to prove that "God's plan for salvation subsumed the whole of history,"[155] drew on Diodorus extensively,[156] and is lavish in his praise of him as "the man of greatest distinction among Greek scholars for having made a single narrative from the whole range of historical works."[157] Justin Martyr

---

[152] The principle was one that Housman (1905, xi) knew and approved: "Either *a* is the source of *b* and *c* and *d* or it is not. If it is, then never should recourse be had to *b* or *c* or *d.* If it is not, the rule ['I have made it my rule to follow *a* wherever possible, and only where its readings are patently erroneous have I had recourse to *b* or *c* or *d*'—still a depressingly popular principle] is irrational; for it involves the assumption that wherever *a*'s scribes made a mistake they produced an impossible reading." The implications, *mutatis mutandis,* for historiography hardly need stressing. Housman's entire discourse on this matter should be of the greatest interest to historians no less than to textual critics, as should his brief remarks (xxviii) on the practice of *Quellenforschung.* In a world where *a* is substantially lost, and we need to deal with *b* and *c* and *d faute de mieux,* Housman's conclusions still have peculiar relevance, and I have used them as a benchmark throughout my career as a historian.

[153] See now the detailed account by P. F. Béatrice ("Diodore de Sicile chez les apologistes," in *Les apologistes chrétiens et la culture grecque,* ed. B. Pouderon and J. Doré [Beauchesne, 1998], 219–235), who points out how such writers adapted and utilized Stoic and even Euhemeristic elements in Diodorus for their own purposes.

[154] See, e.g., S. Runciman, *A History of the Crusades,* vol. 3, *The Kingdom of Acre and the Later Crusades* (Cambridge, 1955), 122ff. For the riches of the libraries in Constantinople, and the disastrous losses incurred as a result of the 1204 sack, see L. D. Reynolds and N. G. Wilson, *Scribes and Scholars,* 3d ed. (Oxford, 1991), 69–70, 72–73. The authors quote a (somewhat improbable) claim by Constantine Lascaris that a complete copy of Diodorus' *Bibliotheke* miraculously survived—only to be destroyed later by the Turks!

[155] Averil M. Cameron, in *OCD,* 576.

[156] Chamoux et al. 1993, cxxv–cxxviii, analyzes all references.

[157] Euseb. *Praep. Ev.* 1.6.9: ὁ Σικελιώτης Διόδωρος, γνωριμώτατος ἀνὴρ τοῖς Ἑλλήνων λογιωτάτοις, ὡς ἂν ὑπὸ μίαν συναγηοχὼς πραγματείαν ἅπασαν τὴν ἱστορικὴν βιβλιοθήκην. Cf. also 2. *proem.* 6.

and Julius Africanus show similar enthusiasm.[158] To the sixth-century John Malalas of Antioch, himself the author of a universal chronicle based on Christ's incarnation, Diodorus was "the wisest" (ὁ σοφώτατος).[159] The *Suda* cites him over sixty times. In his introduction to the first complete edition of the *Bibliotheke's* Greek text (Geneva, 1559), Henri Estienne [Stephanus], though underwhelmed by Diodorus' prose style, likened his historical preeminence to that of the sun among stars.[160] Stephanus' edition excited other scholars to similar hyperbolic admiration.[161] Poggio Bracciolini translated his first five books into Latin in 1449, and about 1486 John Skelton made a hyperaureate English version of the early books from Bracciolini.[162] As late as the mid-eighteenth century, that great scholar Peter Wesseling's commentary "was still respectful of the worth of the *Bibliotheke* as a historical source."[163]

As early as 1670, however, Diodorus' probable dependence on Polybios had been noted,[164] and Wesseling himself pointed out similarities to the earlier historian in Diodorus' general preface. But then came Niebuhr and his successors. If these nineteenth-century German scholars who applied their principles of *Quellenforschung* to the *Bibliotheke* had restricted themselves to establishing its derivative nature, relating its text to earlier *surviving* sources, and evaluating its findings in terms of historical probability, ἀπὸ τῶν εἰκότων, as Greek orators would say, they would have performed a necessary and useful function. Instead, they declared primary (i.e., earlier) texts by definition more trustworthy than later ones, assumed mindless direct copying by the lat-

---

[158] Chamoux et al. 1993, xxv; Hornblower 1981, 18 n. 3.

[159] Chamoux et al. 1993, lxvii, cf. cxxxii.

[160] See Dindorf's 4th ed. (Leipzig, 1868), vol. 5, 331, where Estienne's eulogy is quoted: "quantum enim solis lumen inter stellas, tantum inter omnes quotquot ad nostra tempora peruenerunt historicos (si utilitatis potius quam uoluptatis aurium habenda sit ratio) noster Diodorus eminere dici potest."

[161] See, e.g., the exclamatory praise of Rhodoman, cited by Hornblower 1981, 18: "quem ubi primum legere coepi, dicere non possum, quantos in animo statim meo hic scriptor amores excitarit! in quantam sui admirationem me rapuerit!"

[162] *The* Bibliotheca Historica *of Diodorus Siculus, translated by John Skelton,* ed. F. M. Salter and H. L. R. Edwards, Early English Text Society (London, 1956–57). Of this extraordinary euphuistic translation I remarked, in my monograph *John Skelton* (London, 1960), 10: "For rank periphrastic prolixity, rhetorical curlicues, and expansion of its original text, this work must stand almost without rivals."

[163] Rubincam 1998a, 506. The subsequent editor of Wesseling, J. N. Eyring, was at pains to defend Diodorus "contra iniquas adversariorum reprehensiones" (Wesseling and Eyring 1793, vol. 1, cvff.).

[164] By J. H. Boecler, in an essay entitled "Diodori Siculi Imitatio Polybiana," included in his *Lectiones Polybianae:* Hornblower 1981, 19.

ter, erected an elaborate house of academic cards to prove derivation from largely nonsurviving sources (which they then evaluated on the basis of ancient *parti pris* gossip and dubious fragments), and attempted to prove their scholarly rigor and objectivity by the skepticism with which they treated the late sources, Diodorus in particular, and the fusillade of insults they hurled at him.

Here Niebuhr set the fashion right from the beginning, damning Diodorus as "naïve, unlearned, totally spiritless, without judgment, silly, incompetent even as an epitomiser," and one of the "worst historians who has come down to us in either of the languages of antiquity from any period."[165] How far this extraordinary outburst—repeated, in equally emotional terms, by numerous later scholars—was provoked by Diodorus' elevation of moral *ethos* over historical *praxis,* and the (largely fortuitous) Christological baggage that his text acquired in consequence, it is impossible to say. As should by now be tolerably clear, however, this verdict (not to mention the methodology behind it) not only was mistaken, but encouraged historians to shelve, or misjudge, a great many historical problems that demanded serious attention[166]—something I have constantly borne in mind throughout the present work.

## THE PERSIAN WARS AND THE PENTEKONTAETIA

As Spoerri rightly reminds us, that section of the *Bibliotheke* dealing with the period from 480 to 431 is, or should be, of the greatest interest to ancient historians.[167] In the circumstances, the lack of basic scholarship is remarkable. The only modern English translation of Books 11–12 hitherto available has been that of Oldfather (1946) in the Loeb series, while the nearest approach to a commentary on them, in any language, has been that provided by the (necessarily brief) notes of Casevitz (1972) and, more expansively, by Haillet (2001) in the Budé edition. Haillet in particular has taken careful note of recent scholarship, and some of his comments have helped me considerably. Alois Scherr's dissertation, *Diodors XI. Buch Kompositions- und Quellenstudien*

---

[165] Cited (with approval) by Hornblower (1981, 19).

[166] For typical, and egregious, examples, see (a) the arguments of the traditionalists in attempting to explain the discrepancy of terminal dates for the ending of the *Bibliotheke* (Appendix A); and (b) the accusations of chronological ignorance discussed in the proem to Book 12 (1.5).

[167] Spoerri (1991, 312), listing the many periods, including those of Philip II, Alexander, the early *Diadochoi,* and Dionysios I of Syracuse, "présentant un intérêt majeur pour les historiens," duly includes the years Diodorus covers in Books 11–12.

(1933), on the other hand, promises more than it delivers. Though Scherr is uneasily aware that the *Bibliotheke* draws on testimony over and above the main block sources regularly posited by Volquardsen and his successors, he still treats Diodorus, in essence, as a slavish copyist[168]—but one who inserted numerous additions to his main source so unintelligently that a watchful *Gelehrte* could easily spot them by the inconcinnities and contradictions that their mindless introduction created.

In the first instance, then, my aim has simply been to fill a regrettable gap. But to achieve that end—as should by now be all too clear—I have had to grapple with the daunting task of rescuing Diodorus as a historical source from a century and a half of systematic, and highly misleading, misrepresentation.[169] It may therefore be advantageous to recapitulate at this point the various conclusions, discussed above, that I have reached in the course of my investigations, with a view to calculating their possible impact on my attitude to, and interpretation of, the Diodoran historiography of the Persian Wars and the Pentekontaetia. Inevitably, these findings will have been dictated at least in part by purely personal beliefs and judgments, and I hope that—especially in the final one or two points I raise—I have made proper allowances for this.

(1) Though quite capable of error, and no more than an average secondary-source historian, Diodorus was not the mental defective that critics from Niebuhr on have regularly portrayed him as: he planned and carried out a vast undertaking with excellent organization and economy, and in his cross-referencing within and between book rolls compares well with other similar writers.[170] Result: Numerous historical problems can no longer be shelved with a dismissive allusion to his stupidity, but demand re-examination in rational terms. Obvious inconsistencies in his work probably indicate rough alternative drafts that he did not live to revise.

(2) The *Bibliotheke* does not consist of near-verbatim extracts from one source for each historical period (however convenient this would be for historians). Result: The old assumption that throughout Books 11–12 he is vir-

---

[168] Scherr announces (1933, vii) that he intends to disprove the prevalent theory that "Diodor . . . seine Quellen mehr oder minder mechanisch ausgeschrieben und nur in seine Sprache übertragen hat, weshalb ihm auch der Vorwurf eines gedanklosen Ab- und Ausscheibers nicht erspart blieb," but in fact his own thesis merely reinforces the accusation of *Gedanklosigkeit*.

[169] My debt to earlier scholars in the field is, it goes without saying, considerable: see the Preface above for acknowledgments.

[170] Rubincam 1987, 1989, 1998c.

tually transcribing Ephoros must be abandoned, and a great many passages
hitherto listed as Ephoran fragments removed from the canon. Ephoros may
indeed have been his primary source for these books, but this tells us much
less than has hitherto been assumed: see (3) and (7).

(3) Some basic assumptions of *Quellenforschung* need serious modification.
Even were we able to prove beyond a shadow of doubt (which we cannot) that
a passage of Diodorus was, in fact, more or less copied from Ephoros, what
does that tell us? Since we do not have Ephoros' text, but only out-of-context
extracts (and not many of those), plus the *parti pris* judgments of ancient critics and rival historians, it tells us very little, and what it does say is highly unreliable. The suspicion arises that this process was simply designed to minimize the value of late secondary sources by comparison with Herodotos and
Thucydides.

(4) A corollary to (3) is the equally fallacious assumption that the testimony
of Herodotos and Thucydides is always *by definition* to be preferred over that
of a late source such as Diodorus. But this involves the illogical assumption
(duly castigated, *mutatis mutandis*, by Housman) that every time the late source
differs from Herodotos or Thucydides, the late source gets it wrong. It also,
now, comes up against the demonstrable fact[171] that though writers such as
Diodorus embellish their narrative with rhetoric, they are at pains to transmit
the original author's *facts* accurately. It is the *contemporary* sources—whose
findings later texts transmit—that put the prejudicial spin on their version of
events. Result: The facts recorded by the *Bibliotheke* must thus be evaluated
*on the same basis as* those in Herodotos or Thucydides—that is, on their intrinsic plausibility. *All* sources, Herodotos and Thucydides included, must
be checked as far as possible for contemporary bias. This will obviously be
easier in the case of the two surviving historians of contemporary or near-
contemporary events; see (5).

(5) I am on record[172] as distrusting Thucydides' motives in writing his *History* and finding his reputation for objectivity greatly exaggerated. This, again,
goes against conventional wisdom and underlies some of the judgments in my
commentary: unlike many, I have no difficulty in preferring what scholars,
with exquisite contempt, have labeled "the vulgate tradition"[173] wherever the

---

[171] Bosworth 2003.

[172] See, for example, Green 2004, 72 and 103.

[173] Here, of course, Ephoros enjoys a prominent representative position: described by
Macrobius (5.18.6) as "notissimus scriptor historiarum," he largely "represented throughout Antiquity the 'vulgate' version of Greek history down to the age of Alexander" (Schepens 1977, 96–97).

facts would appear to warrant it. Nor, I hope, has my temperamental prefer-
ence for Herodotos blinded me to *his* prejudices where detectable. Even when
every allowance has been made for nationalistic fervor (that still-flourishing
phenomenon known to a modern Greek as *ethnikismós*), not all of Plutarch's
charges in the *De malignitate Herodoti* are moonshine.

(6) As noted in (2), Diodorus, far from copying his sources slavishly, put
his own stamp on the material he used, eliminating both the original author's
style and many of his personal insights.[174] It thus becomes impossible, using
these criteria, to deduce with any certainty where he has—or, perhaps more
important, has *not*—consulted a particular source, and all claims thus advanced (not least those in *FGrH*) need to be re-examined with a high degree
of skepticism.

(7) The assertion that Diodorus did not read the major authors he cites,
but drew his information on them solely through allusions in later sources,
can no longer be sustained. For Books 11–12 he cites Herodotos, Ephoros, and
Thucydides, and the present work proceeds on the assumption that he was directly familiar with, and drew upon, the texts of all three (as well as some—
e.g., Ctesias—whom he does not cite by name there). The surviving evidence
further suggests that, far from "leaning on [Ephoros] like Hope on her anchor
and trusting to heaven that no harm will come of it"—to adapt Housman's
critique of the superior-manuscript theory[175]—Diodorus, though he often
used Ephoros, frequently preferred other sources and was, in fact, sharply critical on occasion of Ephoros' methods and accuracy. His text also confirms
careful study of, and methodological help from, all of his other various predecessors (discussed above, pp. 16–23), from Theopompos to Poseidonios.

(8) The conclusion that not one word that Diodorus tells us about his travels or his working methods can be believed, on the apparent basis that a congenital fool must also be a congenital liar, and the bigger the fool, the more
all-pervasive his lies, does not stand up to critical scrutiny. With ordinary allowance made for authorial self-promotion, there is no reason not to take his
claims, by and large, at face value. What he reports about the production of
the *Bibliotheke* also strongly suggests (a) that the early non-annalistic books
were published—and pirated—before the rest, and (b) that the annalistic
books, in particular Books 11–20, never received their final revision, and may,
in places, have still consisted of a rough text with competing draft notes.

(9) While the factual matter Diodorus reports can with fair confidence be

---

[174] Cf. Lévy 2001, 341, on his treatment of Thucydides.
[175] Housman 1905, v.

trusted as a more or less accurate transcript of his primary sources,[176] the personal profile that can be built up from an overall reading of the *Bibliotheke* should always be borne in mind when assessing Diodorus' (like any other historian's) preferences: *suppressio veri,* mostly by omission in a crowded field, always remains a significant factor. His obsession with moral exempla; his fascination with the oddities of myth; his sourness about women; his dislike of philosophers and rhetoricians (he seems to have shared Ephoros' objections to long Thucydidean-style historical speeches); his admiration for Caesar (and other monarchical rulers); his personal coolness, as a Sicilian, toward Octavian; his repeated pleas—also as a Sicilian—for φιλανθρωπία and ἐπιείκεια; perhaps above all his discernible partiality for ad hominem motivation in analyzing political cause and effect:[177] these are factors to remember when assessing his judgments, and I hope I have always done so.

(10) Lastly, an important general point. Historical verdicts are made, too often for comfort, on the basis of what I like to call the Moral Exclusionary Syndrome: that is, an action or event is believed or rejected on the basis of what its protagonists (in the historian's view) either could or, more commonly, "could not possibly" have done. A notorious example of this practice at its most extreme is Sir William Tarn's appendix on the sex life of Alexander the Great.[178] Consciously or (more often) unconsciously, historians retroject their own moral principles into admired figures such as Sokrates or Perikles; American scholars get more uptight than their Mediterranean colleagues over the financial dealings of Themistokles; Athenian democracy is credited with various modern virtues that would have astonished the hard-scrabble politicians who hammered it out. The past century, in my firm belief, has taught us (what men like Thucydides knew well) that there is no political deceit too gross, no military atrocity too vile, no financial dishonesty too outrageous for educated, civilized, well-principled men to embrace when inflamed by ideology and ambition, greed and creed, in pursuit of what the Greeks called *kleos,* that heady mix of glory, success, and renown. If at several points in the historical period covered by the present volume I have challenged conventional interpretations, this belief will, more often than not, be the chief reason.

---

[176] Bosworth 2003.

[177] As Prof. Marincola reminds me (*per litt.*), this habit is "quite in keeping with the vast majority of ancient historians, who often explain 'great' events by recourse to personal motivation: cf. Herodotus' explanation of the origins of the Ionian revolt, or indeed Thucydides' narrative of the Harmodius and Aristogeiton affair."

[178] W. W. Tarn, *Alexander the Great* (Cambridge, 1948), vol. 2, app. 18, "Alexander's Attitude to Sex," 319–326.

Dealing with the Persian Wars and the Pentekontaetia *primarily* from Diodorus' viewpoint leaves the historian with two constant reminders that neither Herodotos nor Thucydides can (as they too often are) be treated as offering the final and virtually unchallengeable word on these crucial periods. The first—more often felt when making comparisons with Thucydides—is a regular ongoing awareness of the wider world, particularly that of the West: not only its military history and leaders (e.g., Gelon, whose involvement in the Persian Wars is stressed at the outset of Book 11, and who is compared to Themistokles at 23.1–3), but also its political and intellectual developments (e.g., the legal codes of Charondas and Zaleukos, 12.11.4–21.3). One undoubted value of the *Bibliotheke*, irrelevant to its accuracy over historical detail, is thus the synoptic perspective it offers of the larger Greek world in the fifth century, and the consequent adjustments entailed to Thucydides' overly parochial view of *polis* patriotism and internecine city-state conflict.

The second, more complex, infinitely more problematical, and frustratingly underdocumented phenomenon, which no researcher into this period is allowed to forget for long, is the presence, at every turn, of the "vulgate tradition," not just—as scholars sometimes imply—in such regrettable but easily discountable forms as melodramatic rhetoric, romantic anecdotage, disprovable historical fictions, and overworked popular *Märchen*, but encapsulating a specific factual, and per se credible, record at odds with Herodotean or Thucydidean testimony, and, in general, with an Athenocentric interpretation of events. As should by now be clear, the still too-common historiographical practice of regularly rejecting such conflicting "vulgate" evidence on principle is in essence flawed: as in the cognate case of rival manuscript readings, the notion of the "better" source should only be invoked (and then as a *pis aller*) in a case where there is nothing to choose, on the face of it, between two discrepant views.[179] To do otherwise is to ignore the obvious truism that even the most untrustworthy source—Ctesias, say, or the Alexander Romance—does not, by definition, get *everything* wrong; that nuggets of good testimony survive amid the dross, and that the historian's business, working ἀπὸ τῶν εἰκότων, on the basis of probability, is to find them. There are no shortcuts.

This is particularly true when we try to isolate, let alone evaluate, alternative primary sources for the Persian Wars and the Pentakontaetia. One of the

---

[179] As Housman pointed out (1905, xv): "In thus committing ourselves to the guidance of the best MS we cherish no hope that it will always lead us right: we know that it will often lead us wrong; but we know that any other MS would lead us wrong still oftener." The same is essentially true of all historical testimony.

few positive leads we have is Thucydides' clear statement (1.97.2) that no previous writer, except for Hellanikos, had dealt with the Pentekontaetia, and that Hellanikos only covered this period briefly in his *Atthis* and was vague about dates.[180] Yet in that case, on whom, apart from Hellanikos (most of whose few surviving *Atthis* fragments are mythological, not historical),[181] were Ephoros and Diodorus' other secondary sources, not to mention Plutarch, depending when they differed (as they frequently do) from the Thucydidean version of events? We simply do not know, and speculation merely confuses the issue. All that seems likely, given the facts of the case, is that Thucydides' claim to be first in the field was, for whatever reason, mistaken.[182] This is hardly a helpful conclusion. Yet as we shall see, the "vulgate tradition," often highly critical of Athenian methods,[183] in fact by and large confirms, in unflattering detail, Thucydides' thesis of Athens' steadily increasing naval imperialism as a prime cause of the Peloponnesian War.

We are little better served as regards the Persian Wars, though it is at least known that a number of contemporary writers dealt with them, that their accounts often differed in detail from that of Herodotos, and that they probably, like him, exploited the various possible sources well described by Macan:[184] the oral evidence of eyewitnesses, in particular naval and military personnel, whether Athenian, Spartan, or other; local tradition, especially about earlier events (e.g., Marathon), and speeches made on notable occasions; autopsy of battle sites and related terrain, together with ethnographic

---

[180] Thucydides' words are βραχέως καὶ τοῖς χρόνοις οὐκ ἀκριβῶς ἐπεμνήσθη: this need not imply actual false dates, but a more general lack of chronological specificity, which seems far more probable: cf. Pearson 1939, 224: "Evidently no records were kept in Athens, and Hellanicus had no documents to which he could refer to verify the dates of events." In any case, as neither Gomme (1945, 280) nor Hornblower (1991, 148) was slow to point out, and my commentary should amplify, this criticism by Thucydides was very much a case of pot calling kettle black.

[181] Pearson 1981, 1–26, esp. 24. If Hellanikos' Ἀττικὴ Ξυγγραφή (Thuc. 1.97.2) really covered all of Athens' history to the end of the Peloponnesian War in no more than two books, one can understand Thucydides' objection.

[182] Plut. *Them.* 27.1 cites Charon of Lampsakos (*FGrH* 162 F 11) for the date of Themistokles' flight to Asia Minor; but Charon (of whom more in a moment) seems to have been fond of digressions, and this could be one such inserted during a narrative of the Persian Wars: Pearson 1939, 148.

[183] Here a parallel may be drawn with the criticisms launched (probably in the 440s: Bowersock 1968, 443–445) by that cynical (and economically acute) critic the "Old Oligarch," in particular as regards Athenian financial ruthlessness in the matter of tribute from the "subject-allies" (Ps.-Xen. 1.14–15, 2.11–12).

[184] Macan 1895, vol. 1, Intro. §20, lxxiv–xc.

observations; the monumental testimony of trophies, tombs, and other memorials, including the inscriptions on them; the literary evidence both of
poets (Aeschylus, Simonides) and of prose writers (Hekataios); the record
of oracles, official edicts (κηρύγματα), and assembly votes; and, where possible—most often through the efforts of bilingual Asiatic Greeks serving the
Achaimenid court—material, such as military rolls, extracted from the Persian archives.

Among those known to have composed Persian histories (Περσικά) that
included some account of the great conflict with the Greek states,[185] only two
have left even a bare minimum of discussable evidence. Charon of Lampsakos[186] was a slightly older[187] contemporary of Herodotos, writing (cf. Plut.
*Them.* 17.1) not earlier than the late 460s. Athenaios refers to his account
of the wrecking of Mardonios' fleet off Mt. Athos.[188] Plutarch, in the *De malignitate Herodoti* (chs. 20 and 24),[189] twice quotes him verbatim to "correct"
Herodotos: the first time on the fate of Paktyes (Hdt. 1.156–160), the second
on the Athenian retreat from Sardis (Hdt. 5.99–102). In both cases Charon's
text is simply too brief to have room for the kind of comment to which Plutarch objects in Herodotos: of Paktyes, all he says is, "When Paktyes learned
that the Persian forces were approaching, he fled, first to Mytilene, then to
Chios; and it was there that Cyrus caught him."[190] Bowen's comment (1992,
8)—"Examination of the two passages suggests that if we had a full text of
Charon, we should use it only where Herodotus fails"—is risky. One late piece
of evidence suggests that Charon was more like Herodotos than we might
otherwise have guessed: Tertullian[191] reports that he similarly recorded Astyages' prophetic dream (cf. Hdt. 1.107–8) about his daughter Mandane. But

---

[185] Mostly prior to 450, after which interest in the topic seems, understandably, to have
faded (Pearson 1981, 6–7): but this meant that those who researched the topic could consult and debrief eyewitnesses and participants.

[186] Testimonia and fragments: *FGrH* 262, 687b; the most balanced account is still that
of Pearson (1939, ch. 4, 139–151). See also the useful articles of Moggi (1977) and Piccirilli (1975). Dionysios of Halikarnassos (*Thuc.* 5.1) places Charon "before the Peloponnesian War."

[187] Plut. *Mor.* 859B; Tertull. *De anim.* 46 = *FGrH* 262 T 3d.

[188] Athen. 9.394e = *FGrH* 262 F 3.

[189] Plut. *Mor.* 859B, 861C–D (*De malign. Herod.* ch. 36) = *FGrH* 262 F 9–10.

[190] His Greek is pithy and archaic: Πακτύης δ' ὡς ἐπύθετο προσελαύνοντα τὸν στρά-
τον τὸν Περσικὸν ᾤχετο φεύγων ἄρτι μὲν εἰς Μυτιλήνην, ἔπειτα δὲ εἰς Χίον· καὶ αὐτοῦ
ἐκράτησε Κῦρος (Plut. *Mor.* 859B = *De malign. Herod.* ch. 20).

[191] Tertull. *De anim.* 46 = *FGrH* 262 T 3d.

whether either Herodotos or Ephoros actually used Charon's *Persika*, or in what their approaches might have differed, cannot, in default of adequate evidence, be determined.

The other *Persika* that should be mentioned here is that by Hellanikos, though concerning it, too, as Pearson confessed ruefully,[192] "there is not much useful information to be found," and most of what there is deals with the early period prior to the Persian Wars, mythical as well as historical. However, that Hellanikos' narrative covered Xerxes' invasion is shown by Plutarch, who cites both Hellanikos and Ephoros to refute Herodotos' figures for Naxos' contribution in ships to the allied cause at the time of Salamis.[193] (In fact, over names, numbers, and genealogical details, Hellanikos tended to be out of step with tradition.[194]) That his *Persika* was in circulation earlier than Herodotos' *Histories* is highly probable.[195] It is also recorded that Hellanikos mentioned two queens called Atossa, though the passage paraphrasing his description[196] has nothing to say about the Atossa, known to us from both Aeschylus and Herodotos, who was Darius I's wife. That is all we know, and as a tool for historiographical criticism, whether of Diodorus, Ephoros, or Herodotos, it is virtually useless.

In other words, to sum up, adequate evaluation of the "vulgate tradition" in terms of its early sources is, for any effective or reliable purpose, impossible, which may in part explain the popular shibboleth regarding the inherent and invariable superiority of the Herodotean and Thucydidean tradition (strikingly different in methods and assumptions though those two historians themselves are). The shibboleth may also have been encouraged by the case of Ctesias, who can be—and has been—presented as a kind of *reductio ad absurdum* of all the faults (inaccuracy, romanticism, ad hominem motivation, lurid rhetoric, uncritical acceptance of anecdotes, chronological confusion, etc.) that historians enjoy attributing to the "vulgate tradition" as a whole. It may therefore be of use, finally, to take a quick look at Ctesias' case: though

---

[192] Pearson 1939, 203: his account (203–209) still remains (as so often with Pearson) the most useful and well-balanced one.

[193] Plut. *Mor.* 869a (*De malign. Herod.* ch. 36).

[194] Pearson 1939, 206–207, with refs.

[195] Aul. Gell. 15.23; Dion. Hal. *Ep. ad Pomp.* 3.6. Cf. Pearson (1939, 208), who argues that had it appeared *after* Herodotos' work had been recognized as "the standard work on 'barbarian matters,'" it would have taken the opportunity to criticize Herodotos wherever possible, and that Plutarch would have used all such criticisms in his own diatribe. But (Marincola *per litt.*) how soon would Herodotos, in fact, have been recognized as "standard" or "authoritative"?

[196] *FGrH* 4 F 178a.

born just late enough to use Herodotos (and thus to qualify as a secondary, rather than a primary, historian), he still had access to the tail end of the primary tradition, was cited in antiquity as a serious historian, lived at the Persian court for some years, left his mark on Ephoros and others, and surfaces at various points during the period covered by my commentary as an often maddening but not always entirely disregardable witness.[197]

Ctesias was from Knidos in Caria, not too far from Halikarnassos, the birthplace of Herodotos; both thus shared the cosmopolitan and trade-conscious outlook natural to Asiatic Greeks. The chronology of his life is hard to establish. He was probably born between 450 and 440, early enough to catch the last remnants of the oral tradition following the Persian Wars. Diodorus, who drew heavily on his work, and almost certainly at first hand,[198] though most prominently in the early books, had this to say about him: "Ctesias of Knidos lived at the time of Cyrus' expedition against his brother Artaxerxes; he was taken prisoner, was then retained by the king because of his medical skill, and for seventeen years was held in great honor by him."[199] The passage has occasioned much debate,[200] but most of the difficulties are removed if we assume, with Eck, that Ctesias' capture took place in 415/4, rather than in 401 at Cunaxa, thus allowing his seventeen-year sojourn in Persia to terminate—as we know it, and his *Persika,* did—in 398/7.[201]

[197] Jacoby's *RE* account (1922, cols. 2046–2047) is still the most detailed, though in places outdated, and overly dogmatic in its dismissal of Ctesias' value as a serious Persian-based witness. His account is echoed by Oldfather, in the introduction to his translation of Books 1–2.34 (1933, xxvii). This attitude persists: Dorati (1995, 35–36) argues that Ctesias' alleged residence at the Persian court was his own invention to promote the reliability of his work. Recent useful studies, presenting a more balanced picture, include those of Bigwood (1976, 1978, and 1980), the last on Ctesias' use by Diodorus; Brown (1978) and Eck (1990) on his life; Lenfant (1996) on his relationship to Herodotos; Alonso-Núñez (1996), Sancisi-Weerdenburg (1987), and Eck (2003, xviii–xxx) for general estimates. For a good bibliography, see K. Karttunen, "Ctesias in Transmission and Tradition," *Topoi* 7.2 (1997): 635–646.

[198] Well argued by Bigwood (1980, 196) and Eck (2003, xv–xvii) against an earlier tradition that, predictably, promoted various intermediaries (Kleitarchos, Agatharchides, Ephoros) as Diodorus' direct source. Both Schwartz (1903, col. 672) and Drews (1973, 195 n. 32) agree that Diodorus used Ctesias directly.

[199] 2.32.4: Κτησίας δὲ ὁ Κνίδιος τοῖς μὲν χρόνοις ὑπῆρξε κατὰ τὴν Κύρου στρατείαν ἐπὶ Ἀρταξέρξην τὸν ἀδελφόν, γενόμενος δὲ αἰχμάλωτος, καὶ διὰ τὴν ἰατρικὴν ἐπιστήμην ἀναληφθεὶς ὑπὸ τοῦ βασιλέως, ἑπτακαίδεκα ἔτη διετέλεσε τιμώμενος ὑπ᾽ αὐτοῦ.

[200] See Eck 1990, 428–434, for details, and the most plausible explanation of the passage's ambiguous chronology.

[201] D.S. 14.46.6 (= *FGrH* 3c T 9), during Ol. 95.3, in the archonship of Ithykles (14.44.1). Artaxerxes II Mnemon only ascended the throne in 405/4, but (*pace* Eck) there

The actual writing of Ctesias' twenty-three-book work, beginning with those semi-legendary figures Ninos and Semiramis, took place on his return to Greece: final publication was between 393 and 385.[202] He was thus in a position to make full use of Herodotos; all of those other shadowy historians of the Persian Wars discussed above; and possibly Thucydides. He could also draw on his own unique position as a trusted figure at the Persian court. Yet the fragments and excerpts that survive suggest—to the frustrated irritation of modern historians—a mere romantic popularizer, a purveyor of salacious tales of decadent court intrigue. Oldfather's reaction is typical: "It is astonishing to observe that a writer with the opportunities which Ctesias enjoyed should have been content to do little more than pass on the folk tales which constitute the 'history' of the Assyrian Empire."[203] How far is such a verdict in fact true?

Ctesias was certainly resident in Persia. He emphasizes (though of course this is no guarantee of his accuracy) that he personally both saw (αὐτόπτης) and heard (αὐτήκοος) what he reported.[204] He spent time in Babylon, and his description of that city,[205] however exaggerated and in places careless, undoubtedly reveals autopsy, and at times corrects Herodotos.[206] Diodorus also (again, in Book 2) records Ctesias' claim to have consulted the royal Achaimenid archives.[207] This claim is often denied. Though Jacoby conceded that Ctesias might, in fact, have been privy to inside information,[208] he regarded his work, in essence, as a falsified rehash of Herodotos that could have been written without residence in Persia.[209] In 1973 Drews similarly evoked a backstairs scene of scandalous gossip and tall stories "in which Ctesias, his fellow

---

is no reason why he should not have taken a proprietary interest in this skilled Greek physician before that.

[202] Eck 1990, 433–434.

[203] Oldfather 1933, xxvii.

[204] *FGrH* 688 T 8 (Phot. *Bibl.* 72, p. 35b).

[205] Summarized by D.S., 2.7.2.–2.9.2 = *FGrH* 688 F 1.

[206] See the excellent article by J. M. Bigwood, "Ctesias' Description of Babylon," *AJAH* 3.1 (1978): 32–52. For a recent argument in favor of the reliability of some of Ctesias' evidence, see Dalley 2003, 182.

[207] D.S. 2.32.4: οὗτος οὖν φησιν ἐκ τῶν βασιλικῶν διφθερῶν . . . πολυπραγμονῆσαι τὰ καθ᾽ ἕκαστον: cf. 2.22.5, where they are referred to as ἀναγραφαί. Whether—granted that Ctesias did "consult" them—this was in person (presuming fluency in written Persian) or through the mediation of a bilingual interpreter is not germane to my discussion.

[208] Jacoby 1922, col. 2035.

[209] Jacoby 1922, cols. 2046–2047; cf. most recently Dorati 1995, passim. Even Eck (1990, 412) concedes that these "archives" could have been fictional.

physicians, the cooks, the translators, and the functionaries of the royal court whiled away their leisure time."[210] Sancisi-Weerdenburg systematically disparaged the value of Ctesias both as an eyewitness and as a reporter of facts from Persian sources: "Ctesias," she argues, "is probably at best considered as an unskilled informant, who has preserved more of the literary tradition than of the factual history of Persia."[211] More recently she has written: "Both in antiquity and modern times his work has been found unreliable, albeit entertaining."[212] This is the general view.

Of the unreliability there can be no doubt. The most famous, and egregious, instance is Ctesias' relocation of the battle of Plataia—well discussed by Bigwood[213]—*before* that of Salamis. Short though his narrative was[214] (and allowing for whimsical excerpting by Photius), it apparently made no mention of Artemision, Mykale, or the Ionian Revolt.[215] His accuracy over names (even making allowances for later scribal error) is less than encouraging: where Herodotos, checked against the Behistun inscription, gets five of Darius' six fellow conspirators more or less right, Ctesias manages only one.[216] His numbers are equally suspect. Herodotos' apparent belief (7.83, 215) that all 10,000 Immortals climbed the Anopaia path under Hydarnes to cut off Leonidas at Thermopylai is improbable enough; Ctesias, grotesquely, bounces this figure to 40,000.[217] By comparison, his much-criticized partiality to court intrigue, especially to that involving the vindictive, and murderous, activities

---

[210] Drews 1973, 107, also cited by Sancisi-Weerdenburg 1987, 36.

[211] Sancisi-Weerdenburg 1987, 43.

[212] Sancisi-Weerdenburg, in *OCD*, 412.

[213] Chs. 25–26 Henry = *FGrH* 688 F 13 (p. 463); Bigwood 1976, 3–4, and 1978, 19. The error can be neither attributed to Photius (always a careful excerptor: Bigwood 1976 and further sources cited at pp. 20–21 n. 11) nor explained by Ctesias deliberately not reporting events in strict chronological order (Hignett 1963, 9).

[214] Books 12–13 covered the reigns of Kambyses, Darius, and Xerxes, Persian Wars included: cf. Bigwood 1978, 20–21 with n. 6.

[215] See Bigwood 1978, 21–22: "Did this historian from Asia Minor have no knowledge at all of Ionia's attempt to shake off the Persian yoke?"

[216] Lenfant 1996, 352–353; Bigwood 1976, 6–7 with n. 24. In a couple of cases, Ctesias seems to have confused father and son, which at least suggests a consultation of records.

[217] Ctes. ch. 24 = *FGrH* 688 F 13 (p. 463). Cf. Bigwood 1978, 26 with n. 27. Ctesias' splenetic determination not only to out-sensationalize Herodotos (with Hdt. 1.84–86 on the capture of Sardis, cf. *FGrH* 688 F 9, pp. 455–456), but also to challenge him at every conceivable point (see Lenfant 1996, 354ff., and Bigwood 1978, 22–24, for some egregious instances) certainly on occasion led him to misrepresent what the earlier historian wrote (e.g., compare Hdt 3.24 with Ctes. ap. D.S. 2.15.1–2). In this case I suspect there may be another explanation (see below).

of royal women such as Amestris or Parysatis, seems relatively harmless.[218] But does all this mean that we should discount his evidence entirely?

In fact, most of these criticisms, valid enough in the specific instance, can be countered or offset. There have always been scholars who—while not necessarily agreeing with the evidence thus adduced—accepted Ctesias' claim to have drawn on Persian sources, both oral and written:[219] recent work on the cuneiform texts, collected and assessed by Lenfant, has reinforced this verdict.[220] Ctesias' plain lack of detailed knowledge about the Persian Wars, with Herodotos at hand to consult as well as to refute, is more of a puzzle than has generally been supposed: if we had his full text it might be easier to understand.[221] Even his failure to match the names of Darius' co-conspirators as recorded on the (conveniently inaccessible) Behistun inscription may indicate not lack of knowledge but, on the contrary, alertness to the political winds of change blowing through the Achaimenid court in the late fifth century.[222] If we apply Hignett's persuasive myriarch/chiliarch theory[223] to Ctesias' count

---

[218] See the catalogue of texts assembled by Sancisi-Weerdenburg 1987, 40, esp. *FGrH* 688 F 14 (44), 15 (52, 54, 55, 61), 16 (66–67), 27 (69, 70).

[219] E.g., Jacoby 1922, col. 2035; Drews 1965, 138ff.; Momigliano 1969, 196; other sources listed by Eck 1990, 411 n. 12.

[220] Lenfant 1996, 364–379. One telling example occurs at *FGrH* 688 F 13 §14 (p. 460 ad fin.). Kambyses sacrifices, but the blood fails to flow from the victim, and the king takes this as a bad omen—something that, as Lenfant points out (1996, 372 with n. 114), is unknown in the Greek tradition, but corresponds to Persian hepatoscopic practice: cf. Finkelstein and Hulin 1964, n. 231, with E. Reiner's transcription, *JNES* 26 (1967): 186–188; and J. Bottéro's French translation in *Mythes et rites de Babylone* (Paris, 1985), 36.

[221] In this context it is worth remembering that in antiquity, Herodotos and Ctesias were most often regarded as being on an equal footing as regards the allocation of both praise and blame: Lenfant 1996, 349–352. Both Strabo (11.6.3, C.507–508) and Lucian (*VH* 2.31) attack them impartially for retailing lies and fantasies in the pursuit of an entertaining story. The thought has often occurred to me that it would not be hard to excerpt Herodotos in such a way as to make him seem a mirror-image of the popular view of Ctesias: cf. Lenfant 1999. This, of course, leaves the evaluation of Ctesias himself wide open and, in default of a full text, virtually insoluble.

[222] Lenfant 1996, 373–379, pointing out that Persian oral tradition, especially among the rival great families, was far from averse to revising the new dynasty's list of founder-heroes, so that even by Herodotos' day the evolutionary process had begun, with Aspathines replacing Ardumanish. In Ctesias, two of the original conspirators (Gaubaruva/Gobryas and Otanes/Utana) have been replaced by their sons, Mardonios and Onophas.

[223] The theory (suggested to Hignett by an anonymous "Oxford scholar" who deserves more credit than he got) is that "some of these estimates may have been due to a genuine misunderstanding, that the Persian unit of calculation may have been a chiliad, misinterpreted by the Greeks as a myriad, so that all figures derived from Persian official sources were automatically multiplied by ten": Hignett 1963, 351. The immediate objection in this case is that such a misunderstanding presupposes no knowledge of Persian on Ctesias' part,

for the number of Immortals who climbed the Anopaia path, we get the very plausible figure of 4,000. Finally, modern, no less than Hellenistic, comparisons suggest that his accounts of dynastic intrigue are not only credible, but precisely what we might expect to find in groups accustomed to the exercise of virtually limitless power: it was this systematic and arbitrary abuse of power to which Herodotos objected throughout his *Histories.* The "literary tradition" was based on brute fact.

Thus we see that even in an extreme case, such as that which Ctesias presents, blanket dismissal of the source as evidence becomes out of the question. Every nugget of information must be considered and evaluated separately, on its inherent probability. Though Diodorus used Ctesias primarily in his early books, he also consulted him on occasion for later episodes of Persian history. Where the present work is concerned, this applies in particular—but not exclusively—to the much-debated narrative of Athens' campaign in Egypt at the time of Inaros' revolt from Persia.[224] In evaluating this and other such testimony, I hope I have always borne in mind Marc Bloch's wise advice, given long ago, on the eve of the first World War, to prizewinners at the Amiens *lycée:* "There are virtually no 'bad' witnesses. A highly flawed narrative can contain useful information. . . . A source does not consist of an indivisible whole that must be adjudged true or false. To criticize it means breaking it down into its component parts, which have then to be tested individually, one after the other."[225]

---

combined with a quite staggering lack of interest in military affairs; but neither of these presuppositions is by definition impossible.

[224] See 11.71.3–36, 74–75, 77.1–5, with commentary ad loc.

[225] Bloch 1950, 5: "Il n'y a guère de mauvais témoins. Un récit très imparfait peut renfermer des renseignements utiles. . . . Un témoignage ne forme pas un tout indivisible qu'il faille déclarer véridique ou faux. Pour en faire la critique, il convient de la décomposer en ses éléments, qui seront éprouvés, l'un après l'autre." I am grateful to Dominique Lenfant (1996, 360 with n. 52) for alerting me to the existence of this remarkable speech.

# BOOK 11: 480–451 B.C.E.

1. The preceding book, the tenth overall, concluded with the events of the year immediately prior to Xerxes' crossing into Europe, and the public debate held in the general assembly of the Hellenes at Corinth to discuss an alliance between Gelon and the Greeks [481 B.C.E.].[1] In the present book we shall fully narrate the subsequent course of events, beginning with Xerxes' expedition against the Hellenes, and concluding with the year before the Athenians' expedition to Cyprus commanded by Kimon [451 B.C.E.].

[2] When Kalliades was archon in Athens [480/79], the Romans elected Spurius Cassius and Proculus Verginius Tricostus consuls.[2] The 75th Olympiad, in which Astylos of Syracuse won the *stadion,* was celebrated at Elis.[3] It was in this year that Xerxes launched his expedition against Greece, for the fol-

---

[1] Book 10 fr. 33, a résumé of Hdt. 7.153.1, 157–163.1. The embassy (sometimes doubted, but for no compelling reason: Lazenby 1993, 107–108 with n. 16) was to solicit Gelon's aid against Persia. Gelon had seized Syracuse in 491 B.C.E. and had immense reserves of wealth and manpower. He refused to help, ostensibly because denied a share in the command, in fact because he was already threatened by Carthage. His victory at Himera (480) made him virtual lord of all Sicily: D.S. 11.20–26 passim. Cf. *CAH* iv, 766–775; Green 1996a, 82–84.

[2] For Diodorus' chronology, see above, pp. 9–12. While his archon-year is correct, the consuls he ascribes to 480/79 (full titles Sp. Cassius Vicellinus and Proculus Verginius Tricostus Rutilus) in fact belong to 486 B.C.E. (Broughton 1951, 20). The error is due to his consulting consular *Fasti* that did not list various interregna when there were no consuls. Diodorus is thus seven years ahead of the Roman (Varronian) chronology, and so remains until 11.41.1. From ch. 48.1 until ch. 91.1, the gap is reduced to six years, at which point it increases to seven once more.

[3] Astylos, originally from Kroton, had won this race twice already (Dion. Hal. *AR* 8.1.1), in the 74th Olympiad as a Syracusan, after changing cities at the request of Hieron (Paus. 6.13). The actual celebration of the 75th Olympiad coincided with the defense of Thermopylai (Hdt. 7.206)—one alleged reason for Sparta's allies sending only advance parties up north at the time. Cf. ch. 4 below.

lowing reason. [3] The Persian Mardonios[4] was Xerxes' cousin and brother-in-law, and because of his intelligence and bravery enjoyed high esteem among his fellow countrymen. This man, being high in his own conceit and at the peak of his youthful strength, passionately desired to command a great military expedition. He therefore persuaded Xerxes that he should enslave the Greeks, who had always been in a state of enmity with the Persians. [4] Xerxes was convinced by him, and determined to uproot all the Greeks from their homeland. He therefore sent envoys to the Carthaginians to propose a joint undertaking, and made an agreement with them, that while he campaigned against the mainland Greeks of Hellas, the Carthaginians should simultaneously raise a large force and subdue those Greeks living in Sicily and southern Italy.[5] [5] In compliance with this treaty, the Carthaginians raised large sums of money and hired mercenaries from Italy and Liguria as well as from Galatia and Spain, conscripting in addition to these forces citizen-soldiers from throughout Libya, as well as from Carthage itself. Finally, having spent three whole years in nonstop preparations, they mustered over 300,000 men and a fleet of 200 vessels.[6]

2. Xerxes, meanwhile, competing with the zeal of the Carthaginians, surpassed them in all his preparations, to the degree that he outstripped them in the sheer number of peoples over whom he ruled. He initiated a ship-building program throughout the entire coastal region subject to him: in Egypt,

---

[4]Mardonios, son of Gobryas, was Darius I's nephew through his mother, one of the king's sisters and thus Xerxes' cousin; he became his brother-in-law by marrying Darius' daughter Artazóstra. He had first held command at an early age, following the Ionian Revolt (c. 492). Diodorus' picture of him as "the moving spirit of Xerxes' invasion" (OCD 924) agrees with Herodotos (e.g., at 7.6–7). Xerxes was in fact returning to his father Darius' plan to conquer Greece (Hdt. 7.1). Nor should it be forgotten that Mardonios himself led an earlier expedition (in 492) that ended in ignominious failure: he had a reputation to save. Cf. Briant 2002, 525–526.

[5]Cf. Timaios fr. 94 = Polyb. 12.26b, Ephoros fr. 186 = schol. Pind. Pyth. 1.146b (which claims that Xerxes ordered (προστάσσοντας) the Carthaginian assault on Sicily), Just. 19.1.10–13. This embassy is not mentioned by Herodotos. Diodorus picks up the Carthaginian narrative at 11.20.1. The Persian-Carthaginian alliance has been doubted (D. Asheri in CAH iv, 774), but is reasonable (Ephoros ibid.; cf. How and Wells 1912, 2:201; Haillet 2001, 120 n. 3).

[6]On these activities, cf. Hdt. 7.165. "Galatia" is probably southwest France. Xerxes' preparations began in the spring of 484 (Hdt. 7.20), and Gelon's may be regarded as having gotten under way soon after. Though the land forces are greatly exaggerated (probably ten times, giving a reasonable figure of 30,000: see below, notes 82 and 86), 200 warships are acceptable for a mainly maritime nation. If they were also used as transports, this would allot 150 men to each vessel.

Phoenicia, and Cyprus, as well as Cilicia, Pamphylia, and Pisidia, not to mention Lycia, Caria, Mysia, the Troad, the cities on the Hellespont, Bithynia, and Pontos. During the three years that he, like the Carthaginians, spent on his preparations, he put into commission more than 1,200 warships.[7] [2] In this task he was helped by his father Darius, who before he died had himself been assembling powerful armaments; for having been worsted by the Athenians at Marathon [490 B.C.E.] (Datis being the commander on that occasion), he continued to bear a grudge against them because of their victory. Darius, however, when on the point of crossing [the Hellespont] against the Greeks, was caught short by death. Thereupon Xerxes, moved both by his father's plans and by the recommendations of Mardonios, as was stated earlier, decided to make war on the Greeks.[8]

[3] When everything had been made ready for his expedition, he ordered his admirals to assemble their fleets at Kyme and Phokaia,[9] while he himself, after marshalling the infantry and cavalry contingents from all the satrapies, set out from Sousa. On reaching Sardis, he dispatched heralds to Greece, with orders to visit every Greek city-state and demand earth and water of the inhabitants.[10] [4] He then divided his forces, sending ahead sufficiently large detachments both to bridge the Hellespont and to dig a channel through the Athos peninsula at its narrowest point, thus not only making the passage safe and short for his armies, but also (he hoped) dumbfounding the Hellenes with the vastness of his achievements.[11] As a result, those who were detailed

---

[7] Hdt. 7.89–95 gives a very similar list, in much the same geographical order: Phoenicians, Syrians, Egyptians, Cypriots, Cilicians, Pamphylians, Lycians, Carians, Ionians, islanders, Aiolians, Hellespontines, and Bosphorans. Diodorus' total of 1,200+ agrees with the estimates of Hdt. 7.89.1 (1,207), Aesch. *Pers.* 341–343 (1,207), and Lys. 2.27 (1,200). The figure is reasonable, especially if we take it to have included 674 galleys used in the bridging of the Hellespont: Green 1996, 60–62.

[8] Marathon: Burn 1984, 236–257; Lazenby 1993, 45–80; Green 1996, 30–40. Darius' preparations up to his death in 486: Hdt. 7.1. Causes of Xerxes' invasion: Hdt. 7.8; Thuc. 1.18.2; Lys. 2.27. These—including the ad hoc reasons alleged by Diodorus (sources in note 5 above)—can be subsumed under the general heading of Achaimenid imperialism. See now, for a balanced view of Achaimenid policies and culture, Briant 1996, 531ff. = Briant 2002, 515ff.; and Scherr 1933, 1–2, on Diodorus' use of diverse sources.

[9] See Map 2, and cf. *BA* 56, D4. Sardis, *BA* 56, G5.

[10] I.e., as a token of their complete submission. Darius had made similar demands in 491 B.C.E. (Hdt. 6.49–49), when both the Athenians and the Spartans had killed the Persian heralds delivering the demand (Hdt. 7.133); Xerxes therefore excepted them from his new mission. Herodotos (7.131–132.1) gives a list of those states which complied.

[11] Hdt. 7.22ff. makes it clear that these major works—certainly the canal—had been in progress for three full years before the expedition, together with the establishment of supply depots along the coast from Thrace to Macedonia.

for the implementation of these tasks soon completed them, since such a swarm of laborers was pressed into service.[12] [5] When the Greeks became aware of the vast size of the Persian expeditionary force, they dispatched 10,000 hoplites into Thessaly to occupy the passes by Tempe: the Spartan contingent was commanded by Euainetos, and the Athenian by Themistokles.[13] These two dispatched envoys to the <neighboring> states,[14] asking them to send troops to share in the defense of the passes, for they were hopeful that every Greek city-state would take part in the defense, and make common cause with them in this war against the Persians. [6] However, since both the Thessalians and most of the other Greeks who dwelt in the area of the passes had given earth and water to Xerxes' envoys at the time of their visit, the Greek generals, seeing that the defense of Tempe was a lost cause, withdrew to their own territories.[15]

3. At this point it may be profitable to identify those of the Hellenes who chose to side with the barbarians, in the hope that the shame here visited upon them may, by the sheer force of its obloquy, deter any [future] traitors to the cause of common freedom.[16] [2] The Ainianians, Dolopians, Malians, Perrhaibians, and Magnesians were already lined up with the barbarians while

---

[12]Xerxes' march: Hdt. 7.26–32. The canal: Hdt. 7.22–25; Lys. 2.28–29; cf. Müller 1987, 156–161. Much of its course is now determinable as a result of aerial photography. The bridging of the Hellespont: Hdt. 7.33–36; Lys. 2.28–29; cf. Hammond and Roseman 1996. The canal was cut to avoid a repetition of Mardonios' losses in 492 while rounding the Athos peninsula (Hdt. 6.44).

[13]Hdt. 7.172–174, cf. Lazenby 108–111, Burn 1984, 339–344. The name Euainetos is supplied from Hdt. 7.173: the MSS of Diodorus (in which the corruption of proper names is a regular feature) read "Synetos."

[14]It is likely that τὰς πλησιοχώρους has dropped out of the manuscript after τὰς πό-λεις. Cf. §6, τῶν ἄλλων Ἑλλήνων τῶν πλησιοχώρων.

[15]The Thessalians, except for the powerful clan of the Aleuadai (Hdt. 7.6, 132), medized reluctantly (Hdt. 7.172.1, who in general is hostile to them), but when the Greeks abandoned their northern defense-line, they had no other option. Cf. Haillet 2001, 7 n. 1, with refs. The second pressing reason for withdrawal (cf. Plut. *Them.* 7.1–2) was the discovery that the Tempe position could be turned via at least two passes, those of Petra and Voluṣtana: Green 1996, 86–87; Lazenby 1993, 109–110; Blösel 2004, 108–120.

[16]Diodorus here, as elsewhere in Book 11 (e.g., 23, 38.5–6, 46.1–4, 53.1–3, 58.4–59, 67.2–6), applies the clear-cut moral judgments he sets out in the preface to Book 1 (see esp. 1.1.5–2.3). "[Future] traitors": Vogel, not seeing any "common freedom" in the late Roman Republic, emended γενομένους of the MSS to γενησομένους (1890, ad loc.). Haillet (2001, 122 n. 3) sees rather a sly allusion to the civil wars then raging. Even if (Marincola *per litt.*) Diodorus simply lifted the sentiment from Ephoros (which may well be true), the textual correction seems justified: the deterrent is aimed at *prevention*, it is not a comment on actions already taken.

the defense force was still stationed at Tempe; the Phthiotic Achaians, the Lokrians, the Thessalians, and most of the Boiotians went over to them as soon as it had pulled out.[17] [3] The Greeks, who were in joint session at the Isthmus [of Corinth],[18] voted to make those Hellenes who voluntarily supported the Persian cause pay a tithe to the gods once the war was won, and to send envoys to those who remained neutral, exhorting them to join in the struggle for their common freedom.[19]

[4] Some of the latter wholeheartedly threw in their lot with the alliance; but others procrastinated for a considerable time, with concern for nothing but their own safety, and keeping a close watch on the likely outcome of the war.[20] The Argives sent ambassadors to the allied congress, announcing that they would join the alliance if offered a share of the command. [5] To which the delegates responded in plain terms that if the Argives thought it worse to have a Greek general than a barbarian master, they were right to remain neutral; but if they aspired to take over the leadership of the Hellenes, they should (said the delegates) have performed deeds deserving of such an honor before applying for it.[21] Afterward, when ambassadors from Xerxes came to Greece demanding earth and water, all the states [included in the alliance] made very clear their zeal for the cause of common freedom.[22]

[6] When Xerxes was informed that the Hellespont had been bridged and a channel dug through Athos, he set out from Sardis and marched for the Hellespont; and when he reached Abydos, he led his forces across the connecting bridge into Europe. During his advance through Thrace, he swelled his ranks with numerous recruits from the Thracians themselves and other neighboring Greeks.[23] [7] When he reached the city called Doriskos, he summoned his naval forces there, so that both fleet and army were assembled in

---

[17] See Maps 1 and 5 for these states, and cf. *BA* 50, 55. Hdt. 7.132 lists an almost identical group.

[18] On this Congress, the nearest thing to a centralized Greek higher command, see Hdt. 7.132, 145; Arist. *Ath. Pol.* 22.8; cf. Haillet 2001, 123 n. 7. Its members were very probably the thirty-one states listed on the Serpent Column of victory with the characteristically laconic inscription: "These fought in the war." Cf. Hignett 1963, 96–104. Diodorus refers to the Congress frequently: 11.2.5, 3.3, 4.1, 14.2, 16.3, 29.2.

[19] The tithe: Hdt. 7.132; Polyb. 9.33; cf. 11.29.3, 65.5 below. Neutrals included Argos (Hdt. 7.150–152), Corcyra, and Crete (Hdt. 7.168–171, and below, 11.15.1). On Medism and collaboration in general, see Gillis 1979 and Graf 1984.

[20] In particular, Corcyra (below, 11.15.1) and Gelon (Hdt. 7.163–164).

[21] For a slightly different account of this face-off, see Hdt. 7.148–149.

[22] Not least Athens and Sparta (Hdt. 7.133): at Sparta the envoys were thrown into a well and told to collect earth and water from the bottom.

[23] For the synchronization of the naval and military advance, see Hdt. 7.58. The crossing: Hdt. 7.54–56.

one place. He also conducted a roll call of the entire expeditionary force: his land forces totaled more than 800,000 men, while the full count of his warships was more than 1,200, of which 320 were Greek, with the Greeks supplying the crews and the Great King the vessels. All the rest were listed as barbarian: of these the Egyptians supplied 200, the Phoenicians 300, the Cilicians 80, the Pamphylians 40, the Lycians the same; and in addition to these the Carians provided 80 and the Cypriots 150. [8] Of the Greeks, the Dorians from the coast of Caria, together with the Rhodians and the Koans, sent 40 ships; the Ionians, together with the Chians and Samians, provided 100, the Aiolians, together with the Lesbians and the men of Tenedos, 40; the Hellespontines and those settled along the coast of Pontos, 80; and the islanders 50, for the Great King had brought over to his side all islands within the area bounded by the Kyanean Rocks, Cape Sounion, and Cape Triopion. [9] The total I have enumerated consisted entirely of triremes; there were also 850 horse transports and 3,000 triakonters. Thus was Xerxes occupied with the tallying of his forces at Doriskos.[24]

4. When reports reached the Greek delegates [at the Isthmus] that the Persian forces were near, they voted for the immediate dispatch of the fleet to Artemision in Euboia, seeing that this site was well placed for resisting the enemy, and of a strong hoplite force to Thermopylai, to occupy the passes at their narrowest point ahead of the barbarians and thus block their further advance into Greece.[25] They acted thus in their eagerness to include those who had chosen the cause of the Hellenes within their defense-line, and to safeguard their allies to the best of their ability.[26] [2] The commander-in-chief was Eurybiades the Lacedaemonian, and the contingent dispatched to Thermopylai was led by the Spartan king Leonidas, a man much concerned with his own courage and generalship. When he took up his command, he proclaimed that only a thousand men should follow him on this campaign.

---

[24] Cf. the full account in Hdt. 7.53–100 passim, with *CAH* iv, 534–538, and Haillet 2001, 123–124. Thracian recruits: Hdt. 7.108–110. The Greek fleet contingents in fact add up to 310, not 320. The Kyanean Rocks (known to Odysseus and the Argonauts as the Clashing Rocks, Συμπληγάδες) were at the Black Sea mouth of the Bosphoros. Of the two capes mentioned, Sounion is at the southern tip of Attica, and Triopion at the southwestern corner of Asia Minor, by Knidos.

[25] See Map 5, and cf. *BA* 55 D3 (Thermopylai), E2 (Artemision). Topography, plans, and photographs: Müller 1987, 310–315 (Artemision), 369–384 (Thermopylai).

[26] Cf. Hdt. 7.175–177 and the Troizen Decree (Green 1996a, 98–114): both make it clear that this was to be an amphibious holding operation. Topography: Kraft, Rapp, et al. 1987; Müller 1987, 310–314 (Artemision), 369–384 (Thermopylai); cf. Lazenby 1993, ch. 6, 117–150.

[3] The ephors told him that this was altogether too small a force to take against a mighty armament, and ordered him to levy a larger company. To which he replied, behind closed doors, that for stopping the barbarians getting through the passes they might be too few, but for the action to which they were now bound, they were amply sufficient. [4] Finding his response enigmatic and unclear, the ephors demanded of him whether he thought he was leading his men on some unimportant mission. He replied that officially he might be leading them to the defense of the passes, but in fact to die for the cause of common freedom. Thus if a thousand men were to march [north], Sparta would gain greater renown by their deaths; but if the Lacedaemonians took the field in full force, Lacedaemon would perish utterly, since not one man there would dare to cut and run in order to save his own life.[27] [5] So the contingent was made up of 1,000 Lacedaemonians, including[28] 300 Spartiate [citizen-warriors]: these, together with 3,000 other Greeks, were now ordered to Thermopylai.

[6] So Leonidas with his 4,000 troops advanced to Thermopylai. Now the Lokrians living near the passes had given earth and water to the Persians, and were under an obligation to occupy these passes before the Greeks; but when

---

[27] Cf. Plut. *Mor.* 866B–D. This is clearly an *ex post facto* rationalization of Leonidas' sacrificial defeat after the pass had been turned, taken from rhetorical accounts such as Isokr. 4.90 or Lys. 2.30. Leonidas in fact took an advance force of no more than 1,000 Lacedaemonians because it was thought that they, together with 3,000 Greek allies, would be sufficient to hold the pass until major reinforcements arrived: Hdt. 7.206; Lazenby 1993, 134–136; Green 1996a, 111–112. Diodorus does not here mention the purported Delphic oracle (Hdt. 7.220.3–4, Just. 2.11.88) which, at the outset of the war, declared that either Sparta or a Spartan king must be destroyed in the conflict. Nor does the implied self-sacrifice seem to have been in Leonidas' mind until he dismissed the allies prior to his last stand: he was, after all, there in the first instance to *block Xerxes' advance,* not to obligingly let the Persian king through into southern Greece while getting himself, together with a large number of first-class Spartan warriors, killed in the process. Thus there is no good reason to dismiss the oracle itself as a forgery *post eventum* (Fontenrose 1978, 77–78, 319): cf. Hammond 1996, 5–7.

[28] The Greek is καὶ σὺν αὐτοῖς. That this phrase is inclusive has been well demonstrated by Flower (1998, 367). Herodotos (7.202) mentions a total of 3,100 Peloponnesian troops, of which only 300 are Spartan; but he also elsewhere (7.228.1) cites an epitaph stating that 4,000 men from the Peloponnese fought at Thermopylai. Diodorus (11.4.5–6) confirms this epitaph: he gives Leonidas a force totaling 4,000, of whom 3,000 were "other Greeks," leaving 1,000 as Lacedaemonians, and at 4.2 he states specifically that Leonidas chose to take only 1,000 Lacedaemonians. Of these, 300 were Spartiates; the remaining 700 were *perioikoi* ("dwellers round about") from the frontier settlements of Lakonia. Isokrates (4.90, 6.99) also gives 1,000 as the total. Flower explains Herodotos' omission of the *perioikoi* on the grounds that they did not stay and fight to the death with Leonidas and his 300. This is plausible.

they heard that Leonidas was coming to Thermopylai, they had second thoughts and went over to the Greeks. [7] Thus there also arrived at Thermopylai 1,000 Lokrians, the same number of Malians, not much short of 1,000 Phokians, together with up to 400 Thebans of the opposition (for the inhabitants of Thebes were split into opposing parties regarding their alliance with the Persians).[29] Those Greeks, then, who were mustered with Leonidas, to the number stated above, took up station in and around Thermopylai, awaiting the arrival of the Persians.

5. After the tallying of his forces, Xerxes advanced with the entire land army, while as far as the city of Akanthos the whole fleet sailed alongside the line of march. From there the ships were piloted through the channel that had been dug for them, safely and speedily, into the sea beyond. [2] However, when [Xerxes] reached the Malian Gulf, he found that the enemy had already occupied the passes. So after enrolling the forces [waiting for him] there, he then summoned his allies from Europe, who were not much short of 200,000 men, so that the overall number of his troops was now not less than 1,000,000, not counting the naval complement. [3] The total figure of those who served as crews aboard his warships, together with those who transported his commissariat and other supplies, was at least as great as those already mentioned, so that the common reports of the multitudes assembled by Xerxes should occasion no surprise, with their claims that perennial rivers were drunk dry by the never-ending columns of troops, and that the seas were hidden by the sails of his vessels. Certainly the greatest military forces of any for which historical records have survived were those that marched with Xerxes.[30]

[4] When the Persians had set up camp by the Spercheios River, Xerxes sent messengers to Thermopylai, who were to find out, among other things, the attitude of the [Greeks there] to the war against him. He ordered them to make the following proclamation: "King Xerxes orders everyone to surrender their arms, to go back under safe-conduct to their native country, and to be allies of the Persians; and if they do this," the proclamation continued, "he will grant them more and better land than that they now possess." [5] But

---

[29] Theban Medism became a pressing problem: see Hdt. 7.132, 205, 9.86, and elsewhere; Thuc. 3.62.2–4; Paus. 9.3.6; Plut. *Arist.* 18.6–7; cf. Haillet 2001, 124.

[30] The Persian advance to Therme: Hdt. 7.121–130. Xerxes' European levy: Hdt. 7.185, who puts it at 300,000 troops and 120 ships. Troops and animals drinking the rivers dry: Hdt. 7.109. The inflation of Persian troop figures by Greek historians is a constant problem. Hammond (1986, 228) suggests, on logistical grounds, a top limit of c. 500,000, and this seems reasonable. For one plausible explanation of the inflated figures, see notes 82 and 86 below; cf. above, Introduction, pp. 46–47, with n.223.

when Leonidas and his companions heard what the messengers had to say, they replied that if they were to be the king's allies, they would be of more use to him fully armed, and if they were compelled to wage war against him, they would do battle for freedom all the better through keeping their weapons; and as for the lands he promised to give them, it was a tradition with the Greeks to gain lands not by cowardice but by valor.[31]

6. Having heard from his messengers what replies the Greeks made, the king summoned Demaratos, a Spartan who had come to [the Persian court] when exiled from his own country; and after a mocking dismissal of the replies, he asked the Laconian: "Will these Hellenes flee faster than my horses? Will they dare to face such vast armaments in battle?" [2] To which, they say, Demaratos replied: "You yourself do not lack knowledge of Greek bravery, for you use Greek troops to reduce any of the barbarians who revolt. Do not, therefore, suppose that men who fight better than Persians on behalf of your rule will be less ready to risk their lives against the Persians for the sake of their own freedom." But Xerxes laughed derisively at Demaratos, and ordered him to remain in attendance, so that he might watch the Lacedaemonians in full flight.[32]

[3] Xerxes then advanced with his forces against the Greeks at Thermopylai. He stationed the Medes ahead of all other peoples, either because he ranked them first for courage, or through a desire to destroy them all; for the Medes still retained their pride, since it was only recently that their ancestral supremacy had been toppled.[33] [4] It so happened that there were among the Medes brothers and sons of those who had died at Marathon; Xerxes made this fact known to them, in the belief that they would thus be sharpened in their desire for vengeance against the Greeks.[34] So the Medes, after being de-

---

[31] Herodotos (7.208) reports this mission in very different terms: for him it was designed to observe troop dispositions in the pass and generally to gather military intelligence: Lazenby 1993, 137–138. Diodorus describes another proposal, from Mardonios in 479, very similar in its conditions to that made by Xerxes here: see below, II.28.1–2.

[32] For Demaratos, the Eurypontid king of Sparta (reigned 515–491 B.C.E.), and the circumstances of his exile from Sparta on a trumped-up charge of illegitimacy organized by his Agiad co-king and rival Kleomenes, see Hdt. 6.50–70 passim. Herodotos (who may have interrogated Demaratos' descendants in the Troad) also describes Xerxes' exchange with him, but in very different terms, leaving Demaratos with much the better of the exchange: 7.209.

[33] Media had fallen to Cyrus the Great of Persia in 550/49. See Hdt. 1.123–129, with CAH iv, 6–46; Kuhrt 1995, 647–659; Olmstead 1948, 34–38.

[34] The Greek of 6.4 is badly corrupt: see Haillet's note (2001, 125). I follow his reconstruction, except that in line 5 I read αὐτούς rather than τούτους.

ployed in this manner, fell upon those defending Thermopylai; but Leonidas was well prepared, and massed the Greeks in the narrowest part of the pass.

7. A fierce battle then took place.[35] Since the barbarians had the Great King as observer of their fighting spirit, while the Greeks were mindful of their freedom and were being urged on in the conflict by Leonidas, the result was a quite extraordinary struggle. [2] Since the battle line was shoulder-to-shoulder, the fighting hand-to-hand, and the combatants in dense array, for a long time the issue hung in the balance. But the Greeks had the advantage, both in their bravery and in the great size of their shields, and so the Medes were gradually forced back: a large number of them were killed, and not a few wounded. A contingent of Kissians and Sakai, specially picked for valor, who had been posted as reinforcements for the Medes, now took their place in the front line. Being fresh troops joining battle against exhausted opponents, for a little while they held their own; but Leonidas' men inflicted heavy casualties on them and pressed them hard, so that they, too, gave way. [3] The reason was that the barbarians employed small shields and targets, which gave them an advantage in open terrain, allowing them to move easily. On a narrow front, however, they found it difficult to wound foemen who stood close-packed side by side, their huge shields protecting their entire bodies, while they themselves, at a disadvantage because of the lightness of their protective armor, suffered countless wounds.

[4] In the end, Xerxes, seeing the whole region around the passes strewn with corpses, and the barbarians failing to stand up to the fighting spirit of the Greeks, ordered up those picked Persian troops known as the Immortals, who were reputed to be preeminent among their fellow soldiers for bravery in action. But when these, too, retreated after no more than a brief period of resistance, and night was falling, they broke off the battle, with heavy casualties among the barbarians, but only light Greek losses.[36]

8. The next day Xerxes, since the battle had turned out contrary to his expectations, selected from all the peoples in his army those with the highest reputation for courage and daring. He then made them a speech, indicating

---

[35] According to Herodotos (7.210.1), only after Xerxes had waited four days, in the expectation that the Greeks would cut and run, a nice instance of action dictated by belief in one's own propaganda. Cf. Lazenby 2001, 137.

[36] Cf. Hdt. 7.210–211. The Kissians formed, with the Medes and Persians, the core of the Achaimenid empire: they occupied Darius' Eighth Satrapy, with its capital at Sousa. The Sakai were central Asiatic nomads. The Immortals: Hdt. 7.83, 211. Their number was maintained at 10,000. In 480 their commander was Hydarnes.

the high expectations he had of them, and informing them that if they forced the entrance to the pass, he would give them gifts of great note, but that the penalty for retreat would be death. [2] So these troops launched a violent massed charge against the Greeks; but Leonidas and his men closed ranks, making a solid wall of their defense line, and threw themselves into the struggle with a will. So great, indeed, was their zeal that the customary rotation of troops out of the front line no longer took place: they all stayed in place, and by their unbroken endurance took out many of these picked barbarian warriors. [3] The whole day long they continued in this struggle, vying one with another: for the older soldiers challenged the vigor of the young men in their prime, while the young in turn set themselves to equal the experience and reputation of their elders. When, finally, Xerxes' crack troops, too, broke and fled, those barbarians holding the support line formed a barrier and would not let the picked troops withdraw, so that they were forced to turn back and renew the fight.[37]

[4] The king was now at a complete loss, and was convinced that not a man of his would dare to join battle again; but at this point there approached him a Trachinian, a native of those parts, who was familiar with the local mountainous terrain. When he came into Xerxes' presence, this man offered to guide the Persians along a certain narrow and precipitous path, which would bring those accompanying him out in the rear of Leonidas' position: the defenders, being thus surrounded and penned in, could then be destroyed without trouble.[38] [5] The king was beside himself with joy, loaded the Trachinian with rewards, and dispatched a force of 20,000 troops with him under cover of darkness. But a man in the Persian camp named Tyrrhastiadas, a Kymaean by birth, a person of high principles and upright conduct, deserted from the Persian encampment that night, went to Leonidas' position, and told the Greeks (who had known nothing of it) about the Trachinian's action.[39]

---

[37] Cf. Hdt. 7.212. Herodotos makes no mention of Xerxes' threats and promises; but he describes Spartan tactics that Diodorus omits, and has Xerxes thrice leaping up from his throne in alarm for his troops.

[38] Cf. Herodotos (7.213–214), who names the informant as Ephialtes of Malis. The mountain path, known as Anopaia, began at the Asopos River and ended at Alpenos: Hdt. 7.215–216; cf. Paus. 1.4.2, 10.2–8. Topography: Müller 1987, 294–302; Burn 1977; Green 1996a, 125, 137–138. See Map 5. The Anopaia route and the site of the skirmish with the Phokaians are currently under exploration by the Leonidas III Expedition led by Professor A. Yiannakis of the University of Connecticut. Its 2001 report can be viewed at http://playlab.uconn.edu/pylae.htm.

[39] Herodotos (7.215) names "Hydarnes and Hydarnes' command," i.e., the Immortals, as the troops sent over Anopaia. These were 10,000, not 20,000, in number, and the actual force sent over the mountain may well have been much smaller: see above, Introduc-

9. The Greeks, on hearing this, held a meeting about midnight to take counsel concerning the dangers now threatening them. Some, then, declared that they should abandon the pass right away, and save themselves by falling back on their allies, since if they stayed where they were they had no hope of survival. But Leonidas, the Lacedaemonian king, who was ambitious to win high glory for himself and his Spartiate warriors, ordered all other Greeks to pull out and save themselves, so that they might fight with their fellow Hellenes in battles yet to come; but the Lacedaemonians themselves, he said, must stay behind and not abandon the defense of the pass, since it was fitting that the leaders of Hellas should be prepared to die while striving for the prize of honor.[40] [2] So all the rest departed at once, leaving Leonidas and his fellow citizens to perform heroic and incredible deeds. Though the Lacedaemonians were few in number—of the rest Leonidas had retained only the Thespians—so that he had not more than 500 men with him all told, he was ready to face death for the sake of Hellas.[41]

[3] After this, the Persians accompanying the Trachinian, having made their way round over very difficult terrain, suddenly caught Leonidas and his men from the rear. The Greeks abandoned any thought of saving themselves, and instead opted for glory, with one voice calling on their commander to lead them against the enemy before the Persians learned that their own troops' encircling strategy had succeeded. [4] Leonidas welcomed his soldiers' readiness, and told them to make a quick breakfast, since they would be dining in Hades.[42] He himself took nourishment in accordance with the orders he had

---

tion, pp. 45–47. He also identifies Leonidas' informants, unnamed, as (a) deserters and (b) his own look-out men. Tyrrhastiadas was one of the former, and his being from Kyme (as was Ephoros) suggests that here Diodorus may have been using Ephoros' account as well as that of Herodotos. Cf. Brown 1952, 343.

[40] Similar debate, and attitude of Leonidas, implied at Hdt. 7.219–221. Diodorus omits any mention of the Phokians detached to guard the summit of Anopaia (Hdt. 7.217). Veh and Will (1998, 307) ascribe the last-minute dismissal of the non-Spartan troops, too, to Spartan propaganda: according to them, Leonidas simply missed the right moment to retreat. More probably he was determined to give the retreating troops a head start against eventual pursuit, especially by the Persian cavalry.

[41] Hdt. 7.222 states that the Thebans as well as the Thespians remained, "but unwillingly," kept by Leonidas as hostages. This was an unmerited slur (cf. Plut. Mor. 865A–E): the 400 Thebans who stayed were "of the [anti-Persian] opposition," D.S. 11.4.7. Contra, Hammond 1996, 19–20. Justin (2.11.11–15), like Diodorus, omits them here. Thus the total force was not 500, but nearer 900–1,000. Cf. Lazenby 1993, 146.

[42] This famous mot is also recorded by Plutarch (Mor. 225D) and Cicero (Tusc. Disp. 1.42.101), but not by Herodotos.

given, thinking that by so doing he would be able to husband his strength for a longer period, and better endure the business of holding firm in battle. Then, when they had hastily refreshed themselves and all were ready, he ordered his troops to make a raid on the Persian camp, killing all they met, and to aim for the Great King's own pavilion.

10. So they in accordance with his commands formed a tight column under cover of darkness and charged into the Persian encampment, with Leonidas himself at their head. The barbarians, taken by surprise and not knowing what was happening, with loud shouts came running pell-mell from their tents: getting the idea that the contingent with the Trachinian had been destroyed, and the Greeks' entire force was now upon them, they panicked. [2] As a result, many fell victim to Leonidas and his men, and many more perished at the hands of their own people, who, failing to recognize them, took them for enemies, since the darkness made correct recognition impossible. The resultant confusion, which spread through the entire encampment, understandably caused considerable slaughter: with no orders from a commanding officer, no demands for the password, and a general failure to restore logical thinking, the circumstances did not permit careful scrutiny, and so they kept killing one another. [3] Thus if the king had stayed in his royal pavilion, he himself might easily have been killed by the Greeks, and the entire war would have reached a quick conclusion; but in the event, before the Greeks burst into the pavilion and slaughtered almost everyone they found still there, Xerxes had hastened out to confront the uproar. [4] So long as it remained dark, they (very understandably) ranged through the length and breadth of the encampment looking for Xerxes; but when day dawned and the whole situation became clear, the Persians, noting that the Greeks were few in number, made light of them.[43] Yet they still did not confront them face to face,

---

[43] The night raid described by Diodorus (the probable date was 19–20 August) is absent from Herodotos, but not necessarily to be dismissed as a fabrication on that account. It is confirmed in detail both by Plutarch, who, in his essay *On the Malice of Herodotos* (*Mor.* 866A), upbraids Herodotos for omitting Leonidas' "greatest deed," and by Justin (2.11.12–18). Flower (1998, 370ff.) argues for the lyric encomium excerpted by Diodorus at 11.6 as the source. In the circumstances it made excellent sense. Diodorus has, however, run it confusingly into the final engagement described by Herodotos (7.223–233) as taking place in the pass the next morning "about the market hour," i.e., 9–10 A.M. This may be due (Flower 1998, 373–375) to Diodorus and/or his source(s) emphasizing nocturnal activities, whereas for Herodotos it is dawn that signifies the beginning of the final act in the drama. In fact they were quite separate actions. The non-Herodotean tradition of the raid-

through fear of their valor, but instead grouped themselves on their flanks and in rear of them, from where, with a rain of arrows and javelins, they slew them all. Such, then, was the end met by those who guarded the pass of Thermopylai with Leonidas.[44]

11. Who would not be amazed by these men's prowess? With united determination they did not abandon the post to which Greece had assigned them, but willingly gave up their own lives for the common salvation of the Greeks, and chose to die with honor rather than live in ignominy. Nor could anyone doubt the sheer consternation experienced by the Persians. [2] For which of the barbarians could have grasped what had taken place? Who could have foreseen that a group numbering five hundred would dare to attack a million? As a result, what man of a later age would not aspire to emulate the courageous achievement of these warriors? Rendered powerless by the magnitude of the crisis, they may have been physically beaten down, but remained unconquered in spirit: and thus alone among those of whom record survives, they have become more renowned in defeat than all who have won even the finest victories. Brave men should be judged, not by the outcome of their deeds, but rather by their intentions; [3] for the first is governed by chance, whereas it is right intention that garners esteem. Who would reckon any men braver than these, since though not numerically equaling a thousandth part of the enemy, they nevertheless dared to set their valor against such incredible multitudes? With no expectation of defeating so many tens of thousands, they still reckoned on surpassing all their predecessors in courage; and though they were fighting the barbarian, they reckoned the true contest, with the prize for valor, was in competition with all those who had ever excited amazement on account of their bravery. [4] For they alone of those commemorated down the ages chose to preserve the traditions of their city-state rather than their own lives: not resentful of the fact that so great a peril hung over them, but convinced that for those who practice valor, nothing could be more desirable than exposure to contests of this kind. [5] Moreover, anyone who argued that these men were also more responsible for achieving the freedom of the Greeks

---

ing party's dawn annihilation is not incompatible with the final last stand (Hdt. 7.223–228), commemorated *in situ* by a stone lion and the burial there of the Spartan dead—though this does raise the question of where, in fact, Leonidas himself met his end.

[44] It should by now be clear that Flower (1998, 376) is right in his assertion "that neither we, nor our sources, have sufficient information to reconstruct *what* took place during the last night and day at Thermopylae with as much certainty and precision as many moderns lay claim to."

than the victors in subsequent battles against Xerxes would be in the right of it;[45] for when the barbarians recalled their deeds, they were terror-struck, whereas the Greeks were encouraged to attempt similar acts of bravery.[46]

[6] Generally speaking, these men alone of their predecessors [and contemporaries] were immortalized because of their exceptional valor. As a result, not only historians, but also numerous poets hymned their courageous deeds, including Simonides, the lyric poet, who composed a celebratory ode (enkomion) worthy of their valor, from which these lines are taken:

> Of those who died at Thermopylai
> renowned is the fortune, noble the fate:
> Their grave's an altar, their memorial our mourning,
>       their fate our praise.
> Such a shroud neither decay
> nor all-conquering time shall destroy.
> This sepulcher of brave men has taken the high
> renown of Hellas for its fellow occupant, as witness
> Leonidas, Sparta's king who left behind a great
> memorial of valor, everlasting renown.[47]

12. Now that we have discoursed sufficiently on the theme of these men's valor, we shall continue our narrative from the point at which we abandoned it. By gaining control of the passes in the way previously described, which gave him (as the proverb has it) a "Kadmeian" victory only,[48] Xerxes had caused very few enemy casualties, while losing countless numbers of his own

---

[45] A hint, here, of the engrained class prejudice that exalted Athens' land battles (fought by hoplites, led by aristocrats) against the naval victories of the "sailor rabble" (ναυτικὸς ὄχλος); for an egregious example, see the remarks by the Athenian Stranger in Plato's Laws (707B–C; cf. Green 1996a, 291).

[46] "It should be noted, however, that Thermopylae has no such effect on the Greeks in D.'s narrative: cf., e.g., 16.2–3 below, where the Greeks are petrified" (Marincola per litt.).

[47] Diodorus alone records this encomium. Hdt. 7.228 cites, tellingly, the brief and famous epitaph on the common Spartan grave in situ: "Go tell the Spartans, thou that passest by, / That here obedient to their laws we lie." As Haillet notes (2001, 127–128), the Simonidean tribute was either for a cenotaph or for the reburial of the ashes of the dead in Sparta. Cf. below, II.33.2, with notes.

[48] I.e., a victory in which the victor lost as much as the defeated, the name being taken from the fratricidal combat of the Seven Against Thebes (cf. Aeschylus' play of the same name), in which both Eteokles and Polyneikes, sons of Oedipus and thus descended from Kadmos, died. Diodorus describes this encounter at 4.65, and explains the proverb at 22.6.1–2. Cf. Hdt. 1.166.

troops. So, having thus obtained control of the passes with his land forces, he decided to make trial now of his navy, and force the issue at sea.[49] [2] He therefore promptly sent for Megabates, the high admiral of the fleet, and ordered him to sail out against the Greek squadrons: his instructions were to make every effort, with all the ships at his disposal, to force the Greeks into a sea battle. [3] Megabates, in accordance with the king's briefing, set sail from Pydna in Macedonia toward the promontory of Magnesia known as Cape Sepias. At this point a huge storm got up, and he lost more than three hundred warships, as well as a large number of horse transports and other vessels. When the storm died down, he put to sea again, making for Aphetai in Magnesia. From there he ordered out 200 triremes, instructing the captains to follow a roundabout sailing route, keeping Euboia to starboard, and thus to outflank the enemy.[50]

[4] The Greeks were anchored at Artemision in Euboia, and had a total of 280 triremes, of which 140 were Athenian, and the remainder contributed by the other Greeks.[51] Their admiral was Eurybiades the Spartan, but it was Themistokles the Athenian who was actually in charge of the disposition of the fleet, since on account of his sharp intelligence and strategic skill he had the confidence, not only of the Greeks throughout the fleet, but also of Eurybiades himself: he was the man to whom everyone looked for guidance, and whose word they eagerly accepted.[52] [5] When a council of ships' captains was held to discuss naval strategy, all the rest advocated holding station and waiting for the enemy to attack; only Themistokles expressed the opposite opinion, demonstrating that it would be to their advantage to sail out against the enemy in a single body, with the whole fleet. He argued that in this way they would prevail, since they would be going in close formation against an enemy whose line must inevitably be broken and in disarray, with squadrons emerging from a number of harbors at some distance one from the other. Finally the Greeks accepted Themistokles' advice and sailed against the enemy with their

---

[49] In fact, the war at sea had been going on concurrently with the assault on the pass, and (Hdt. 8.15, Lys. 2.31) the battles of Artemision and Thermopylai traditionally took place on the same day.

[50] According to Herodotos (7.183), the Persian fleet left Therme for Pydna and Magnesia only eleven days after Xerxes marched from the same city. The episode of the storm (Hdt. 7.188–193) took place about 13–14 August, at least a week before the last stand of Leonidas. Aphetai: Hdt. 7.193, 196, 8.6. The Persian outflanking movement around Euboia: Hdt. 8.7–8 (also 200 triremes): cf. Lazenby 1993, 140–141. See Map 1, and cf. *BA* 55.

[51] Hdt. 8.1–2 puts the total at 271, with 127 of these Athenian. Cf. Green 1996a, 143–144.

[52] On the uneasy relationship between these two leaders, cf. Hdt. 8.4–5 and Plut. *Them.* 7.2–6.

entire fleet.[53] [6] Now since the barbarians did indeed have to put out from numerous separate harbors, to begin with Themistokles engaged with scattered groups of Persian [ships], sank a good number of them, and forced not a few others to turn tail, pursuing them landward. Later, however, when the entire fleet had gathered, a hard-fought battle ensued: each side gained the upper hand with part of their complement, yet neither could win a total victory, so as night fell they broke off the engagement.[54]

13. After this sea battle, a great storm arose that destroyed a large number of vessels riding at anchor outside the harbor, so that it seemed as though divine providence was taking the side of the Greeks, and by reducing the numbers of the barbarian fleet was making the Greek forces a fair match for them, and a worthy opponent in any sea battle. Consequently the Greeks became steadily bolder, while the barbarians faced each successive conflict with increasing timidity.[55] Despite this, when they had recovered from the effects of the shipwreck, they put out against the enemy with their whole [surviving] fleet. [2] The Greeks, their numbers now augmented by fifty [new] Athenian triremes, moved into position facing the barbarians. The naval engagement that followed much resembled the skirmishes at Thermopylai; for the Persians were determined to force back the Greeks and win passage through the Euripos channel, while the Greeks were blocking the narrows and fighting to safeguard their allies in Euboia and beyond. A fierce battle took place, with heavy loss of vessels on both sides, and only the onset of darkness forced them to put about and return to their respective harbors. In both engagements, as is reported, the prize for conspicuous bravery went on the Greek side to the Athenians, and on that of the barbarians to the men of Sidon.[56]

---

[53] Cf. Hdt. 8.4–9 and Plut. *Them.* 7.4–6, both of whom allege bribery by Themistokles to bring his fellow commanders (Eurybiades, Adeimantos of Corinth) around to his viewpoint. Intelligence reconnaissance showed some Persian confusion after the storm, and a reduction of strength with the detachment of 200 triremes to outflank Euboia: these were decisive factors in shaping Greek strategy.

[54] Cf. Hdt. 8.9–11, which gives a more detailed account of the tactics employed (the bows-out circle, the *kyklos*) and the result (thirty Persian vessels captured). *Pace* Haillet 2001, 128–129, the two versions are compatible.

[55] Cf. Hdt. 8.12–13, from where we learn that the storm also wrecked the 200-strong Persian outflanking squadron off the Hollows (τὰ Κοῖλα) of Euboia. Herodotos, like Diodorus, ascribes this to the aid of divine providence.

[56] Herodotos (8.14) mentions a skirmish (not referred to by Diodorus) against some Cilician vessels the day after the first battle. The second battle here described (cf. Hdt. 8.15–18) was fought on the third day, at the same time as Leonidas' last stand at Thermop-

[3] After this the Greeks, on hearing what had happened at Thermopylai, and learning besides that the Persians were advancing on Athens overland, lost heart. They therefore sailed away to Salamis and took up station there.[57] [4] Meanwhile the Athenians, perceiving that the whole population of Athens was in imminent danger, embarked on boats their women and children, together with all useful objects for which there was room, and conveyed them to Salamis.[58] [5] The Persian admiral, on learning of the enemy's retreat, sailed for Euboia with his entire complement, where he stormed the city of the Histiaians, after which he looted and ravaged their territory.[59]

14. Simultaneously with these events, Xerxes struck camp and marched from Thermopylai, advancing through the territory of the Phokians, sacking their cities and destroying their rural holdings. The Phokians had thrown in their lot with the Greeks, but now, seeing they were not strong enough to offer resistance, they abandoned all their cities en masse and sought refuge in the rugged terrain around Mt. Parnassos. [2] After this, the king traversed the territory of the Dorians and did it no harm, since they were the Persians' allies. He left there one part of his army with orders to march on Delphi, burn the precinct of Apollo, and pillage the votive offerings, while he himself with the rest of the barbarian host advanced into Boiotia and set up camp there. [3] Those detailed for the robbing of the oracle had gotten as far as the temple of Athena of the Foreshrine [*Pronaia*] when a heavy rainstorm, accompanied by incessant thunder and lightning, unexpectedly fell from heaven. What was more, the tempest broke loose huge rocks and dropped them on the barbarian encampment: as a result, many of the Persians perished, and all the survivors,

---

ylai. Herodotos (8.15) gives the number of vessels in the new squadron of reinforcements as fifty-three. He also singles out the Egyptians rather than the Sidonians for valor, and names the bravest Athenian as Kleinias, father of Alcibiades. Cf. Lazenby 1993, 149.

[57] Nevertheless, the final sea battle at Artemision was seen as an Athenian victory: Hdt. 8.76; Simonides and Pindar ap. Plut. *Them.* 8.2, 5; cf. Haillet 2001, 129 n. 3, with later refs. With the amphibious Thermopylai-Artemision line broken, Salamis was the prearranged fallback and second line of defense. Cf. Green 1996a, 144–148.

[58] For the evacuation of noncombatants (women, children, the elderly, slaves) and movable property from Attica to Troizen, Aigina, and Salamis, cf. Hdt. 8.40–41, Paus. II.31.7, Front. *Strat.* 1.3.6, and Plut. *Them.* 10.1–4. The Troizen Decree makes clear that the main evacuation had been ordered and had taken place, two months earlier, in June: Green 1996a, 97–105, 156–161: what happened now (?24 August) was a final emergency exodus of those still remaining. Thus the decree and the literary sources (Herodotos in particular) are not, in fact, incompatible: cf. Meiggs-Lewis no. 23, p. 52; Nikolaou 1982, 147.

[59] Cf. Hdt. 8.23.

terror-struck at this intervention by the gods, fled the region.[60] [4] Thus the oracle at Delphi, by some divine dispensation, escaped being plundered. The Delphians, wanting to leave for later generations an eternal memorial of this epiphany of the gods, set up a trophy by the temple of Athena of the Fore-shrine, on which they carved the following elegiac quatrain:

> In memory of defensive action and as witness to victory
>     the Delphians set me up, in gratitude to Zeus
> and Phoibos, for their repulse of the Medes' city-sacking column
>     and rescue of the bronze-crowned shrine.[61]

[5] Xerxes meanwhile, on his march through Boiotia, ravaged the territory of the Thespians and burned Plataia, which was empty of inhabitants, since the population of both cities had fled en masse into the Peloponnese. After this he pressed on into Attica, ravaging the countryside, burning the temples of the gods, and razing Athens to the ground. While the king was occupied with these matters, his fleet sailed from Euboia to Attica, sacking both Euboia itself and the Attic coast as it went.[62]

---

[60] A more detailed account of the Persian advance can be found in Hdt. 8.25–34. The march through Phokis, and the Phokian retreat to Parnassos: ch. 32. The division of forces: chs. 34–35. The raid on Delphi, and its repulse: chs. 35–39. Herodotos agrees on the falling rocks and adds other marvels, including a volley of well-aimed thunderbolts and pursuit by a pair of larger-than-life heroes. Some (e.g., Veh and Will 1998, 308) see here a post-war fiction promulgated by Delphic authorities anxious to avoid the taint of Medism. Athena Pronaia ($\Pi\rho o\nu\alpha\iota\alpha$, or $\Pi\rho o\nu\eta\iota\eta$ in Ionic), Athena of the Foreshrine (cf. Hdt. 8.37, 39, 1.92; Aesch. *Eum.* 21), seems to be the better-authenticated epithet. However, Diodorus' MSS, confirmed by Paus. 10.8.6 and accepted by Haillet (2001), read *Pronoias* ($\Pi\rho o\nu o\iota\alpha\varsigma$), i.e., Athena-as-Forethought. Whether both titles were always in use, or the second was a corruption of the first that established itself independently over time, remains quite uncertain.

[61] To whom is the victory ascribed? By the manuscript tradition to the Delphians: $\dot\alpha\pi\omega$-$\sigma\dot\alpha\mu\epsilon\nu o\iota$, $\dot\rho\upsilon\sigma\dot\alpha\mu\epsilon\nu o\iota$. But some critics (Oldfather 1946, 162 n. 1, contra Haillet 2001, 25) argue that, on the *non nobis, Domine* principle, gratitude to the gods must be for divine rescue (well attested in the tradition) achieved *by the gods themselves,* and therefore read $\dot\alpha\pi\omega\sigma\alpha\mu\dot\epsilon\nu o\iota\varsigma$, $\dot\rho\upsilon\sigma\alpha\mu\dot\epsilon\nu o\iota\varsigma$. I have tried to leave the ascription ambiguous in my translation. Peek (1978) regards the epigram as a fourth-century forgery, Ebert (1982) as a commemorative dedication on the 100th anniversary of the Persian repulse from Delphi, i.e., in 380. Neither offers a compelling reason for rejecting its authenticity.

[62] Cf. Hdt. 8.50–53 for Xerxes' advance into Attica and the sack of Athens. Background: Hignett 1963, 193–204; Burn 1984, 425–435; Green 1996a, 165–167; Camp 1986, 59–60. Herodotos (8.66) allots six days only for the Persian fleet to reach Piraeus, and makes no reference to coastal raiding, of either Euboia or Attica.

15. About this same time the Corcyraeans, who had fitted out sixty triremes, were waiting off the Peloponnese. The reason they themselves give for this is that they were unable to round Cape Malea; but according to certain historians, they were watching to see how the war turned out, so that, if the Persians won, they might offer them earth and water, whereas if the Greeks secured the victory, Corcyra would be credited with having offered them support.[63] [2] The Athenians waiting on Salamis, however, when they saw Attica ablaze and heard that the precinct of Athena had been destroyed, were terribly disheartened. (Considerable panic likewise possessed those other Greeks, fugitives from every quarter, who were now crowded into the Peloponnese.[64]) They therefore decided that all those appointed to commands should hold a joint meeting and take counsel as to what kind of site would best suit their plans for a naval engagement. [3] After many and various arguments had been put forward, the Peloponnesians—thinking solely of their own security— said that the struggle should take place at the Isthmus, since it had been strongly fortified, and thus if the sea battle produced any setback, the losers would be able to take refuge in the Peloponnese, the handiest sanctuary available. On the other hand, if they boxed themselves up in the little island of Salamis, they would be beset by dangers from which it would be hard to rescue them. [4] Themistokles, however, urged that the naval battle should take place off Salamis, arguing that in the narrows those with fewer ships to deploy would have a great advantage over a vast fleet. He also demonstrated, in general terms, that the Isthmus would be an altogether unsuitable venue for this sea battle; for there the fight would take place in open waters, and the Persians, having ample room to maneuver, would easily overcome a small flotilla with their countless vessels. By similarly advancing many other arguments germane to the situation, he persuaded everyone to vote in support of the plan he had recommended.[65]

---

[63] For Corcyraean opportunism regarding the outcome of the war, cf. Hdt. 7.168. This could well have been one of the passages to which Diodorus refers.

[64] Refugees included—apart from the Athenians—the Thespians (Hdt. 8.50) and the Plataians (Hdt. 8.44), and probably also the families of the anti-Persian opposition party in Thebes (D.S. 11.4.7) and of the Megarians (Hdt. 8.45).

[65] On this crucial debate, cf. Hdt. 8.56–63 and Plut. *Them.* 11.2–12.3; cf. Green 1996a, 166–171, and Lazenby 1993, 154–163. Diodorus alone mentions here the (very cogent) argument about the potential danger of being cut off on Salamis, though Herodotos (8.70) makes clear that he was well aware of it; he also emphasizes that there was general agreement on retreating to the Isthmus before the meeting was even held. The Spartans, moreover, land-based and strategically imperceptive, remained obsessional in their devotion to an "Isthmus defense" (see below). Both Herodotos and Plutarch stress the cunning with which Themistokles finally got his way.

16. When finally a general decision had been taken to fight at sea off Salamis, the Greeks began making preparations to face the Persians and the challenge of battle. Eurybiades therefore, taking Themistokles with him, undertook the task of exhorting the crews and filling them with zest for the impending struggle. But the crews refused to pay any attention; in fact, since they were all in a state of panic because of the size of the Persian armaments, not a single man took the slightest notice of the commanders, since every one of them was desperate to sail away to the Peloponnese. [2] The Hellenic land forces likewise were equally terrified by the enemy's vast armaments: the loss at Thermopylai of their most distinguished fighters utterly dismayed them, while the disasters taking place in Attica before their very eyes reduced the Greeks to a state of deep despair.[66] [3] The delegates to the Greek congress, observing the confusion of the masses and the general atmosphere of panic, voted to build a wall across the Isthmus. The work was soon completed, due to the eagerness and the vast number of those taking part in it. However, while the Peloponnesians were reinforcing this wall, which stretched for forty stades [about five miles] from Lechaion to Kenchreai,[67] those waiting on events at Salamis, together with the entire fleet, were so demoralized that they no longer obeyed the orders given by their officers.[68]

17. Themistokles, seeing that the naval commander Eurybiades could do nothing to overcome the state of mind of his forces, but also that the cramped space on Salamis might contribute largely to achieving victory, devised the following scheme. He persuaded a certain man to approach Xerxes in the guise of a deserter, and assure him, as certain knowledge, that the ships at Salamis were going to pull out from there and reassemble at the Isthmus.[69] [2] So the king, believing him because of the plausibility of the news he brought,

---

[66] Hdt. 8.74 clearly refers to this panic-stricken episode, but in very guarded and general terms. It is not mentioned elsewhere, but carries conviction.

[67] For this Isthmus wall, cf. Hdt. 8.71–72, Isokr. 4.93–98. Müller 1987, 777–778, has photographs of surviving stretches of a great defense-wall from the right area; though this may date only to Justinian's day, nevertheless (as Müller says), the 480 wall must have followed the same line, and may indeed have provided some of its material. Cf. Nikolaou 1982, 148.

[68] Both Herodotos (8.74) and Plutarch (*Them.* 12.3) agree with Diodorus in making the Sikinnos episode (see note 69 below; Diodorus does not name him) Themistokles' way of coping with this general despair and panic in the Greek camp.

[69] Sikinnos was the school escort (*paidagogos*) of Themistokles' children. The trick is also reported by Aeschylus (*Pers.* 355ff., without naming Themistokles), Herodotos (8.75–76.1), and Plutarch (*Them.* 12.3–5): Hignett (1963, 403–408) disbelieves it, but for no good reason.

hurried to prevent the Greeks' naval forces from linking up with the troops they had stationed ashore. To this end, he at once dispatched the Egyptian squadron, with orders to block the channel between Salamis and the territory of the Megarid.[70] The remaining bulk of his fleet he ordered to Salamis, with instructions to join battle with the enemy and decide the issue at sea. His triremes were stationed in successive ethnic groups, so that a common language and mutual recognition might speed cooperation between them. [3] This deployment of the fleet was so arranged that the right wing was held by the Phoenicians, and the left by those Greeks who were fighting with the Persians.[71]

The commanders of the Ionian squadrons sent a Samian over to the Greeks to inform them of all of Xerxes' decisions, and of his entire battle plan, and that they, the Ionians, planned to desert from the barbarians during the course of the battle. [4] When the Samian had swum across unobserved, and had briefed Eurybiades on these matters, Themistokles, overjoyed that his stratagem had worked out as planned, rousingly encouraged the crews for the fight ahead, while the Greeks as a whole took heart from the news about the Ionians; and though circumstances were forcing them to fight at sea against their own inclinations, they came down readily from Salamis to the shore to engage in this naval battle.[72]

---

[70] Diodorus' phrasing somewhat obscures the fact that Xerxes' strategy, in the light of Sikinnos' message, was also to bottle up the Greek fleet in the Bay of Eleusis and prevent it escaping (cf. Hdt. 8.76, Aesch. *Pers.* 363–371, Plut. *Them.* 12.5). Note that Diodorus and Plutarch emphasize regrouping at the Isthmus, whereas Herodotos and Aeschylus speak only of precipitate flight by "the Greeks." One suspects pro-Athenian propaganda here. On the other hand, Diodorus is our only source specifically to report the (very probable) blocking of the western (Megarian) exit—modern Troupika—by the Egyptian squadron (Plut. *Them.* 12.4–5 and *Arist.* 8.2 imply it), and Deman (1985, 54) is wrong to dismiss this evidence (well supported by Bengtson 1971, 89–94). The other exits were at either end of the island of Psyttáleia (modern Lipsokoutali): see Hdt. 8.76 passim. Though the Egyptians may well have played a greater part in the battle than Diodorus suggests (Deman 1985, 56–74), only Hdt. 8.85, of the texts cited, lends any kind of support to Deman's argument.

[71] This agrees with Hdt. 8.85.1.

[72] The story of the Samian deserter is unique to Diodorus. We do not know his source for it: it could well be true, with the Ionians hedging their bets on the outcome. (Conventional wisdom ascribes the anecdote to Ephoros, and speculates that it was propaganda on his part to make his fellow Ionians look better: see, e.g., Frost 1998, 132–133; but Diodorus is equally positive about Ionian pro-Greek behavior at Mykale: 11.36.2–5). The improved morale can be ascribed not only to this, but to certain arrivals that had taken place shortly before the battle, as described by Herodotos (8.79–83) and Plutarch (*Them.* 12.6–7, *Arist.* 8.2–6). These were: (a) Aristeides from Aigina, with news of the blockade, necessitating a fight on the spot; (b) a shipload of Tenian deserters with the same news; and (c) a trireme from Aigina (probably the one bringing Aristeides), with the sacred images of Aiakos (lord of Aigina) and his sons Telamon (mythical king of Salamis) and Peleus (fa-

18. Eurybiades, Themistokles, and their staff finally completed the disposition of the [Greek] forces. The Athenians and Lacedaemonians held the left wing, which would thus be matched against the Phoenicians; for the Phoenicians enjoyed a sizable advantage both on account of their numbers and through the experience in naval matters that they had from their ancestors. [2] The right wing went to the crews of Aigina and Megara, since these were reputed to be the most skilled sailors after the Athenians, and would, it was thought, evince the best fighting spirit, since alone of the Greeks they would have no refuge anywhere should there be any setback during the battle. The center was held by the rest of the Greek forces.[73]

So they sailed out drawn up in this manner, and occupied the strait between Salamis and the shrine of Herakles;[74] [3] and the king gave the order to his admiral to sail against the enemy, while he himself moved to a spot directly opposite Salamis, from where he could observe the development of the battle.[75] [4] As they sailed, the Persians could, to begin with, hold their battle

---

ther of Achilles), heroic figures to whom the Greeks had prayed for victory (cf. Plut. *Them.* 15.1 for the heroes' alleged response). Themistokles' speech: Hdt. 8.83, and cf. Aesch. *Pers.* 401–405, which may enshrine his famous peroration.

[73] At 11.19.1–3, Diodorus indicates that the Persian center was held by the Cilician, Cypriot, Lycian, and Pamphylian squadrons. Herodotos (8.85) agrees with Diodorus in the main, but gives the right wing to the Lacedaemonians rather than to Aigina and Megara. How and Wells (1912, 2:264; also Lazenby 1993, 185) assume without question that Herodotos is right here. Yet the Spartans lacked any serious naval experience, and to deploy them with the Athenians would be a good face-saving measure while entrusting the other wing (as Diodorus sees) to veteran and experienced sailors. Diodorus' order of battle is surely the correct one. The bibliography on the battle of Salamis is enormous. Roux (1974, 51–94) is essential; in English, a representative selection of differing views would be: Burn 1984, ch. 21, 450–475 (still in my opinion the best analysis); Hignett 1963, ch. 4, 193–239; Lazenby 1993, ch. 7, 151–197; Green 1996a, 162–198; Hammond 1973, ch. 8, 251–310; Frost 1998, 118–151.

[74] This shrine was on the Attica coast opposite the island of Aghios Georgios (see Map 6), i.e., at modern Perama: cf. Frost 1998, 133 with refs. This implies an east-west line of battle: Herodotos (8.85), dealing with the entrance to the straits, assumes the same. It is objected (e.g., by Lazenby 1993, 185) that Diodorus' evidence requires a north-south alignment. But the topography makes clear that such arguments are meaningless. The line began east-west, swung around to near north-south beyond Psyttáleia and C. Kynosoura, and was back to east-west again as it neared Aghios Georgios. In other words, as Burn (1984, 457ff.) and, in particular, Roux (1974, 80–85) realize, against the majority of scholars, the line was transverse (coast-to-coast) and not longitudinal (parallel with coast): essential if the outnumbered Greek fleet were to take advantage of the narrows. Like the majority of modern topographers, e.g., Burn, Wallace, and Lazenby (1993, 179 n. 44), I take Psyttáleia to be modern Lipsokoutáli, rather than, as argued by Hammond (1956, 32–54), Aghios Georgios.

[75] This was on the slopes of Mt. Aigaleos (see Map 6): Hdt. 8.90, Plut. *Them.* 13.1. The position made an excellent command-post. Contrary to general belief, Xerxes' seat was not

line, since they had ample room; but when they came to the narrows, they were forced to pull out some of their ships, and this caused considerable confusion. [5] The admiral, who was ahead of the line and leading it, and had been the first to engage, was killed after putting up a gallant fight.[76] When his ship sank, there was chaos in the barbarian fleet, since those giving orders were many, but there was no agreement over the commands. In consequence they halted the advance, backed off, and began to retreat toward open water. [6] The Athenians, perceiving the confusion among the barbarians, drove ahead against the foe, ramming some of their vessels and shearing off the oar banks of others; and since their rowers could now no longer operate, many of the Persian triremes turned broadside onto the [enemy's] rams, and in consequence again and again suffered crippling damage. Because of this they stopped backing water, instead putting about and retreating in headlong flight.[77]

19. While the Phoenician and Cypriot vessels were being worsted by the Athenians, those of the Cilicians and Pamphylians—as well as the Lycian squadron, stationed in their rear—to begin with offered a strong resistance; but when they saw the most powerful ships in retreat, they, too, abandoned the struggle. [2] On the other wing a fierce engagement took place, and for some while the battle hung in the balance; but the Athenians, once they had driven the Phoenicians and Cypriots ashore, turned back, and pressed the barbarians hard, so that they broke line and fled, losing many of their ships.[78] [3] With such tactics, then, the Hellenes triumphed, winning a most notable naval victory over the barbarians. During this battle forty Greek vessels were

---

a throne, but a gilded stool (*diphros*, δίφρος); Demosthenes (who also so describes it, 24.129) adds the detail that it had silver feet.

[76] His name was Ariabignes (Hdt. 7.97, 8.89); Plutarch (who calls him Ariamenes) gives a detailed account of his defeat and death at *Them.* 14.3. See also 11.27.2 below with note 114. For the beginning of the battle, cf. Aesch. *Pers.* 408–411. Confusion in the narrows: Hdt. 8.89, Plut. *Them.* 15.2.

[77] The Athenian tactics seem to have included the "breakthrough" (*diekplous*, διέκπλους), i.e., shooting through between two enemy ships on momentum, oars shipped, if possible shearing off the enemy's oarbanks, and then turning to ram them in flank or rear. Cf. Hdt. 6.15, Thuc. 1.49, 7.36; Morrison et al. 2000, 42–43 and elsewhere; Morrison and Williams 1968, 137–139, 314–319. The turning broadside-on of the Persian vessels is partly to be explained by a morning breeze and swell in the straits: Plut. *Them.* 14.2.

[78] §1 describes the engagement of the Greek right and center. The "other wing" is the Greek right, held by the Megarians and the Aiginetans, and opposed to the pro-Persian Ionians. (The latter were at least suspected of treacherously changing sides, as Diodorus claims they promised to do, 11.17.3–4: see Hdt. 8.90.)

lost, but of the Persian fleet over 200, not counting those captured with their crews.[79]

[4] The king, being thus worsted against his expectations, put to death the most culpable of those Phoenicians who had first fled, and threatened to visit the rest with the punishment they merited.[80] The Phoenicians, scared by his threats, initially sought refuge further down the coast of Attica, and then, as soon as it was dark, hoisted sail for Asia. [5] Now Themistokles, who was credited with responsibility for the victory, thought up another stratagem no less ingenious: since the Greeks were scared of engaging in a land battle against such a vast number of Persians, by the following device he greatly reduced the size of the Persian army. He sent his own sons' tutor to Xerxes, with the message that the Greeks intended to sail [to the Hellespont] and break down his bridge [of boats]. [6] Consequently the king, convinced by this report because of its plausibility, became panic-stricken in case he might be cut off—with the Greeks now dominant at sea—from his line of retreat back to Asia.[81] He therefore resolved to make the crossing from Europe into Asia with all speed, leaving Mardonios in Greece with the pick of his infantry and cavalry, to the total number of not less than 400,000. In this way Themistokles, by employing the two ruses described, brought substantial benefits to the Greeks.[82] Such was the course of events in Greece during this period.

---

[79] The battle began early in the morning and lasted all day (Aesch. *Pers.* 384–386, 428; Hdt. 8.83). It remained long in doubt; Lysias (2.35–39) gives a vivid picture of Athenian anxieties: "Knowing their own ships to be few, and seeing how many those of the enemy were, well aware that their city had been laid waste, that their land was being ravaged and overrun by barbarians, that their temples were being burnt, and that every kind of terror threatened them." Diodorus omits the hard-fought sweep of the island of Psyttáleia by Aristeides and the hoplites: Aesch. *Pers.* 445–471; Hdt. 8.95; Plut. *Arist.* 9.1–2. On the other hand, he is the only source to give Greek losses, and a reasonable figure (though Burn [1984, 467] doubts even this) for those of the Persians (Ctesias [fr. 13 ch. 26] claims 500 vessels destroyed, Plutarch [*Mor.* 349A] 1,000!). Haillet (2001, 29 n. 1) reminds us that disproportionate losses can be explained up to a point by the fact that Greeks could swim, whereas Persians could not.

[80] Hdt. 8.90, cf. Aesch. *Pers.* 369–371.

[81] Some form of this second message to Xerxes by the hand of Sikinnos is vouched for by all of our main sources (Hdt. 8.108–110, who names Sikinnos but adds others unnamed; Thuc. 1.137.4: Themistokles later claiming responsibility for the bridge *not* having been destroyed; cf. Plut. *Arist.* 9.3–4, *Them.* 16, naming a captured royal eunuch, Arnakes, as messenger). Cf. Frost 1998, 147–148, for an excellent discussion. Other modern scholarship has been unnecessarily skeptical: see the survey in Lazenby 1993, 199–200.

[82] Despite horrific details of the land withdrawal in Hdt. 8.97–120 and Aesch. *Pers.* 480–512, Xerxes in fact retreated at leisure (forty-five days to the Hellespont: Hdt. 8.115)

20. Now that we have discoursed at sufficient length on events in Europe, we shall transfer our narrative to the affairs of another nation. The Carthaginians had reached an agreement with the Persians to reduce the Greeks in Sicily at the same time [as Xerxes was invading the Greek mainland],[83] and had amassed large quantities of such materials as were useful for fighting a war.[84] And when all their preparations were complete, they chose as their general Hamilcar, on the grounds that no other man among them enjoyed a higher reputation.[85] [2] He took over the command of vast forces, both naval and military, and sailed from Carthage with an army of not less than 300,000 men and over 200 warships, quite apart from a fleet of 3,000 and more merchantmen for transporting supplies.[86] While crossing the Libyan Sea, he was hit by a storm and lost the craft transporting his horses and chariots.[87] When he

---

and with an intact army. The force left with Mardonios is estimated by Herodotos (9.32.2) at 300,000; both his and Diodorus' guesses are far too high (see below, note 118). Hignett (1963, 351), as we have seen (see pp. 46–47, with note 223, in the Introduction above), argued that Greeks frequently mistook a Persian chiliad (1,000) for a myriad (10,000), and this may well have been the case here: a force of 30,000–40,000 would have been a practical answer to Mardonios' needs. Cf. Green 1996a, 206–211.

[83] This agreement has often been doubted, e.g., by Meister (1970, 607ff.; cf. Devillers 1998, 152–153), but without any really cogent reasons: the notion of Hellenism versus barbarism as a rallying cry (rather than as *ex post facto* propaganda) is not in itself implausible.

[84] Cf. 11.1.4 with note 5. Sicily at this time was divided into pro- (Selinous, Himera) and anti- (Syracuse, Akragas) Carthaginian tyrannies. Carthage already held several cities, including Panormos and Motya, in the north and west of the island, and was eager to extend its power eastward, not least for commercial reasons: Warmington 1969, 48–52; Asheri in *CAH* iv, 769–771; Consolo Langher 1997, 16–23. As elsewhere, much time and energy have been expended here on trying to identify Diodorus' sources, with little substantive gain: Timaios, Philistos, and Ephoros all have their advocates (Devillers 1998, 150 with n. 6 gives a handy rundown). Certainty is impossible and, in default of these authors' actual texts, would be useless even if established.

[85] Hamilcar (Abd-Melkart) was the grandson of Mago, the founder of the Magonid dynasty, and was either king himself or a *suffete* (elected ruler, judge), noted for his "manly courage" (ἀνδραγαθίη) and for his Syracusan mother, Hdt. 7.166.

[86] Hignett's "chiliad/myriad theory" (see note 82 above) can be tested here. Assuming that numbers under 1,000 are not liable to this kind of inflation, we can accept 200 warships as a reasonable fleet. How big an army could it transport? To move 300,000 men would mean putting 1,500 in each vessel, which is manifestly absurd; but one-tenth of that figure, i.e., 150, is exactly right. Three hundred merchantmen (including small boats) would also make more sense than 3,000.

[87] In Sicily, his loss of cavalry mounts was to be made good by Selinous: see 11.21.4, and Haillet 2001, 136 n. 3.

reached port in the Sicilian harbor of Panormos,[88] he had, he said, concluded the war; for he had been afraid that the sea would save the Siceliotes from peril. [3] He spent three days resting his troops and repairing the damage that the storm had wreaked on his ships, and then advanced with his entire force against Himera, while the fleet accompanied him off-shore. When he reached the aforementioned city, he set up two encampments, one for his land forces, the other for the navy. All the warships he hauled ashore and surrounded with a deep ditch and wooden palisade. He reinforced the army's encampment by relocating it to face the city and extending it along the [line of the] naval defense works as far as the surrounding hills. [4] In general, after occupying the entire western quarter, he unloaded all the supplies from the merchantmen, and then immediately sent them off again, with orders to bring grain and other goods from Libya and Sardinia. [5] He himself then took the pick of his troops and marched on the city. He routed those of the Himerans who ventured out against him, killing many of them. This caused panic among the city's inhabitants. It also scared Theron, the ruler of Akragas, who with a fair-sized force was standing guard over Himera, into sending a hasty message to Syracuse, asking Gelon for immediate reinforcements.[89]

21. Gelon had similarly put his forces in readiness for action, and when he learned of the Himerans' plight, he force-marched from Syracuse, at the head of not less than 50,000 infantry and over 5,000 cavalry.[90] He covered the distance in short order, and as he approached the Himerans' city, he gave heart to those who until then had been dumbfounded by the might of the Cartha-

---

[88] See Map 3, and cf. *BA* 47 C2 (Panormos) and D3 (Himera), both on the northern coast. Diodorus (himself a Sicilian) elsewhere (22.10.4) describes Panormos (Palermo) as "the finest harbor in Sicily."

[89] Theron had been tyrant of Akragas (modern Agrigento) since 489. About 483/2 he drove out Terillos, then tyrant of Himera, and took over the city, aligning it with Syracuse. This was the immediate excuse for a Carthaginian invasion, since Terillos, who had been Hamilcar's guest-friend, appealed to him for assistance. Similarly, Theron called on Gelon of Syracuse as his son-in-law, Gelon having married Theron's daughter Damarete (Asheri in *CAH* iv, 771–772; Haillet 2001, 31 nn. 1–2).

[90] On Gelon, see 11.1.1 with note 1. Ephoros (*FGrH* 70 F 186 = schol. Pind. *Pyth.* 1.146b) puts his forces at 200 ships, 10,000 infantry, and 2,000 cavalry: more reasonable, but still formidable. He also had support from his younger brother Hieron, tyrant of Gela since 485 B.C.E., and Ainesidemos, tyrant of Leontinoi (Haillet 2001, 135 n. 3). As Haillet says, the battle of Himera was a decisive showdown between Magonid Carthage and a powerful group of Hellenic *tyrannoi* for domination in Sicily. See now Kukofka 1992, 49–75.

ginians. [2] He began by making his own encampment, adapting it to the terrain outside the city, and fortifying it with a deep ditch and a palisade. He also dispatched his entire cavalry force against a number of the enemy who were roaming the countryside in search of easy plunder. These horsemen, appearing out of the blue to troops scattered over the countryside in no kind of order, rounded up as many prisoners as each could drive before him. When over 10,000 captives[91] had been thus shepherded to the city, Gelon was in high regard, and the inhabitants of Himera began to despise the enemy. [3] Gelon followed up what he had already achieved by unblocking all the gateways that Theron and his men had previously bricked up out of fear, and even built some extra ones that it might be handy to utilize in an emergency.

In general, then, Gelon—a man of outstanding generalship and subtle insight—at once began looking for a way in which, without risk to his own troops, he might outwit the barbarians and utterly destroy their power. His own ingenuity was greatly helped by a stroke of pure accidental luck, through the following circumstances. [4] He had planned to set fire to the enemy's fleet; and while Hamilcar was busy in the naval encampment with the preparations for a lavish sacrifice to Poseidon,[92] horsemen arrived from the countryside, bringing to Gelon a courier who was delivering letters from the people of Selinous. In these letters it was written that they would send their cavalry on the day that Hamilcar in his letter had asked them to. [5] Since the day was that same one on which Hamilcar intended to offer up his sacrifice, when it arrived, Gelon sent out cavalry of his own, with orders to take a wide loop outside the immediate area, and to ride up to the naval encampment at dawn, as though they were the allies sent from Selinous. Once they were inside the wooden stockade, they were to kill Hamilcar and set fire to the ships. He also sent scouts up into the hills overlooking [the city], with instructions to give the signal when they saw the horsemen actually inside the stockade. He himself mustered his forces by dawn and waited for the signal from the scouts.

22. So at sunrise the cavalry detachment rode up to the Carthaginians' naval encampment and were admitted by the guards, as supposed allies. They then galloped across to where Hamilcar was occupied with his sacrifice, killed him, and set the ships ablaze, at which point the scouts gave the signal, and Gelon advanced with his entire army, in close order, against the Carthaginian

---

[91] Another estimate that would carry more conviction if divided by ten.

[92] As Haillet says (2001, 32 n. 2), a surprising deity for Hamilcar to be cultivating. While the Carthaginians did adopt certain Greek deities (or their equivalents), Poseidon was notably absent from the list.

encampment. [2] The leaders of the Phoenicians in the camp at first led out their troops to resist the Siceliotes, and when the lines met they fought fiercely. At the same time, trumpets in both camps sounded the alarm for battle, and shouting arose from both sides in turn, each determined to outdo the adversary in the volume and loudness of their cheers. [3] The death toll was heavy, and the battle was surging to and fro: then suddenly the flames from the ships shot high into the air, and reports began to circulate of the general's death. At this the Greeks took fresh courage, and, their spirits raised both by these reports and by their hopes for victory, they assailed the barbarians with increasing fury, while the Carthaginians, disheartened and giving up all hope of victory, turned tail and fled.[93]

[4] Since Gelon had given orders to take no one alive, a mass slaughter of the fugitives ensued: before it was over no less than 150,000 of them had been butchered.[94] The remainder who escaped got to a stronghold where at first they held out against their attackers, but the site they had occupied was waterless, and the pressure of thirst forced them to surrender to the victors. [5] Gelon, victorious in a most extraordinary battle, won first and foremost by his own generalship, gained a reputation that spread abroad not only among the Siceliotes, but among all other [Greeks] as well; [6] for there is record of no man before him who employed such a stratagem, or slew more barbarians in a single onset, or took so vast a number of prisoners.

23. As a result, many writers compare this battle with that fought by the Greeks at Plataia,[95] and Gelon's strategy with the clever ideas of Themistokles; and because of both men's surpassing excellence, some allot first place to the

---

[93] Herodotos (7.166–167) confirms the duration and toughness of the battle; but he makes no mention of Gelon's stratagem, and has Hamilcar alive still until the rout, sacrificing for favorable omens, and finally in despair immolating himself. Gelon wanted his body, yet "neither alive nor dead was it anywhere to be found." For a general account of the battle, see Green 1996a, 147–149 (with plan). Detailed analysis: Pareti 1914, 113–172. Cf. Polyaen. 1.27.2.

[94] Diodorus undoubtedly exaggerates the figures of the Carthaginians killed and captured in a mood of Sicilian patriotism (which also leads him to boost Himera at the expense of the Persian War victories by the mainland Greeks): cf. 13.5.9, where his estimate is 150,000 dead and the same number captured; 11.25.2–3, 5; and note 96 below. Since none of these are Persian forces, Hignett's chiliad/myriad theory cannot be applied; yet, as so often, decimation produces a reasonable figure. A figure of 30,000 either killed or wounded would be quite impressive enough.

[95] On which, see chs. 34–36 passim. Scherr (1933, 12–13) points out that comparisons between Plataia and Himera can be confused with comparisons between Himera and Salamis. Cf. Brown 1952, 349.

one and some to the other. [2] And indeed, at a time when both Greeks and Greek Sicilians were dumbfounded by the vast size of the barbarian forces, it was the Sicilians whose earlier victory raised the spirits of the Greek main-landers when they heard of Gelon's triumph.[96] As for those who held supreme command on each occasion, in the case of the Persians the Great King escaped, and a great host with him; but in that of the Carthaginians, not only did the commanding general perish, but all who took part in that campaign were butchered too, and, as the saying goes, not a man was left alive to carry the news back to Carthage.[97] [3] What is more, of the two most distinguished Greek commanders, Pausanias and Themistokles, the first was put to death by his own countrymen because of his arrogant ambition and treasonable dealings, whereas the second was forced out of Greece altogether, and sought refuge with Xerxes, his most determined enemy, on whose bounty he lived until his dying day.[98] Gelon, on the other hand, after the battle stood ever higher in the esteem of the Syracusans, grew old in his kingship, and died with his popularity still undiminished. So powerful was the goodwill felt by the citizens toward him that the rule of his house continued under three further relatives.

However, now that these men's well-justified renown has been augmented by befitting encomia from us, we shall return to the continuation of our previous narrative.

24. Gelon's victory happened to take place on the same day as Leonidas' final battle against Xerxes at Thermopylai, as though heaven had deliberately arranged for the finest victory and the most famous of defeats to take place simultaneously.[99] [2] After the battle outside Himera, twenty warships man-

---

[96] We know, from a scholiast on Pindar (schol. Pind. *Pyth.* 1.146b = *FGrH* 70 F 186 ad fin.), that Diodorus not only drew on Ephoros for this statement, but carefully modified his source's hyperbole. What Ephoros claimed was that Gelon διαμαχησάμενον μὴ μόνον τοὺς Σκελιώτας ἐλευθερῶσαι, ἀλλὰ καὶ σύμπασαν τὴν Ἑλλάδα ("by his victory *freed* not only the Sicilians, but all of Greece"). "It makes an additional argument that D. was not an uncritical reader of Ephorus, since D. says merely [and surely correctly] that it raised their spirits": Marincola *per litt.* I am grateful to Marincola for bringing this little-noticed passage to my attention.

[97] But see 11.24.2 for exceptions—though these were not drawn from the combatants actually engaged in the fighting.

[98] Diodorus clearly has in mind here Thucydides' famous excursus on Pausanias and Themistokles, 1.128–138. Cf. his own excursuses at 11.44.1–47.8, 54.1–59.4.

[99] Such coincidences are not impossible, but we should be wary of them: the "myth of simultaneity" was popular in antiquity, and another tradition (Hdt. 7.166, Arist. *Poet.* 23.1459a: implication of mere accident in both cases) has Himera fought on the same day as Salamis! Cf. Haillet 2001, 137 with further refs.; How and Wells 1912, 2:201. Brown (1952, 350) suggests that the "Herodotean synchronism of Himera and Salamis" was changed "to

aged to make their escape, being a detachment that Hamilcar had <not> [100] hauled ashore, but kept available for routine errands. For this reason, though virtually all his men were either killed or taken prisoner, these vessels put out to sea before they were noticed. However, they took aboard numerous fugitives, and being thus overburdened, they ran into a storm and were all lost. Only a few survivors got safely home to Carthage in a small skiff, and broke the news to the citizen body with a brief statement, to the effect that all who had made the crossing to Sicily had perished.

[3] The Carthaginians had thus, contrary to all expectation, suffered a major disaster, and were so panic-stricken that night after night they remained wakeful, guarding the city, convinced that Gelon had decided to sail against Carthage at once, with his entire armament. [4] Because of the huge number of casualties, the city went into public mourning, while privately the homes of individual citizens were filled with grief and lamentation. Some were inquiring after the fate of sons, some of brothers; while innumerable children who had lost their fathers, and were now orphans bereft of support, lamented both the death of their begetters, and their own lack now of anyone to make provision for them. So the Carthaginians, fearing lest Gelon should steal a march on them by crossing over into Libya, at once dispatched to them as ambassadors plenipotentiary their most persuasive public speakers and counselors. [101]

25. After his victory, Gelon honored with rich gifts the horsemen who had slain Hamilcar, and bestowed decorations for valor on those others who had displayed outstanding bravery in action. The best of the booty he kept in reserve, desiring to adorn the temples of Syracuse with the spoils; of what remained, he nailed a good deal to the most notable of the Himeran shrines, and the rest, together with the prisoners, he shared out among the allies, proportionately to the number that had served under him. [2] The cities chained

---

give the Sicilian Greeks the priority claimed for them in ch. 23." Cf. Sacks 1990, 123–124. At the same time, as Prof. Rubincam reminds me, "the multiplicity of Greek lunar calendars plus the lack of fast communication made precision and accuracy about synchronisms very difficult."

[100] The insertion here of a negative missing from our manuscripts (οὐκ before ἐνεώλκησε), first suggested by Rhodoman and accepted by Vogel (1890), Oldfather (1946), and Haillet (2001), is logical: the Carthaginian ships drawn up on shore had been burned (11.22.1), and the other transport vessels already had been dispatched for supplies to Libya and Sardinia (11.20.4): Haillet 2001, 35 n. 3.

[101] The public mourning is understandable, and almost to the end of the century the Carthaginians refrained from attempts at expansionism in Sicily. Yet apart from their losses in men and equipment, the only further setback they suffered was the 2,000-talent indemnity imposed on them by Gelon (11.26.2–3, where their relief is made clear).

the captives thus divided among them and employed them as laborers on public works. An especially large number went to the Akragantines, who used them for the embellishment both of their city and of the surrounding country-side: indeed, so great was the multitude of war captives they received that many private citizens had 500 [*sic*] fettered prisoners at their disposal. One supplementary reason for the vast number of these captives, in addition to the fact that [the Carthaginians] had sent out so many troops, was that when the rout took place, many of the fugitives fled into the interior, and particularly into the territory of the Akragantines; and since the Akragantines captured every single one of them, the city was overflowing with prisoners of war. [3] The bulk of them were turned over to the state; and it was these men who quarried the stones that went to build, not only the biggest temples of the gods,[102] but also the subterranean conduits used to drain off water from the city, which are of such a size that their construction amply merits inspection—though because it was done on the cheap it tends to be underrated. The overseer of this work, a man by the name of Phaiax, used the fame of his undertaking to ensure that these underground conduits were named *phaiakes* after him.[103] [4] The Akragantines also built an extravagant swimming-pool, seven stades [just short of a mile] in circumference and twenty cubits [about thirty feet] deep. They piped water from both rivers and springs into it, and [later] turned it into a fish-pond, which supplied fish in great quantities both as food and for pleasure. Swans in abundance also settled on its surface, and the scene it presented was enchanting.[104] In later years, however, it became silted up through neglect, and in the course of time it ceased to exist; [5] but the area remained fertile, and the inhabitants planted it thickly with vines and [orchard] trees of every sort, so that they drew a substantial income from it.

After dismissing the allies, Gelon led his citizen-soldiers home to Syracuse. Because of the magnitude of his achievement, he was highly regarded not only among his fellow citizens, but also throughout Sicily; for he brought with him

---

[102] In particular, the gigantic temple of Olympian Zeus, or Olympieion (though work on this may have begun before 480): see 13.82.1–5 for Diodorus' detailed description, based on autopsy. Other smaller temples begun now were those of Demeter (now incorporated into the church of S. Biagio) and of Athena, on the citadel, its remains visible under the church of S. Maria dei Greci: schol. Pind. *Ol.* 2.15d; Polyaen. 6.51; cf. Dinsmoor 1950, 101–105, 108–109.

[103] See A. di Vita, Caratelli 1996, 294–296. The water was channeled from Rupe Atenea and the Girgenti hills in what has been estimated as twenty-three branch conduits for a total length of about 9 miles. Akragas reveals urban grid planning that predates the work of Hippodamos (who supposedly introduced it, at Piraeus among other places) by several decades.

[104] Diodorus returns to this artificial pool at 13.82.5.

such a mass of captives that it seemed as though all Libya had been taken prisoner by their island.

26. Also, ambassadors from those cities and rulers that had previously opposed him made haste to seek audience, begging forgiveness for past errors and assuring him that in future they would execute his every command.[105] He showed restraint to them all, and concluded alliances with them, bearing his good fortune with proper moderation: this attitude embraced not them alone, but even his worst enemies, the Carthaginians. [2] For when the envoys who had been dispatched from Carthage appeared before him, and implored him with tears to show humanity in his treatment of them, he granted them peace, on condition that they paid the cost of his campaign, 2,000 talents of silver; in addition, he required them to build two temples, in which they had to deposit [copies of] the peace treaty. [3] The Carthaginians, having thus against all expectation achieved their deliverance, accepted the outlay required of them, and, further, offered the gift of a gold crown to Gelon's wife Damarete, since it had been Damarete who, at their behest, did most toward achieving the peace treaty. When she received the crown from them, of 100 gold talents, she used it to mint a coin for circulation, the Damareteion, that was named after her. This was the equivalent of ten Attic drachmas, and because of its weight was called by the Sicilian Greeks a *pentekontalitron*.[106]

[4] Gelon treated all men equitably, in the first instance because this was his natural disposition, but in no small degree because of his eagerness to secure the loyalty of all by acts of benevolence. [5] Now he was preparing to sail

---

[105] Certainly Selinous and Rhegion; Haillet (2001, 38 n. 1) suggests that Sicel communities of the interior may also have been included.

[106] Diodorus has got the weight and value of the Syracusan decadrachm exactly right. The Attic drachma weighed 4.36 g; ten times that is 43.6 g. The Sicilian silver *litra* (λίτρα) weighed 0.87 g; $50 \times 0.87 = 43.5$ g (cf. Arist. fr. 476, 510 Rose). A good example of this famous and beautiful coin is printed by Kraay (1966, frontis., pls. 26–27, figs. 78–80). Unfortunately, most numismatists are now in agreement that the surviving examples must be dated at least fifteen to twenty years later than the victory at Himera: Kraay 1976, 204–206; Haillet 2001, 138 n. 3, with earlier scholarship. If true, this means one of three things. Either (a) no example of the 480/79 Damareteion has survived, and existing specimens are later and different issues, or (b) the specimens we have are indeed Damareteia, but Diodorus got their date and the circumstances of their minting wrong (a predictably popular theory), or (c) the entire story of the post-Himera minting and Damarete is later propaganda, probably invented by Hieron II (Rutter 1993, 171–188). I still would like to believe that Diodorus in fact got it right (numismatists are not infallible), and indeed that Damarete may have modeled for the adorable Arethusa on the specimens still surviving; but if forced to choose between the above alternatives, I would pick (a) as the likeliest in historical terms.

to Greece with a large force, and ally himself with the Hellenes against the Persians. When he was already on the point of putting to sea, some men arrived from Corinth with the news that the Greeks had won the sea battle off Salamis, and that Xerxes and part of his host had retreated from Europe. He therefore canceled his departure.[107] Delighted by the enthusiasm of his soldiers, he summoned an assembly, with orders that all should attend fully armed. He himself, however, came to the assembly not only unarmed, but not even wearing a tunic, and simply wrapped in a mantle. Then, coming forward, he gave an accounting of his entire life, and of all he had done for the Syracusans. [6] At each act he mentioned, the crowd applauded; they appeared absolutely astonished that he had presented himself thus defenseless for anyone who might so wish to assassinate him. In fact, so far was he from suffering the retribution due to a tyrant, that with one voice they proclaimed him Benefactor, Savior, and King.[108] [7] It was after these events that Gelon built notable shrines to Demeter and Kore [Persephone] from the spoils of war, and also fashioned a golden tripod worth sixteen talents, which he set up in the sacred precinct at Delphi as a thank-offering to Apollo.[109] He later planned to erect a temple to Demeter at Aitna, since none existed there; but fate cut short his life, and so this aim remained unfulfilled.[110]

---

[107] Hdt. 7.163 and 165 are ambivalent about Gelon's attitude: the first has him a hard-faced opportunist hedging his bets and waiting to see who wins; the second has him pro-Greek. After the news of Salamis (not to mention his own victory at Himera), the two are not necessarily incompatible, and he may actually have made a show of setting out to impress the mainland Greeks. Cf. Ephoros *FGrH* 70 F 185.

[108] D.S. 16.20.6 records a similar tribute in Syracuse to Dion (though in his case the assembly drew the line at "King"). Oldfather (1946, 194 n. 1) correctly specifies that "this acclaim recognized [Gelon's] rule as constitutional, not 'tyrannical.'" Cf. Ael. *VH* 6.11, 13.37. The second of these references has Gelon acting thus to thwart a conspiracy. Polyaen. 1.27.2 makes him strip naked in the *ekklesia* [!] before being acclaimed, not as king, but as general (στρατηγός). Bravo 1993, 80ff., analyzes these passages at length.

[109] No shrines to Demeter and Persephone are known in Syracuse; but Gelon and his descendants were hereditary priests of these chthonian deities (Hdt. 7.153), so the claim is plausible. Diodorus does not mention the great temple of Athena on Ortygia, also begun after Himera, and today incorporated into the structure of Syracuse Cathedral (Dinsmoor 1950, 108 with n. 1; Guido 1963, 36–43). On Gelon's dedication in the Pythian shrine at Delphi, and those of his brothers, see Meiggs-Lewis no. 28, pp. 60–61 (the inscribed base survives), and the dedicatory epigram (by Simonides?) of Gelon and his brothers, fr. 106 Diehl (printed with translation by Oldfather [1946, 194–195 n. 3]). Cf. Devillers 1998, 150–151 with nn. 9–10.

[110] The phrase "since none existed there" translates Vogel's (1890) emendation of the text, νεὼς ἐνδεούσης, the most satisfying reconstitution of the nonsensical †ἐννηὼς δὲ οὔσης† of the MSS. Haillet (2001) finds no emendation adequate and leaves it as a *locus desperatus*. Gelon died in 478 B.C.E. (11.38.7).

[8] Of the lyric poets, Pindar was at his peak during these times.[111] Such, by and large, are the most noteworthy events that took place during this year.

27. During the archonship of Xanthippos in Athens [479/8], the Romans appointed as consuls Quintus Fabius Silvanus <Vibulanus> and Servius Cornelius Tricostus <Maluginensis>.[112] At this time the Persian fleet, except for the Phoenicians, after being worsted in the sea battle of Salamis, lay in port at Kyme, where it spent the winter. At the beginning of summer it coasted down to Samos to keep a weather eye on Ionia: the total number of vessels at Samos was over 400, and their job was to keep watch on the cities of the Ionians, who were suspected of anti-Persian sympathies.[113]

[2] After the battle of Salamis, the Athenians were generally believed to have been responsible for the victory, and as a result got a very high opinion of themselves. Indeed, it became clear to everyone, throughout Greece, that they meant to challenge the Lacedaemonians for leadership at sea. This was why the Lacedaemonians, foreseeing what was liable to happen, exerted themselves to humble the Athenians' pride. Thus when a contest was proposed for the allocation of prizes for valor, through their powerful influence they saw to it that the highest award to a city was bestowed on Aigina, while the individual thus honored was Ameinias the Athenian, brother of Aeschylus the poet, since he had been the first trireme commander to ram the Persian flagship, which he in fact sank, killing the admiral.[114] [3] When the Athenians reacted

---

[111] Pindar was born in 518 B.C.E. (C. M. Bowra, *Pindar* [Oxford, 1964], app. 2, "Pindaric Chronology," 406), and his *floruit aet.* 40 thus falls in 478.

[112] The Roman consuls listed are in fact those for 485 B.C.E. (Broughton 1951, 21): Diodorus is still seven years ahead in his *Fasti* chronology. The mangling of "Vibulanus" into "Silvanus" (like many such errors) may well have been due (Perotti 1984, 162) to an editor or scribe who "propriam significationem cognomini tribuere studeret," was ignorant of the cognomen Vibulanus, and felt that "Silvanus" solved the problem nicely. Cf. ch. 41.1 below for a virtually identical error.

[113] Herodotos (8.130) gives a more detailed account, stressing that the Persian fleet (300 vessels, he claims) dared not venture westward into the Aegean, but remained guarding the Asia Minor coast.

[114] First prize to Aigina: Hdt. 8.93, Plut. *Them.* 17.1, Ael. *VH* 12.10. Ameinias' action: Hdt. 8.84, Plut. *Them.* 14.3, and above, 11.18.5. Diodorus' explanation for the award of prizes is not found in our other sources. Cf. Nikolaou 1982, 154. The Aiginetans were reputedly the best and most experienced sailors, even before the Persian Wars, and if the Spartans did lobby on their behalf, it was in all likelihood because of their actual superiority, as well as to counter vigorous Athenian propaganda claiming Salamis as a virtually exclusive Athenian victory. Marincola points out (*per litt.*) that this is an excellent instance of the thesis argued by Bosworth (2003): that while later historians may use spin, they tend to preserve facts. Diodorus notes the Aiginetan victory, but implies it was undeserved.

badly to this undeserved slight, the Lacedaemonians, fearing lest Themistokles, out of resentment at the outcome, might plot some great harm to them and the Hellenes generally, honored him with double the number of gifts that those awarded the prizes had received. But when Themistokles accepted these gifts, the Athenian people stripped him of his generalship and transferred the office to Xanthippos son of Ariphron.[115]

28. When the alienation of the Athenians from the Greeks generally became public knowledge, ambassadors arrived in Athens both from the Persians and from the Hellenes. Those sent by the Persians brought a proclamation to the Athenians from Mardonios, the general, in which he declared that if they would come over to the Persian side, he would give them any land in Greece they chose, rebuild their walls and temples, and leave Athens autonomous. Those sent by the Lacedaemonians, however, urged them not to be persuaded by the barbarians, but rather to preserve their goodwill toward the Hellenes, who were their kin and with whom they shared a common tongue. [2] The Athenians' response to the barbarians was that the Persians had neither good enough land nor sufficient gold to induce the Athenians to desert their fellow Hellenes. To the Lacedaemonians they declared that, for their own part, they would endeavor to maintain in the future the same concern for Hellas as they had exercised in the past; and what they asked of [the Lacedaemonians] was that they, with all their allies, should come to Attica as quickly as possible, for it was all too clear that Mardonios, now that the Athenians had proclaimed their opposition to him, would march on Athens in strength.[116] [3] This is what in fact happened: for Mardonios, who was waiting in Boiotia[117] with his army, at first tried to suborn certain cities in the Peloponnese by channeling funds to their chief officers; but afterward, upon learning of the Athenian response, he became enraged, and led his entire field force into Attica. [4] Besides the army left him by Xerxes, Mardonios himself had enrolled

[115] Cf. Hdt. 8.124–125, Plut. *Them.* 17.1–2. Again, the motives ascribed by Diodorus are not found elsewhere. In our other sources, the Spartans are making up to Themistokles for his lack of recognition in the prize-giving, and there is no mention of Athens depriving him of his generalship (a fact doubted, on no compelling grounds, by Podlecki 1975, 30). Motives: Green 1996a, 211–214.

[116] Mardonios' embassy to Athens (using Alexander I of Macedon as intermediary): Hdt. 8.136.1, 140; Plut. *Arist.* 10.2; cf. Green 1996a, 219–226. Spartan embassy: Hdt. 8.141–142, Plut. *Arist.* 10.3. Athenian response: Hdt. 8.143–144, Plut. *Arist.* 10.4–6, cf. Isokr. 4.94. The Athenians could use Mardonios' promises to put pressure on Sparta: they also knew that Xerxes himself was occupied with the revolt of Babylon (Haillet 2001, 41 n. 1).

[117] At various times, Mardonios seems to have had his winter quarters in Macedonia, Thessaly (Hdt. 8.126, 133; Plut. *Arist.* 10.2), and Boiotia (D.S. 28.3, Plut. *Arist.* 10.2).

many other troops from Thrace and Macedonia and the other allied states, more than 200,000 men in all.[118] [5] With such a vast force advancing into Attica, the Athenians sent couriers to the Lacedaemonians asking for their help. But since the latter procrastinated, and the barbarians had already entered Attica, they panicked, and, once more taking wives, children, and of their possessions only what could be quickly shifted, they abandoned their fatherland and once more sought refuge on Salamis.[119] [6] Mardonios in his fury at them laid waste the entire countryside, leveled the city, and totally destroyed any temples that had been left standing.[120]

29. After Mardonios and his force returned to Thebes, the Greeks met in congress and voted to succor the Athenians; to march out in full strength to Plataia and fight to the death for freedom; and to make a vow to the gods that, if they should emerge victorious, the Hellenes would, on that day, celebrate a festival of freedom (*eleutheria*) and hold the games of the festival in Plataia.[121] [2] When the Greek forces were mustered at the Isthmus, they all voted to take an oath concerning the war, designed to strengthen the concord between them and make them nobly endure the hazards of battle. The oath went roughly as follows:

[3] "I will not value life above freedom, nor will I desert the leaders, whether living or dead; but I will bury all of the allies who have died in the fighting; and if in this war I vanquish the barbarians, I will not overthrow any of the cities that engaged in the conflict, nor will I rebuild any of the burnt and demolished temples, but will leave them untouched, as a memorial to future generations of the impiety of the barbarians."[122] [4] When they had

---

[118] Mardonios' attempted bribery and march: Hdt. 9.1–5. His local recruitment figures can almost certainly be decimated in the same way as those for his original army corps: a total of 20,000 men from Thrace, Macedonia, and the other pro-Persian states is still high, but not impossible. This would give him a working force of about 50,000 all told.

[119] Hdt. 9.6–7, 8; Plut. *Arist.* 10.6. The "procrastination" seems to have been a calculation that with the Isthmus wall built, and Mardonios lacking a fleet, Athens could be hung out to dry with impunity (Hdt. 9.7, cf. Lys. 2.44–45). A threat by Athens to use its own fleet to help Mardonios had the desired effect.

[120] The second, total, destruction of Athens: Hdt. 9.13. Mardonios had entered the city ten months after its prior capture in September 480, i.e., midsummer 479, and will have leveled it about a month later (after a second abortive approach to the Athenians, Hdt. 9.4–5).

[121] Mobilization and marching of the Spartans: Hdt. 9.9–11, Plut. *Arist.* 10.6–11.1. The Greeks at the Isthmus: Hdt. 9.15.1. Festival and games: Plut. *Arist.* 21.1–5 (who places the decision, more plausibly, *after* the victory); Strabo 9.2.31, C.412; Paus. 9.2.6.

[122] The Oath of Plataia survives in three versions, conveniently correlated by Robert 1938, 307–316, and Conomis 1958, 112: (a) that recorded by Lykourgos *In Leocr.* §81;

sworn the oath, they marched into Boiotia by the pass over Kithairon, and after coming down as far as the foothills near Erythrai, they pitched camp there. The leader of the Athenians was Aristeides, and the overall command was held by Pausanias, the guardian of Leonidas' son.[123]

30. On learning that the enemy forces were advancing on Boiotia, Mardonios set out from Thebes; and when he reached the Asopos River, he established his camp, which he reinforced by means of a deep ditch and surrounded with a wooden palisade. The total number of the Greeks was close to 100,000, that of the barbarians to half a million.[124] [2] The first to en-

---

(b) that given here by Diodorus; and most important, (c) that on a stele from Acharnai. For (c), see Tod 1948, no. 204, pp. 303–307 (text); Burn 1984, 512–515; Fornara 1983, no. 57, pp. 56–57 (translation). Versions (a) and (b) are in effect paraphrased digests. Often dismissed as spurious (e.g., by Hignett [1963, 460–461]), the Oath is probably, like the Troizen Decree, a late version of a genuine document (Burn 1984, 512–515; Barron in *CAH* iv, 604). The notion of tithing medizers, specified by (a) and (c), is placed by Diodorus much earlier (see above, 11.3.3). A full and judicious commentary on the text(s) is offered by Conomis (1958, 113–120), who dates them, in their present form, to the fourth century at the earliest. While allowing for the possibility of rhetorical contamination, he concedes the probable original reality of the Oath (124). Of the divergent views on where the Oath was sworn (Lykourgos says Plataia), Diodorus' choice of the Isthmus is the likeliest. Conomis, oddly, plumps for Thermopylai (Hdt. 7.132), a guess by Jacoby (1913, col. 453) for what is quite evidently an oath taken on an earlier and different occasion.

[123] On the campaign and battle of Plataia in general, see Burn 1984, 516–546; Lazenby 1993, 221–247; Green 1996a, 241–277; Barron in *CAH* iv, 598–611. Topography: Müller 1987, 546–571 (photography excellent, maps misleading and confusing). Pausanias, son of the Agiad king Kleombrotos, and Leonidas' nephew, was to achieve considerable notoriety (whether deservedly or not is still debated) in the decade following Plataia. See note 170 below.

[124] Diodorus' overall figures are in the same rough area of inflation as the totals given by Hdt. 9.30 and 32 (110,000 Greeks, 350,000 Persians and allies), though Diodorus has forgotten that above, at 11.19.5 and 28.4, he reports figures putting the Persians at 600,000 rather than a half million. Can we reduce fantasy to reality here? For the Persians, Hignett's chiliad/myriad theory (see note 82) produces a total—bearing all estimates in mind—of between 35,000 and 60,000. What about the Greeks? Here we are lucky. Hdt. 9.28–29.1 gives a detailed breakdown of the infantry, city by city, state by state, clearly based on a genuine muster-roll. Total: 37,800, which carries instant conviction. At this point, clearly seeing that not even Greek heroes could beat more than ten-to-one odds in an open plain, Herodotos hastily flings in 35,000 helot batmen and 34,500 light-armed troops, of whom we hear singularly little in the subsequent battle. There are no figures for cavalry on either side. If we add 10% for the Greeks, making a total, with the infantry, of 42,570—say a round 43,000—we will probably not be far out. If we assume that the lower Persian estimates exclude cavalry, then a total force of 50,000+ seems reasonable. How far, if at all, these figures should be rounded upward to allow for light-armed troops, it is impossible to

gage were the barbarians, who sallied out against [the Greeks] at night, and charged the [Greek] encampment with all the cavalry they had. The Athenians saw them coming and, forming up in close order, confronted them boldly. There ensued a hard-fought battle. [3] At length, all the other Greek units routed the barbarians brigaded against them; only the Megarians, who had to stand up to the cavalry commander himself and the pick of the Persian horsemen, and were hard pressed in the fighting (but did not break ranks), sent some of their men over to the Athenians and Lacedaemonians, asking for immediate reinforcements. [4] Aristeides at once dispatched the picked Athenians who acted as his personal bodyguard: these charged the barbarians in close formation, rescued the Megarians from the danger threatening them, killed large numbers, including the Persian cavalry commander, and put the rest to flight.[125]

Now that the Greeks had so brilliantly prevailed in, as it were, a qualifying round, they became optimistic about final overall victory. After this skirmish they shifted their camp from the foothills to another site, better located for such a decisive showdown. [5] For on their left was a high hill, and to their right the Asopos River,[126] while the area between was occupied by the camp, itself defended by the natural lie of the land and the protection it offered.[127] [6] The Greeks had calculated sensibly: the restricted field contributed greatly to their victory, since the Persians' battle line could not be far extended, and

---

tell; but at least we are now in the realm of the plausible. The Persians indeed retain numerical superiority, to the tune of over 10,000 men, which would give their battle line a very real advantage, but not an insuperable one.

[125] See Hdt. 9.20–24, from which we learn that the Persian cavalry commander was Masistios (and get a detailed account of his splendid armor and death). It is not said there (though Plut. *Arist.* 14.3 confirms it) that the 300 Athenian picked troops under Olympiodoros were Aristeides' bodyguard, or that the attack took place at night.

[126] Diodorus' manuscripts reverse these positions, placing the Asopos to the left and the hill to the right of the Athenian position: ἐκ μὲν τῶν δεξιῶν γεώλοφος ὑψηλός, ἐκ δὲ τῶν εὐωνύμων ὁ Ἀσωπὸς ποταμός. No critic to my knowledge has been bothered by this. But even a glance at the map, let alone knowledge of the site, shows clearly that Pyrgos Hill is away to the Athenians' northwest, and the loop of the Asopos east-northeast of them. While it is possible that Diodorus mixed up his compass-points, absent-minded metathesis at some early point by a possibly dyslexic scribe strikes me as far more likely. I therefore reverse the positions of δεξιῶν and εὐωνύμων, and translate accordingly.

[127] On the Greek change of position, see Hdt. 9.25: one major reason for the move was the proximity of a good spring. What Diodorus omits is the eleven-day stand-off that followed. As the seers of both sides emphasized (Plut. *Arist.* 15.1), a defensive policy was best. This made sense. Mardonios could not take cavalry into the foothills; Pausanias could not risk his hoplites being outflanked in the open plain. Each hoped the other would attack, and Pausanias could, marginally, afford to wait longer: Green 1996a, 251–254.

in consequence, as indeed it turned out, no use could be made of the barbarians' vast numbers.[128] So Pausanias, Aristeides, and their staff, emboldened by the terrain, led their forces out to battle and, after assuming a formation appropriate to their circumstances, advanced against the enemy.[129]

31. Mardonios, being thus compelled to [narrow and] deepen his battle line, disposed his troops as seemed to his best advantage, and advanced, with much shouting, to meet the Greeks. He had a bodyguard of picked soldiers, and at the head of these he charged the Lacedaemonians brigaded against him, fighting gallantly and slaying many Greeks. But the Lacedaemonians resisted stubbornly, and met every challenge of battle with a will, so that the death toll among the barbarians was heavy. [2] Now so long as Mardonios and his picked detachment continued to bear the brunt of the fighting, the barbarians faced all dangers with a good heart; but when Mardonios, still fighting furiously, fell,[130] and of his picked troops some were killed and others incapacitated by wounds, their courage failed them and they took to flight. [3] When the Greeks pressed them hard, the majority of the barbarians sought shelter behind the wooden palisade;[131] of the remainder, the Greeks serving with Mardonios retreated to Thebes, while the rest, over 400,000 in all, were taken charge of by Artabazos, a man of high repute among the Persians, who retreated by the other route, advancing by forced marches toward Phokis.[132]

---

[128] Diodorus omits all the complex maneuvers in the days prior to the final engagement: Hdt. 9.41–58, Plut. *Arist.* 15–17. Much of this does not reflect well on Pausanias' command of the situation. It is worth noting that Diodorus throughout credits the Greeks with more unity, confidence, and good planning than Herodotos' account (or the probable facts) would seem to warrant.

[129] The essential difference between Diodorus and Herodotos (9.58–61) on the opening of the battle proper is that in the latter account it is Mardonios, not the Greeks, who presses forward on the attack. But the two historians agree (Hdt. 9.62–63) on the Spartans having to deal with the toughest and best of Mardonios' troops.

[130] Cf. Hdt. 9.63, Plut. *Arist.* 19.1–2, with Haillet 2001, 45 n. 1.

[131] Hdt. 9.65, 70, cf. Plut. *Arist.* 19.3–4.

[132] There were, as Haillet rightly reminds us (2001, 142 n. 2), only two escape routes available for the Persians: one north to Thebes, the other northwest by way of Haliartos into Phokis (Hdt. 9.66). Thus Oldfather's "in the opposite direction" for εἰς θάτερον μέρος is incorrect: "by the other route" seems more appropriate for a retreat in the same quarter of the compass. Herodotos (9.66) and Plutarch (*Arist.* 19.4) confirm Hignett's chiliad/myriad theory by estimating the force with Artabazos at 40,000, but even so, this is far too high: the figure may well represent the *total* count of survivors: Green 1996a, 270–271. For Artabazos, see below, note 288, and Book 12, note 11. Herodotos implies that Artabazos' force got away unnoticed; since Diodorus does not relate whether the Corinthians and the rest ever caught up with them, the odds are that they did not.

32. Just as the barbarians took different routes in their flight, so, too, the mass of the Greeks was similarly divided. The Athenians, Plataians, and Thespians took off in pursuit of those who had set out toward Thebes; the Corinthians, Sikyonians, and Phliasians, together with some others, followed after the force retreating with Artabazos; while the Lacedaemonians and the rest chased down those who had taken refuge behind the wooden palisade, and laid into them with a will. [2] Meanwhile the Thebans took in the fugitives, added them to their strength, and attacked their Athenian pursuers. A sharp battle took place under the walls, in which the Thebans performed with dazzling panache: not a few fell on both sides, but finally they were outfought by the Athenians, and all once more fled for refuge back inside Thebes.[133]

[3] After this, the Athenians moved off to join the Lacedaemonians, and with them proceeded to assault the palisade in pursuit of those who had taken refuge in the Persian encampment. Both sides put up a tremendous struggle, the barbarians resisting strongly from their fortified positions, while the Greeks battered at the wooden walls. In this desperate engagement many fell wounded, and not a few met death bravely, overwhelmed by a storm of missiles. [4] However, the violent onset of the Greeks could be halted neither by the sheer number of the barbarians, nor by the defensive palisade they had built, and all resistance was forced to yield; for the leaders of Hellas, the Lacedaemonians and the Spartans, were now vying with one another, on top of the world because of their earlier victories, and confident in their own tried valor. [5] In the end the barbarians were overcome by main force, and, despite their pleas to be taken prisoner, they received no mercy. For Pausanias, the captain-general of the Hellenes, seeing how numerically superior the barbarians were, was at pains to prevent any unforeseen accident, due to so great a disparity: because of this he had given orders to take no prisoners, and as a result there was soon a quite incredible death-toll. In the end, it was only after the Greeks had butchered over 100,000 barbarians that they reluctantly stopped this slaughter of their enemies.[134]

33. Such was the outcome of this battle. When it was over, the Greeks buried their fallen, to the number of 10,000 and more.[135] The booty they shared

---

[133] Cf. Hdt. 9.67−69; Plut. *Arist.* 18.6, 19.2−3.

[134] A figure of 10,000+ would fit well with a total survival of c. 40,000 on the basis of an original force in the neighborhood of 50,000+ (see above, II.19.6 with note 82).

[135] Diodorus' estimate for overall Greek losses, in what was clearly a savage and hard-fought battle, is the most realistic we have: nor, applied in a Greek context, would it be subject to Hignett's chiliad/myriad theory. Plutarch (*Arist.* 19.4) puts the total at no more than 1,360, but makes it clear that he is talking about *hoplite* losses only: he criticizes He-

out proportionately to the number of their troops, after which they voted on the awards for valor. At Aristeides' urging, they gave the award for cities to Sparta, and the individual prize to Pausanias the Lacedaemonian. [Meanwhile] Artabazos, with up to 400,000 of the retreating Persians, marched through Phokis into Macedonia, taking advantage of the speediest routes, and got these troops safely back to Asia.[136]

[2] The Greeks took a tithe of the spoils[137] to build a golden tripod, which they set up in Delphi as a token of gratitude to the god, with the following elegiac couplet inscribed on it:[138]

> The saviors of spacious Hellas set up this offering
> having saved their cities from hateful slavery.

Epitaphs were also composed for the Lacedaemonians who died at Thermopylai:[139] this for the whole body of them in common:

---

rodotos' absurdly low figure (9.70: 91 Spartans, 52 Athenians, 16 Tegeans, for a total of 159) not per se, but simply for omitting other participants. Even for hoplites alone, Plutarch's total remains suspiciously low.

[136] Oldfather (1946) and Haillet (2001) both accept Post's persuasive emendation Ἀριστείδου κελεύσαντος for †χαριτίδου κελεύσαντες† of the MSS: cf. Plut. *Arist.* 20.1. I translate accordingly. On the prize-giving generally (which generated much rivalry and ill will), see Plut. *Arist.* 2–3, cf. Hdt. 9.70–71. Though all agree on Pausanias, Plutarch reveals that the Athenians balked at the award to Sparta, and that the Council of the Hellenes, called on to adjudicate, gave the prize to Plataia as an acceptable *tertius gaudens*. Artabazos' march through Phokis: Hdt. 9.66, 89.

[137] Herodotos (9.81) reports two further "tithes," from which were made (a) a ten-cubit bronze Zeus at Olympia, and (b) a seven-cubit bronze Poseidon for "the god of the Isthmus" (i.e., Poseidon). Pausanias (5.23.1) states that the offerings were for Plataia alone; in fact (Meiggs-Lewis no. 27, pp. 57–60; Thuc. 1.132), they commemorated the entire war.

[138] For the golden tripod, mounted on an eighteen-foot bronze column of three intertwined serpents, and inscribed with the names of thirty-one states, stating briefly (coil 1), "These fought in the war" (το[ίδε τὸν]/πόλεμον [ἐ]-/πολ[έ]μεον), see Meiggs-Lewis no. 27, pp. 57–60 (= Fornara 1983, no. 59); and How and Wells 1912, 2:321–324, which gives parallel lists of participating states from (a) the Serpent Column, (b) the statue of Zeus at Olympia (Paus. 5.23.1), and (c) Hdt. 8.43–48, 9.28–30.77, noting omissions in (a) and (b). The base is still *in situ* facing the eastern front of the temple of Apollo. The golden tripod was stolen in 355 B.C.E. by the Phokians (Paus. 10.13.9); Constantine I carried the bronze column off to the Hippodrome in Constantinople, where it remains. Some, including Meiggs-Lewis (no. 27, p. 60) and Haillet (2001, 143 n. 3), doubt, on no clear grounds, whether Diodorus' epigram was the original replacement for the boastful distich first incised on the tripod by Pausanias (Thuc. 1.132, [Dem.] 59.97, Plut. *Mor.* 873C, *Suda* s.v. Pausanias), but promptly erased by his fellow Spartans.

[139] Both of these epitaphs (the second deservedly famous) are known to Herodotos (7.228), who reports correctly that they were set up at Thermopylai. His text of the sec-

> Here once against two hundred myriad there fought
> four thousand from the Peloponnese.

and this for [the Spartans] alone:

> O stranger, report to the Lacedaemonians that here
> we lie, obedient to their laws.

[3] The citizens of Athens adorned in a like fashion the tombs of those who had fallen in the Persian War: they also then held the Funeral Games for the first time, and made a law that specially chosen speakers should deliver eulogies over those buried at the public charge.[140]

[4] After these events, Pausanias the captain-general mobilized his army and marched to Thebes, where he demanded for punishment those men responsible for [the city's] alliance with the Persians. The Thebans were so dumbfounded, both by the number of these enemies and by their reputation as fighters, that those most responsible for their defection from the Hellenes voluntarily agreed to be handed over, and duly received punishment at Pausanias' hands: every one of them was put to death.[141]

34. There also took place a great battle between Greeks and Persians in Ionia, fought on the same day as the final action at Plataia; and since we propose to describe it, we shall take up the tale of it from the beginning.[142] [2] After the battle of Salamis, the commanders of the naval arm, Leotychidas the Lacedaemonian and Xanthippos the Athenian, mustered the fleet off Aigina, and after spending several days there sailed for Delos with 250 triremes. While they rode at anchor there, there arrived from Samos ambassadors calling upon them to liberate the Greeks of Asia. [3] Leotychidas and his officers consulted their captains, and when they had heard the Samians out, they agreed to lib-

---

ond differs slightly from Diodorus': instead of "obedient to their laws," πειθόμενοι νομίμοις, he has "obedient to their *instructions*," ῥήμασι πειθόμενοι. Though Cicero's Latin translation clearly used Diodorus' text, there can be no doubt that what Herodotos had was the original version. Cf. Veh and Will 1998, 312. For other sources, and minor variants in the texts, see Haillet 2001, 143 nn. 3–4, and the brief note of How and Wells 1912, 2:230.

[140] Tombs at Plataia: Hdt. 9.85. For the institution of the Funeral Games and public eulogy at this time in Athens, see Thuc. 2.34; full discussion in Loraux 1986, esp. ch. 1, "The Funeral Oration in the Democratic City," 15–76.

[141] A more detailed and nuanced account in Hdt. 9.86–88. Pausanias first had to lay siege to Thebes.

[142] For modern accounts of Mykale, see Burn 1984, 547–551; Hignett 1963, 247–259; Green 1996a, 277–283; Barron in *CAH* iv, 613–616.

erate the [eastern Greek] cities, and at once set sail from Delos.[143] As soon as
the Persian admirals who were stationed on Samos heard about the approach
of the Greek fleet, they put out from Samos with their entire complement,
and made landfall at Mykale in Ionia. Seeing that their ships were in no condition for a sea battle, they hauled them ashore and ran a wooden palisade and
a deep ditch round them. Nonetheless, they also summoned troops from Sardis and other nearby cities, and rounded up in all about 100,000 men. They
also laid in every other sort of handy military equipment, being convinced
that the Ionians, too, would defect to the enemy.[144]

[4] Leotychidas and his men sailed in on the barbarians at Mykale with his
whole fleet dressed for action, and sent ahead a vessel carrying a herald who
had the most powerful voice of anyone in the navy, and who was instructed
to approach the enemy and proclaim, loudly, that the Hellenes, having conquered the Persians, were now come to free the Hellenic cities of Asia. [5] Leotychidas and his staff took this action in the belief that those Greeks fighting
alongside the barbarians would defect from the Persians, causing great confusion in the barbarian camp; and this is just what happened. For the moment
that the herald sailed up close to the ships that had been hauled ashore and
made his announcement, the Persians began to mistrust the Greeks, and the
Greeks began to take counsel among themselves about defecting.[145]

35. When the Greeks [of the fleet] sensed the mood prevalent among those
[ashore], they disembarked their forces. The next day, while they were making ready for combat, a rumor reached the camp that the Hellenes had defeated the Persians at Plataia. [2] At this, Leotychidas and his staff summoned
an assembly and encouraged their troops for battle, among other things
<hinting at> a Plataian victory. This they did on the assumption that it would
embolden those who were going into battle. The outcome was, indeed, remarkable, for later both battles—that at Mykale and that at Plataia—were re-

---

[143] Hdt. 8.131, 9.90–92, 96.1. Herodotos gives the total of the Greek fleet at Aigina as
110 vessels only; but Will (1994, 121) is surely right in arguing that the bulk of the Athenian
fleet only joined Leotychidas after Mardonios' withdrawal from Attica to Thebes.

[144] Hdt. 9.96–97. Persian numbers, once more, benefit from decimation (Green 1996a,
278, with earlier scholarship). Diodorus' total figure includes a land force of 60,000(?) under Tigranes, an Achaimenid who had come to Greece in command of the Medes (Hdt.
9.96.2). If we think of a body of c. 10,000, including a badly reduced force of 6,000
(Tigranes as chiliarch rather than myriarch), we shall probably not be far out.

[145] Hdt. 9.98 reports the same piece of subversive propaganda by Leotychidas and his
herald.

vealed to have taken place on the same day. [3] Thus Leotychides and his staff would appear to have not yet learned of the victory, but to have made the story up themselves as deliberate propaganda, since the great distance between the two sites demonstrates the impossibility of getting a message through in time.[146] [4] Meanwhile the Persian commanders, now thoroughly distrustful of their Greek [allies], disarmed them and gave their weapons to those on whose loyalty they could rely. They then mustered all of their troops and told them that Xerxes himself with a great host was coming to their aid, thus encouraging them for the coming battle.[147]

36. When both sides had drawn up their troops in line and were advancing against each other, the Persians, reacting to the enemy's scanty numbers with scorn, raised a loud shout and charged them. [2] Now the Samians and the Milesians had all agreed beforehand to help the Greeks, and were coming on ahead together at the double. When their advance brought them in view of the Greeks, the Ionians assumed that their appearance would be cause for encouragement; in fact, it had exactly the opposite effect. [3] Leotychidas and his men thought that Xerxes had arrived from Sardis with his army, and that it was they who were now coming at them.[148] The result was panic and con-

---

[146] Diodorus' account has one night pass before the battle; Herodotos makes it take place that afternoon. "Hinting at" translates παραδηλοῦντες, my suggestion for the impossible †παρῳδοῦντες† ("parodying") of the MSS. Vogel (1890) suggested τραγῳδοῦντες, "hamming it up," accepted by Oldfather (1946); but as Haillet says (2001, 145 n. 2), this does not sound like normal Spartan laconic sobriety. Leotychidas could indeed have been inventing a victory; but this time it is just possible that the simultaneity with Plataia was real, and that news of the latter reached the Spartan and his men by means of an Aegean beacon chain: Green 1996a, 281–282. In either case there would have been enough doubt to make hints rather than a certain declaration desirable.

[147] Cf. Hdt. 9.99. The "great host" will have been that commanded by Tigranes: clearly the Persians, too, were not above stretching the truth a little to produce battle fervor.

[148] Herodotos (9.99, 103–104) reports that the Persians, immediately before the battle, (a) disarmed the Samians, and (b) sent the Milesians to guard the passes. We thus, according to Diodorus, have a group of Greeks, most of them unarmed, doubling forward in front of the Persian shield-line toward Leotychidas and his men. This is improbable, but not out of the question. That the Spartans mistook them for Persian warriors, however, really defies belief. Herodotos (9.103–104) has the Samians helping where and as they could, and the Milesians leading the fleeing Persians on a wild-goose chase in the hills. His version also has *the Greeks* rather than the Persians, Athenians in particular, advancing to the attack, against the barricade of shields, while the Spartans execute an outflanking movement via the lower slopes of the mountain. Thus Diodorus' version favors the Ionians, but we need not assume (as is generally done, e.g., by Hignett [1963, 257] and Oldfather [1946,

fusion in the ranks, with some saying that they should run for the ships and get away fast, while others argued that they should stay, hold their line, and tough it out. While all was still hubbub and disorder, the Persians came into sight, equipped in a manner calculated to inspire panic, and bore straight down on them, shouting. [4] The Greeks, thus given no time for [further] deliberation, were forced to face up to this barbarian attack.

To begin with, both sides fought fiercely, and the battle hung in the balance, with numerous casualties on both sides. But when the Samians and Milesians made their allegiance plain, the Greeks found new strength, while the barbarians, terrified, turned and fled. [5] A great slaughter then took place. The troops of Leotychidas and Xanthippos pressed hard on their beaten foes and pursued them to the camp; and once the outcome was certain, the Aiolians, as well as many other East Greeks, joined in the battle, since a passionate urge for freedom now swept through the city-states of Asia Minor. [6] In consequence, few of them gave any thought to the hostages they had given or the oaths they had taken, but along with the other Greeks began killing the barbarians as they fled. In this manner, then, were the Persians defeated, with a death toll of more than 40,000. Some of the survivors took refuge in the camp, while others retreated to Sardis.[149] [7] When Xerxes learned of the defeat at Plataia, as well as the rout of his own troops at Mykale, he left part of his forces in Sardis to pursue hostilities against the Hellenes, while he himself, in a state of shock, set forth with the rest of his army on the long march to Ekbatana.[150]

37. Leotychidas and Xanthippos and their men now sailed back to Samos, where they made alliances with the Ionians and Aiolians, after which they tried to persuade them to abandon Asia and migrate to new homes in Europe, offering to expel those peoples who had sided with the Medes and to make them [the eastern Greeks] a present of their lands. [2] If they stayed in Asia, the argument ran, they would always have the enemy at their gates, with mil-

221 n. 1]) that this has to be because he got it from Ephoros of Kyme (whose local partisanship is taken for granted on little or no evidence). If we reject it in favor of the Herodotean account, it is simply and solely because the latter is more intrinsically plausible.

[149]Cf. Hdt. 9.102–103, 105–106.1.

[150]Cf. Hdt. 9.108, where Xerxes' destination is given as Sousa, the Achaimenid winter capital. Mykale was fought about mid-August. Ekbatana, to the north of Sousa and another royal residence, may have been an autumn way-station on this occasion. Cf. also Ctesias, FGrH 688 F 13 32–33 (p. 464).

itary strength far superior to their own; their allies, being across the sea, would not be able to come to their aid in an emergency. When the Aiolians and Ionians heard these assurances, they decided to accept the Greek offer, and began preparing to sail with them to Europe. [3] The Athenians, however, changed their minds and offered them contrary advice, saying they should stay where they were, since even if no other Greeks came to their assistance, the Athenians, as their kinsmen, would do so by themselves. (The conclusion they had come to was that if the Ionians were relocated by the Greeks as a whole, they would no longer consider Athens their mother-city.) This was why the Ionians changed their minds and chose to remain in Asia.[151]

[4] Somewhat later than these events, circumstances brought it about that the forces of the Greeks were divided: the Lacedaemonians sailed back to Laconia, while the Athenians, together with the Ionians and the islanders, set out for Sestos. [5] As soon as Xanthippos, as general, made landfall there, he assaulted the city, took it, and put in a garrison. He then dismissed the allies, and with his citizen-militia returned to Athens.[152]

[6] This, then, was the end of the so-called Median [Persian] War, which had lasted two years. Among the authors [describing it] is Herodotos, who, beginning at a point before the Trojan War, composed in nine books an account of just about all public events that took place in the inhabited world,

---

[151] Thucydides' brief reference (1.89.2) does not mention this Samian council at all. Herodotos (9.106) differs from Diodorus over several points: (a) Diodorus has alliance offered to "the Ionians and Aiolians" *before* the council meeting, Herodotos to the islanders only (though including, *pace* Meiggs [1972, 414], members of both groups) and—more plausibly than Diodorus—*after* the meeting. (b) Herodotos has Athens oppose the proposed population transfer of the Ionians *ab initio,* as well as objecting to Sparta making decisions about Athenian colonies; in Diodorus' version, the Athenians initially agree, but change their minds for fear of losing mother-city influence over their colonists. Both Diodorus and Herodotos imply strong disagreement between Athenians and Peloponnesians. These accounts are essentially reconcilable. (c) Herodotos has the entire Greek fleet sail for Sestos to break down the bridges, and Leotychidas take his contingent home from there when the bridges are found to be down already (9.114); Diodorus places the parting at Samos. Here again, Herodotos is more plausible. Both agree that the Spartans pulled out *before* the siege of Sestos, which was Xanthippos' sole responsibility. Raccuia (1990) has a detailed and sensible review of the scholarship.

[152] Diodorus abbreviates Hdt. 9.114–121 very considerably. The siege lasted for several months, until the defenders were near starvation. The Persian commanders tried to escape, but one, Oiobazos, was killed in Thrace, while the other, Artaÿktes, was captured and crucified by Xanthippos. Oiobazos had brought the great cables of the bridges to Sestos: these were taken back home by the Greeks and subsequently dedicated at Delphi.

bringing his account to a close with the battle between the Greeks and the Persians at Mykale, and the siege of Sestos.[153]

[7] In Italy, the Romans fought a campaign against the Volscians, and defeated them in battle, with heavy casualties. Spurius Cassius, who had been consul the previous year [actually 486] and was thought to be aiming at a tyranny, was found guilty and executed.[154]

Such, then, were the events that took place during this year.

38. In Athens, Timosthenes was archon [478/7], and in Rome, Caeso Fabius and Lucius Aemilius Mamercus succeeded to the consulship.[155] During their time in office, the island of Sicily enjoyed almost continuous peace, now that the Carthaginians had finally been humbled and Gelon's equitable rule over the Sicilian Greeks was bringing their cities a highly stable regime as well as an abundance of essential goods.[156] [2] Now the Syracusans had, by [sumptuary] law, abolished extravagant funerals, and banned the customary expenses incurred on behalf of the deceased, including in this decree even totally neglected burial practices.[157] King Gelon, through his desire to encourage the public's civic zeal in all matters, applied the law relating to burials impartially in his own case. [3] When he fell ill and his life was despaired of, he handed over the monarchy to Hieron, the eldest of his brothers, and in the matter of

---

[153] Diodorus is the first writer to mention the division of Herodotos' history into nine books. Note that he ignores the final digression (9.122) on the ecological wisdom of Cyrus.

[154] For the consuls of this year [actually 485], see 11.27.1 and note 112. Dionysios of Halikarnassos (*AR* 8.82.1) confirms that one of them, Q. Fabius Vibulanus, attacked the Aequi and the Volscians (a campaign that dragged on until early in the third century B.C.E.). The prosecution of Sp. Cassius (cf. 11.1.2 and note 2 above) for *perduellio* (treason): Livy 2.41.11, Dion. Hal. *AR* 8.77.2–80.1; other sources in Broughton 1951, 20 and 22. Cassius seems to have won favor with the plebs by means of an agrarian law at the expense of the patricians.

[155] L. Aemilius Mamercus and Caeso Fabius Vibulanus were in fact consuls for 484 (Broughton 1951, 22): Diodorus is still seven years ahead of the Varronian *Fasti*.

[156] The prosperity of Sicily under Gelon after Himera is well supported (Consolo Langher 1997, 27–33; Asheri in *CAH* iv, 775ff.; Caven in *OCD* 628; Haillet 2001, 146 n. 2): we do not need to ascribe Diodorus' judgment (Meister 1967, 44) to mindless copying of the pro-Gelan Timaios.

[157] The text of the final clause is uncertain: I read καὶ τῶν παντελῶς ἠμεληκότων ἐνταφίων. This is Vogel's text (1890) except for the crucial reversal of the last two words. Haillet (2001) agrees with Vogel, and then translates in a way that has the Syracusans, nonsensically, both imposing these laws and at the same time neglecting them. Oldfather (1946), following an emendation of Capps, reads καὶ τῶν παντελῶς λιτῶν ἐνταφίων, and translates "even the altogether inexpensive obsequies."

his obsequies gave orders that the letter of the law was to be strictly observed. Consequently, when he died, his successor as king held his funeral in precise accordance with his instructions. [4] His body was laid to rest on his wife's estate, in the building known by the name of Nine Towers, famous for the massive solidity of its construction. The entire population accompanied his cortège from the city, though the site was some twenty-five miles distant. [5] Here Gelon was buried, and a fine tomb built for him at public expense, and civic honors granted him of the sort proper for heroes; later, however, his monument was torn down by the Carthaginians during a campaign against Syracuse, while Agathokles out of envy demolished the towers.[158] Yet neither the hostility of the Carthaginians nor the mean-spiritedness of Agathokles nor any other cause has ever been able to deprive Gelon of his renown. [6] The just testimony of history has preserved his fame unblemished, proclaiming it worldwide for all eternity. It is indeed both just and advantageous for any society that, of those who have held office, the mean should bear the weight of history's outrage, whereas the generous should be immortalized in memory; for in this way above all, it will be seen, many men of later generations will be motivated to work for the common benefit of mankind.[159]

[7] Gelon was king for a period of seven years [485–478 B.C.E.], while Hieron, his brother and successor in power, reigned over the Syracusans for eleven years and eight months [478–467].[160]

39. In Greece the Athenians, after the victory at Plataia, conveyed their women and children back to Athens from Troizen and Salamis, and at once set about fortifying the city, busying themselves with every possible precaution that might contribute to their greater security. [2] The Lacedaemonians, however, seeing that the Athenians had acquired a great reputation through

---

[158] Gelon's illness was dropsy: schol. Pind. 1.46a Drachmann; Plut. *Mor.* 403C. His respect for the laws: Ael. *VH* 6.11, 13.37. His three younger brothers were Hieron, Polyzelos, and Thrasyboulos. Destruction of his tomb in 396 by the Carthaginians under Himilco: 14.63.3. Agathokles (361–289 B.C.E., tyrant of Syracuse from 316): D.S. bks. 19–20, passim; cf. Meister in *OCD* 37.

[159] History as embodying a series of educative moral exempla is a recurrent leitmotif of Diodorus. Cf. above, 11.3.1, and below, 11.46.1 (apropos Pausanias); also 1.4–2.8 passim, 14.1.1–3, 15.88.1, and elsewhere. See above, Introduction, pp. 3–4, 13. Devillers (1998, esp. 153ff.) has a very interesting analysis of Diodorus' portrait of Gelon, suggesting that, in addition to the royal attributes of Hellenistic monarchy, he was allusively comparing the Syracusan ruler to (the recently deceased) Julius Caesar. Diodorus' liking for kingship (a term he uses very loosely) makes this both plausible and suggestive.

[160] These dates are correct: cf. Haillet 2001, 147 n. 2.

the activities of their navy, eyed their increasing power with suspicion, and resolved to stop them from rebuilding their city-walls. [3] They therefore at
once sent ambassadors to Athens, who were to counsel them against fortifying their city at this time, ostensibly because to do so would not be to the general advantage of the Greeks: should Xerxes, they argued, return with a still
larger field force, he would have walled cities handy outside the Peloponnese,
from which he could make forays and easily subjugate them all. When their
advice was ignored, the ambassadors approached the builders and ordered
them to stop work at once.

[4] The Athenians were at a loss as to what they should do; but Themistokles, who at the time enjoyed the greatest prestige among them, advised them
to do nothing, pointing out that if they resorted to force, the Lacedaemonians
and Peloponnesians could easily mobilize against them and prevent them
from completing their fortification of the city. [5] But he informed the Council, confidentially, that he and some others would go on a mission to Sparta
to explain this business of the wall-building to the Lacedaemonians; and he
instructed the archons, when envoys should reach Athens from Lacedaemon,
to detain them until he himself returned from there, and meanwhile to set all
hands to work on fortifying the city. In this way, he explained to them, they
would succeed in their endeavor.

40. The Athenians agreed to this proposal, and, while Themistokles together with his fellow envoys set off for Sparta, they set about building the
walls with enormous enthusiasm, sparing neither houses nor tombs [for ma-
terial]. Children and women joined in the work, as indeed did every non-
citizen and slave, with no lack of zeal all round. [2] Thus the work advanced
at astonishing speed, due to the multitude of laborers and the enthusiasm they
all brought to their task. Themistokles was summoned by the authorities [in
Sparta] and admonished regarding the building of the walls; but he denied
any such construction was going on, and advised them not to listen to base-
less rumors, but rather to send reliable envoys to Athens, from whom they
would learn the truth of the matter. As a surety for them he offered himself
and those who had accompanied him on his mission. [3] The Lacedaemonians agreed to Themistokles' proposal, put him and his fellow envoys under
guard, and dispatched to Athens their most distinguished citizens to investigate anything that aroused their urgent concern. But some time had now
passed, and the Athenians were well advanced with their work on the walls.
Thus when the Lacedaemonian ambassadors reached Athens and began to
denounce their actions and threaten them with violent reprisals, the Athe-

nians arrested them, saying they would [only] release them when the Spartans released Themistokles and his party. [4] In this way the Lacedaemonians were outmaneuvered and forced to let the Athenian envoys go in order to get their own back. Themistokles, having by this ingenious trick built up his country's defenses quickly and without risk, won a high reputation among his fellow citizens.[161]

[5] At the same time as these events were taking place, the Romans fought a war against the Aequi and the citizens of Tusculum. They brought the Aequi to battle, defeated them, and killed a large number of the enemy, after which they besieged and captured Tusculum and occupied the city of the Aequi.[162]

41. After the end of the year, the archon in Athens was Adeimantos [477/6], while in Rome Marcus Fabius †Silbanus† and Lucius Valerius †Publius† were elected as consuls.[163] During their term, Themistokles, on account of his strategic skill and sharp-wittedness, was [still] in high repute, not only among his fellow citizens but throughout Greece.[164] [2] As a result, he became puffed up by his own fame, and embarked on many other larger projects, aimed at the enhancement of his country's increasing power. For example, the port known as Piraeus was not at that time a harbor at all; instead,

---

[161] For the rebuilding of Athens' city-walls, the Spartans' objections to this, and Themistokles' diplomatic role in deceiving them, cf. Thuc. 1.89.3–93.2, and the brief reference in Plut. *Them.* 19.1–2 (where Theopompos is cited for the claim that Themistokles bribed Sparta's ephors into not opposing the project). See Frost 1998, 154–156; Lenardon 1978, 87–97; Gomme 1945, 1:258–261; Podlecki 1975, 30–32, 182–183; Hornblower 1991, 135–138. Stretches of the Themistoklean wall have been found (and confirm the emergency cannibalization of existing material: see, e.g., Wycherley 1978, 7–25, esp. 11ff.), but no sure trace of the pre-479 circuit has yet surfaced. Spartan distrust of Themistokles (and subsequently of Athens' imperial aspirations) dates from this episode. The importance attached to it by Thucydides is also significant: the walls became, in a very real sense, a power base, and bred unease in Sparta and its allies by that fact alone.

[162] Diodorus seems to be running two campaigns into one here. Aemilius fighting the Aequi (and Volscians): Livy 2.42.3, Dion. Hal. *AR* 8.84.1–87.1. Capture of Tusculum: Livy 3.23. The two main cities of the Aequi at this time were Tibur and Praeneste (see Map 4): which of them now fell is unknown.

[163] Diodorus remains seven years ahead of the Varronian *Fasti:* these are the consuls for 483. Valerius' cognomen was Potitus, not Publius; that of Fabius was Vibulanus. Cf. II.27.1 and note 112.

[164] At the Olympic Games of 476 (Plut. *Them.* 17.2, Paus. 8.50.3, Ael. *VH* 13.43), no one had eyes for anyone else. Yet in fact he was clearly already persona non grata with the Spartans, and there are signs that his enemies at home had begun to ease him from power.

the Athenians were utilizing as their roadstead the limited space provided by Phaleron Bay. Themistokles therefore got the idea of converting Piraeus into a harbor, since it would need only a little remodeling to turn it into the best and largest harbor of any in Greece.[165] [3] He hoped, too, that with the addition of this facility, the city would be able to compete for the leadership at sea, since at that time the Athenians possessed the largest number of triremes, and from a long succession of sea battles had also acquired experience and prestige as experts in naval warfare. [4] In addition, he figured that they would be able to count on the Ionians through ties of kinship, and through them would get to free the other Greeks of Asia, who because of this benefaction would likewise turn in goodwill toward the Athenians; and that then all the islanders, in amazement at the size of their naval arm, would promptly align themselves with those who could bring them both the greatest trouble and the greatest advantages. [5] For the Lacedaemonians, he saw, well organized though their land forces might be, lacked all natural aptitude for combat at sea.[166]

42. After thinking these matters through, he decided not to make any open declaration of his plan, knowing for sure that the Lacedaemonians would try to prevent it. He therefore announced to his fellow citizens in assembly that there were certain large concerns, of advantage to the city, that he wanted to introduce, and about which he had advice for them. However, to discuss them openly was not in the public interest: the proper course would be to implement them through the agency of a limited number of individuals. He therefore asked the *demos* to choose two men in whom they had complete confidence, and authorize them to act in this matter. [2] The majority agreed, and the *demos* chose as the two men Aristeides and Xanthippos, whom they picked not only for excellence of character, but also because they saw both as active competitors with Themistokles in the pursuit of public renown and

---

[165] Detailed account (esp. of the great Piraeus circuit-wall, not mentioned by Diodorus, but see below, 11.43.1–3) in Thuc. 1.93.3–8. This plan was initiated during Themistokles' archonship (493/2), but for whatever reason was long shelved, and only fully developed in the aftermath of Salamis, when Athens' vastly enlarged fleet would have provided a pressing reason for developing a good harbor. Cf. Frost 1998, 156–158; Lenardon 1978, 35–39; Garland 1987, 14–21, 163ff. On the chronology of this period, Pelekidis 1974, 421ff., has many useful insights.

[166] Diodorus' comments in effect sum up the military, and hint at the commercial, advantages of the Athenian imperial regime that developed from the Delian League (see 11.46.5 with note 179 below). Whether this was Themistokles' brainchild *ab initio* remains uncertain: it was undoubtedly the kind of long-term practical scheme at which he excelled.

leadership, and for this reason as liable to oppose him. [3] So these men were privately informed about his plan by Themistokles, and then declared to the *demos* that what Themistokles had told them was indeed important, of advantage to the city, and feasible.[167]

[4] The *demos*—which, while admiring the man, also suspected that he might be entertaining such large and weighty schemes with the idea of setting himself up in a tyranny—demanded that he state openly what it was he had decided. But he repeated that it was not in the public interest that his intentions should be openly discussed. [5] At this people were all the more admiring of his cleverness and intellectual stature, and bade him reveal his plans to the Council in secret session, with the assurance that if that body determined what he told them to be both feasible and advantageous, then their advice would be for the implementation of his proposal. [6] As a result, when the Council heard all the details, and determined that Themistokles' recommendations were both feasible and advantageous, the *demos* promptly endorsed the Council's findings, and he was granted the authority to do whatever it was he wanted. Every man left assembly filled with admiration for the man's high ability, as well as with elated expectations concerning the outcome of his plan.

43. Having thus obtained authority to act, together with every kind of ready assistance in his undertaking, Themistokles once more thought up a way to out-maneuver the Lacedaemonians, knowing full well that just as they had attempted to block the fortification of the city, so they were sure to try, in the same way, to disrupt the Athenians' plans for undertaking the construction of the harbor.[168] [2] He therefore decided to send ambassadors to the Lacedaemonians, to make them see how it furthered Greece's common interests to possess a first-class harbor as defense against the new expedition that the Persians were certain to mount. Having in this manner taken the edge off the Spartan urge to interfere, he applied himself personally to the task, and since everyone was only too eager to cooperate, the work was speedily ac-

---

[167] The rivalry between Themistokles and Aristeides is well attested: Hdt. 8.79; Arist. *Ath. Pol.* 23.3–4; Plut. *Them.* 3.1–2, 5.5, *Arist.* 2.1–3, 3–4 passim. Xanthippos' ostracism in 484 (*PA* 2:153, no. 11169) was probably engineered by Themistokles: Green 1996a, 56. If this secret plan of Themistokles' is historical, it contained a second, and more notorious, proposal: as well as the development of a new harbor in Piraeus, the burning of the Spartan fleet, then at Pagasai; see Plut. *Them.* 20.1–2, *Arist.* 22.2 (Cic. *De Off.* 3.49 and Val. Max. 6.5 ext. 2 locate the fleet at Gytheion). This proposal was firmly vetoed.

[168] Thuc. 1.93.3–7 provides an account of this construction: cf. Garland 1987, 163–165; Frost 1998, 156–158.

complished, and the harbor ready before anyone expected. [3] He also persuaded the *demos* every year to construct twenty triremes as additions to the existing fleet, and to make resident aliens and craftsmen tax-free, the object being to bring crowds of immigrants into the city from every quarter, and thus to provide manpower for a greater number of skilled occupations. Both these acts he regarded as vital to the building up of the naval arm.[169] These, then, were the matters with which the Athenians were occupied.

44. The Lacedaemonians appointed Pausanias, the commanding general at Plataia, as their admiral of the fleet, and instructed him to free all Greek cities that were still guarded by permanent barbarian garrisons.[170] [2] He therefore took fifty triremes from the Peloponnese, and sent to Athens for thirty more, under the command of Aristeides. He then sailed first of all to Cyprus, where he freed those cities that still had Persian garrisons, [3] and after that to the Hellespont. Here he took Byzantion, which had been held by the Persians.[171] Of the other barbarians there, he killed some and expelled the rest,

[169] Diodorus is our only source for these two measures. The annual building of fresh triremes (which had a comparatively short life) is plausible. There had been a tradition since Solon's day of encouraging craftsmen (τεχνίται) to immigrate on advantageous terms; but as Meiggs says (1972, 263), it is unlikely that a blanket exemption was ever given to them, or to metics (who had to pay a special tax for resident aliens, the *metoikion*). What Themistokles may well have encouraged were individual exemptions, on easy terms.

[170] As he does later, at even greater length, for Themistokles (54.1–59.4), Diodorus here, clearly influenced by the Thucydidean excursus on both men (1.128.1–138.6), writes his own account of Pausanias entirely under the archon-year 477/6, as a kind of extended footnote. Pausanias in fact embarked on his original mission, as described here, at least as early as 478. (I am not convinced by Loomis' down-dating of the fall of Byzantion to spring 477.) In fact, 477 probably marks the date of his first recall, acquittal, and return to Byzantion (Badian 1993, 86ff., 99, 132ff.), where he remained for seven years (Just. 9.1.3; cf. Smart 1967, 137; Pelekidis 1974, 422 with n. 46; Fornara 1966, 257–258; Badian 1993, 206–207 with n. 54), with tacit Spartan approval, keeping Byzantion out of Athenian hands. But when he was expelled by Kimon in 471, his final recall and condemnation followed swiftly (cf. 11.54.1–2). By the end of 470 (Keaveney 2003, 8, argues for 469), he was, almost certainly, dead: *pace* White (1964), who argues for a date c. 467/6, on the dubious grounds that (a) Themistokles' move to Ephesos and (?) Artaxerxes came almost immediately after Pausanias' death, and (b) Pausanias is unlikely to have sired three sons in five years (between 475 and 470). Much of this whole episode (including Thucydides' dating of so much to Pausanias' *first* sojourn in Byzantion) is still fiercely debated.

[171] Cf. Thuc. 1.94.1–2, cf. 128.5–6; Nep. *Paus.* 2.1–2, *Arist.* 2.2; Justin 2.15.13–14, with Meiggs 1972, 38–41; Hammond 1973, 321–325; Hornblower 1991, 140–141. Diodorus also comments on the strategic location of Cyprus at 14.98.3. Pausanias' appointment and instructions must have come de jure from the Hellenic league, though de facto Sparta probably did dictate both. "All Greek cities" suggests those of Asia Minor, whereas both Cy-

thus liberating the city; but many high-ranking Persians whom he captured in Byzantion itself he handed over to Gongylos of Eretria to guard. Now ostensibly he was to hold these men pending future punishment, but in fact his business was to get them back safely to Xerxes, since he [Pausanias] had concluded a secret treaty of friendship with the Great King, and was going to marry Xerxes' daughter, with the intention of betraying the Greeks. [4] The intermediary in this business was the general Artabazos, who was secretly furnishing Pausanias with large cash subventions for the purpose of suborning Greeks in key positions.[172]

Pausanias, however, was exposed and punished in the following manner. [5] Because he aspired to emulate the luxurious Persian life-style, and behaved like a despot to his subordinates, everyone resented him, in particular any of the Greeks who had been appointed to some [junior] command. [6] There was, then, a great deal of gossip in the army, among both ethnic and civic groups, highly critical of Pausanias' harsh discipline. Certain Peloponnesians actually deserted him and sailed back home, from where they sent envoys [to Sparta] with a formal bill of indictment against him. Aristeides the Athenian shrewdly took advantage of this opportunity to win over various cities during official discussions, using his personal influence to bring them into the Athe-

---

prus and Byzantion were relatively remote. But both controlled major trade-routes, the first to Egypt and the Levant, the second to the Black Sea, the Crimea, and the great wheat-fields of the Ukraine. Grain imports took priority over the Ionians. Pausanias' small fleet's remarkable successes hint at either Phoenician demoralization, or withdrawal from the Cyprus area, or both (Miller 1997, 9); by the mid-460s the island had once more passed under Persian control. Thucydides agrees on thirty Athenian vessels, but puts the Peloponnesian contingent at twenty, with "a mass of other allies," which will account for the remaining thirty. It is worth noting that the Athenian commanders were Aristeides and Kimon (Plut. *Arist.* 23.1, *Cim.* 6.1)—not Themistokles, already in bad odor with the Spartans and (not surprisingly) with their Athenian supporters. Podlecki (1976, 293–294) explains his absence by theorizing that he was "still occupied with the completion of the city and Peireius fortifications" (above, 11.41.2).

[172] Thuc. 1.128.5–129.1; Nep. *Paus.* 2.2–4. On Gongylos, cf. Xen. *Hell.* 3.1.6 and *Anab.* 7.8.8. Herodotos (5.32) says that Pausanias ("if the tale is true") actually married the daughter of the Daskyleion satrap, i.e., either Megabates or Artabazos as his replacement. Thucydides and Nepos both cite improbable alleged correspondence between Pausanias and Xerxes. Pausanias' supposed Medism, the account of which follows here (Diodorus draws throughout, often almost verbatim, on Thuc. 1.128–135.1), has often been seen as a frame-up—most notably by Fornara (1966), Cawkwell (1970, 51), and Badian (1993, 130–132), and cf. Hornblower (1991, 219) and Haillet (2001, 151 n. 1 with further refs.)—Pausanias' real offense being his supposed favoring of the Helots. It is also possible that the Athenians and Ionians used Pausanias' highhandedness (of which complaints were lodged with Sparta) as a lever to undermine Spartan leadership: Hdt. 8.3; Plut. *Cim.* 6.1–3, *Arist.* 23.1–5. But the whole truth remains irretrievable.

nian alliance.[173] Yet the Athenians benefited even more from a stroke of pure luck, as a result of the following circumstances.

45. Pausanias had arranged that the couriers who carried correspondence from him to the Great King should not return, and thus be in a position to betray his secrets. They were, therefore, being done away with by those to whom they delivered the letters, which was why none of them ever returned safely. [2] One of these couriers, putting two and two together from their nonappearance, opened the letters, and found that his guess concerning the elimination of their bearers was indeed the truth. He therefore turned them over to the ephors as evidence. [3] They, however, were suspicious because the letters had come to them already opened, and demanded more, and more convincing, proof. The courier then offered to confront them with Pausanias acknowledging his actions in person. [4] He therefore traveled to Tainaron[174] and seated himself as a suppliant at the shrine of Poseidon. He also set up a double-roomed tent, in which he concealed the ephors and certain other Spartans. When Pausanias approached him and inquired the reason for his being a suppliant, the man blamed Pausanias himself, inasmuch as the latter had included in the letter directions for his execution. [5] Pausanias then apologized and asked forgiveness for past mistakes, going so far as to beg the man to keep the incident secret, promising him lavish gifts. They then parted.

The ephors and those with them, despite having discovered the whole truth of the matter, at that time kept quiet and took no action. Later, however, when the Lacedaemonians were, with the ephors' assistance, investigating the matter, Pausanias was forewarned and, anticipating them, took refuge in the shrine of Athena of the Brazen House.[175] [6] The Lacedaemonians were in a quandary as to whether, now that he was a suppliant, they should punish him. The story goes that Pausanias' mother came out to the shrine, but neither said nor did anything except to pick up a brick and put it at the entrance, after which she went back home; [7] at which point the Lacedaemonians, in compliance with the mother's verdict, proceeded to wall up the entrance, and

---

[173] For Aristeides' role in establishing the Delian League, see 11.47.1–3 with notes 179–180. Other tributes to his cleverness and shrewd diplomacy: Arist. *Ath. Pol.* 23.4; Plut. *Arist.* 23.1–2, *Cim.* 6.3.

[174] Tainaron (today C. Matapan) lies at the southernmost tip of the central Peloponnesian peninsula of Taygetos. Near the temple of Poseidon was a cavern by way of which Herakles supposedly brought up the three-headed dog Kerberos from the underworld (the whole area is riddled with subterranean limestone caves and waterways).

[175] This temple (also known as that of Athena Poliachos) was located on the Spartan acropolis, to the north of the theater: Haillet 2001, 62 n. 1.

in this way forced Pausanias to end his life through starvation. Now though the body of the deceased was handed over to his kin for burial, divine displeasure still manifested itself at this violation of the sanctity of suppliants: [8] for when the Lacedaemonians were consulting the oracle at Delphi about some quite different matters, the god gave them an oracular response bidding them return her suppliant to the goddess. [9] The Spartans regarded this sacred injunction as impracticable, and for some while were thus at a loss, being unable to carry out the order the god had given them. Resolving, however, to do what they could, they had two bronze statues of Pausanias made, and set these up in Athena's shrine.[176]

46. Since all through our history we have regularly augmented the high repute of good men with the eulogies we pronounce over them, and at the deaths of base persons have similarly uttered the appropriate obloquies, we shall not let Pausanias' vileness and treachery pass uncondemned. [2] Who, indeed, would not be astounded at the folly of this man? By his victory at Plataia, and through the performance of many other highly praised deeds, he became the benefactor of Greece. Yet he not only failed to maintain the esteem in which he was held, but through his passion for Persian wealth and luxury brought shame on his existing reputation. [3] Puffed up by his successes, he came to loathe his Laconian upbringing, and to ape the licentiousness and luxury of the Persians, though he least of all had cause to emulate the customs of the barbarians, since he had not learned about them at second-hand, but had made trial of them in fact and in person, and knew well how much more his ancestral way of life inclined toward high achievement than did the luxury of the Persians.[177]

---

[176] Pausanias' death probably took place in 471/0, though the date is much disputed: see note 205 below. Pausanias was removed from the shrine shortly before his death to avoid pollution (Thuc. 1.134.2–3). At first the Spartans planned to throw his corpse into the malefactors' pit (ibid. §4), but then they "decided to bury him somewhere nearby," presumably turning his body over to his relatives for this purpose. The later oracle is mentioned by Thucydides (1.134.4 and 135.1) and by Pausanias (3.14.1, 17.7), both of whom saw the statues, as well as by Plutarch (*Mor.* 560F). This consultation of Delphi may well have been occasioned by the great earthquake (of 469/8 or 464) and the subsequent Helot revolt. The god ordered Pausanias' body to be reburied at the site of his death: Thucydides records that this was done in the "temple forecourt" (προτεμενίσματι).

[177] The question of Pausanias' guilt or innocence remains ambiguous, and is probably insoluble. That he was arrogant there seems no doubt; that he had powerful enemies at Sparta is equally certain. As Herodotos says (9.64), he had won νίκην . . . καλλίστην ἀπασέων τῶν ἡμεῖς ἴδμεν, "the finest victory of any known to us," and this must have engendered jealousy among his peers. Podlecki (1976, 310) makes the point that "as a regent who

[4] It was, indeed, through his own vileness that he not only got the punishment he deserved, but also was responsible for his countrymen losing their supremacy at sea. By way of contrast, the diplomacy of Aristeides in his dealings with the allies—among other virtues, his amiability toward his subordinates—attracted much attention, and led everyone, as though driven by the same impulse, to incline toward the Athenian cause. [5] Because of this, they no longer paid any heed to the leaders sent from Sparta,[178] but in their admiration for Aristeides eagerly took his word over everything, thus ensuring that he was assigned the supreme command at sea without needing to fight for it.[179]

47. Aristeides at once counseled the allies, who were meeting in general assembly, to designate Delos as [the location for] their common treasury, and to deposit there all the revenues they collected; also, against [the cost of] the war

---

was unlikely ever to become king, he might have been willing to take any steps necessary to perpetuate his power." Both Podlecki and earlier scholars plausibly associate the odium he incurred at home with his supposed plans to enfranchise or militarize some portion of the Helot population. All of our evidence (including that of Thucydides) gives off the unmistakable smell of *parti pris* propaganda.

[178] Cf. Thucydides (1.95.6), who names the Spartan Dorkis as one of these leaders.

[179] Diodorus now gives his version of the (still much-debated) foundation of the breakaway so-called Delian League under Athens' leadership, in 478/7, according to Aristotle (*Ath. Pol.* 23.5, archonship of Timosthenes): doubtless the process extended over several years. It should be noted that what Aristotle places in 478/7 is Aristeides' tribute assessment, which implies a fairly advanced stage in the breakaway. His narrative (*Ath. Pol.* 23.2–4) suggests that the earliest steps could have been taken as early as 479. Other main sources: Thuc. 1.95–96; Hdt. 8.3.2; Plut. *Arist.* 23–25.1, *Cim.* 6.2–3; Nep. *Arist.* 2.2–3; Aristodem. in *FGrH* 104 F 7 (= HMA 18). Cf. Meiggs 1972, 42–49; *ATL* 3:225–243; French 1971, 26–30, 79–86; Rhodes 1985, 5–11; Hornblower 1991, 143–147 and 2002, 13–18.

Postwar conflict between Athens and Sparta was virtually inevitable. Since the mid-sixth century, Sparta, by virtue of its military preeminence, had been the natural leader of the Greek states. Now, as the result of the Persian Wars, Athens had emerged as a powerful rival—and, worse, the one thing Sparta could never be: a strong naval power. Even while the war was still undecided, this had produced strain over leadership. Once it was over, there were many states—the islands and eastern Greek cities not least—that would jump at the chance to free themselves of Sparta's dominance and go in under Athens' naval umbrella. Hence the anxiety at Sparta over the rebuilding of Athens' walls, and the (justified) suspicions of Themistokles (whose proposal to burn the Spartan fleet is unlikely to have remained secret). At Thuc. 1.95.7 we find a restatement of the Athenian line: that Sparta was only too glad to get rid of the leadership and have Athens exercise it instead. This is at odds not only with other evidence (Hdt. 8.3.2, Arist. *Ath. Pol.* 23.2, the debate below reported by Diodorus in ch. 50), but also with Thucydides himself a bare three chapters earlier (92). Had this inconsistency been Diodorus', we should not have had to wait for Hornblower (1991, 142–143) to point it out.

that they anticipated being renewed by the Persians, to levy a tax on all the cities according to their means, with the total collected amounting to 560 talents. [2] When he himself was appointed as assessor of the various sums to be levied, he calculated the division [of responsibilities] so accurately and fairly that every one of the cities approved it. Consequently, since he was regarded as having achieved an impossibility, he gained a very high reputation for justice, and on account of his surpassing excellence in this area, he became known as "the Just." [3] Thus at one and the same time the villainy of Pausanias deprived his countrymen of supremacy at sea, while Aristeides' all-around excellence enabled Athens to win the leadership hitherto denied her.[180]

These, then, were the events that took place during this year.

48. During the archonship of Phaidon in Athens [476/5], the 76th Olympiad was celebrated, in which Skamandrios of Mytilene won the *stadion*, while in Rome the consuls were Caeso Fabius and Spurius Furius †Menellaeus† <Medullinus?>.[181] [2] During their period of office, Leotychidas, the Lacedaemonian king, died after a reign of twenty-two years. His successor was Archidamos, who reigned for forty-two years.[182] There also died Anaxilas, the

---

[180] Delos (cf. Thuc. 1.96.2; Aristodem. in HMA 18) was chosen as occupying a central point in the Aegean; it was also an international Ionian religious center. The exact annual amount of the tax ($\phi \acute{o} \rho o s$) imposed is still debated. Thucydides (1.93.2), Plutarch (*Arist.* 24.3), and Nepos (*Arist.* 3.1) agree on the figure of 460 talents per annum: Diodorus' 560 talents may well have been the same figure originally, corrupted in transmission. However, comparison with the (very ill-preserved) tribute lists suggests that the actual sum collected was appreciably less than 460 talents. Various explanations have been offered (e.g., that part of the assessment was in ships rather than in cash, or that the figure of 460 may well have been a projection never in fact realized). Yet (Meiggs 1972, 65) by 431 there was a 6,000-talent *reserve* in the Athenian treasury, after all expenses had been met, which would imply a 125-talent annual *surplus* over a regular income of 460 talents. The problem remains. Aristeides, too, may not have been quite so simon-pure politically as Athenian propaganda made him out: one contemporary, Kallaischros—"Shameful Beauty," an odd name—described him as "foxier by nature than by deme" ($\mu \hat{\alpha} \lambda \lambda o \nu \ \tau \hat{\omega} \ \tau \rho \acute{o} \pi \omega \ ' A \lambda \omega \pi \epsilon - \kappa \hat{\eta} \theta \epsilon \nu \ \hat{\eta} \ \tau \hat{\omega} \ \delta \acute{\eta} \mu \omega$); Meiggs 1972, 41; Lenardon 1978, 161.

[181] Though Diodorus has the correct archon for 476/5 (cf. Dion. Hal. *AR* 9.1.1, Plut. *Thes.* 36.1), he has lost the consuls for 482, Q. Fabius Vibulanus and C. Iulius Iullus, and in consequence is now, and through ch. 88, six, rather than seven, years ahead of the Varronian *Fasti*. The consuls for 481 were C. Fabius Vibulanus and Sp. Furius Fusus. Diodorus' corrupt $M \epsilon \nu \acute{\epsilon} \lambda \lambda \alpha \iota o s$ *could* hint at "Medullinus," but this is uncertain (Broughton 1951, 24). "Furius" is an early, obvious correction for $\Phi \rho o \acute{\upsilon} \rho \iota o s$ of the MSS (the latter probably chosen because it gave the sense of a guard or protector: Perotti 1984, 163).

[182] Leotychidas II was *exiled* in 476/5; he did not die until 469/8, in Tegea. This has occasioned confusion. His grandson Archidamos became Eurypontid king, as Diodorus says. But when? Was the date of his accession calculated from the date of his grandfather's exile,

*tyrannos* of Rhegion and Zankle, after holding power for eighteen years; he was succeeded in his tyranny by Mikythos, who was entrusted with the office on the understanding that he would hand it over [in due course] to the sons of the deceased, who were still underage.[183] [3] Hieron, king of the Syracusans after the death of his brother Gelon, seeing the popularity of his brother Polyzelos among the Syracusans, and convinced he was simply waiting to usurp the kingship, very much wanted to get him out of the way; meanwhile, by enrolling foreign troops and surrounding himself with a foreign bodyguard, he reckoned he could safely hold on to the throne. [4] So when the Sybarites, who were being besieged by the Krotoniates,[184] asked for his help, he enrolled a large number of troops for the campaign and put his brother Polyzelos in command of them, on the assumption that he would be killed by the Krotoniates. [5] When Polyzelos, suspecting this, refused to undertake the campaign, his brother was furious with him; and when he fled for protection to Theron, the tyrant of Akragas, Hieron began preparations for a war against Theron.[185]

---

or that of his death? Now at 12.35.4, under 434/3, Diodorus notes Archidamos' death, again after a forty-two-year reign. This takes us back to 476/5. But in fact Archidamos died in 427/6, and Diodorus himself records his various activities between those two dates (see 12.42.6, 47.1, 52.1). However, if we count from 469, the *actual* date of Leotychidas' death, we reach, precisely, 427/6. Diodorus' chronological sources show doubts elsewhere over the inclusion or exclusion of years of exile in a Spartan king's reign: cf. 13.75.1, with Gomme 1945, 1: 405–406. There may also be a more specific explanation for the error. The archon for 476/5 was Phaidon, that for 469/8 Apsephion. But evidence exists for a second or alternative archon in 469/8: Phaidon or Phaion (Haillet 2001, 82 n. 2). This is not the only place where Diodorus may have confused them: see note 223 below, and cf. Smart 1967, 136; Sordi 1976, 28 with n. 8.

[183] Anaxilas held power in Rhegion (modern Reggio) from 494. He also repopulated Zankle in Sicily, renaming it Messana (modern Messina). In the Carthaginian campaign of 480, he sided with his father-in-law Terillos of Himera and the Carthaginians against Syracuse and its allies (Hdt. 7.165), but later made his peace with Hieron, marrying his daughter. For Mikythos, once Anaxilas' slave (Just. 4.2.5), see 11.66.1–4 with notes 249–250 below. Cf. Hdt. 7.170, Dion. Hal. *AR* 20.7.1, Paus. 5.26.4.

[184] See schol. Pind. *Ol.* 2.29(b), (d) = HMA 169; cf. Haillet 2001, 153–154; Kraay 1958, 13ff.; and below, 12.10.1 with note 48, for this often-neglected episode in Sybaris' history, between the great Krotoniate destruction of 510/09 and the attempted refoundation of 252/1(?) (see 11.90.3 with note 372 below). See also Sensi Sestito 1976, 244 with n. 4.

[185] Hieron had good reason for wanting Polyzelos out of the way. His young brother, not content with the governorship of Gela, had married Gelon's widow Damarete (see 11.26.3 with note 106), herself the daughter of Theron of Akragas; Polyzelos also married off his own daughter from an earlier marriage to Theron, thus setting up a close alliance with the Akragantine dynasty of the Emmenids (Asheri in *CAH* v, 149). According to two Pindaric scholia (HMA 168–169 = *FGrH* 566 F 93a, b), Polyzelos, far from refusing to

[6] Some time after these events, it happened that Theron's son Thrasydaios, the governor of Himera, was using undue severity in the exercise of his office, to a point at which the Himerans had become totally alienated from him. [7] They turned down the idea of going to his father and formally accusing him, in the belief that they would not get an impartial hearing; instead, they sent ambassadors to Hieron, who were to present their case against Thrasydaios, and [at the same time] offer to make Hieron a present of Himera, and to join him in his attack on Theron. [8] Hieron, however, had already decided to enter peaceful relations with Theron, and so he betrayed the Himerans, briefing Theron on their secret plans. After Theron had investigated this plot and found the charge to be true, he resolved his differences with Hieron, and saw to it that Polyzelos regained [his brother's] goodwill as before. He then arrested the Himeran opposition leaders—there were a good many of these—and put them all to death.

49. Hieron uprooted the inhabitants of Naxos and Katana from their cities and replaced them with settlers of his own, comprising two lots of 5,000 each, brought in from the Peloponnese and from Syracuse. He changed Katana's name to Aitna and commandeered not only this city's territory, but much land adjacent to it, which he parceled out in holdings for all 10,000 settlers. [2] His object in so doing was twofold. He wanted to have solid support available for any emergency, but he also hoped to receive heroic honors from this newly founded city of 10,000 inhabitants. The Naxians and Katanians whom he had uprooted from their native soil he dumped on the citizens of Leontini, with instructions that they should make new homes in that city alongside the local population. [3] When Theron was through with slaughtering the Himerans, he realized that the city now needed new settlers, and brought in a very mixed crowd, granting citizen status not only to Dorians, but to anyone else who applied. [4] These people lived on amicable terms with one another, enjoying excellent government, for fifty-eight years; but then the city was conquered and demolished by the Carthaginians [409/8], and has remained deserted to this day.[186]

---

carry out the campaign, did so with great success, and returned to Sicily in triumph; but he did, nevertheless, have to seek refuge with Theron. The resultant war described in §5 was brought to an end, and the brothers reconciled, through the good offices of the lyric poet Simonides. Details of it survive in Polyaen. 1.29 and schol. Pind. *Ol.* 2.29b–d, conveniently tabulated by Piccirilli (1971, 67–69).

[186] Diodorus is the sole source for the "refoundation" of Himera. Asheri (in *CAH* v, 151: by a slip he refers to Thrasydaios as "Thrasybulus") suggests, plausibly, that Theron was competing with Hieron's similar action in respect to Katana/Aitna. The peaceful coexis-

50. When Dromokleides held the archonship in Athens [475/4], the Romans elected as consuls Marcus Fabius and Gnaeus Manlius.[187] During these officials' term, the Lacedaemonians, having without good cause lost their supremacy at sea, bore that loss extremely ill, and this caused them to show great resentment toward those Greeks who had broken away from them, and threaten them with fitting punishment. [2] Indeed, at a meeting of the Gerousia,[188] they considered declaring war on Athens over this matter of naval hegemony. [3] In the same way, when the general assembly was convened, all of the younger men and a majority of the rest showed eagerness to recover this supremacy: if they succeeded, they thought, they would enjoy great wealth, Sparta as a whole would be made greater and more powerful, and the domestic circumstances of private individuals would enjoy a strong surge in prosperity. [4] They also kept recalling a certain ancient oracle, in which the god bade them watch out lest they find themselves with a "lame leadership":[189] this oracle, they said, referred specifically to nothing other than the present, since their rule would without a doubt be lame if, of their two supremacies, they lost one.

[5] Since almost the entire citizen body was enthusiastically in favor of this argument, and the Gerousia was in session to debate it, no one expected any person to be so presumptuous as to offer a contrary opinion. [6] But a certain member of the Gerousia, one Hetoimaridas, a descendant of Herakles, whose outstanding excellence of character earned him high esteem among his fellow citizens, undertook this course. They should, he counseled them, leave the Athenians in possession of their leadership, since it was not (he asserted) in Sparta's best interests to dispute the rule of the sea with it. This unexpected

---

tence in Himera of this highly mixed Ionian-Dorian population is, as he says, remarkable in an island, and an era, more notable for cruelty and ethnic antagonism. Diodorus gives a more realistic account of Hieron's mass deportations to create Aitna than the encomiastic references by the court poets Pindar and Bacchylides (see, e.g., Pind. *Pyth.* 1.69; Haillet 2001, 155 n. 2; and Asheri in *CAH* v, 150). The new foundation was short-lived: see below, 11.76.3 with note 293 (under 461). For the conquest and destruction of Himera in 409/8, see 13.61–62.

[187] M. Fabius Vibulanus (II) and Cn. Manlius Cincinnatus were in fact consuls for 480 (Broughton 1951, 24).

[188] The Gerousia was the Spartan Council of Elders, an advisory body consisting of twenty-eight nobly born members over the age of sixty, plus the two kings.

[189] It is interesting that this metaphor is also the one used by the philo-Laconian Kimon when arguing in favor of support for Sparta at the time of the great Messenian revolt: Plut. *Cim.* 16.8; cf. below, 11.64.2 with note 238. It recurs again at the accession of Agesilaos: Xen. *Hell.* 3.3.3.

proposal he had no trouble in supporting with highly relevant arguments, so that, contrary to general expectations, he won over both the Gerousia and the people. [7] Thus in the end the Lacedaemonians determined that what He-toimaridas proposed was to their advantage, and gave up this urge they had to go to war with Athens. [8] The Athenians themselves at first expected to have a great war with the Lacedaemonians for supremacy at sea, and as a re-sult were building more triremes, raising substantial funds, and treating their allies reasonably; but when they heard the Lacedaemonians' decision, they were freed from their fear of war, and devoted all their energies to the enhancement of their city's prestige and power.[190]

51. When Akestorides was archon in Athens [474/3], in Rome Kaeso Fa-bius and Titus Verginius succeeded to the consulship.[191] During their period of office, Hieron, king of the Syracusans, was approached by ambassadors from Cumae in Italy, soliciting his aid in the war being waged against them by the Tyrrhenians, at that time in control of the sea, and he dispatched a siz-able number of triremes to their aid. [2] The commanders of this squadron sailed to Cumae, where they joined forces with the local inhabitants and fought a naval campaign against the Tyrrhenians, destroying many of their ships and finally defeating them in a great sea battle. Having thus humbled the Tyrrhenians and freed the men of Cumae from their fears, they sailed back home to Syracuse.[192]

---

[190] Once again, Diodorus is our only source for this highly interesting episode in 475. Many, beginning with Busolt (1897, 71 n. 1), deny its historicity altogether. Meiggs (1972, 40, 454) argues that it must have taken place, if at all, earlier, in 478 or 477, as a direct and immediate response to the foundation of the Delian League, and attributes the supposed misplacement to Diodorus' allegedly cavalier grouping of events under archon-years. Ka-gan (1969, 378–379) and Sordi (1976, 25–41) accept it, though Sordi shares Meiggs' doubts as to the date. Sordi's inference (32–39) that this diplomatic *démarche* may have led to the fall both of Themistokles in Athens and of the arrogant victor of Plataia, Pausanias, is in-triguing but highly speculative. As we have seen, Sparta's resentment and fear at Athens' emergent naval power were very real. The debate (cf. Arist. *Ath. Pol.* 23.2) also hints at something that recurs through the fifth and much of the fourth century: a clash among Spartan policy-makers between conservatives and those who "wanted a more dynamic for-eign policy" (Meiggs 1972, 41). See Thuc. 1.95.7 (cf. 75.2), Xen. *Hell.* 6.5.34, Plut. *Arist.* 23.6.

[191] K. Fabius Vibulanus and T. Verginius Tricostus Rutilus were in fact consuls for 479 (Broughton 1951, 25).

[192] For Hieron's great victory over the Tyrrhenians (Etruscans) off Cumae (about 6 miles northwest of Naples, opposite the island of Ischia, ancient Pithekoussai), see also Pind. *Pyth.* 1.70–75 with schol. 71c (= HMA 174), and Meiggs-Lewis no. 29, p. 62 = Fornara 1983, no. 64, p. 63) for Hieron's dedication of two captured helmets. Cf. Haillet 2001, 156 n. 3.

52. When Menon was archon in Athens [473/2], the Romans elected as consuls Lucius Aemilius Mamercus and Gaius Cornelius Lentulus.[193] In Italy, war broke out between the Tarantines and the Iapygians. [2] Over a period of years these peoples had been quarreling over some land on their marches, with skirmishes and raids into each other's territory. Since the dispute only grew worse with time, and deaths had become frequent, they finally plunged into an all-out conflict. [3] The Iapygians not only mobilized their own forces, but also brought in an allied contingent from their near neighbors, managing in this way to raise a total of over 20,000 men. The Tarantines, on learning the size of the army mustered against them, likewise mobilized their citizen-body, augmenting them with a large number of their allies, the Rhegians. [4] A hard-fought battle took place, with heavy casualties on both sides, but in the end the Iapygians triumphed. The losers in their flight split into two groups, the one retreating to Taras, the other seeking refuge in Rhegion. The Iapygians in similar fashion also divided. [5] Those pursuing the Tarantines—the latter having only a short start—killed a large number of them, but those on the heels of the Rhegians were so enthusiastic that they forced their way into Rhegion[194] along with the fugitives and made themselves masters of the city.[195]

53. The following year [472/1], in Athens the archon was Chares, in Rome those elected as consuls were Titus Minunius <Menenius> and Gaius Horatius †Polyidus†, and the 77th Olympiad, in which Dandes the Argive won the *stadion*, was celebrated by the Eleians.[196] It was during this period that in

---

[193] The consuls (for 478) were L. Aemilius Mamercus and C. Servilius Structus Ahala. How Diodorus came to replace the latter with "Gaius Cornelius Lentulus" is uncertain, especially since (Broughton 1951, 26 n. 1) "the praenomen is foreign to the patrician Lentuli and the cognomen does not appear until much later."

[194] If this is true, it has to be reckoned the most enthusiastic pursuit in all of ancient history, since Rhegion lay well over 200 miles away to the south (see Map 4, and cf. *BA* 45 F4, 46 C5), on the Straits of Messina. Magno (1983, 12) supposes that Diodorus confused "some *oppidum* allied to the Rhegians" with Rhegion itself.

[195] Iapygia was Apulia (modern Puglia) in southeast Italy. For this violent conflict, cf. Herodotos (7.170)—who estimates Rhegian losses at 3,000 and those of Taras (Tarentum, modern Táranto) as "too numerous to count"—Paus. 10.10.6, 13.10, and Arist. *Pol.* 5.1303a3. Cornell (1995, 305) puts the battle in the general context of Italic tribes exerting pressure on Greek coastal colonies, and calls it the latter's most disastrous loss yet recorded.

[196] The consuls (for 477) were T. Menenius Lanatus and C. Horatius Pulvillus (Broughton 1951, 26–27). Once again a scribe or editor, not recognizing the cognomen Pulvillum, seems to have substituted a (similar) Greek term with a recognizable meaning (πολύειδος = multiform): Perotti 1984, 164. Several events of the mid-470s narrated by Thucydides (1.98) in roughly chronological order (e.g., Kimon's reduction of Eion and Skyros, and the campaign against Karystos) are related by Diodorus at ch. 60 below (see note 223 there:

Sicily Theron, the ruler of Akragas, died after a reign of sixteen years, and was succeeded by his son Thrasydaios. [2] Now Theron, whose rule had been fair and unoppressive,[197] was held in high esteem by the Akragantines during his lifetime, and received heroic honors after his death; but his son, even while Theron still lived, was given to violence and murder, and after his death ruled the country in a lawless and tyrannical manner. [3] The result was that he quickly lost the loyalty of his subjects, and had a miserable existence, universally hated and the target of continual plots; and indeed, his life very soon came to a disastrous end well suited to his lawless nature. For after his father Theron's death, he hired numerous mercenaries, as well as mobilizing the citizen-militia of both Akragas and Himera, and in this way raised a total of over 20,000 cavalry and infantry. [4] Since his intention was to use these troops against the Syracusans, King Hieron got together a very considerable force and himself marched on Akragas. A hard-fought battle took place, in which—since here Greeks were matched against Greeks—the casualties were particularly heavy. [5] In this fight the Syracusans prevailed, their dead numbering up to 2,000, whereas the other side lost over 4,000. After suffering this humiliation, Thrasydaios was driven out of office and fled to the city known as "Nisaian" Megara, where he was arraigned, condemned, and put to death [471/0].[198] The Akragantines, after restoring their democracy, sent ambassadors to Hieron and obtained a peace settlement [467/6].[199]

[6] In Italy, war broke out between Rome and Veii, and a great battle took place near the place called Cremera. The Romans got the worst of it, and a large number of them fell, including (as some historians have it) the 300 Fabii, who, being all of the same *gens,* shared an identical family name.[200]

---

the possibility remains that Diodorus' chronology may be correct) in a compressed digression under the archon-year 470/69.

[197] The Himerans (11.48.8, 49.3) might have disagreed; but modern verdicts tend to agree with Diodorus, here and at 10.28.3: see, e.g., Caven in *OCD* 1508: "A just and undespotic ruler." *Contra,* Haillet 2001, 155. The passion of these Sicilian tyrants for heroic honors (cf. 11.49.2 on Hieron) is interesting: it foreshadows the ruler-cults of the Hellenistic era. Theron's failure to leave an adequate successor led to the rapid demise of the Emmenid dynasty in Akragas.

[198] Hiring numerous mercenaries for self-protection or aggression was a regular habit among these dynasts: Gelon (11.72.3), Hieron (11.48.3), and Thrasyboulos (11.67.5) all practiced it. "Nisaian" Megara, so called because of its port of Nisaia on the Saronic Gulf, is given its full title by Diodorus to distinguish it from Megara Hyblaea in eastern Sicily.

[199] Thrasydaios' death was followed by an oligarchy, of the so-called Thousand (Diog. Laert. 8.66): after three years (467/6), this was broken up by the efforts of Empedokles, who restored democracy. Hieron himself died in the same year (11.66.4).

[200] Diodorus' six-year advance on the Varronian *Fasti* shows here: the battle of the Cremera (river, not place: today the Fossa di Valca, joining the Tiber about 5 miles outside

These, then, were the events taking place in the course of this year.

54. When Praxiergos was archon in Athens [471/0], the Romans elected as consuls Aulus Verginius Tricostus and Gaius Servilius Structus.[201] During their term, the Eleians, who had been dwelling in a number of small townships, united to form the one city-state called Elis.[202] [2] The Lacedaemonians, seeing that Sparta (because of the treacherous activities of their general Pausanias) was suffering humiliation, whereas the Athenians were well thought of since none of *their* citizens had been convicted of treason, were desperate to involve Athens in similar unsavory charges. [3] So, since Themistokles was very well thought of by the Athenians, and enjoyed a high reputation for integrity, they accused him of treason, claiming that he had been a great friend of Pausanias, and that together they had planned to betray Greece to Xerxes.[203] [4] They also had discussions with Themistokles' enemies, urging

---

Rome) was traditionally fought in 477, not 471. See Livy 2.48–50, Dion. Hal. *AR* 9.15–21. Cf. Haillet (2001, 71 n. 1) and Oldfather (1946, 262–263 n. 1), who points out that "in some way the Fabian gens dressed up the story so that in later tradition only Fabii and their clients were fighting Rome's battles for 'bridgeheads' on the Tiber." Prof. Rubincam notes (*per litt.*) that Diodorus' "comment on the shared gentile name of the 300 Fabii shows him explaining for Greek readers less familiar than himself with Roman customs this distinctively Roman nomenclature."

[201] The consuls (for 476) were A. Verginius Tricostus Rutilus and Sp. Servilius Structus (Broughton 1951, 27, who in n. 1 to this entry justifies Servilius' praenomen as Spurius [Livy 2.51.4] against the Gaius of Dion. Hal. *AR* 9.25.1, 28.1, as well as Diodorus).

[202] Since Elis had been responsible for the administration of the Olympic Games since 576 B.C.E., this development might be thought overdue. For the uniting (*synoikismos*) of Elis, see also Strabo 8.3.2, C.336. The new regime seems to have been democratic, and the change has often been ascribed (on no evidence) to Themistokles' machinations in the Peloponnese while an exile at Argos (see below).

[203] In fact Themistokles—after the rebuilding of Athens' walls in the face of Spartan objections, and his (doubtless widely publicized) recommendation for the destruction of Sparta's fleet—constituted a far more real danger than a mere affront to Spartiate *amour propre*. This should be borne in mind throughout what follows, since the charges of Medism per se, against both Themistokles and Pausanias (whose real offense may have been an alarming partiality for the Helots), bear every sign of fabrication.

Diodorus, like Thucydides (1.135–138), now devotes an excursus (54.3–59.3) to the exile and final years of Themistokles: this, though retained under the archon-year of 471/0 (which is when the sequence of events described began), stretches, as is Diodorus' custom (cf. 11.59.4 for his own admission on this score), over an extended period, indeed until 459/8, the year of Themistokles' death (APF 214–215). Compare his earlier (11.44.1–46.4) treatment of Pausanias. Readers are warned that the chronology in particular (including that adopted here) is still highly uncertain. The best and most thorough discussion is that of Keaveney 2003. I do not always agree with it, but it has sharpened my own thinking on this vexed topic throughout.

them to bring charges against him and supplying them with money. When Pausanias decided to betray the Greeks, they said, he revealed his private plan to Themistokles and invited him to join in the undertaking. Though Themistokles did not accept the offer, neither did he judge himself obliged to accuse a man who was his friend. [5] Be that as it may, a formal indictment was now brought against Themistokles, though at the time he was acquitted of any treasonable activities. After being thus cleared, he remained very highly thought of by the Athenians, since his fellow citizens loved him dearly because of his achievements. Later, however, those who feared his powerful influence, as well as others who were jealous of his renown, forgot about the benefits he had brought the state, and worked zealously to shrink his power and humble his high opinion of himself.[204]

55. So first they banished Themistokles from Athens,[205] using against him that device called "ostracism," which was established by law in Athens after

---

[204]Themistokles' political opponents (the land-based aristocratic conservatives now led by Kimon, who always maintained close ties with Sparta) and his many personal enemies (see Plut. *Them.* 22–23 passim) were obvious targets for Spartan persuasion and bribery. The early approach by Pausanias to Themistokles (probably during Pausanias' first residence in Byzantion, 478?) has often been denied because at Plut. *Them.* 23.1–2 (reconcilable with Diodorus' account of two procedures, but also used, wrongly, to extract the same sense from Thuc. 1.135.2–3), "it was not until Pausanias saw Themistokles embittered by exile that he invited him to participate in his scheme" (Barrett 1977, 291–295, 298–299). But what the Spartan in fact saw was Themistokles ἐκπεπτωκότα τῆς πολιτείας, which here clearly means simply "excluded from government," a process that began (as with Churchill in 1945) almost as soon as hostilities against Persia were concluded (cf. above, II.27.3). Themistokles was out of office, touting an anti-Spartan policy that was anathema to Kimon and his friends, and reduced to boring everyone with reminders of his own achievements (Frost 1998, 166–167). His general (as opposed to his political) popularity held until 477/6, when he produced Phrynichos' *Phoenician Women* and was a star figure at the Olympic Games (Plut. *Them.* 5,3–4, 17.2). This was his last recorded public appearance (Keaveney 2003, 101). The first trial probably took place in the spring of 472, though it could have been up to a year later (see below). Whether this was identical with the embezzling charges, for which some evidence exists (Carawan 1987, 196–200), is uncertain, and on the whole unlikely. Cf. Podlecki 1976, 299ff.

[205]Thuc. 1.135.3; Plat. *Gorg.* 516D; Nep. *Them.* 8.1, *Arist.* 3.3; Plut. *Them.* 22.3; Cic. *De amic.* 12.42. When was Themistokles ostracized? Diodorus' starting date of 471/0 is generally agreed to refer to either (a) his ostracism or (b) his subsequent condemnation and flight. (Pelekidis' argument [1974, 425–426], that it refers to his first trial in Athens, is hard to square with the evidence.) Lenardon (1959, 23–31) offers strong arguments in favor of (b), but the true course of events seems rather to indicate (a). Now in March 472 there took place the young Perikles' production of Aeschylus' play *The Persians,* with its tremendous indirect tribute to Themistokles. (T. Harrison [2000, 31–48] argues that the play's real hero was the Athenian *demos;* yet even if this is correct in a loosely generalized sense, everyone

the dissolution of the tyranny of the Peisistratids, and worked as follows. [2] Each citizen would write on a potsherd, or *ostrakon,* the name of the man who seemed to him most in a position to subvert the democracy; and he whose name figured on the largest number of *ostraka* was obliged to go into exile from his fatherland for a five-year period. [3] The Athenians would appear to have made this law not for the punishment of evildoers, but rather to humble by means of exile the arrogance of the over-ambitious.[206] Themistokles, then, after being ostracized in the aforementioned manner, went as an exile from his own country to Argos.[207] [4] When the Lacedaemonians learned of these events, it seemed to them that fate had vouchsafed them the ideal

---

in that audience knew who had been the true architect of victory.) This was clearly meant to boost Themistokles' standing, which suggests that he was already facing the kind of Spartan-influenced attack described by Diodorus. The natural inference is that his first trial followed soon after *The Persians* was put on, and the play aimed, inter alia, to influence its outcome. This may, but need not, be the case: the trial could in fact have taken place at any point in 472/1. If, as I believe, what Diodorus places—correctly—in 471/0 (i.e., the early spring of 470) is his ostracism (so, most recently, Keaveney 2003, 104–112), that leaves ample time for his enemies, both Spartan and Athenian, to plan his downfall.

There remains the problem of correlating these events with the arrest and death of Pausanias. As we have seen, Themistokles' supposed involvement with the Spartan could have taken place at any time after 478/7, and Diodorus' narrative strongly suggests that Themistokles' trial and ostracism took place *after* Pausanias' exposure. Now Pausanias, as we have seen (note 170 above), was expelled from Byzantion by Kimon in 471 (Thuc. 1.131.1, Plut *Cim.* 6.5–6, Just. 9.1.3). His recall to Sparta from Kolonai in the Troad, and his death (in sanctuary, by starvation), followed soon afterward: just how soon we do not know. If Diodorus is right, the scandal may well have led to Themistokles' ostracism in 470. Plutarch, however (*Them.* 23.1–4), dates the charges arising against Themistokles (from correspondence discovered by the Spartans after Pausanias' death) to the period of his exile, following ostracism, in Argos. In that case, what we have is part of the evidence for his trial and condemnation in absentia. Even so, Pausanias' death is extremely unlikely to have taken place later than 470.

[206] For ostracism, see Thomsen 1972, Lang 1990, Vanderpool 1973, and the excellent short account by Podlecki (1975, 185–194) with further bibliography. Lang (1990, 102ff.) catalogues the Themistoklean *ostraka.* (More have since been found.) Cf. Haillet 2001, 158 nn. 1, 3. Diodorus' account is standard except for the length of the term of exile, which he halves, from ten to five years, either through a confusion with the similar Syracusan system of petalism (see 11.87.1 with notes 359–360), or perhaps in accordance with a mistaken tradition that had Themistokles return from exile c. 465 to support Ephialtes in his attack on the Areopagos (Arist. *Ath. Pol.* 25.3–4; hyp. Isokr. 7 *[Areopagiticus]* = HMA 126; Cic. *Ad Fam.* 5.12.5).

[207] Cf. Thuc. 1.135.3; Aristodem. *FGrH* 104 F 6.1 = HMA 18; Plat. *Gorg.* 516D; Plut. *Them.* 23.1. Argos, as a traditional enemy of Sparta, was a natural asylum for Themistokles at this point.

opportunity to attack Themistokles. They therefore once again sent ambassadors to Athens, to charge Themistokles with complicity in the treason of Pausanias. Since his misdeeds were the common concern of all Hellas, the ambassadors emphasized, Themistokles should not be tried privately by the Athenians, but before the general congress of the Hellenes, which was customarily due to meet [in Sparta] at about that time.[208]

[5] Themistokles himself, seeing that the Lacedaemonians were eager to humiliate and defame the Athenian state, while the Athenians wanted to clear themselves of the charge that had been thus leveled against them, calculated that he would indeed be handed over to the general congress. [6] This body, as he well knew, rendered its verdicts not according to the dictates of justice, but rather out of favoritism to the Lacedaemonians: this conclusion he based on a number of episodes, in particular the way the judgment had gone in the matter of the Athenians and the Aiginetans. On that occasion, indeed, those in charge of the voting revealed so grudging an attitude to the Athenians that, even though they had provided more triremes than all the other participants in the battle combined, they made them out to be in no respect superior to the rest of the Greeks.[209] [7] These, then, were the reasons why Themistokles came to distrust the delegates to the congress. What was more, it was from Themistokles' own defense speech at his earlier arraignment in Athens that the Lacedaemonians had drawn the basis for their subsequent indictment. [8] In the course of his defense, Themistokles had acknowledged the receipt of letters from Pausanias, urging him to become a party to Pausanias' own

---

[208] Thucydides (1.135.2–3) shows Athens collaborating with Sparta, after their envoys' request, in an attempt to arrest Pausanias, but does not mention any request for a trial before the general congress (logical though this would have been in a case of Medism). For a typical meeting of the congress in 479, see Plut. *Arist.* 21.1. These congresses were normally held at the Isthmus, not Sparta; and one manuscript of Diodorus' text omits the words "in Sparta," as does Oldfather (1946). A public charge (*eisangelia*) was lodged against Themistokles by an Alcmaionid, Leobotes (Plut. *Arist.* 21.1), but whether now or at the time of the earlier trial remains uncertain. Since Themistokles was never in fact brought to trial, we cannot be certain whether the Spartans finally agreed to Athens handling the case. Indeed, though it is generally assumed that he was tried and condemned to death in absentia at Athens (see most recently *OCD* 1498), our only direct evidence for such a trial is Nep. *Them.* 8.3 ("hoc crimine absens proditionis damnatus est"), and even Nepos does not mention the death penalty. From Thuc. 1.138.6, Plut. *Arist.* 26.3, and schol. Aristoph. *Kn.* 84 = HMA 26, it seems clear that the actual sentence was banishment (φυγήν, φεύγοντος, φυγαδευθείς), rather than a death penalty that led to flight.

[209] Reading Wesseling's correction Αἰγινητῶν for Ἀργείων of the manuscripts. Vogel (1890) and Oldfather (1946) prefer Rhodoman's περὶ τῶν ἀριστείων, "in the matter of the awards for valor." For the occasion, cf. above, II.27.2–3.

treasonable activities, and used this as his strongest piece of evidence to establish the fact that Pausanias would not have needed to *urge* him, had he not refused an earlier invitation.

56. It was for these reasons, as was stated earlier, that he fled from Argos[210] to Admetos, the king of the Molossians, and, taking refuge at the king's hearth, became his suppliant.[211] The king at first gave him a friendly reception, bade him be of good cheer, and in general undertook to guarantee his security. [2] However, the Lacedaemonians then sent to Admetos an embassy composed of the most notable Spartan citizens, who demanded the surrender

---

[210] The date is uncertain. Themistokles reached Argos in the spring or early summer of 470. At the latest, his enforced departure is unlikely to have been after 469; Keaveney (2003, 116) improbably postpones it until early 466, but once a case had been put together against Themistokles after Pausanias' death, it is inconceivable that his enemies in Sparta and Athens would have waited four years before taking action against him.

Diodorus in fact nowhere earlier discusses "these reasons." He also omits Themistokles' initial flight to Corcyra, where he enjoyed the rights of a "benefactor" (*euergetes*), including asylum, in return for earlier favors (Thuc. 1.136.1 with schol.; Plut. *Them.* 24.1; Aristodem. 10.1 = HMA 19–20; Nep. *Them.* 8.2–3; cf. Hdt. 7.115). Spartan pressure scared the Corcyraeans, and Themistokles moved on to Epiros. Again, we do not know exactly when: most probably in 469, and surely not later than 468. The story Plutarch retails from Stesimbrotos (Plut. *Them.* 24.4), that Themistokles was en route to Hieron's court with a request to marry his daughter, is improbable, to say the least (Plutarch himself doubts it), but may well have been generated by Themistokles' known interest in, and connections with, Magna Graecia and Sicily (Lenardon 1978, 131–132). Cf. Frost 1998, 179–184. Diodorus, it should be noted, discusses Themistokles' entire career, as a kind of separate insert, under the archon-year 471/0. Badian argues (1993, 28) that what Diodorus found under this year was his ostracism (cf. 11.55.1 with note 205). In any case, for chronological purposes we must for the rest of this chapter rely on other evidence.

[211] Thucydides (1.136.2–137.1), Plutarch (*Them.* 24.1–3), and Nepos (*Them.* 8.4–6) all tell the story of how Themistokles (who had given Admetos good cause to dislike him in the past), either on his own initiative or with the encouragement of the king's wife Phthia, took Admetos' young child with him to the hearth when he made his act of supplication. This has been discredited because it bears too close a resemblance to the plot of Euripides' play *Telephos*. Wecklein (cited by Gomme 1945, 1:439 n. 1) suggests, more plausibly, that Euripides may well have based his plot on the famous historical episode rather than the other way around. See Frost 1998, 182–184; Hammond 1967, 491–492. How long Themistokles stayed with Admetos, as on Corcyra, is uncertain. It all depends on what Diodorus means by "at first" (τὸ μὲν πρῶτον); but this surely was a period measured in months, at most, rather than years, since again, the Spartans would not have been slow to take action. Themistokles was probably in Epiros during the winter of 469/8. By 468/7 he was certainly on the move again.

of Themistokles for punishment, and branded him as the betrayer and de-stroyer of all Hellas. To this they added the threat that, should Admetos not hand him over, they and all the Hellenes would make war on him. At this point the king—scared by their threats, yet full of compassion for his suppli-ant, and anxious to avoid the shame he would incur by surrendering him—persuaded Themistokles to make a speedy departure unseen by the Lacedae-monians, and gave him a large sum in gold as journey-money during his flight. [3] So Themistokles, being hunted from every quarter, accepted the gold and fled the land of the Molossians by night, with all possible assistance from the king in furthering his escape. Finding two young men, Lynkestians by birth, who were engaged in trade and for that reason well acquainted with the roads, he used them as guides on his journey. [4] By traveling only at night, he gave the Lacedaemonians the slip, and through the goodwill of the young men and the trouble they went to on his behalf, he made his way to Asia.[212] There he had a personal friend, Lysitheides by name, much looked up to because of his reputation and wealth, and it was with him that Themisto-kles now sought refuge.[213]

---

[212] The detail of the young Lynkestians (Lynkestis was an upland out-kingdom of Macedonia) is unique to Diodorus. On the other hand, he omits two otherwise well-documented intermediary stages in Themistokles' journey: to Pydna (see Map 1), then part of Alexander I's Macedonia, and from there by sea to Ephesos (Thuc. 1.137.1–3, Nep. *Them.* 8.5–7) or Kyme (Plut. *Them.* 26.1, cf. Frost 1998, 187–189), with a near disaster when a storm threatened to drive the ship to shelter at Naxos, which was at the time (468) under siege by the Athenian fleet. Cf. Frost 1998, 185–190, for some of the textual and chronological problems involved.

[213] There is a still much-debated problem here that hinges on chronology. Our two ear-liest sources, Thucydides (1.135.2–4) and Charon of Lampsakos (*FGrH* 262 F 11 = Plut. *Them.* 27.1, cf. schol. Aristoph. *Kn.* 84), both of whom were in a good position to know the truth (cf. Nep. *Them.* 9.1), state that it was Artaxerxes I with whom Themistokles made contact. However, the numerous later writers in addition to Diodorus (see Plut. *Them.* 27.1, where some are named), who had Themistokles approach his old enemy Xerxes, were not simply after a good dramatic confrontation. The dates are difficult. Artaxerxes did not succeed (11.69.1 with note 265 below) until 465 (Xerxes was assassinated by Artabanos in August, and Artaxerxes narrowly escaped being killed himself: Frost 1998, 192 n. 24 with refs.). Yet Themistokles fled Argos comparatively soon after the death of Pausanias, which cannot have taken place later than 470, and may well have been as early as November or December 471. See Gomme 1945, 1:397–402; Frost 1998, 187–193.

Where, then, did Themistokles spend the next five years? Partly, as we have seen, on Corcyra and in Epiros. His trek from Epiros to Pydna, and then by sea to Asia, can hardly have taken more than two or three months. He *could* have reached Asia by the early fall of 468, and Spartan pressure makes it unlikely that his arrival there can be placed more than

[5] Lysitheides happened to be a friend of Xerxes the Great King, and during Xerxes' passage [through Asia Minor] had entertained the entire Persian expeditionary force. Consequently, since he both enjoyed this close familiarity with Xerxes, and at the same time out of compassion wanted to save Themistokles, he promised the latter that he would do all he could to further his cause. [6] However, when Themistokles asked that Lysitheides bring him to Xerxes, at first the latter refused, making it plain to him that he would suffer retribution for his previous anti-Persian activities; but later, after coming to see the possible advantages, he agreed, and—against all odds—got him safely into Persia. [7] This was because of a custom among the Persians that anyone bringing a concubine to the Great King transported her in a covered wagon, and of those who encountered it none made difficulties about its passage or insisted on inspecting the passenger. So it came about that Lysitheides availed himself of this facility in order to carry out his project. [8] After fitting out the wagon and adorning it with expensive hangings, he put Themistokles in it, and got him all the way through in complete safety.[214] He then approached the Great King, and after some guarded discussion, finally received guarantees from the king that he would do Themistokles no harm. Lysitheides then brought him into the king's presence, and Xerxes gave him leave to speak. When he was persuaded that Themistokles had done him no wrong, the king absolved him from the [threat of] punishment.

---

a year later. In Asia we hear of him being protected not only by Lysitheides (not otherwise known: the man who entertained Xerxes' whole host at Hdt. 7.27 was named Pythios), but also by another wealthy character, Nikogenes, at Aigai in the Aiolid (Plut. *Them.* 26.1–3). It is possible, then, that he lay low in Asia Minor for several years (468/7–465), learning Persian (or possibly Aramaic, the *lingua franca* of the empire) and awaiting his opportunity. Yet Thucydides (1.137.3–4) and Plutarch (*Them.* 26.2–4) both write as though there was virtually no waiting period at all; and Briant (2002, 563, 970), for one, argues forcefully in favor of Xerxes as his benefactor.

Is it possible that *both* traditions are essentially true? Could Themistokles have been introduced to Xerxes by Lysitheides c. 468 (D.S. 11.56.5–8, Plut. *Them.* 28.3–4), incurred the suspicion of Artabanos, Roxanes, and many others (Plut. *Them.* 27.1–5, 29.1–4) as well as the resentment of Mandane (D.S. 11.57.1–5: if true, cf. Briant 2002, 901), been acquitted after a year—during which he learned Persian (c. 467/6: Plut. *Them.* 29.3–4, cf. Thuc. 1.138.1–2, Nep. *Them.* 10.1)—and endowed with honors (D.S. 11.57.5–7, Plut. *Them.* 29.4), but then have been placed in jeopardy by Artabanos' assassination of Xerxes (see above) and forced in 465 to renegotiate his position with Artaxerxes? This at least would make some sense of otherwise irreconcilable and inexplicable testimony. There is a limit to what can be written off as romantic fiction.

[214]Cf. Plut. *Them.* 26.3–4. The practice is well attested: see, e.g., Xen. *Cyr.* 6.4.11.

57. But just as it seemed that, against all odds, he had been rescued by his old enemy, he once more fell into even greater danger, for the following reason. Xerxes had a full sister named Mandane, daughter of that Darius who had slaughtered the Magians,[215] and she was held in high regard among the Persians. [2] This woman had been bereft of her sons on the occasion of Themistokles' victory over the Persian fleet in the sea battle off Salamis, and took the loss of her children very hard. Because of the magnitude of her misfortune, she was the object of considerable public pity. [3] When she learned of Themistokles' presence, she went to the palace arrayed in mourning, and with tears besought her brother to exact retribution from him. When he took no notice of her, she went the rounds of the Persian nobles with her petition, and in a general way incited the people at large to seek vengeance on Themistokles. [4] When the mob ran to the palace and with much shouting demanded his surrender for punishment, the king answered them that he would form a panel of judges from the noblest Persians, and that their verdict would be carried out. [5] This decision met with general approval; and since ample time was allowed to prepare for the trial, Themistokles used it to master the Persian language. He then conducted his defense in Persian and was acquitted of the charges brought against him.[216] [6] The king was delighted by the acquittal, and honored Themistokles with substantial gifts. He gave him in marriage a Persian lady of high birth and outstanding beauty, who was also highly praised for her virtues. He [also provided] a multitude of domestic slaves for his service, as well as drinking-cups of every kind and all other household goods appropriate for a pleasurable and luxurious existence. [7] The king likewise made him a present of three cities well suited to his sustenance and pleasure: Magnesia on the Maiandros [Maeander] River, which had the most grain of all the cities in Asia, for bread; Myous for relish, since its offshore waters teemed with fish; and Lampsakos, with its numerous rich vineyards, for wine.[217]

---

[215] For the supposed Magian usurpation, and its overthrow by a group of seven Persian noblemen led by Darius, who then (522/1) ascended the Achaimenid throne, see Hdt. 3.61–88. Whether the Magian called by Herodotos "Smerdis" (= Bardiya) was a Magian or, in fact, a homonymous son of Cyrus (thus making Darius the usurper, who rewrote the story on accession) is still debated. For a good discussion of the evidence, see Frye 1966, 113–117, cf. Kuhrt 1995, 664–667.

[216] No other source reports this trial, and it is generally rejected as dramatic invention (e.g., in the strongest terms, by Frost 1998, 193; cf. Haillet 2001, 160 n. 3).

[217] For Themistokles' honors (mostly regarding the cities mentioned), cf. Thuc. 1.138.5; Plut. *Them.* 29.4, 7; Nep. *Them.* 10.2–3; schol. Aristoph. *Kn.* 84 = HMA 26; Athen. 1.29f,

58. So Themistokles was now freed of the fear that had threatened him on the Greek side. Equally improbably exiled by those to whom he had brought the greatest benefits, and rewarded by those who had suffered worst at his hands, he spent the rest of his life in the above-mentioned cities, amply supplied with everything that makes for a good life.

After his death, he was given a fine funeral in Magnesia, and a memorial that is still standing to this day.[218] [2] Some writers state that when Xerxes conceived the desire to launch a second invasion of Greece, he invited Themistokles to be his commander-in-chief. Themistokles agreed, and received from the king a sworn guarantee that he would not march against the Greeks without Themistokles. [3] So a bull was sacrificed, and the oaths taken. Then Themistokles filled a cup with its blood, drank it down, and at once died. Xerxes as a result is supposed to have given up his plan; and thus Themistokles, by the death he chose, left behind the best possible argument that in all matters touching the Hellenes he had acted as a good citizen.[219]

---

533d. As governor of Magnesia (Thuc. 1.138.5: probably not as satrap, Hornblower 1991, 215–216), Themistokles struck coinage, a few examples of which survive (Podlecki 1975, 169–172; Keaveney 2003, 81–83). Diodorus is the only source to mention Themistokles' Persian marriage (sometimes doubted, but for no compelling reason). Magnesia was slightly inland on a tributary of the Maeander River; Myous was on the Maeander itself, upriver from Miletos; Lampsakos was situated on the Asiatic side of the Hellespont (see Map 2). Such perquisites were not uncommon: cf. Hdt 2.98, Xen. *Anab.* 1.4.9. There is also the question of divided loyalties: how far were these cities committed to the Delian League, how far still under the control of the Achaimenids? To what extent did they hedge their bets? See the judicious discussion by Frost (1998, 197–199).

[218] The memorial in Magnesia's marketplace is vouched for by Thucydides (1.135.5), Plutarch (*Them.* 32.3), and Nepos (*Them.* 10.3–5). Both Thucydides and Nepos (Plut. *Them.* 32.3), as well as (with variations) the scholiast to Aristoph. *Kn.* 84 (2d version) = HMA 27, claim that Themistokles' bones were at some point spirited away back to Attica, either by his relatives or at a time of national crisis.

[219] Plutarch (*Cim.* 18.5–6) identifies a Persian campaign in Egypt against nationalist rebels supported by an Athenian expedition under Kimon (Thuc. 1.104; see 11.77 below) as the occasion on which Themistokles failed, or refused, to take over the command of the king's forces. There is much that is suspicious about this. (a) The expedition in question was not an invasion of Greece. (b) It was planned and carried out not by Xerxes but by his successor Artaxerxes. (c) If Themistokles committed suicide (itself contradicted by Thucydides) to hold (Arta)xerxes to his word about not marching against Greeks without him, his gesture had singularly little effect: the expedition proceeded as planned. (d) Worst of all, Plutarch, though clearly describing the same campaign as Thucydides (that of 461–?457), mistakenly identifies it as Kimon's second Cypro-Egyptian campaign (450), in which he lost his life, and by which time Themistokles was long dead. The date 459/8 is generally, and rightly, accepted as the date of Themistokles' death, but on quite different grounds: APF 214–215. The widespread legend of his committing suicide by drinking bull's blood

[4] We are now confronted with the death of a very great Greek, about whom disagreement still continues. Was it because he had wronged both his fatherland and the Hellenes at large that he sought asylum with the Persians? Or was it, on the contrary, that his own city and the rest of Hellas, despite the great benefits he brought them, showed him no gratitude, but rather, most unjustly, exposed their benefactor to the gravest perils? [5] If anyone examines this man's character and achievements closely, without prejudice, it will be found that in both respects Themistokles stands head and shoulders above all those of whom we have record. It follows that one well might be astounded at the Athenians' readiness to deprive themselves of a man endowed with such natural brilliance.[220]

59. Who else, while Sparta held supreme power, and the Spartan Eurybiades was in command of the fleet, could by his individual efforts have stripped Sparta of that proud glory? What other man do we find in the annals of history who, by a single act, raised himself above all other leaders, his city above all other Greek states, and the Greeks over the barbarians? During whose term as general (*strategos*) have resources ever been slimmer, or imminent danger greater? [2] Who else, confronted with the whole might of Asia, and with his city evacuated, faced the enemy and won? Who else in peacetime increased the strength of his fatherland with such achievements as his? Who, when a vast war overtook the state, saw it through to safety, and by one single ruse, that involving the bridge [11.19.5–6], reduced the size of the enemy forces by half, so that it fell easy victim to the Greeks? [3] As a result—when we consider the magnitude of his achievements and, examining them individually, find that his own city dishonored this man, whereas it was by *his* deeds that the city itself achieved its high position—we may plausibly infer that the city

---

(not in fact lethal, and in some places a diet staple, Frost 1998, 204) goes back as far as the 420s (Aristoph. *Kn.* 83–84 with schol.), though according to Thucydides (who knew the story), he in fact died of an illness (1.138.4). Various explanations of his alleged suicide exist: a misinterpreted coin icon or posthumous propaganda by Themistokles' family are the most plausible, though I have always been tempted by the idea of a sudden heart attack shortly after the act of libation at a public sacrifice. See Frost 1998, 203–205; and J. Marr, in *G&R* 42 (1995): 159–167.

[220] Podlecki (1975, 34ff.; 1976, 311) argues that the charges, especially that of Medism, were absurd, and that Themistokles in fact fell "through the concerted efforts of his political adversaries," e.g., Kimon, probably Aristeides, and the Alkmaionids. Lazenby (1993, 169) toys with the possibility that he may have been prepared to medize in earnest. In a sense, Podlecki's thesis could be said to imply Lazenby's: in the end, Themistokles turned to Persia because all other doors had been closed against him. There was, quite simply, nowhere else for him to go.

with the highest reputation of all for wisdom and tolerance treated him most harshly.

[4] Though we may have digressed too long on this matter of Themistokles' great worth, we thought it not proper that we should leave that worth unrecorded.

At the same time as these events, in Italy, Mikythos, whose sway extended over Rhegion and Zankle, founded the city of Pyxous.[221]

60. While Demotion was archon in Athens [470/69], the Romans elected as consuls Publius Valerius Publicola and Gaius Nautius Rufus.[222] During their term of office, the Athenians chose as general Kimon son of Miltiades, entrusted him with a strong force, and dispatched him to the coast of Asia [Minor], to render aid to the cities in alliance with them and to liberate those still occupied by Persian garrisons. [2] Kimon picked up the flotilla stationed at Byzantion, sailed to the city known as Eion, which was under Persian control, and captured it. He then took by siege [the island of] Skyros, of which the inhabitants were Pelasgians and Dolopians, installed a colony with an Athenian as official "founder" (ktistes), and divided up the land into cleruchs' allotments.[223] [3] After this, having it in mind to embark on greater enter-

---

[221] On Mikythos, cf. 11.48.2 and note 183 above, and 11.66.1–3 and notes 249–250 below. Pyxous (Roman Buxentum) lay on the western coast of Italy at the northernmost part of Lucania, east of Cape Palinurus on the modern Gulf of Policastro (see Map 4, and cf. BA 46 C1). It had at some point been Greek-occupied before Mikythos' settlement, which did not last long (Strabo 6.1.1, C.253).

[222] The consuls (for 475: Diodorus remains six years ahead) were P. Valerius Poplicola and C. Nautius Rutilus (Broughton 1951, 27–28).

[223] For Kimon's expedition to Byzantion (471), and the capture of Eion and Skyros (470?), cf. Hdt. 7.107; Thuc. 1.98.1–2, 131.1; Plut. Cim. 6.1–3, 5–6, 7–8 passim (including an account of Kimon bringing back the "bones of Theseus from Skyros"); Nep. Cim. 2.2–5; P.Oxy. 13.1610 f.6 = HMA 114 = Fornara 1983, 61 B2 (possibly from Ephoros, cf. 60.1: FGrH 70 F 191); Polyaen. 7.24; Paus. 1.17.6, 8.8.7–9; D.S. 4.62.4; HMA 341. Eion was a key strategic point (access to Thracian mines and Macedonian timber); Skyros had been a notorious hang-out for pirates (Haillet 2001, 79 n. 1). "Cleruchs" were Athenian colonists who kept their Athenian citizenship: Hornblower in OCD 347–348. Thucydides (1.98.3) also mentions, after Skyros, the reduction of Karystos in Euboia; cf. Hdt. 9.105.

The chronology is dubious. Plutarch (Cim. 6.1, 7.1, and 12.1) suggests action soon after the end of the Persian Wars and the reduction of Byzantion; the scholiast to Aeschines (2.31) dates the colonization of Eion in 476 (and thus, possibly, its reduction a year earlier), with the reduction of Skyros following. This is the most generally accepted chronology. But Justin (9.1.3), as we have seen, states that Pausanias held Byzantion for seven years; our other sources (except Diodorus) claim that he was finally ousted from the city by Kimon during this expedition. If true, this would be in 471, still leaving time (above, note 205) for Pausanias' subsequent arrest. In that case, Diodorus' chronology could be roughly cor-

prises, he sailed to Piraeus, where he took on more triremes and organized supplies on a generous scale. At that point, he put to sea with 200 triremes; but afterward, what with requisitions from the Ionians and everyone else, he brought his overall total up to 300. [4] So he sailed with this entire fleet to Caria. Those cities on the coast that had been colonized from Greece he at once persuaded to revolt from the Persians. Those, however, with bilingual populations and resident Persian garrisons he dealt with by force, laying siege to them. After thus bringing over the cities of Caria, he did the same with those in Lycia, again by persuasion. [5] Also, by acquiring extra ships from these new allies as they were enrolled, he increased the size of his fleet yet further.[224]

The Persians drew on their own peoples for their land forces, but their navy they assembled from Phoenicia and Cyprus and Cilicia: the commander-in-chief of all Persian armaments was Tithraustes, a bastard son of Xerxes. [6] When Kimon learned that the Persian fleet was lying off Cyprus, he sailed against the barbarians and engaged them in a naval action, with 250 vessels against the enemy's 340.[225] A fierce battle ensued, in which both sides acquitted themselves with distinction; but ultimately the Athenians were victorious, destroying a large number of the enemy's ships and capturing more than a hundred, together with their crews.[226] [7] The remainder got away to Cyprus,

---

rect: see Smart 1967; Fornara 1966; and Meiggs 1972, 73. But advocates of the alternative chronology can counter that Diodorus may have confused the archons of 476/5 and 469/8 (Smart 1967, 136–137; Pelekidis 1974, 422): for Phaidon/Phaion, see note 182 above. Without further evidence, the problem remains insoluble.

[224] For this expedition, cf. P.Oxy. 13.1610 f.8 = HMA 114 (with which Diodorus is in close agreement: Plut. *Cim.* 12.4 strongly suggests that the author is Ephoros, or an epitome of him); Plut. *Cim.* 12.1; Front. *Strat.* 2.9.10, 3.2.5. Thucydides does not mention it; instead, he refers to the revolt from the Delian League, and reduction by Athens, of Naxos (1.98.4, 137.2; cf. HMA 341). When did these events take place? The *terminus ante quem* is the secession of Thasos in 465 (schol. Aeschin. 2.31, Thuc. 4.102.2–3), before which we must also place the battle of the Eurymedon (below). In 469/8 Kimon and his fellow generals, then in high honor, were asked to adjudicate in the theater (Plut. *Cim.* 8.7). What had been the immediate occasion of that honor? For advocates of the early chronology, the Eurymedon; but this made for difficulties. The late chronology makes Eion and Skyros (with the return of the "bones of Theseus") the obvious choice, and leads straight into the Carian-Lycian campaign (468/7?) and the Eurymedon (466?: so Meiggs 1972, 81, but for different—and incompatible—reasons). Cf. Rhodes 1985, 12–13; Badian 1993, 6–10 (the rise of grain prices at Persepolis from Dec. 467 to Aug. 466 may be relevant); Miller 1997, 12.

[225] Plutarch (*Cim.* 12.5) gives the Persian figures as 600 (Phanodemos) or 350 (Ephoros), and at 12.2 says that Kimon sailed from Knidos and Triopion (see Map 2, and cf. *BA* 61 E4) with 200 triremes.

[226] Thucydides (1.100.1; cf. Nep. *Cim.* 2.2–3) gives the figure as 200; Diodorus' figures agree with those in P. Oxy. 13.1610, frs. 9–10, col. 1; cf. Lycurg. *In Leocr.* 72. This papyrus

where their crews went ashore and took off for the interior; the ships themselves, being emptied of defenders, fell into the hands of the enemy.

61. After this,[227] Kimon, not content even with so substantial a victory, led his entire fleet against the Persian land force, which was then in camp by the Eurymedon River.[228] Having a notion to outwit the barbarians by a stratagem, he embarked the pick of his troops on the captured Persian vessels, giving them tiaras to wear and in all other respects dressing them up as Persians. [2] The barbarians were taken in by the Persian vessels and accoutrements even when the fleet had come close inshore, and therefore, assuming that these triremes were their own, they greeted the Athenians as friends. It was already dark when Kimon landed his troops, and the barbarians welcomed them with open arms.[229] This enabled Kimon to charge straight into their encampment, [3] causing considerable noise and confusion among the Persians. Kimon's troops slaughtered every man in their path, including Pherendates, the Per-

---

fragment figures as fr. 191 of Ephoros in *FGrH* 70; but Ephoros is not named there, and the identification is made solely on a passing resemblance to Diodorus (11.61.1). This, as Brown (1952, 343) tartly observes, only shows that Diodorus and fr. 191 "have a common source, not that Ephorus is that source." Cf. above, Introduction, pp. 26–27.

[227] How long after? Has Diodorus, even roughly, preserved the archontic sequence (470/69), or is this a later event (466, the likeliest date, or even 465, have supporters both ancient and modern: Plat. *Menex.* 241d–e; *Suda* s.v. Themistokles, Kimon; Aristodem. 10.4–11.2; Meiggs 1972, 73; Badian 1993, 100) retrojected into a suitable Kimonian context? Several versions of the Eusebian *Chronicle* (HMA 118), with some unanimity, date the Eurymedon in 461/0. Though this can be convincingly explained as an error caused by some source that collected the main events of Kimon's life under the date of his ostracism, it makes one uncomfortably aware of just how fragile our entire chronological tradition for this period is. (Schreiner [1976–77, 38ff.] in fact is inclined to accept it, but at the cost of far too much questionable interpretation of our other evidence.)

In any case, we have to consider the strong probability that Athens made a nonaggression treaty with Xerxes immediately after the Eurymedon; that an attempt, led by Kallias, to renew this treaty on Artaxerxes' accession, and not later than 464, was rejected, leading immediately to renewed Athenian activity in the eastern Mediterranean and elsewhere, as well as to the removal of the "Delian" treasury to Athens (see note 240 below); that a successful renewal was negotiated, again by Kallias, in 449, at the end of Kimon's second Cypro-Egyptian expedition; and that this renewal was confirmed by Darius on his accession in 424/3 (for which, the so-called Treaty of Epilykos, we have the testimony of Andokides, 3.29). See below, 12.4.4, with notes 19–24.

[228] The Eurymedon River debouches from Pamphylia into the sea near Phaselis (which Kimon also won over: Plut. *Cim.* 12.3–4, cf. Meiggs-Lewis no. 31): see Map 2, and cf. *BA* 65 F4.

[229] Polyaenus (1.34.1) also reports this ruse, but locates the attack on Cyprus rather than at the Eurymedon estuary. Oldfather (1946, 286–287 n. 3) informs us that "great generals do not win battles by such comic-opera stratagems." I fear I lack his confidence.

sians' deputy commander and a nephew of the Great King, whom they seized in his pavilion. Of the rest, they killed some and seriously wounded others: because of the unexpectedness of the attack, they forced every last man of them into headlong flight. By and large the Persians were in such a state of panic and bewilderment that most of them had no idea who it was attacking them. [4] It never occurred to them that the strong force coming against them could be Greek; indeed, they were convinced that the Greeks had no land army at all. They assumed rather that it must be the Pisidians who were responsible for this hostile incursion, since they shared a frontier with them and were embroiled in continual disputes. Because of this, they figured that the enemy attack was coming from inland, and so made for the ships, assuming that these were on their side. [5] The night, being dark and moonless, simply served to increase their bewilderment: not a soul could see the true state of affairs. [6] Because of the confusion in the barbarian ranks, a great slaughter took place. At this point, Kimon—who had given his troops prior orders to come back at the double when he showed them a flaming torch as signal and marker—now raised this signal beside the ships, worried lest the wide dispersion of his men, and the possibility that they might rush off in pursuit of plunder, should produce some unlooked-for setback. [7] However, the soldiers all abandoned their plundering, and duly assembled by the lit torch. They then withdrew to the ships. The next day they set up a trophy, after which they sailed back to Cyprus, having won two outstanding victories, one on land, the other at sea. Never again since has history recorded such great and momentous actions on the same day[230] by a force that engaged both ashore and afloat.[231]

62. Kimon's great successes, achieved through his personal bravery and strategic skill, meant that his fame got noised abroad, not only among his own countrymen, but throughout the rest of the Greek world; for he had captured 340 ships, over 20,000 men,[232] and a very considerable sum of money. [2] The Persians however, after suffering these substantial reverses, built yet more

---

[230] A nice case of symbolic synchronicity (cf. II.24.1 and note 99 above) being defeated by geography: the minimum distance from Cyprus to the Eurymedon is about 130 miles, so that Kimon and his fleet cannot conceivably have made the voyage in less than eight or nine hours, let alone have fought two engagements on the same day.

[231] Other sources for the Eurymedon campaign: Thuc. 1.100.1; P.Oxy. 13.1610 frs. 9–14 = HMA 115; Plut. *Cim.* 12.3–13.2; Nep. *Cim.* 2.2–3; Polyaen. 1.34.1; Paus. 1.29.14. Cf. Meiggs 1972, 74–79; French 1971, 37–39; Hornblower 2002, 22–23; Haillet 2001, 162–163 n. 5.

[232] Curiously, this is the only reference during the Pentekontaetia before 433 B.C.E. to the taking of Persian prisoners; their subsequent fate remains unknown: Pritchett 1974, 78–79.

triremes, in even greater numbers, through their fear at the growing power of the Athenians. Indeed, from this time on, the Athenian *polis* kept building up its power more and more, being in possession of an abundance of wealth, and having acquired a very high reputation for bravery and military skill. [3] The Athenian *demos* dedicated a tithe of the booty to the god, and inscribed the following epigraph on the dedication:

> From the day when first the sea divided Europe from Asia
>    and brash Ares won a hold on the cities of men,
> never yet among earth-dwelling mortals was there such a
>    deed accomplished at once on land, by sea.
> These men on Cyprus wrought many Medes' destruction,
>    taking at sea a hundred Phoenician ships
> crammed full of warriors, and greatly did Asia mourn them,
>    struck down with both hands by the might of war.[233]

63. Such, then, were the events that took place during this year.

When Phaion was archon in Athens [469/8], in Rome Lucius Furius †Mediolanus† and Marcus Manilius †Vaso† succeeded to the consulship.[234] During their term of office, a great and unlooked-for disaster befell the Lacedaemonians: major earthquakes took place in Sparta, so that houses collapsed from their foundations and over 20,000 Lacedaemonians were killed.[235]

---

[233] The god thus honored was Delphic Apollo; the tithe paid for a bronze palm-tree on which stood a Palladion, a gilt statue of armed Athena: Paus. 10.15.4–5; Plut. *Nic.* 13.3, *Mor.* 397F, 724B; Paus. 10.15.4–5. The inscription is generally attributed to Simonides, and is sometimes thought either to combine two separate epigraphs, one for the Eurymedon (1–4), one for Kimon's later victory off Cyprus (5–8: see below, 12.3.3–4 with note 14), or else to have been composed for the Cyprus victory alone, in the spring of 449. This second theory, though unprovable, is very plausible. Badian (1993, 64–66) argues that the encomium was transferred in the fourth century to the Eurymedon, which ousted it in popular imagination. Cf. Haillet 2001, 163 n. 1, and Paus. 10.15.4–5; see also Plut. *Cim.* 13.6 for the sale of booty to pay for the extension of the great southern wall of the Akropolis in Athens.

[234] The consuls (actually for 474) were L. Furius Medullinus and A. Manlius Vulso (Broughton 1951, 28 with n. 1). Cf. 11.48.1 and note 181 above. Furius here is, again, a correction for Φρούριος of the MSS, while Μεδιολανός is a Hellenization of Medullinus. (This kind of Hellenization came in later for some acid comments by Lucian in his essay "On How to Write History," *Hist. Conscr.* 21.) ΟΥΑΣΩΝ = VASO(N) is an easily explainable corruption of ΟΥΛΣΩΝ = VULSO(N): Perotti 1984, 164. The eponymous archon is variously reported as Phaion or Phaidon (Diodorus), or Apsephion (*Marm. Par.* 56). Cf. note 223 above.

[235] Generally dated to 464/3 on the basis of Paus. 4.24.5–6, citing the archon-year; but Sealey (in *Hist.* 8 [1959]: 368–371) accepts Diodorus' date and puts the Helot revolt four to five years later. The evidence, including Diodorus', suggests that in fact there may have

[2] Since the disintegration of their city, with houses collapsing into rubble, went on nonstop for a considerable period, many were pinned by the falling walls, and so perished, while the earthquake damaged no small amount of household property. [3] This evil afflicting them they suffered as though it was the handiwork of some avenging divinity—though they also faced other dangers from human enemies, for the following reasons. [4] The Helots and Messenians, although nursing enmity toward the Lacedaemonians, had hitherto remained quiet, through fear of Sparta's preeminence and power; but when they perceived that the greater part of them had perished in the earthquake, their attitude to the few survivors became one of contempt. They therefore banded together and jointly waged war against the Lacedaemonians.[236] [5] The Lacedaemonian king Archidamos, by his personal foresight, both saw to his countrymen's safety at the time of the earthquake, and fought nobly against the insurgents during the war [that followed]. [6] When his city was paralyzed by the intensity of the seismic shock, he was the first Spartan to grab his armor and hasten from the capital into the countryside, while calling on the other citizens to follow his example. [7] The Spartans obeyed him, and by so doing those who survived [the first shock] were saved. It was they whom King Archidamos rallied into a defense force and trained to fight the rebels.

64. When the Messenians joined forces with the Helots, they at first hurried to attack Sparta, figuring that they would have no trouble capturing it through the city's dearth of defenders. However, when they heard that the

---

been at least *two* earthquakes during this period, one in 469/8, the other in 464/3: see Thuc. 1.101.2, 128.1; Plut. *Cim.* 16.4–6; Paus. 1.29.8, 4.24.6; Polyaen. 1.41.3; Aristoph. *Lys.* 1137–1144 with schol.; Ael. *VH* 6.7. Seismologically this is by no means unlikely. In particular, schol. Aristoph. *Lys.* 1144 clearly describes a situation in 468/7 where there has already been both an earthquake and a Messenian uprising, followed by a (first?) Athenian rescue expedition led by Kimon (Plutarch [*Cim.* 17.2], discussing the 463/2 appeal, which he treats as a *second* plea, clearly implies this). The numerous casualties had a serious effect on Spartan manpower: e.g., they fielded 8,000 hoplites at Plataia in 479, but only 3,000 in 425 during the first phase of the Peloponnesian War. That both Helots and Messenians should have taken advantage of the chaos produced by two successive earthquakes is hardly surprising; there is no need to choose between them.

[236] For this revolt, cf. Hdt. 9.64.2; Thuc. 1.101.2, 103.1–3; Plut. *Cim.* 16–17; Paus. 1.29.8, 4.24.6; Aristoph. *Lys.* 1137–1144 with schol.; Just. 3.6.1–11. The chronology is confused, and is made worse by the dubious article of faith among modern scholars that Thucydides never, in the Pentekontaetia, diverges from a strict chronological sequence. (For a salutary demolition of this shibboleth, see Badian 1993, 73–103, and cf. Walker 1957, passim.) At 1.103.1 Thucydides makes the revolt last over nine years; if we accept 469/8 as the date of the (first?) earthquake *and* the first outbreak of the revolt, we get a cessation date of 459 (confirmed by Diodorus at 11.64.4), which makes excellent historical sense.

survivors were drawn up [under arms] with King Archidamos [at their head], and stood ready to fight for their fatherland, the rebels abandoned this plan, and instead occupied a stronghold in Messenia,[237] from which they made regular sorties to overrun Laconia. [2] The Spartans were driven to solicit aid from the Athenians, who sent them an expeditionary force; they also collected troops from the rest of their allies, and thus got themselves on an equal footing with the enemy.[238] Thus to begin with they had the advantage over them; but later, when a suspicion arose that the Athenians intended to defect to the Messenians, the Spartans repudiated Athens as their ally, saying that the other allies they had offered them sufficient support for the conflict ahead.[239] [3] The Athenians, though regarding this act as an affront, at the time simply withdrew.[240] Afterward, however, being already on unfriendly terms with the Lac-

---

[237] This was Mt. Ithome, not particularly high (2,500 ft.) but dauntingly precipitous, which had once before served the same purpose, in the First Messenian War (Paus. 4.9–13).

[238] To begin with, the Spartans had been very much on the defensive (Xen. *Hell.* 6.5.33). From Athens they got 4,000 hoplites led by Kimon (Thuc. 1.101.1–2); other allies who helped included Aigina, Plataia, and Mantinea. Cf. Plut. *Cim.* 16.7–8, Paus. 1.29.8, Just. 3.6.2.

[239] For the suspicion about the Athenians, cf. Paus. 4.26.4; for their dismissal by the Spartans, see Thuc. 1.102.3; Plut. *Cim.* 17.2; Paus. 1.29.8–9, 4.24.6–7; Just. 3.6.3. The date is uncertain: Diodorus twice emphasizes that it happened "later" (ὕστερον), or "afterward" (μετὰ δὲ ταῦτα), and it would fit well in the context of 463/2, where it is generally placed. This was one of the reasons for the subsequent ostracism of the aggressively pro-Laconian Kimon in 461: Plut. *Cim.* 17.2, *Per.* 9.4; Plat. *Gorg.* 516D; Nep. *Cim.* 3.1.

[240] Justin (3.6.4) reports that one result was the relocation of the League's treasury from Delos to Athens, a move that Aristeides described during debate, accurately, as "improper but advantageous," οὐ δίκαιον μέν, συμφέρον δέ (Plut. *Arist.* 25.3). Though the reason Justin gives—fear that Sparta, breaking from the alliance, might raid Delos and hijack the funds ("ne deficientibus a fide societatis Lacedaemoniis praedae ac rapinae esset")— sounds uncommonly like self-justificatory Athenian propaganda (fear of "the Barbarians" was also alleged, Plut. *Per.* 12.2), nevertheless his actual dating of the move (Robertson 1980, 112), when Athens' ruthless reduction of Thasos, with its unmistakable message of nascent imperial autocracy, had stirred up acute fear and resentment among the subject-allies (see below, 11.70.1–5, under 464/3, with notes 268–271), makes excellent, if unwelcome, sense. (Plutarch [*Per.* 12.2] remarks that Perikles' use of treasury funds for the Parthenon building project finally exposed official reasons for the transfer as false excuses, but this need not be taken as implying that it was the project itself that first elicited them.) It was also a time when Athens' widespread naval and military activities, from Thasos to the eastern Mediterranean, urgently needed the easy availability of large infusions of ready cash. If we place the move in 463/2 or even 462/1 (cf. note 241 below), as opposed to the traditionally accepted date of 454 (for which there is no real evidence, cf. note 302 below), we shall not be far out.

Also, the commencement of recorded ἀπαρχαί to Athena in 454, after a run of crushing military defeats, suggests an atmosphere in which the loyalty of the subject-allies has

edaemonians, they were all the more inclined [because of this incident] to fan the flames of hatred. As a result, they took [the rebuff] as the beginning of the estrangement between them. Later the two states quarreled, and by launching into a series of major wars, filled all Hellas with vast misfortunes. However, we shall write of these matters severally in their proper context [12.38ff.]. [4] At the time, the Lacedaemonians made an expedition with their allies against Ithome, and laid siege to it.[241] Meanwhile the Helots as a whole now revolted from the Lacedaemonians and allied themselves with the Messenians. The fortunes of war favored first one side, then the other: for ten long years they continually attacked and counterattacked, without any final decision being reached.[242]

65. After this [468/7], Theagenides was archon in Athens, while in Rome the consuls who took office were Lucius Aemilius Mamercus and Lucius Iulius Iullus,[243] and the 78th Olympiad was held, in which Parmenides of Poseidonia won the *stadion*. During this period, war broke out between the Argives and the Mycenaeans, for the following reasons. [2] The Mycenaeans, on account of their country's ancient high repute, would not subordinate themselves to the Argives like the other cities throughout the Argolid, but took an independent line and ignored Argive authority. They also had a run-

---

become a matter of great concern, thus making public accountability suddenly desirable. Exactly how much specie was transferred, and when, remains problematic. Thucydides (2.13.3) simply refers to the sum of 10,000 (less 300) talents as the maximum held at any time on the Akropolis before the major Periklean building program. Diodorus (12.38.2) and Isokrates (8.126–127) both put the sum transferred from Delos at 8,000 talents. Two chapters later (12.40.2), so that any absent-minded citing of discrepant sources can be ruled out, Diodorus like Thucydides, refers to an overall total on the Akropolis of 10,000 talents. The context in both cases suggests that the accumulated tribute from Delos became part of a general fund represented by the larger figure, of which some, clearly, existed in Athens prior to the transfer.

[241] In 463/2, by the general consensus of modern scholars. Diodorus (who here moves to and fro in time with more than his usual flexibility) makes it clear that the expedition, in any case, took place *before* the dismissal of the Athenians reported in §2.

[242] For the chronology, see 11.84.6 with note 340 below. Against the various attempts to emend Thucydides' statement (1.103.1) that the Messenian War ended "in the tenth year," see Deane 1972, 23–28, and V. Parker 1993, 129–130.

[243] The consuls are those of 473: Diodorus is still six years out. The name of the second consul is uncertain: Vopiscus Iulius Iullus (Broughton 1951, 29; Bickerman 1968, 171); Opiter Verginius (Samuel 1972, 256, ex Livy 2.54.3). "Iulius" in Diodorus is Dindorf's emendation for the manuscript reading *stoudios* (retained by Haillet [2001]). Cf. Perotti (1984, 165), who argues that Lucius (as the praenomen of other branches of the *gens Iulia*) has ousted Vopiscus.

ning dispute with them about the sacred precinct of Hera, as well as claiming that it was they who should by rights organize the Nemean Games.[244] Furthermore, when the Argives voted not to fight with the Lacedaemonians at Thermopylai unless they were allowed to share the command, the Mycenaeans, alone of those domiciled in the Argolid, fought at the Lacedaemonians' side.[245] [3] The long and short of it was that the Argives regarded the Mycenaeans with suspicion, and were worried lest any increase of strength on their part might lead them, relying on their city's ancient prestige, to challenge the Argives for leadership. For these reasons, then, they were at loggerheads. The Argives had from of old always striven to promote their own city, and at this point they figured they had a fine opportunity, seeing that the Lacedaemonians had been weakened and could not come to the Mycenaeans' assistance. Accordingly, they put together a sizable force, from both Argos and the cities allied with it, and marched against the Mycenaeans. After defeating them in battle and driving them back inside their walls, they laid siege to the city. [4] For a while, the Mycenaeans energetically stood off the besiegers; but later on, as they began to get the worst of it in the war, and the Lacedaemonians were unable to relieve them on account of their own wars and the disastrous impact of the earthquake, and since they had no other allies, they were overpowered through lack of external support.[246] [5] The Argives sold the Myce-

---

[244] The famous Heraion, or sanctuary of Hera, stood on an ancient Bronze Age site about midway between Argos and Mycenae, and served as a common shrine for the whole Argolid (Strab. 8.6.10, C.372). It is easy to see (Haillet 2001, 85) how the two cities clashed over its maintenance. The Nemean Games, first celebrated in 573 B.C.E., had been administered by Kleonai, a town located inside the territory of the Heraion. From 460 (probably as a result of this dispute), the Argives took over control of the games (Paus. 2.15.2).

[245] On Argive neutrality during the Greco-Persian Wars, see Hdt. 7.148–152 (esp. 148 for their insistence on a share of the command), cf. 9.12; and see above, 11.3.4–5. Herodotos (7.202) lists the allied contingents with Leonidas: in addition to eighty Mycenaeans, they included, from the Peloponnese, men of Tegea, Mantinea, Arcadia, Corinth, and Phlious. What Diodorus must mean is that when Hydarnes' approach became known, and the other allies were dismissed to fight another day (Hdt. 7.221–222), the Mycenaeans alone, together with the Thespians and the Thebans, stayed to the end with the Spartans. Herodotos does not name them; that does not necessarily mean they were not there. Haillet (2001, 165) and others list, in refutation of Diodorus, those Peloponnesian towns that appear as postwar Greek allies; but here Diodorus is specifically referring only to Thermopylai, and, evidently, to the final combatants.

[246] After the defeat of Mycenae, the Spartans, though occupied with the Messenian revolt, did send a small force to help Tiryns, similarly threatened by a resurgent Argos (Hdt. 6.83.2; Paus. 2.17.5, 2.25.8, 8.27.1). This force was defeated at the battle of Oinoë (exact location uncertain), and both Argos and, more surprisingly, Athens (Paus. 1.15.1, 10.4.4) commemorated the victory with lavish monuments at home and in Delphi. Argos, clearly, was celebrating its recovery from the crushing defeat by Sparta under King Kleomenes in 494

naeans into slavery, dedicated a tenth part of them to the god, and demolished Mycenae itself. So this city, so fortunate in ancient times, able to boast of great heroes and with notable achievements to its credit, came to the disastrous end described above, and has remained uninhabited to this day.[247]

These, then, were the events that took place during this year.

66. When Lysistratos was archon in Athens [467/6], the Romans elected as consuls Lucius Pinarius Mamertinus and Publius Furius †Fifron† <Fusus>.[248] During their term of office, Hieron, king of the Syracusans, summoned to Syracuse the sons of Anaxilas, who had been tyrant of Zankle. Bestowing rich gifts upon them, he reminded them of the benefactions that their father had received from Gelon, and he counseled them, now that they had come of age, to demand a reckoning from their guardian Mikythos and assume power themselves.[249] [2] So when they returned to Rhegion, they asked their guardian for an accounting of his stewardship. Mikythos, being an honest man, assembled the friends of the boys' father, and made so scrupulous an accounting that everyone present was amazed at his righteousness and good faith; and the boys, now regretting their action, besought Mikythos to reassume authority, and carry out the business of government with all the power and rank that their father had enjoyed. [3] Mikythos, however, would not agree. Instead, after effecting a meticulous transfer of power, he loaded all his personal property aboard a ship and sailed away from Rhegion, accompanied by the

---

at Sepeia (Hdt. 6.76–80). But Athens in 468/7 was still, however reluctantly, an ally of Sparta; and though Kimon's philo-Laconism has been exaggerated (so, rightly, Schreiner 1997, 36–37), it may well be that the Athenian commemoration of Oinoë only came later, with the rebuff of Kimon at Ithome, the consequent break with Sparta, and the alliance with Argos and Thessaly (Thuc. 1.102.4, cf. D.S. 11.64.2–3). In general on Oinoë, see now Schreiner 1997, ch. 2, 21–37, *inter alia* summing up earlier scholarship.

[247] For this war between Argos and Mycenae, cf. Strab. 8.6.10 and 19, C.372, 377; Paus. 5.23.3, 7.25.5–6. Argos was supported by Kleonai and Tegea. It proved impossible to breach the great walls of Mycenae, and the inhabitants were starved out. (Diodorus' Greek, κατὰ κράτος ἥλωσαν, is ambiguous, but could suggest that the city was stormed, and is so translated by both Oldfather [1946] and Haillet [2001].) Over half of the survivors took refuge with Alexander I of Macedon. Both Mycenae and nearby Tiryns were now razed to the ground, and never reoccupied.

[248] The consuls (actually for 472) were L. Pinarius Mamercinus Rufus and P. Furius Medullinus Fusus (Broughton 1951, 29). φίφρωνα (F) is retained by Haillet; PS M read Φιλοσόφαν (sic). Cf. Perotti 1984, 165.

[249] Picking up from 11.48.2. Hieron's determination to hold Mikythos to his agreement may have been due in part to the latter's ambitious colonizing activities (above, 11.59.4) and the debacle in which he was involved with Taras (Táranto) in attempting to oust the Iapygians (Hdt. 7.170; above, 11.52.3).

good wishes of the populace. When he reached Greece, he spent the rest of his life in Tegea in Arcadia, the object of general esteem.[250] [4] Hieron, the king of the Syracusans, died in Katana, and received heroic honors, having been the founder of the city. He had ruled for eleven years, and he left the kingdom to his brother Thrasyboulos, whose reign over the Syracusans lasted one year only.[251]

67. When Lysanios was archon in Athens [466/5], the Romans elected as consuls Appius Claudius and Titus Quinctius Capitolinus.[252] During their term of office, Thrasyboulos, king of the Syracusans, lost his throne. Since we are describing this episode in detail, we need to go back a little in time and narrate the whole story in clear detail from the beginning.[253]

[2] Gelon son of Deinomenes, a man who far excelled all others in courage and generalship, outfought and defeated the barbarians of Carthage in a great battle, as has been narrated above [11.21ff.]. Now since he treated with moderation all those whom he vanquished, and in general behaved with humanity to all his near neighbors, his reputation among the Sicilian Greeks stood very high.[254] [3] Being, then, loved universally on account of his mild rule, he continued to enjoy a peaceful life until he passed away. But when Hieron, the next oldest brother, inherited the kingdom, his manner of rule over his subjects was very different, [4] he being avaricious, violent, and, in sum, of a character wholly opposed to honesty or nobility.[255] As a result, many

---

[250] That Mikythos did, in fact, hand over power to Anaxilas' sons (one of whom was named Leophron) we know from Dion. Hal. *AR* 20.7.1, Athen. 1.3c, and Just. 21.3.2–3, where Leophron appears as *tyrannos* of Rhegion.

[251] Hieron reigned for eleven years and eight months: 11.38.7 above. His death may be more accurately described as having taken place in Aitna, founded by Hieron himself, after the destruction of Katana (11.49.1–2), as that city's replacement. Thrasyboulos, overthrown in 466/5, ruled, according to Aristotle (5.9.23, 1315b38), for not quite eleven months.

[252] The consuls (actually for 471) were Ap. Claudius Crassinus Inregillensis Sabinus and T. Quinctius Capitolinus Barbatus (Broughton 1951, 30).

[253] See Asheri 1980, 145ff., and the same author's shorter account in *CAH* v, 154ff.; cf. Sinatra 1992, 347–353; Manganaro 1974–75, 9–10.

[254] Gelon's popularity, both during and after his lifetime, is widely attested. In addition to Diodorus (11.26.4–6, 13.22.4, 14.66.1–5), cf. Haillet 2001, 166 n. 6 and sources collected there. This despite his record of the mass transfer of populations for Syracuse's benefit, and the selling off into slavery of Megara Hyblaia's inhabitants (Hdt. 7.155–156).

[255] Diodorus is clearly not impressed by Hieron's very considerable record as an enlightened patron of the arts, whose guests included Pindar, Bacchylides, Simonides, Xenophanes of Kolophon, and Aeschylus, or indeed by his chariot victories at the Olympian and Pythian Games (Paus. 6.12.1, 8.42.9; cf. Pind. *Ol.* 1, *Pyth.* 1).

were eager to revolt, but restrained themselves on account of Gelon's reputation and his benevolence to all Sicilian Greeks. [5] But after Hieron's death, his brother Thrasyboulos succeeded to the throne,[256] and in the matter of wickedness he outdid his predecessor. A man not merely violent but murderous by temperament, he unjustly executed many citizens, and forced not a few into exile through false accusations, impounding their property for the benefit of the royal treasury. Since, by and large, those whom he wronged detested him as much as he did them, he hired a large number of foreign mercenaries, thus setting up an opposition force with which to counter the citizen-militia. [6] Indeed, since he continually exacerbated the hatred of the citizens by the numerous outrages he perpetrated on them (including not a few murders), he finally drove his victims to rebellion. The Syracusans, then, chose men to be their leaders, and united in their determination to bring down the tyranny. Once these leaders had organized them, they clung with tenacity to the pursuit of freedom. [7] When Thrasyboulos saw that the whole city was on the warpath against him, he at first tried to check the revolt by diplomacy; but when he realized that the momentum of the Syracusans' [uprising] was unstoppable, he mustered all his allies, including those colonists that Hieron had settled in Katana, as well as a vast number of mercenaries,[257] raising in all something like 15,000 men. [8] He then seized the quarter of the city known as Achradine, together with the Island [of Ortygia], which was fortified, and from these bases waged war against the rebels.[258]

68. The Syracusans began by occupying the quarter called Tyche,[259] and from this base sent out ambassadors to Gela and Akragas and Selinous, as well

---

[256] Why did he succeed? Presumably because his older Deinomenid brother, Polyzelos, had fled the country (cf. 11.48.3–6); but Aristotle (*Pol.* 5.8.19, 1312b10–16) identifies the heir as a son of Gelon (unnamed), whom his uncle Thrasyboulos, as a preparation for seizing power himself, deliberately urged into self-indulgent frivolities.

[257] The presence of so many mercenaries had been one of the grievances against both Hieron and Thrasyboulos: Consolo Langher 1997, 44.

[258] For Syracuse, see Map 3; for the topography, see Guido 1963; Fabricius 1932; Drögemüller 1969; and Green 1971, 183–186. Ortygia (originally an island, now linked to the mainland) was the oldest quarter; Achradine, immediately to the north and northwest of Ortygia, formed the city's earliest extension. Freeman 1891, 304–314 has a useful narrative of the events leading to Thrasyboulos' removal; cf. Consolo Langher 1997, 44–45. Thrasyboulos' command of Ortygia and Achradine meant that he controlled both of Syracuse's harbors.

[259] The identity, name, and location of this quarter have been much debated. Diodorus' MSS read Ἰτύκην, which is clearly corrupt. The obvious correction is to Τύχην, since there is good evidence for the later existence of a quarter named Tyche on the coast im-

as to Himera and the Sicel cities of the interior, asking them to come quickly
and join with them in liberating Syracuse. [2] All responded with a will, and
lost no time in dispatching aid. Some sent cavalry and infantry detachments,
others warships fully equipped for battle, and so in a very short time a considerable force had been put together to back the Syracusans. As a result of
this, the Syracusans manned their fleet and brought their land force to battle
stations, thus demonstrating that they were ready and willing to pursue the
struggle to its end both on land and at sea. [3] Thrasyboulos, being abandoned by his allies, had to base his hopes on the mercenaries. All he held was
Achradine and the Island: the rest of the city was controlled by the Syracusans. He then led his fleet out against the enemy, and after being worsted in
a sea battle and losing numerous triremes, retreated to the Island with those
that remained. [4] In a like manner he sallied out from Achradine with his
land force and fought an engagement in the suburbs, which he lost. After suffering heavy losses, he was forced to withdraw back into Achradine. Finally he
abandoned his claim on the tyranny, negotiated a deal with the Syracusans,
and, having come to terms with them, withdrew under truce to [Epizephyr-
ian] Lokroi.[260] [5] The Syracusans, after freeing their city in this manner, gave
the mercenaries their *congé* from Syracuse, then freed those other cities which
either were ruled by tyrants or had garrisons, and restored democratic government in them.[261] [6] From now on, Syracuse had peace and greatly in-

---

mediately east of Achradine. But how early was it established? Haillet (2001, 167 n. 1)
doubts whether it existed in 466/5, and considers the possibility of Συκῆ (*Syke*, "The Fig-
Tree"), mentioned by Thucydides (6.98.2) as the site of the Athenians' fort during the 415
siege of Syracuse. But this was actually on the heights of Epipolae above the city, and the
researches of Fabricius (1932; cf. Green 1971, 183–186) conclusively demonstrated that at no
time did Syracuse extend up onto this plateau, so that Syke cannot in fact be considered as
a quarter at all. Guido (1963, 13–14) has no difficulty in dating the creation of Tyche to
Gelon's reign, and this seems the only viable solution. Oldfather (1946, 301 n. 3) accepts
Tyche, but places it to the *west* of Achradine, probably a slip induced by the Syke argument. Vogel (1890) and Haillet (2001) both read the meaningless Τύκην, also found as a
variant in one manuscript for the Thucydidean Συκῆν.

[260] Epizephyrian Lokroi was on the southeastern coast of the Bruttian peninsula, almost
at the toe of Italy (Map 4 and *BA* 46 D5). Hieron had earlier forced Anaxilas of Rhegion
to stop his attacks on the city (Haillet 2001, 167 n. 3), which was now repaying this favor.
Aristotle (*Pol.* 1312b19) suggests that other members of the Deinomenid clan turned against
Thrasyboulos in the hope of saving the regime.

[261] As Haillet rightly points out (2001, 90 n. 1), this process was in fact both lengthy and
convulsive, something Diodorus himself makes very clear in subsequent chapters (chs. 72–
73, 76, 78, 86, 88, 91–92). See now Robinson 2000, 189–205. Cf. Euseb. *Chron.*, which
agrees with Diodorus in dating the restoration of "democracy" in Syracuse (cf. note 276)
to 463/2 or 462/1, four or five years later. But Thrasyboulos' fall did in fact bring down the

creased prosperity, preserving its democracy for almost sixty years, until the tyranny of Dionysios.[262] [7] Thrasyboulos, who had inherited an excellently established kingdom, lost it in a shameful manner through his own wickedness and, after fleeing to Lokroi, lived out his days there as a private citizen.

[8] Simultaneous with these events, in Rome for the first time there were now elected four tribunes: Gaius Sicinus, Lucius Numitorius, Marcus Duillius, and Spurius Acilius.[263]

69. When this year had run its course, Lysitheos became archon in Athens [465/4], while in Rome the consuls elected were Lucius Valerius Publicola and Titus Aemilius Mamercus.[264] During their term, in Asia Artabanos, a Hyrkanian by race, a man of the highest authority in King Xerxes' court and the commander of the palace guard, decided to eliminate Xerxes and transfer the royal power to himself.[265] He made the eunuch Mithridates privy to his plot:

---

whole carefully constructed political edifice of the Deinomenid dynasty. The process had already begun at Akragas (Agrigento) (11.53.2) with the fall of Thrasydaios in 472/1. As for the mercenaries, not more than 3,000 left; over twice that number stayed on, and (11.72.3–73) their exclusion from citizenship caused a major crisis. Cf. Sinatra 1992, 352–353.

[262] For the accession to power of Dionysios I, see 13.91–96.

[263] In 471 (Livy 2.55.10–58.2) = 466/5 by Diodorus' reckoning, a bill was passed to transfer election of tribunes (first constituted as an office in 493, at the time of the First Secession of the Plebs) to the Comitia Tributa, and to create either five or four urban tribunes. Livy lists those chosen as Gnaeus Siccius, Lucius Numitorius, Marcus Duillius, Spurius Icilius, and Lucius Maecilius: the first four, with only minor variations, correspond to Diodorus' list. (The names of Siccius, Icilius Numitorius, and Duillius also, suspiciously, recur in connection with the *second* Secession to the Aventine in 450/49.) As Haillet says (2001, 168 n. 4), four urban tribunes is a more logical number when we match them against the four urban tribes. Cf. Broughton 1951, 30–31.

[264] The consuls (actually for 470) were L. Valerius Potitus and Ti. Aemilius Mamercus: cf. Broughton 1951, 31.

[265] The assassination of Xerxes is also recorded by Ctesias (§§29–30: *FGrH* 688 F 13–14, p. 464) and Justin (3.1.1–8), who, with variations, tell roughly the same story. Aristotle (*Pol.* 5.8.14, 1311b36–40) claims that Artabanos moved through fear: he had hanged Darius contrary to Xerxes' instructions. This sounds highly improbable, and is contradicted by our other sources' agreement that Darius was in fact the conspiracy's second victim after Xerxes himself. A Babylonian eclipse text (sources in Badian 1993, 188 n. 7) establishes that Xerxes died between 4 and 8 August 465, but the claim that Artaxerxes did not succeed him until December (Haillet 2001, 91 n. 2; Briant 2002, 566), though it may be very roughly true, is not, as was once believed, supported by Babylonian evidence. Even so, there may just be something to Eusebius' claim that Artabanos actually usurped the throne for seven months. Briant (2002, 563–567) has an otherwise exemplary analysis of the evidence for this episode. But his observation that all three sources "are built on common heroic-literary motifs" (564) does not necessarily (as he later concedes) put them out of court. Such mo-

this person, besides being the king's chamberlain and enjoying his absolute trust, was also Artabanos' kinsman as well as his friend, and therefore lent himself to the plot. [2] Artabanos was brought by him at night into the [king's] bedchamber, and killed Xerxes. He then moved against the king's sons. These were three in number: the eldest, Darius, and Artaxerxes were both resident in the palace, but the third, Hystaspes, was abroad just then, in charge of the Bactrian satrapy. [3] So Artabanos came to Artaxerxes while it was still dark, and told him that his brother Darius had murdered his father and meant to seize the throne for himself. [4] He advised Artaxerxes, therefore, before Darius could consolidate his power, to look to it that he did not, through mere passive indifference, suffer enslavement: let him rather take vengeance on his father's killer and himself become king. He also promised to bring him the royal guard as accomplices to this end. [5] Artaxerxes was convinced, and at once, with the royal guard's cooperation, assassinated his brother Darius. At this point Artabanos, seeing how well his plan was going, summoned his own sons to his side, and told them that now was the moment to win the throne. He then struck Artaxerxes a blow with his sword. [6] Artaxerxes, however, though wounded, was in no way incapacitated by this assault: he defended himself vigorously against Artabanos, and struck him a shrewd blow that killed him. Thus Artaxerxes survived against odds, avenged his father's murder, and succeeded to the Persian throne. Xerxes, then, died in the aforesaid manner, having reigned over the Persians for more than twenty years, and was followed by Artaxerxes, who ruled for forty.[266]

70. When Archidemides was archon in Athens [464/3], the Romans elected as consuls Aulus Verginius and Titus Minucius [Numicius], and the 79th Olympiad was held, in which Xenophon the Corinthian won the *stadion*.[267] During their term, the Thasians revolted from the Athenians through a disagreement about certain mines: but the Athenians reduced them by siege

---

tifs most often developed on the basis of observed or reported fact. The details of Xerxes' murder remain uncertain. But that dynastic assassination was a common factor in Achaimenid history is undeniable.

[266] Xerxes reigned 486–465 B.C.E., Artaxerxes 465–425/4. Diodorus' estimates are correct. The name Artaxerxes proved popular after Artaxerxes II Mnemon's long and successful reign: his successor Ochos also adopted it—as, with less success, the satrap Bessos also did after murdering Darius III. Cf. D.S. 15.93.1.

[267] The consuls (actually for 469) were T. Numicius Priscus and A. Verginius (Broughton 1951, 31). Minucius in Diodorus' MSS is a clear metathesis of Numicius. The victory by Xenophon of Corinth was celebrated by Pindar in *Ol.* 13.

and forcibly brought them back under their control.[268] [2] Similarly, when the Aiginetans rebelled, the Athenians put Aigina under siege with the object of reducing them to servitude; for this *polis*, having fought numerous successful sea battles, was full of arrogant self-confidence, besides being well supplied with cash reserves and triremes. Thus, generally speaking, it was at permanent odds with the Athenians.[269] [3] The latter therefore made an expedition against [the island], laid waste its territory, and besieged [the city of] Aigina, making every effort to take it by storm; for it was generally true that, since their current great gains in power, the Athenians no longer treated the allies equitably, as they had done earlier, but were subjecting them to a rule as harsh as it was arrogant. [4] In consequence, most of the allies, unable to tolerate their severity, were discussing the idea of revolt with one another, whereas some of them, in defiance of the general congress [of the Delian League], were acting as though they were independent.[270]

---

[268] Cf. Thuc. 1.100.2, 101; Plut. *Cim.* 14.2; Nep. *Cim.* 2.5. No workings have been found on Thasos itself: the mines were probably the rich ones, yielding both gold and silver, of Mt. Pangaios on the mainland (which would also explain the expedition against Amphipolis and Thrace, 11.70.5), over which the Thasians had established control. A naval assault force against Thasos was led by the Athenian general Kimon, who then laid siege to its city. Thasos surrendered in the third year of this siege, i.e., 463, the year under which Diodorus records the event: the beginning of the operation will have been in 465 (cf. Thuc. 4.102 and schol. Aeschin. 2.31). Thasos appealed for help to Sparta; the latter's favorable response was annulled by the major earthquake of 464 and the consequent renewed Helot and Messenian revolt.

[269] Thuc. 1.105.2 and *IG* I³ 928 = Meiggs-Lewis no. 33 clearly place action against Aigina in 459, at the same time as the expedition against Egypt, and this is generally regarded as an error on Diodorus' part, especially since the Aiginetans are spoken of as having *rebelled* (ἀποστάντες), which they could not have done until 459/8, when they were forcibly enrolled in the Delian League. But three points are worth noting here: (a) Diodorus is drawing a comparison only, and does not place this revolt in 464/3; (b) Thucydides (ad loc.) leaves the date of the first outbreak of hostilities between Athens and Aigina open: the sea battle is merely located at some point after that; (c) it is Diodorus himself (11.78.4) who furnishes the fact, and the date, of Aigina's forcible enrollment. It seems reasonable to assume that Athens and Aigina may well have been at war for several years before the island's final reduction.

[270] This general assessment of nascent Athenian imperialism exactly agrees with the conclusions reached by Thucydides (1.98–99 and elsewhere) and others: see the useful note by Haillet (2001, 169–170—who, however, finds Diodorus' estimate of general rebelliousness among the subject-allies "surprising"; since several actual revolts were in the process of breaking out, it is hard to see why). It is in this context that, contrary to general belief, we should place the removal by Athens of the League treasury from Delos to Athens: cf. 11.64.3 with note 240 above.

[5] Simultaneously with these events, the Athenians, as masters of the sea, sent out 10,000 colonists, recruited in part from their own citizen body, and in part from the allies, to Amphipolis. They parceled out the land in cleruchies, and for a while kept the Thracians in subjection; but afterward, when they penetrated deeper into Thrace, those thus invading the country were wiped out to the last man by a people called the Edones.[271]

71. When Tlepolemos was archon in Athens [463/2], the Romans elected as consuls Titus Quinctius and Quintus Servilius Structus.[272] During their term, Artaxerxes, the Great King of Persia, who had recently regained the throne [11.69.5–6], first of all—after punishing those involved in the assassination of his father—reordered the government of the realm to his own advantage. [2] Of the satraps then in office, he dismissed those personally hostile to him, and replaced them with friends of his chosen for their proven competence. He also turned his attention to the revenues and to military preparations generally; and since his administration of the kingdom as a whole was, by and large, equitable, he was held in high esteem by the Persians.[273]

---

[271] Thucydides (1.100.3, cf. 4.102) places this expedition to the Strymon area at "about the same time" as the reduction of Thasos, and twenty-eight years before the successful colonization of Amphipolis by Hagnon in 437/6 (12.32.3 with note 164 below), i.e., c. 464. Herodotos (9.75) refers to one Sophanes who, *subsequent to* taking part in the siege of Aigina in 459, died fighting the Edones "for the gold mines," which gives us at least a loose *terminus post quem* for the final destruction of this ill-fated venture. Schol. Aeschin. 2.31 more specifically dates it in the archonship of Lysikrates, i.e., 453/2. (For various a priori efforts to backdate this event, see Badian 1993, 81–86.) The colony thus lasted about twelve years. The actual site of the disaster (mentioned by Pausanias and Thucydides) was Drabeskos, somewhere near modern Drama, and perhaps 25 miles from Amphipolis (Badian 1993, 82–85). Cf. Isokr. 8.86, D.S. 12.68.2, Paus. 1.29.4–5 (who reports that the dead were returned to Athens for public burial in the Kerameikos).

[272] The consuls (actually for 468) were T. Quinctius Capitolinus Barbatus and Q. Servilius Structus Priscus (Broughton 1951, 32).

[273] On Artaxerxes' early reforms, cf. Plut. *Them.* 29.4, *Mor.* 173d–e, 565a, *Art.* 4.1; Joseph. *AJ* 11.185. A good general discussion can be found in Briant 2002, 569–573. The chronology here presented suggests that Artaxerxes took up to two years to establish himself in full control of the Achaimenid realm, and this may well be true. It is thus likely that the Argive and Athenian embassies reported by Herodotos (7.151) can be dated to 464 (Badian 1993, 4) as part of a general resumption of foreign diplomatic activity in Sousa. The Athenians—described, maddeningly but significantly as being in Sousa "on other business," ἑτέρου πράγματος εἵνεκα, by Herodotos, who seems to have thought the nature of their mission better unspecified—will undoubtedly have been counting on the Eurymedon victory (11.61.1–7 with note 227 above) to convince the new Great King of the need to renew the treaty made with Xerxes two or three years earlier. In this, it seems clear, they were unsuccessful, which would explain Herodotos' reticence. The Argives, as he notes,

[3] But when the Egyptians got wind of Xerxes' death, with the whole business of the attempt on the throne, and the resultant confusion throughout the Persian realm, they decided to make a bid for their freedom. So they promptly raised an army and revolted from the Persians, expelling those Persians stationed in Egypt to collect tribute, and setting up their own king, one Inaros by name. [4] Inaros began by enlisting troops from among the native inhabitants, but later also gathered mercenaries from a variety of countries, and thus built up a very sizable army.[274] He also dispatched ambassadors to the Athenians to discuss the matter of an alliance, promising them that if they would [help] liberate the Egyptians, he would open his kingdom to them and offer them in return benefits far greater than their service to him. [5] The Athenians decided that it would be to their advantage to cut the Persians down to size as far as they could, and to use the Egyptians as a handy bulwark against the random vicissitudes of fortune. They therefore voted to come to the Egyptians' aid with a fleet of 300 triremes.[275] [6] So the Athenians, with great enthusi-

---

were similarly checking on whether the treaty of friendship established with Argos by Xerxes remained in force. It did. It is also very likely that the diplomats of both missions got together and laid the foundations of the Athenian-Argive *entente* achieved a year or two later, after the ostracism of Kimon (Thuc. 1.102.4). Cf. Fornara and Samons 1991, 174–175 (though their date for the Sousa embassies is too late if the Athenian expedition to Cyprus and Egypt began in 462). See 12.4.5–6 with notes 21–22.

[274] Egypt had long been resentful of Persian control, ever since the conquest by Kambyses in 525 (Hdt. 3.1–45 passim). An earlier attempt at secession (486/5) had been put down by Xerxes after the death of Darius (Hdt. 7.1.3, 7.5.1, 7.7.1), and the country was turned over to Xerxes' brother Achaimenes as governor. Achaimenes was still in charge at the time of Inaros' rebellion, which, as Briant correctly (despite Thuc. 1.104.1) emphasizes (2002, 575), was restricted to the Delta and the adjacent western marshes extending into Libya. Here was where Inaros established his base, perhaps in association with Amyrtaios (Thuc. 1.110.2; Ctes. §32.27 Henry; cf. Briant 2002, 575–576). As the son of Psammetichos, Inaros clearly presented himself as a national (Saïte) pharaoh. The uprising was carefully planned over a long period. Xerxes' assassination took place in summer 465. Though the subsequent events leading to Artaxerxes' succession, and his settling in as Great King, must have been common knowledge in Memphis by the summer of 464 at the latest, the actual decision to revolt may only have come in the fall, with winter 464/3 given over to planning and the raising of an initial military force. None of the actual events described in §§1–6 precede the summer of 463. It is then, or more probably in the fall, that we should date the removal of the tribute-gatherers (i.e., the resident Persian administration), together with their (clearly inadequate) military guard. Inaros was then proclaimed pharaoh. However, he must have known that Persia would, eventually, act against him: the winter of 463/2 and the spring of 462, as is clear from Diodorus and Thucydides (1.104), were spent recruiting troops and making diplomatic approaches to various potential foreign allies.

[275] Inaros only appealed to Athens *after* he had established himself (Thuc. 1.104.1, ἄρχων γενόμενος). According to Thucydides (1.104.2), the Athenians already had a flotilla

asm, set about the preparation of this expedition. When Artaxerxes learnt of the Egyptians' rebellion and their preparations for war, he figured that he would need to outstrip the Egyptians in the size of his forces. He therefore at once began to enlist troops from all the satrapies, lay down ships, and busy himself with every other sort of preparation.

Such were the events of this year in Asia and Egypt.

72. In Sicily, no sooner had the Syracusan tyranny been abolished, and every city on the island liberated, than Sicily as a whole began moving very quickly toward an increase in general prosperity.[276] The Sicilian Greeks were

---

200 strong (their own and their allies') en route for Cyprus when the appeal reached them, thus during the 462 campaigning season, and arguably (Plut. *Cim.* 15.1 is ambiguous) once more under Kimon's command. Whatever was then voted, the decision needed to be conveyed to the fleet—this alone would take a month or more—and the revised plans implemented: it is unlikely (see below, note 284) that an Athenian flotilla could have reached Egypt before late fall.

We are nowhere told what so vast a force was supposed to be doing in the eastern Mediterranean. The obvious answer would seem to be protecting the Egyptian and Levantine trade routes against potential Persian aggression (Plut. *Them.* 31.3 would seem to support this): despite Kimon's earlier efforts (11.44.2), Persia had regained Cyprus as a naval base (11.60.5–7). There is good epigraphical evidence (Meiggs-Lewis no. 33) for military action on, or off, Cyprus, as well as in Egypt and Phoenicia, at about this time.

The degree of Athenian involvement in Egypt also presents problems. Ctesias (§32.37–40 Henry), for once a minimalist, puts the size of the Athenian squadron at forty ships only, and this is both realistic and attractive. Thucydides' figure of 200 triremes (1.104.2) would perhaps be reasonable for a fleet patrolling the eastern Mediterranean. Can they have *all* been diverted to Egypt? It seems highly unlikely (and Thuc. 1.104.2 does not preclude this), though the possibility that they were also looking for safe grain-markets (Green 1971, 33; Meiggs 1972, 95) should not be forgotten. As for Diodorus' figure of 300, it is most likely a mere slip for 200, unless he has added the two detached squadrons of forty and fifty to the original total, and then rounded up.

[276] Thrasyboulos, and the Deinomenid tyranny, had fallen in 466/5 (11.68.4–6), after which Syracuse granted the other cities their independence—thus stimulating a marked breakaway in coinage from the Syracusan model—so that autonomy and pluralism became the general watchword (Consolo Langher 1997, 47ff.), in a system of republican government that lasted until the Congress of Gela in 424. Diodorus describes the new system as "democracy," but it was in fact rather (in Thucydides' apt phrase, ὀλιγαρχίαν ἰσόνομον, 3.62.3) a limited or "isonomous" oligarchy, where the aristocracy (Gamoroi) and middle-class hoplites ruled through the council (*Boule*), with the *demos* generally restricted to an assembly (*ekklesia*) that lacked genuine executive power. Aristotle (*Pol.* 1316a32–33) confirms the transition from tyranny to democracy; but he elsewhere (*Pol.* 1304a27–29) claims that in 413, after the defeat of the Sicilian Expedition, Syracuse changed its constitution from a *politeia* to a democracy. These statements are not necessarily incompatible: rule between 466 and 413 was "democratic" only in a very limited elective sense. Cf. Robinson

now at peace, and the land they cultivated was rich. The abundance of their produce soon enabled them to increase their holdings, so that they filled the countryside with servants and cattle and other manifestations of prosperity, accumulating vast revenues, while at the same time spending nothing on the wars to which they had previously grown accustomed. [2] Later, however, they once more plunged into wars and civil strife, for the following reasons.[277] Having overthrown the tyranny of Thrasyboulos, [the Syracusans] convened an assembly. After debate concerning the [implementation of] their own democracy, they voted with one accord to put up a colossal statue of Zeus the Liberator [*Eleutherios*], and, on the day on which they had overthrown the tyrant and freed their native city, to celebrate an annual Festival of Liberation [*Eleutheria*], with sacrifices and high-class games, at which they would slaughter 450 bulls in honor of the gods and use them to furnish meat for the citizens' public feast.[278] [3] All the offices of state they allotted to those who were citizens by birth: the aliens enfranchised in Gelon's time they did not consider for this honor, because they either deemed them unworthy, or else distrusted them as men who, being acclimatized to tyranny and, indeed, as former veterans of the tyrant, might well attempt a revolution. This in fact was precisely what happened: for Gelon had put more than 10,000 foreign mercenaries on the citizen rolls,[279] and at the time of which we are speaking, over 7,000 of them were still left.

---

2000, 193ff. Not until 412, with the reforms of Diokles, was Syracuse to achieve full democracy (13.34.5–35). It is thus not surprising to find the post-Deinomenid government busy with that time-honored oligarchic device, the purging of the citizenship rolls. Cf. Sinatra 1992, 355 with n. 36. Manganaro (1974–75, 12) argues that much of what Diodorus describes here, e.g., the Eleutheria decree and the exclusion of *xenoi* from office, in fact belongs to 466/5, and more properly forms an extension of ch. 68. This is plausible.

[277] Periods of undisturbed peace in Sicily were in fact rare, though Diodorus emphasizes them where he can: cf., e.g., 12.26.2–6 (442/1) and 16.83 (339/8, under Timoleon). As he makes clear here, it was only five years from the abolition of the tyranny before internal strife once more reared its head.

[278] Diodorus' text suggests unanimity on all else, but disagreement over the nature of the proposed democracy: Syracuse's subsequent history makes this very plausible. Pindar refers to the Himeran dedicatee of *Ol.* 12, composed about this time, as "son of Zeus the Liberator." For a comparable annual celebration of freedom, cf. 11.29.1 and note 121 above for that established at Plataia after the allied victory in 479. Haillet (2001, 171 n. 3) points out that the size of the sacrifice (450 bulls) reveals not only the Syracusan wealth of cattle, but also the size of the citizen population.

[279] For this regular practice by *tyrannoi* to shore up their support, see Haillet 2001, 95 n. 1. It is not certain whether the exclusion decree applied to all foreigners admitted by Gelon (and Hieron), or was directed solely against the (very considerable) number of mercenaries now assimilated into the citizen body.

73. These men much resented being thus excluded from the dignity of office, and with one accord revolted from the Syracusans.[280] They then seized two quarters of the city, Achradine and the Island, both of which possessed their own excellent fortifications. [2] The Syracusans, being thus once more plunged into disorder, [nevertheless] held the rest of the city, and the quarter facing toward Epipolai they walled off, thus achieving a high level of security for themselves; for by so doing, they at once easily cut off the rebels' access to the countryside, and very soon had them short of provisions. [3] Now though these foreigners were fewer in number than the Syracusans, in military experience they far exceeded them, so when attacks and isolated skirmishes took place at various points throughout the city, the foreigners invariably came off best in such encounters. However, since they were cut off from the countryside, they lacked supplies and went short of food.[281]

Such were the events during this period in Sicily.

74. When Konon was archon in Athens [462/1], in Rome the consulship was held by Quintus Fabius Vibulanus and Tiberius Aemilius Mamercus.[282] During their term, Artaxerxes, the Great King of Persia, appointed as commanding general for the campaign against the Egyptians Darius' son Achaimenes, who was also his own uncle.[283] He handed over to him a force of over 300,000 troops, inclusive of both cavalry and infantry, with orders to crush the Egyptians utterly. [2] On reaching Egypt, Achaimenes encamped near the

---

[280] Manganaro (1974–75, 9ff.) and Sinatra (1992, 354–355 with nn. 28–32) both emphasize the date—i.e., that civil *stasis* broke out, as Diodorus says, in 463/2. For Gelon's earlier moves to enfranchise these elements, see above, 11.25.1 and 4, with Sinatra 1992, 356–358 and notes. La Genière (2001) attempts to demonstrate that these *xenoi* were all non-Greek (*barbaroi*), but this seems most unlikely.

[281] See Map 3. It should be noted that though the mercenaries held Achradine and Ortygia (which gave them control of both harbors, 11.67.8 with note 258 above), they could be deprived of both food and supplies when cut off on the landward side. This suggests that they had neither ships nor naval expertise. It is, indeed, possible (cf. 11.68.3) that when Thrasyboulos left, he was allowed to take his naval flotilla with him.

[282] The consuls (actually for 467) were Q. Fabius Vibulanus and T. Aemilius Mamercus, as Diodorus correctly reports.

[283] Achaimenes is known to us from Herodotos (3.12.4, 7.7, 236), who confirms his name and relationship to Artaxerxes (he was Darius' son and thus Xerxes' brother), and also gives us the valuable information that he was still in 462/1 holding the governorship of Egypt to which Xerxes had appointed him in 485 (Ctes. §32 calls the appointee of 462/1 Achaimenides and Artaxerxes' brother, thus implying that he was the governor Achaimenes' son: if this is not a simple scribal error, it may well be a case of Ctesias' zeal to "correct," i.e., contradict, Herodotos wherever possible: Bigwood 1976, 7–9).

Nile, and rested his troops after their long march.[284] He then made preparations for battle. The Egyptians, however, who had been assembling an army
from Libya and Egypt itself, were still awaiting the allied contingent from
Athens.[285] [3] The Athenians finally made landfall in Egypt with 200 ships,
and drew up their battle line alongside the Egyptians against the Persians. A
fierce struggle ensued. For a while the Persians had the better of it because of
their superior numbers, but later the Athenians went on the attack and routed
the forces opposed to them, killing a good number. The rest of the barbarians
thereupon turned and fled. [4] Considerable slaughter took place during the
retreat, until finally, after losing the greater part of their army, the Persians
sought refuge in the so-called White Fort. The Athenians, who had secured
victory by their own courageous actions, pursued the barbarians as far as this
stronghold, and had no qualms about laying siege to it.[286]

[5] When Artaxerxes heard about the defeat of his troops, his first thought
was to dispatch some of his friends, with large sums of cash, to Lacedaemon,
with a request that the Lacedaemonians make war on the Athenians, suppos-
ing that thus those Athenians who were winning in Egypt would surely sail
back to Athens to rescue their homeland. [6] The Lacedaemonians, however,
neither took the money nor paid the slightest attention to the Persians' pro-

---

[284] If Achaimenes was resident governor at the time of Inaros' rebellion, it is clear that
he was summoned to Sousa after the initial successful revolt by Inaros, since we find him
(§2) returning to Egypt at the head of an army. This is what we would expect. He reported
the situation to his nephew and was provided with a force to deal with it. This Diodorus
places in the late summer of 462. The size of the force (Ctes. §32 puts it at 400,000) is obviously exaggerated: Hignett's decimating myriad/chiliad theory (1963, 351, cf. note 82
above and elsewhere) may well apply in this case. An expeditionary force of 30,000 would
make excellent sense. But if it had to be assembled, and then march to Egypt from Sousa,
it could hardly be in place by the Nile before late fall 462 at the very earliest, and it is possible that the resting of the troops was in winter quarters.

[285] See above, notes 274–275. The engagements that followed were probably fought, on
balance, at the very end of the 462 campaigning season; but the early spring of 461 cannot
be ruled out.

[286] Ctes. §32 (*FGrH* 688 F 14, p. 465) clearly distinguishes two separate actions: a military engagement on land, during which Achaimenes lost his life, and the naval assault led
by the Athenian Charitimides and his forty triremes, which sank or captured fifty out of
eighty Persian vessels. Herodotos (3.12.4, 7.7) places the land engagement in the Papremis
district, immediately north of Memphis. The Athenian squadron sailed up the Nile (Thuc.
1.104.2), probably by the Kanopic branch, and proceeded to blockade the White Fort,
which was in Memphis itself. (See Map 8, and cf. *BA* 74 C2, E4–5; 75 E1.) "Charitimides"
is otherwise unattested as an Athenian name: Bigwood 1976, 9 with n. 31. This does not
necessarily invalidate it.

posal.[287] So Artaxerxes, giving up any hope of getting aid from them, set about raising a new force of his own. As joint commanders of it he appointed Artabazos and Megabyzos, men highly distinguished for skill and valor, and sent them off to campaign against the Egyptians.[288]

75. When Euthippos was archon in Athens [461/0], the Romans elected as consuls Quintus Servilius and Spurius Postumius Albinus.[289] During their term, in Asia Artabazos and Megabyzos, who had been sent out to prosecute the war against the Egyptians, took the road from Persia with a field army of cavalry and infantry totaling over 300,000. [2] When they reached Cilicia and Phoenicia, they rested their land forces after the march, and sent orders to the Cypriots and Phoenicians and Cilicians to provide ships for them. Three hundred triremes were supplied, which they then manned with their finest fighting marines, providing also arms, missiles, and everything else of use in naval warfare. [3] So these men were busy with their preparations, and spent nearly the whole year training their troops and inuring them all to the business of warfare. [4] Meanwhile the Athenians in Egypt were [still] laying siege to the troops that had fled for refuge to the White Fort near Memphis; but these Persians mounted a vigorous defense, so that the Athenians failed to storm the stronghold, and continued to besiege it for the rest of the year.[290]

---

[287] Thucydides (1.109.1–2) identifies the Persian emissary as Megabazos; he also indicates that the money, or some of it, was accepted, though the Spartans (still preoccupied with the Helot revolt and the aftermath of one or more shattering earthquakes) indeed took no action on Megabazos' proposal. Nevertheless, it is significant that in the spring or summer of 461, Persian understanding was that they well might.

[288] Artabazos is probably the same general whom we found earlier (11.44.3) acting as contact between Xerxes and Pausanias, and, like Megabazos, handing out bribes for the corruption of Greek officials. Megabyzos (more correctly Megabyxos) was the son of Zopyros, the heroic (and self-mutilated) captor of Babylon (Hdt. 3.153–160), and grandson of a still more famous Megabyxos, one of the original Seven Conspirators (Hdt. 3.70) who removed Smerdis and put Darius I on the throne of Persia. He himself had been one of Xerxes' top commanders in 480 (Hdt. 7.82, 121). Cf. below, 12.3.2 and note 11.

[289] The consuls (actually for 466) were Q. Servilius Priscus and Sp. Postumius Albus Regillensis (Broughton 1951, 33).

[290] Ctesias (§33) estimates this relief force at 200,000 troops and 300 ships. If Artabazos and Megabyzos marched in July 461, the one to Phoenicia, the other to Cilicia, they will not have reached these points before September. They then rested their troops and sent out orders commandeering ships. It would be surprising if the ships arrived before the early spring of 460. The remainder of 461/0 (§3) was taken up with training, as Diodorus makes clear. The siege of the White Fort in Memphis was similarly still continuing in the summer of 460.

76. In Sicily, the Syracusans were still fighting their rebellious foreign [mercenaries]. They made continual assaults on both Achradine and the Island, and also defeated the rebels in a sea battle, but on land proved unable to dislodge them from the city because of the excellent fortifications protecting these two strongholds. [2] Later, however, when an open engagement took place outside the city—in which both sides fought vigorously, and both suffered not a few casualties—final victory went to the Syracusans. After the battle they bestowed the crown of valor on the picked force of 600 men who were responsible for the victory, and presented each one of them with a *mina* of silver.[291] [3] Simultaneously with these events, Ducetius, the native Sicel leader,[292] who bore a grudge against the inhabitants of Katana for robbing the Sicels of their land, led a force against them. Now it happened that the Syracusans had also mounted an expedition against Katana; so they and Sicels shared out the land between them in allotments, and together made war on those settlers who had been sent out by Hieron as ruler [of Syracuse]. The Katanians fought back, but were defeated in a series of battles and driven out of Katana, subsequently taking possession of what is now Aitna, but formerly was known as Inessa. Thus after many years, the original inhabitants of Katana recovered their native city.[293]

---

[291] This civil war between old and new citizens included those who had been exiled (and dispossessed of their property) by the Deinomenids—at the expense of their new supporters—and were now determined to reclaim what they had lost; it also extended to cities other than Syracuse (e.g., Gela and Akragas, below, §4). The old landed gentry resisted *any* radical distribution of land: they were no more eager to see it go to returning middle-class exiles (with whom their alliance in 461 was temporary and adventitious only) than to ex-mercenary squatters. On Ortygia, where the oldest families had been long established, this problem was particularly acute. Cf. Consolo Langher 1997, 52–56. The suspicion also arises that the "picked force of 600 men" may well have been mercenaries themselves, who were bribed to change sides: one *mina* = 100 drachmas, i.e., one-sixtieth of a talent, and ten talents was an extraordinarily heavy outlay, bearing in mind the fact that even the best mercenaries seldom asked more than two or three drachmas per diem.

[292] This is the first mention of the remarkable Sicel nationalist for whom Diodorus is our sole ancient source, and whose name was still being invoked in Sicily in the late 1940s in connection with his modern epigonos Salvatore Giuliano (cf. Gavin Maxwell, *God Protect Me from My Friends*, rev. ed. [London, 1972]). As Sinatra (1992, 360) points out, his joint action with Syracuse was a natural consequence of the suppression of the mercenaries and their supporters.

[293] See 11.49.1–2 with note 186 above. Hieron had expelled the Katanians and relocated them in Leontinoi; he renamed Katana Aitna, and transferred there 10,000 new colonists, half from Syracuse and half from the Peloponnese, giving them land-holdings not only in the city but through a wide swathe of the surrounding countryside (Manganaro 1974–75,

[4] After these events, [other] groups who had been expropriated from their own cities during Hieron's reign, finding themselves now with support in the struggle, returned to their several homelands and drove out those who had unjustly seized the property of others. Among them were the inhabitants of Gela, Akragas, and Himera.[294] [5] In a similar manner, the Rhegians and Zanklians together expelled the sons of Anaxilas who were then ruling them, and liberated their native cities.[295] Somewhat later the Geloans, who had been the original settlers of Kamarina,[296] divided up that city's territory into allotments. Virtually all the cities, in their eagerness to put an end to these wars, with one accord agreed to come to terms with their resident bodies of foreign [mercenaries].[297] They then took back the exiles and returned the cities to their original citizens. All those foreigners who, at the behest of former tyrannical rulers, had been left in possession of cities not their own, they gave leave

---

11). Hence the Sicel resentment on which Ducetius capitalized. The Syracusan attack on Katana/Aitna in 461 was part of the general determination to evict Deinomenid beneficiaries: clearly the original inhabitants of the city joined in the attack en masse. The Katanians (more properly the Aitnaean settlers) thus driven out settled at Inessa, about ten miles away on the rocky foothills of Etna, and (confusingly for modern research) renamed that Aitna too. Cf. Strab. 6.2.3, C.268; Haillet 2001, 173 n. 2; Asheri in *CAH* v, 131.

[294] Forcible mass evictions and transferences of populations were the special hallmark of the early fifth-century Sicilian *tyrannoi*. Gelon destroyed Kamarina and repopulated it with Geloans; the inhabitants of Kamarina (c. 485) and over half the population of Gela—primarily the artisan class—he shifted to Syracuse (Philistos *FGrH* 556 F17; Hdt. 7.155–156; Thuc. 6.5.3). As Herodotos (7.156.3) makes very clear, Gelon's prime motivation in much of this was political and class-based: he acted "in the belief that the *demos* was a thankless lot to live with" (νομίσας δῆμον εἶναι συνοίκημα ἀχαριώτατον).

[295] Cf. above, 11.48.1–2 with note 183, 11.66.1–3 with notes 249–250. The sons of Anaxilas had only taken over from their guardian Mikythos in 467/6. Justin (4.3.1–3) reports violent internal factionalism in Rhegion at the time, which probably explains why it, and Zankle, were the last Greek Sicilian cities to break loose from tyrannical overlordship (Haillet 2001, 174 n. 4).

[296] Cf. Timaios (*FGrH* 566 F19a–b = schol. Pind. *Ol.* 5.19), who puts the foundation by Gela in Ol. 42 (612/608). Against this, Thucydides (6.5.3) gives the founder as Syracuse and the date as 599/8 (which suggests that Diodorus may have been using Timaios here). However, since Thucydides agrees that Kamarina was refounded at least twice, it is possible to reconcile the two accounts if we concede (which Thucydidean fundamentalists do not) that he may have missed the earliest settlement: Timaios was, after all, a Sicilian himself. Pearson (1987, 48) argues, flatly but unconvincingly, that either "the scholiast on Pindar must be wrong or the text corrupt in giving Timaeus' date for this event as the forty-second Olympiad."

[297] We get a glimpse of some of these conflicts in a fragmentary papyrus (P.Oxy. 665 = *FGrH* 577 F, further edited and emended by Heichelheim 1955, 88ff.) involving Akragas, Gela, and Kamarina. Cf. Manganaro 1974–75, 13–14 with nn. 11–12.

to remove all their personal property, and to settle in Messenia.[298] [6] Thus the civil strife and anarchy that had plagued the Sicilian cities were brought to a close; and the cities themselves, after extirpating such alien forms of government as had been introduced, almost all shared out their separate territories in the shape of allotments for the entire citizen body.[299]

77. When Phrasikleides was archon in Athens [460/59], the 80th Olympiad was held, in which the *stadion* was won by Toryllas of Thessaly, and the Romans elected as consuls Quintus Fabius and Titus Quinctius Capitolinus.[300] During their term, in Asia the Persian generals who had marched across country to Cilicia fitted out 300 ships, equipping them fully for armed combat. They then took their land force and advanced through Syria and Phoenicia, and thus, with the fleet hugging the coast alongside the army, reached Memphis in Egypt.[301] [2] Their first act was to break the siege of the

---

[298] This arrangement seems not to have aroused comment, but it is certainly striking, since it came when Messenia was still in revolt against Sparta; the natural assumption is that the deportees, almost all experienced mercenaries, were welcomed by Sparta as a useful instrument in helping to put down the insurrection, and were granted land tenure in return for their services, acting thereafter as, among other things, rural slave-masters.

[299] Cf. Diodorus' similar remarks (16.83) on the later (339/8) removal of tyrants by Timoleon. The general extirpation of authoritarian rule throughout Greek Sicily is hinted at by commemorative issues and symbolic changes in the currency of the various cities: cf. Consolo Langher 1997, 53–56 with pls. ix–xxiv; Haillet 2001, 174–175 n. 1. As we have seen (above, §2), a less-than-radical political democratization followed. Aristotle (*Pol.* 5.3.6, 1304a27–29) remarked that after Syracuse's victory over Athens in 413, the *demos,* having been responsible for that victory, "changed from a commonwealth to a democracy" (ἐκ πολιτείας εἰς δημοκρατίαν μετέβαλεν): there was a considerable gray area as to what really constituted democracy. Thucydides (7.55.2), like Diodorus, thought the Syracusan government against which the Athenians fought was, in fact, a democracy comparable to theirs. We can see its oligarchical bias; but then, that was not something of which Thucydides disapproved (8.97). Manganaro (1974–75, 12) argues that much of what Diodorus describes here had been going on since 463/2.

[300] The consuls (actually for 465) were Q. Fabius Vibulanus and T. Quinctius Capitolinus Barbatus (Broughton 1951, 33).

[301] The chronology is uncertain here. If the Persians only began fitting out their large fleet (Ctes. §33 confirms the number of ships) in Cilicia by late summer 461, they are unlikely to have moved until the early spring of 460, and the amphibious advance from there down the eastern Mediterranean coast can hardly have reached Egypt, at the most optimistic estimate, until June of that year. How their arrival can have come as a surprise is hard to see. Their approach will have been from the east, by Pelousion (see Map 8, and cf. *BA* 74 H2). Thucydides (1.109.3–4) speaks *only* of an overland march, and says nothing of the large Persian fleet. He also agrees with Ctesias (§33) in reporting, first, a major land

White Fort, [their arrival] having dumbfounded the Egyptians and Athenians; subsequently, however, they implemented a more cautious policy, refusing any head-on encounters, and doing their utmost to end the war by means of various stratagems.[302] Therefore, since the Athenian fleet was moored at

---

battle with "the Egyptians and their allies," which he carefully distinguishes from the subsequent assault on the Greeks besieging Memphis.

Inaros and the survivors of this defeat, according to Ctesias, fled to an Egyptian "stronghold" (πόλις ἰσχυρά) called Byblos. There is no record of such a town, and the name (which means "papyrus") suggests that, if the report is true, what Inaros did was to join Amyrtaios in the impregnable western marshes. (It is not necessary to assume—as, e.g., Bigwood [1976, 9–10, cf. 23–25] does—that Inaros joined the Athenians at Prosopitis.) The Persians will then have marched westward to Memphis along the line of the Pelousiac branch of the Nile, a distance of about 140 miles. They will certainly have been accompanied by a small part of the fleet. Apart from supply vessels, some naval *appui* will have been needed to dislodge the besiegers of the White Fort. At the same time, as the course of events makes very clear, they were forced, ultimately, to deal with the Greek squadron *from the land,* and we should never forget (Holladay 1989, 176, with earlier bibliography) that "the Nile is too narrow for a full fleet action by triremes."

[302] This entire passage suggests fairly drastic compression by Diodorus for the last part of the Egyptian expedition. It also implies that the Persians had real problems dealing with the Greek force. Ctesias (§33, 40b11–12) reports the death in action of the Athenian naval commander Charitimides: since at the time of the final surrender there was no fighting, it seems likely that he lost his life when the Athenians were forced to abandon their blockade of the White Fort. If we allow the rest of the 459 campaigning season for the various activities to which Diodorus alludes, we can place the beginning of the Prosopitis siege around October, and its end (eighteen months later, Thuc. 1.109.4) in April or May 457. Allow two months for the canal-digging and diversion of the Nile, and we have June 457 (when the Nile would be at its lowest ebb) for the final reduction of the Greek expeditionary force. This time scheme covers six campaigning seasons, agreeing with Thucydides' estimate (1.110.1, ἓξ ἔτη πολεμήσαντα). Interestingly, this is the date offered (though without explanation) by Appelbaum (1979, 31). It is also the schema presented by Reuss (1896b, 653), working solely from the ancient evidence.

The usual modern dating of the Egyptian expedition (460–454), however, now hallowed by long acceptance, depends not on evidence, but on theory: the interrelated assumptions that (a) Thucydides narrates all events of the Pentekontaetia in strict chronological order, and (b) the Delian League treasury was transferred from Delos to Athens in 454—the same year (calculating six years from 460) as the disaster in Egypt—on the grounds that this is the year when the first Athenian tribute-list, with its tithes (ἀπαρχαί) to Athena, was set up. (This claim was originally argued in *ATL* 3:160–162, renewed, at great and elaborate length, by Buonocore [1980, 51–127], and maintained as an article of faith by D. M. Lewis [in *CAH* v, 499–505]; cf. e.g., Meiggs [1972, 109]; Raubitschek [1966, 37], and Samons [2000, 100–102], who argues that it would have taken twenty-two or twenty-three years from 477 at 460 talents per annum [i.e., to 454!] to accumulate the 9,700 talents mentioned by Thucydides [2.13.2] as having been the maximum held.) Neither of these claims is ultimately compelling. On the first, see, e.g., Walker 1957, 27–38; Badian 1993, 6, 78ff., 106; and Parker 1993, 129–130. Parker remarks, sensibly: "In point of

the island known as Prosopitis, they dug canals to divert the river that flowed past both sides of this island, thus making the island an island no longer. [3] When the ships were in this way suddenly stranded on dry land, the Egyptians panicked, abandoned the Athenians, and cut a deal with the Persians.[303] The Athenians, now bereft of allies and seeing that their ships had been rendered useless, set fire to them to stop their falling into the hands of the enemy. They then, no whit perturbed by the serious situation they were in, encouraged one another to do nothing unworthy of their triumphant past struggles. [4] So, their fighting spirit surpassing in valiance those who died for Hellas at Thermopylai, they stood there prepared to fight it out to the death with the enemy. However, Artabazos and Megabyzos, the Persian generals, observing the enemy's courageous determination, and reckoning that they could not wipe out men such as these without losing a vast number of their own, made a truce with the Athenians, which would allow them to pull out of Egypt

---

fact Thucydides nowhere says or implies that he will recount all the events of the Fifty Years in an absolute chronological order. It is very difficult to imagine why he would (if indeed he could) have"—except, of course, to give modern scholars a tidy yardstick. As regards the second claim, there is no reason why transfer of the treasury (on which see note 240 above) should not have long preceded the arrangement initiated in 454/3; and such evidence as there is (Just. 3.6.1–4 with D.S. 12.38.2, and above, II.70.1–5 with note 270) points clearly to late 463/2 or early 462/1. Samon's argument is vitiated by several facts: (a) Thucydides (2.13.2) cites annual tribute as 600 talents, and (b) makes clear that the treasury had various other sources of income; while (c) neither in Thucydides nor in Diodorus is there any clear indication of the actual date of the transfer. For the sums involved, see note 240 above. The chronology here adopted owes a good deal to Robertson (1980, 112–119). An almost identical dating scheme (462–456 B.C.E.) is advanced by Paršikov (1970) on very similar grounds, and hinted at by Yardley and Develin (1994, 50 n. 10).

[303] Prosopitis was probably located at least sixty miles north of Memphis—considerably further if the windings of the Kanopic branch of the Nile, up which the Athenian squadron sailed, are taken into account—in the Prosopitean nome: see Map 8, and cf. BA 74 D4. Ctesias (§34) claims that the Greeks, as well as Inaros and his men, came to terms with Megabyzos, who acted thus on the grounds that "Byblos," i.e., probably the western marshes (either the area known as Sketis, due west of the Prosopitean nome, or the larger region southwest of Memphis and north of the "Libyan Mount," cf. BA 74 C-D 4, 75 C-D 2), where they took refuge, was difficult of access, and a mopping-up operation would result in heavy losses among his own troops. Thucydides (1.109.4) states that Megabyzos "crossed on foot and took the island," but does not mention a prior breakout. Diodorus' suspect rhetoric about Thermopylai—whether his own or his source's—does seem designed to mask some kind of less than heroic deal with the Persians, whether struck at Prosopitis or from the vantage-point of the marshes. Inaros was later (after five years, says Ctesias [§36]) betrayed and impaled (Thuc. 1.110.3). Bigwood (1976, 19–21) argues that Ctesias is biased in favor of Megabyzos, which is possible, but also that his account of the expedition in general is a tissue of lies, duplications, and anachronisms, and here what evidence there is does not bear her out.

without let or hindrance. [5] So the Athenians, having secured their safety by virtue of their own fighting spirit, departed from Egypt, and marching by way of Libya and Cyrene finally, against all expectation, came safely home.[304]

[6] Simultaneously with these events, in Athens,[305] Ephialtes son of Sophonides—a demagogue who had sharpened public hostility to the Areopagite Council—persuaded the *demos* to vote for a reduction in the council's powers, thus annulling many famous ancestral traditions.[306] He did not, however, escape unscathed after undertaking such lawless actions, but was assassinated one night, it never being clear afterward just how his death came about.[307]

78. When this year had run its course, in Athens the archon was Philokles [459/8], while in Rome, Aulus Postumius †Regulus† and Spurius Furius †Mediolanus† succeeded to the consulship.[308] During their term, war broke out between Athens and an alliance of Corinth and Epidauros: the Athenians marched against the latter and, after a sharp engagement, were victorious. [2] They then with a large fleet put in at a port called Halieis, disembarked in the Peloponnese, and killed not a few of the enemy. But the Peloponnesians rallied, assembled a sizable force, and joined battle with the Athenians off the

---

[304] On the vexed question of Athenian losses during this campaign, see Appendix B.

[305] We have a firm date for Ephialtes' stripping the Areopagos of its major powers: 462/1, in the archonship of Konon (Arist. *Ath. Pol.* 25.1–2, where this event is also calculated as having taken place seventeen years after the Persian Wars). Diodorus has probably (after juxtaposing it with a sequence in which, as we have seen, several years were compressed) entered this item in the year of Ephialtes' recorded death.

[306] Our sources agree in treating this move as a radical democratic attack, inspired by Perikles and the naval imperialists, on that Athenian conservatism, strongly defended by Kimon, of which the ancient Areopagos Council was a leading symbol: see Arist. *Ath. Pol.* 25, 27.1, 35.2; Plut. *Per.* 7.5–6, 9.3–4, *Mor.* 812d, *Cim.* 10.7–8, 15.1–2. The only serious power left to the Areopagos was jurisdiction in certain murder trials: Dem. 23, §§22, 66; Philochoros *FGrH* 328 F 64b. The ostracism of Kimon (462/1) and the removal of the Delian League treasury to Athens at about the same time (cf. notes 240 and 302 above) can be seen as part and parcel of the same political agenda.

[307] For Ephialtes' assassination, see Arist. *Ath. Pol.* 25.4, Plut. *Per.* 10.6–7. The actual killer was Aristodikos of Tanagra, but our sources indicate that he was simply a hired hitman. The late-fifth-century orator Antiphon (5.68) stated that those responsible had never been identified, but it seems a safe bet to look for them among Athens' ultra-conservatives, if not in the Areopagos itself.

[308] The consuls (actually for 464) were A. Postumius Regillensis and Sp. Furius Medullinus Fusus (Broughton 1951, 34). On the reasons for these corruptions, see 11.48.1 and note 181 above.

[island] called Kekryphaleia. Here once more the Athenians were victorious.[309] [3] After these successes, seeing that the Aiginetans not only had a high opinion of themselves because of their past achievements, but also were hostile to Athens, [the Athenians] determined to subjugate them by force, [4] and therefore sent out a strong fleet against them. The Aiginetans, who had great experience in (and a great reputation for) fighting at sea, were not disturbed by the Athenians' superiority [in numbers]. Since they possessed a reasonable number of triremes, and had besides laid down some new ones, they met the Athenians in a naval engagement, but were crushingly defeated, with the loss of seventy vessels. Their confidence broken by the magnitude of this disaster, they were forced to join Athens' league, and pay tribute. This was accomplished for the Athenians by their general Leokrates, who spent nine months all told fighting the Aiginetans.[310]

[5] Simultaneously with these events, in Sicily Ducetius, the king of the Sicels, scion of a famous family and at the time enjoying considerable influence, founded the city of Menaenum, and shared out the territory around it

---

[309] These encounters marked the beginning of the so-called First Peloponnesian War, on which see Meiggs 1972, ch. 6, 93ff. Athens had recently broken off its alliance with Sparta (thus repudiating Kimon's pro-Laconian policy) and made treaties with Thessaly and Sparta's Peloponnesian archrival, Argos (Thuc. 1.102.4, 2.22.3; Paus. 1.29.9, 4.24.7). A Spartan attack on Argos had been repulsed at Oinoë (Paus. 12.15.1, 10.10.4; Meiggs 1972, 96), and the Spartans had apparently seized Halieis (Hdt. 7.137.2). Thucydides (1.105.1) does not mention the first of Diodorus' battles, and reports that the Athenians lost at Halieis (which Diodorus does not specifically deny). Halieis, modern Porto Cheli, has a fine harbor; it offered convenient access to Argos, and made a useful base for raids. Kekryphaleia (modern Angistri) is a small island west of Aigina. The mention of Halieis in Meiggs-Lewis (no. 33), which specifically places all of its casualties within the same archon-year, combined with this passage, places the year as 459/8. The emphasis on the size of Athens' naval forces reinforces the assumption that the losses in Egypt cannot have been crippling.

[310] Cf. above, II.70.2–3 with note 269: whether Athens and Aigina had actually been at war since 464/3 is uncertain, but there can be no doubt about the running hostility. This campaign is reported by Thucydides (1.105.2–4, 108.4) in very similar terms (also confirming the role of Leokrates), but raising a tricky point of chronology. He states that after the naval defeat, Leokrates laid siege to the city. He also places Aigina's final surrender *after* the battles of Tanagra and Oinophyta, dated by Diodorus (11.81–83.1) in 457/6. If we accept the nine-month siege (as Badian 1993, 213, argues), then we have to assume that Diodorus (as so often) has concluded a narrative under one archon-year that should more properly have been continued in the next. If the actual siege was not enforced until, say, October 458 (Badian 1993, 213), then we can posit a final surrender in July or August of 457, very shortly after Tanagra and Oinophyta. As always, the break of the archon-year in the middle of the campaigning season can (and in antiquity often did) cause confusion.

between the settlers. He also campaigned against the notable city of Morgantina and reduced it, thus winning high renown among his Sicel fellow-countrymen.[311]

79. When the year drew to a close, in Athens †Bion† was archon [458/7], while in Rome Publius Servilius †Structus† and Lucius Aebutius †Albas† succeeded to the consulship.[312] During their term, a dispute arose between Corinth and Megara over some frontier land, and the two cities went to war. [2] To begin with they kept raiding each other's territories and skirmishing in small groups; but as their differences grew more acute, the Megarians, who continually got the worst of it and as a result were now afraid of the Corinthians, contracted an alliance with Athens.[313] [3] This made the cities once

---

[311] Ducetius is described as "king" (βασιλεύς) of the Sicels only here: elsewhere (11.76.3, 88.6, 91.1) he is referred to simply as the "leader" or "commander" of a union or federation (*synteleia, συντέλεια*) of Sicel communities (Wentker 1956, 54–55). But he had learned a lot from the Deinomenid and other Sicilian *tyrannoi;* his political methods and concepts, though aimed at the creation of a powerful Sicel *tiers état,* were thoroughly Hellenized, as his establishment of Menaenum makes clear (Menai, modern Mineo: a dramatic description of the lofty site, based on autopsy, in Freeman 1891, 362–365; Adamasteanu 1962, 174–181; Sjöqvist 1973, 52; Manganaro 1974–75, 16). His central power-base lay in the wild mountain region northwest of Syracuse that the *tyrannoi* had never subjugated (see Map 3, and cf. *BA* E-F 3). His earlier collaboration with Syracuse (11.76.3 with notes 292–293 above) had been one of convenience only; his ruthless and violent destruction of Morgantina was so thorough that it took that city a century and a half to recover (Sjöqvist 1973, 51). It is almost certain that many of the dismissed mercenaries (some of whom were Sicels) found their way into his service. Morgantina's obstinate resistance shows how the individualism of autonomous cities in Sicily could override Ducetius' goal of a federated ethnic *synteleia* (Consolo Langher 1997, 65). Hybla, too, stood out against him (11.88.6). On Ducetius in general, Freeman 1891, 361–387, is still well worth reading.

[312] The archon's name was Habron [Ἄβρων], established by *IG* ii² 2318.52 (ἐπὶ Ἀβρωενος). It is easy to see how, if the initial Ἀ- were lost or misaligned, -βρων would almost inevitably be corrected to the more common Βίων. The consuls (actually for 463) were P. Servilius Priscus and L. Aebutius Helva (Broughton 1951, 34). Structus was a cognomen in the *gens Servilia.*

[313] Cf. Thucydides (1.103.4): he places the dispute in the context of the end of the ten-year struggle of Sparta against the Messenians, thus incidentally increasing support for 458/7 as the date for that, and the resultant freeing up of Spartan troops for other activities. This quarrel about boundaries makes more sense when we realize that Megara's two ports of Nisaia (on the Saronic Gulf) and Pegai offered the only alternative to Corinth's at Kenchreai and Lechaion for a controlled passage between the Saronic and Corinthian gulfs (see Map 1, cf. *BA* 58 D-E 1), and that (as Thucydides goes on to tell us) Athens baited its offer of alliance to Megara with the fortification of both ports, and the construction of Long Walls from Nisaia to Megara (cf. Green 1971, 32–33). So long as this alliance existed, Athens could bypass Corinth, patrol the Gulf of Corinth, and keep its vital trade-route to

more of equal strength for the contest; and so when the Corinthians, accompanied by some other Peloponnesians, marched into the Megarid[314] with a strong force, the Athenians sent a task force to the aid of the Megarians, led by Myronides, a man much admired for his valor.[315] A long, hard-fought battle took place, in which each side matched the other in deeds of bravery, but in the end the Athenians triumphed, and slew many of the enemy. [4] A few days later another fierce battle took place at the place called Kimolia, where once again the Athenians were victorious.[316]

---

Sicily open without serious opposition from the Peloponnesian bloc. Corinth's resultant hostility to Athens, duly noted by Thucydides (1.103.4), is hardly surprising. The commercial and the military threats together were enough to alarm a far less contentious city-state than Corinth.

[314] Since the Megarid is the final theater of war included in the casualty list of 459/8 (see below, App. B, ad fin.), it follows that the initial engagement there was in May or June of 458; but since the campaign almost certainly extended into 458/7 (i.e., until July or August), it may well be that casualties for the whole season were included under the same rubric. Thucydides (1.105.3–4) reports that (a) the Corinthians acted in the belief that Athens would be unable to aid Megara because so many of its men were away at Aigina and in Egypt, and (b) Myronides was in command of a scratch force consisting of "the oldest and youngest," i.e., those over fifty and under twenty, Athens' Home Guard (this detail is rhetorically embroidered by Lysias in his *Funeral Oration*, 2.48–53). Myronides himself, son of Kallias (II.81.4), had been a young ambassador and commander in 479 (Plut. *Cim.* 10.8, 20.1), and was thus now in his early sixties. His activities in the next two years (458–456 B.C.E.) show him to have been a first-class general (cf. II.83.4 and note 336 below). Aristophanes (*Lys.* 801, *Eccl.* 301) praises him for his old-fashioned virtues.

[315] The current belief (see, e.g., Haillet 2001, 180 n. 1; *OCD* 1016–1017; *DNP* 8:599) that the Myronides of the Persian Wars is not the one of Tanagra and Oinophyta derives from a fragment of Eupolis' *Demes* (412: Page *SP3*, 202–217) where, it is argued, he is shown as *recently dead,* thus precluding the identification on chronological grounds. But (a) the text (98) reads *-yronides,* which 52 shows to be *Pyronides;* and (b) even if this *is* Myronides (brought back from the dead along with other worthies to give good advice), he appears in the company of Aristeides (another emendation, but a likely one), the contemporary of Themistokles. There is thus no evidence whatsoever for his "recent death," and no need to doubt that this (very successful) reserve general of 458–456 was in roughly the same age-bracket as the veterans under his command. Cf. *PA* 2.109 (no. 10509).

[316] At the close of this sentence, the MSS first repeat the phrase with which §3 ends ("and slew many of the enemy," καὶ πολλοὺς ἀνεῖλον τῶν πολεμίων), and then that with which §4 begins ("A few days later another fierce battle took place," μετὰ δ' ὀλίγας ἡμέρας πάλιν γενομένης ἰσχυρᾶς μάχης), a splendid example of careless, or drunken, dittography. Like Oldfather (1946, 330–331 with n. 1), I excise the doublet *in toto.* Haillet (2001) and Vogel (1890) confuse matters by leaving parts in.

The exact location of Kimolia is unknown, but it must have been somewhere along the disputed frontier territory between Corinth and Megara. Comparison with Thuc. 1.105.6–106 suggests that this second engagement was in fact that described—in unusually full de-

The Phokians went to war with the Dorians, these being the ancestors of the Lacedaemonians, who dwell in the three cities of Kytinion, Boion, and Erineon, situated below the hill [*sic*] known as Parnassos. [5] To begin with they overcame the Dorians by force and occupied their cities; but subsequently the Lacedaemonians, because of their kinship, sent out Nikomedes son of Kleomenes to help the Dorians, with 1,500 Lacedaemonians and 10,000 men from other parts of the Peloponnese.[317] [6] Nikomedes, then, the guardian of King Pleistoanax, who was still a child, brought this large force to the Dorians' aid and, after thrashing the Phokians and recovering the cities, made peace [winter 458/7] between the warring parties.[318]

80. When the Athenians learned that the Lacedaemonians had wound up the war against the Phokians and were about to return home, they decided to strike at them while they were on the march [early spring 457].[319] They there-

---

tail—by Thucydides as having been fought over the battle trophies of the first, and that Kimolia (possibly in the foothills of the Geranian mountains?) was the site of both.

[317] The Messenian War had almost certainly concluded in the fall of 458; this released Spartan and allied troops (cf. Just. 3.6.8) to deal with what was seen as the serious threat posed by the Athenians' fortification of the Isthmus crossing in the Megarid, as well as the beginning of the Long Walls linking the city with Athens' port of Piraeus (Thuc. 1.107.1, 3–4), thus creating a virtually impregnable bastion. The large size of the force suggests that the Spartans may have anticipated the possibility of Athens and Megara blocking their line of retreat.

[318] Cf. Thuc. 1.107.2 (with which Diodorus is in substantial agreement), Plut. *Cim.* 17.3. The three towns mentioned here (Diodorus' text is corrected from that of Thucydides) were located in the northern foothills of Parnassos, about 15 miles from Delphi (see Map 1, and cf. *BA* 55 C3). Plutarch claims that the Lacedaemonians freed Delphi itself from the Phokians at the same time, but this is unlikely, and sounds like a slip made by Diodorus or his source writing with the later Third Sacred War of 356–347 in mind, when the Phokians notoriously did occupy—and despoil—Delphi. Thucydides confirms the efficacy of the kinship claim: was it so striking (Hornblower 1991, 168) that such claims still had validity in the mid-fifth century? Nikomedes is reported by Thucydides as son of Kleombrotos, not of Kleomenes, but Diodorus could be right (Lewis 1952, 140). Pleistoanax was the eldest son of Pausanias, the victor of Plataia, and succeeded as a minor (in the Agiad line) in 458, on the death, without issue, of Pleistarchos, son of the famous Leonidas who died at Thermopylai in 480. Kleombrotos, who himself assumed the regency for Pleistarchos on the death of Leonidas, was the full brother of Leonidas and half-brother to Kleomenes: thus whichever of the two was Nikomedes' father, Nikomedes would still be Pleistoanax's uncle. The question remains (Andrewes 1985, ap. White 1964, 140 n. 3): Why was it Nikomedes rather than the experienced Eurypontid king Archidamos who commanded? Andrewes suggests that it may have been because Archidamos was dealing with the final winding-up of the Messenian campaign, and this had priority.

[319] Cf. Thuc. 1.107.4–6, and see note 313 above for the likelihood of more Spartan troops being available after the termination of the Messenian Revolt. Thucydides suggests,

fore set out [at once], taking Argive and Thessalian contingents with them, and occupied the passes about Mt. Geraneia, intending to fall upon [the Lacedaemonians] with fifty ships and 14,000 men.[320] [2] But the Lacedaemonians, being forewarned of the Athenians' intentions, changed their route, marching to Tanagra in Boiotia.[321] The Athenians also made their way to Boiotia, and the two sides confronted each other in a fierce battle. Even though during the fighting the Thessalians defected to the Lacedaemonians, the Athenians and the Argives battled on no less determinedly, and not a few fell on both sides before darkness broke off the engagement.[322] [3] Later, when a large supply convoy was being brought to the Athenians from Attica, the Thessalians decided to attack it, taking their evening meal early and intercepting the convoy at night. [4] The Athenian guards on the convoy thought the Thessalians were still on their side and therefore received them as friends, so that numerous skirmishes, of various kinds, took place over the supplies. To begin with, the Thessalians, being welcomed by the enemy out of ignorance, proceeded to slay anyone they encountered, and being a disciplined group tangling with men thrown into complete confusion, inflicted heavy casualties. [5] However, when the Athenians in camp learned of the Thessalian

---

as an additional motive—both for this expedition and for the Spartan decision to wait in Boiotia—the threat of a pro-Spartan secret plot in Athens, aimed at "putting a stop to democracy and the building of the Long Walls" (ἐλπίσαντες δῆμόν τε καταπαύσειν καὶ τὰ μακρὰ τείχη οἰκοδομούμενα, 1.107.4). The first objective could mean no more than the ousting of the Periklean radicals and the return of Kimonian conservatism. The second was also tied to the Periklean naval program (and Sparta had similarly objected to the rebuilding of Athens' city-walls after the Persian Wars, cf. 11.39–40 with note 161 above and sources there cited). Whether the rumor was true or not, such anti-radical sentiments clearly existed, and were in great part responsible both for Kimon's ostracism in 462/1 (Plut. *Cim.* 17.2–4, *Per.* 9.4, 10.1–3; Nep. *Cim.* 3.1; Plat. *Gorg.* 516d) and for his summary rejection when, still exiled, he tried to join his tribe and fight at Tanagra (see below).

[320] Thucydides (1.107.5) mentions neither the ships—which at this time would have had to sail round the Peloponnese to take up their station, probably at Naupaktos (§3, cf. Buck 1970, 218 n. 16)—nor the occupation of the Geranian passes at the Megara-Corinth frontier (see Map 1, cf. *BA* 58 D-E 1–2). The Argives were 1,000 in number (Thuc. 1.107.5), and the epitaph of their dead survives (Meiggs-Lewis no. 35). Cf. Paus. 1.29.7, 5.10.4.

[321] See Map 1, and cf. *BA* 55 C-F 3–4. It is striking that Tanagra lies nearly 20 miles *east* of Thebes. Why, one wonders, did the Spartan force take up position there rather than in the Theban plain, north of the Asopos? We know (but not from either Diodorus or Thucydides) that Boiotians fought at Tanagra (Plat. *Alcib. I* 112c; Paus. 1.29.90), and the Spartans (11.81.3) were going out of their way to win Theban support.

[322] Cf. Thuc. 1.108.1, Paus. 1.29.7. Pausanias reports that an Argive incipient victory was nullified by the onset of night and subsequent betrayal by the Thessalians (which Thucydides confirms). The heaviness of the losses is suggested by Meiggs-Lewis no. 35, where Argive casualties are in the neighborhood of 400, i.e., a staggering 40%.

attack, they charged up at the double, routed the Thessalians straight off, and slaughtered a large number of them. [6] The Lacedaemonians, in battle array, now came to the rescue of the Thessalians, so that a pitched battle ensued between all the various forces, with such fierce rivalry that on both sides the death toll was heavy. The fight finally ended in a draw, with both the Lacedaemonians and the Athenians claiming victory. However, since night then intervened with the victory still in dispute, they exchanged embassies[323] and concluded a four months' truce.[324]

81. When this year had run its course, in Athens Mnesitheides became archon [457/6], while in Rome the consuls elected were Lucius Lucretius and Titus Veturius Cicurinus.[325] During their term the Thebans, humiliated because of the alliance they had struck up with Xerxes,[326] were looking for some way by which they could recover their ancient influence and prestige. [2] Thus, since the Boiotians generally now despised the Thebans and no longer paid heed to them, the latter appealed to the Lacedaemonians to assist them in gaining for their city supreme control over the whole of Boiotia. In return for this favor, they offered to wage war single-handed against the Athenians, thus

---

[323] Several sources (Plut. *Cim.* 17.6, *Per.* 10.3–4; Nep. *Cim.* 3.3; Andoc. 3.3; and in particular Theopompos *FGrH* 115 F 88) claim that because the Athenians feared a retributive Spartan attack the following year, the philo-Laconian Kimon was recalled from exile five years early, possibly on Perikles' motion, to lead the embassy to negotiate peace. Unless granted a special dispensation rescinding his ostracism altogether (which is by no means impossible), he could not in fact have represented his city politically, but would have remained without civic rights (*atimos*) and thus capable of doing no more than giving advice and helping behind the scenes (Badian 1993, 17–18, perhaps hypercritical).

[324] Diodorus is our only source for this night battle precipitated by the turncoat Thessalians. Though both Herodotos (9.35.2) and Plutarch (*Cim.* 17.6) unequivocally give victory to the Spartans and their allies, it is easy to see, especially from Pausanias' account, how both sides could have claimed victory at the time (Aristodemus [12.2], for what little he is worth, gives the victory to Athens). The four-month truce, again, is vouched for only by Diodorus, but is likely—granted the heavy casualties and the ambivalent outcome of the battle—to be authentic. Enough was enough, for both sides. Thus it will explain Thuc. 1.108.2, where the Spartan force returns home via the Geranian passes and the Isthmus without encountering any opposition. (Gomme [1945, 316] argues that the Athenians must have redeployed the bulk of their forces from there to Tanagra in order to have a combined force of 14,000 in the field, but this is dubious.) The battle of Tanagra was fought in the spring (May or June) of 457.

[325] The consuls (actually for 462) were L. Lucretius Tricipitinus and T. Veturius Geminus Cicurinus (Broughton 1951, 35).

[326] Cf. above, 11.4.7, 21.3, 22.1, 32.2, and 33.4, for Thebes' Medism during the Persian Wars, and the allied response to it.

making it unnecessary for the Spartans to go on taking troops beyond the limits of the Peloponnese.[327] [3] The Lacedaemonians, figuring that this proposal was to their advantage, and in the belief that a stronger Thebes would be a counterbalance to the [increasing power] of Athens, <agreed>.[328] So, since they then had a large force in readiness near Tanagra, they strengthened the circuit wall around Thebes, and forced the cities of Boiotia to submit themselves to Theban overlordship.[329] [4] The Athenians, however, being anxious to cut short this project of the Lacedaemonians, mustered a large force and chose as its general Myronides son of Kallias. Myronides enrolled the necessary number of citizens and gave them his orders, stating the day on which he intended to set out from the city. [5] When the deadline came, and some of the soldiers failed to show up on the appointed day, he mustered those who had reported, and with them advanced into Boiotia. Some of his officers and friends said he ought to wait for the laggards; but Myronides, who was a shrewd man as well as a forceful general, said he would not do so, explaining that those who chose to be late for departure would also prove ignoble and cowardly in battle, and thus would not face up to the perils of war in defense of their fatherland either, whereas those who presented themselves in all readiness on the appointed day clearly would not desert their posts during the war.[330] And indeed, so it turned out: the force he led was few in number, but the bravest of the brave, so that when he matched them in Boiotia against a far larger army, he outfought and defeated his opponents.

82. This action seems to me in no way to fall short of those other engagements fought by the Athenians in earlier times; for the victory at Marathon and the overcoming of the Persians at Plataia and all the other famous achievements of the Athenians in no respect outshine this victory won by Myronides

---

[327] This bargain is confirmed by Justin (3.6.10–11), and accepted by Badian (1993, 213 n. 50). It makes very good sense in the circumstances.

[328] The main verb is missing here in the MSS: Oldfather (1946, 334 n. 2) suspected a lacuna; cf. Haillet 2001, 105 n. 2.

[329] This paragraph makes it clear that Diodorus' preliminary background to his account of Myronides' campaign in Boiotia refers back to the period immediately *before* Tanagra, the only time when the Spartans had "a large force in readiness" there. All the (very plausible) activity here described will have taken place then. This at once removes numerous inconsistencies (of which far too much has been made, e.g., by Buck [1970, 219ff.] and Walters [1978, 189]).

[330] As Haillet points out (2001, 106 n. 1), this sentiment (cf. Plut. *Mor.* 185e) was a rhetorical platitude variously attributed to Leonidas (Plut. *Mor.* 225d) and Timotheos (Polyaen. 3.10.3).

over the Boiotians. [2] For of those [earlier battles], some were against the barbarians, while others were finished off with the help of allies; but this engagement was won by the Athenians alone, in pitched battle, fighting against the
best of the Hellenes — [3] since for firmness against odds and in all the ordeals
of warfare, the Boiotians are reputed second to none. At any rate, it remains
true that in a later age, at Leuktra and Mantinea,[331] the Thebans stood alone
against all the Lacedaemonians and their allies, winning the highest reputation for courage, and unexpectedly emerging as the leaders of all Hellas. [4] Yet
although this battle has become famous, no writer has given an account either
of the way it was fought or of the positioning of the troops [that took part in
it]. Thus Myronides, after defeating the Boiotians in so famous an engagement, became a rival to the most legendary commanders before his time, men
such as Themistokles, Miltiades, and Kimon. [5] After this victory, Myronides took Tanagra by siege, demolished its walls, and then made his way right
through Boiotia, cutting [down trees and vines] and laying [the land] waste.
The spoils he divided among his soldiers, lavishing abundant booty on them
all.[332]

83. The Boiotians, infuriated by the ravaging of their territory, joined up
to the last man, and, when they were fully mustered, put a large army in the
field. A battle was fought at Oinophyta in Boiotia, and since both sides with-
stood the shock of conflict with a courageous spirit, they went on fighting all
day.[333] But the Athenians, with a great effort, [finally] put the Boiotians to

---

[331] At Leuktra in southwestern Boiotia in 371, the Theban general Epaminondas inflicted a crushing defeat on the Spartans, which ended their long military domination and
reduced them to a second-class power: Xen. *Hell.* 6.4.4–15, D.S. 15.55–56, Plut. *Pelop.* 23.
At Mantinea in eastern Arcadia, in 362, Theban victory was nullified by the death of
Epaminondas: Xen. *Hell.* 7.5.18–27, D.S. 15.84–88.
[332] A comparison with Thuc. 1.108.2–3 shows that the engagement Diodorus has described is undoubtedly that of Oinophyta (well established by Busolt 1897, 319 n. 2). There,
too, the victory (dated very precisely to sixty-two days after Tanagra, i.e., in August or early
September of 457) is immediately followed by the demolition of Tanagra's city-walls (cf.
Haillet 2001, 107 n. 2, with earlier bibliography, for the archaeological evidence) and the
establishment of control over Boiotia. There would be no problem were it not for what follows in 11.83.1, on which see note 333.
[333] If the battle described in 11.81.4–6 and 82.4–5 is that of Oinophyta, how are we
to explain this second, immediately juxtaposed, account of it, apparently motivated by
Boiotian resentment of Athenian activities consequent on the first? Setting aside theories
according to which Diodorus was too mindless to understand plain evidence (for an egregious example, see Andrewes 1985, 189ff.), we have the following possibilities: (a) Diodorus took his longer, encomiastic account from either an *Atthis* (account of Attica: so Busolt 1897) or an *epitaphios logos* (funeral oration: so Walters [1978], following Strasburger),

flight, and Myronides became master of every city in Boiotia except Thebes.[334] [2] After this he took his troops out of Boiotia and marched against the so-called Opountian Lokrians. These he overcame at their first encounter, and, after taking hostages from them, he struck into Parnasia. [3] He dealt with the Phokians in much the same way as he had with the Lokrians, overpowering them and then taking hostages.[335] Next he marched into Thessaly, criticizing

---

perhaps that of Lysias (2.48–53) or something similar, that did not clearly identify Oinophyta, and thus led Diodorus to assume a third battle. (b) Diodorus found a source, either (a) or another, which itself reported two encounters and explained Oinophyta as being provoked by the territorial ravaging that followed its predecessor: Plat. *Menex.* 242b places Oinophyta three, rather than sixty-two (Thuc. 1.108.2), days after Tanagra. (c) Diodorus noted down two separate accounts of Oinophyta, but died before he could combine them in his final revision. (d) The evidence of (b), in particular the striking, and precise, chronological discrepancy between Thucydides' and Plato's accounts, suggests that there were actually *two* engagements fought at or near Oinophyta, one about two months after the other. Of these explanations (d) strikes me as by far the most likely, but certainty is impossible. It is worth noting that the "motivation" for Oinophyta does not have to be a prior battle: Myronides' initial incursion (doubtless accompanied by raiding and plunder) will in itself have sparked more than adequate resentment.

[334] Cf. Thuc. 1.108.3, 113.1; 3.62.5; 4.92.6; [Xen.] *Ath. Pol.* 3.11; Plat. *Menex.* 242b; Hornblower 1991, 172–173. This incursion in fact marked the beginning of Athens' brief "land empire," an aggressive move in line with the transfer of the League treasury (which itself surely helped pay for all this active campaigning in various theaters of war) from Delos to Athens, Ephialtes' gutting of the Areopagos Council's authority, the ostracism of Kimon, and Perikles' rise to power as spokesman for the "naval radicals." For the possibility that Boiotian inland towns were made tributary in or before 453, see Hornblower 1991, 172–173, with further refs. Aristotle (*Pol.* 1302b29–32) writes that "at Thebes, after the battle of Oinophyta, the democracy was destroyed as a result of bad government." This has been taken by some (e.g., Buck 1970, 223 n. 32, with earlier refs.) as a reason for rejecting Diodorus' exception of Thebes from Athens' control. But we simply do not know about the vicissitudes of Theban internal *stasis*, or what government during this period was in power when; and even if Athens did briefly gain control of Thebes, it is clear, from Aristotle himself, that it very soon lost it again. Athens was also quite capable, as the Old Oligarch points out ([Xen.] 3.10–11), of supporting Boiotian *oligarchies* when it suited, though this policy brought little advantage in the event.

[335] Cf. Thuc. 1.108.3, Polyaen. 1.35.2. See Map 1, and cf. *BA* 55 C-D 3–4. The Opountian Lokrians (so called from their capital, Opous) were located on the Euboic Gulf, due east of Elateia, and southeast of the Epiknemidian Lokrians. "Parnasia" is the region of Phokis around Mt. Parnassos. Thucydides specifies that the Lokrian hostages were a hundred of their wealthiest citizens. What was this about? At some point not too long before (Thuc. 12.103.3, νεωστί, "lately," cf. Hornblower 1991, 160 with refs.), Lokris had colonized Naupaktos on the Corinthian Gulf west of Delphi (Meiggs-Lewis no. 20, pp. 35–40). Its occupants became known as "Ozolian" (i.e., western) Lokrians. Badian (1993, 163–169) acutely deduced that the hostage-taking was an advance measure to ensure the removal of these colonists by the mother-city, to make room for the relocation of the Messenians af-

[the Thessalians] for their earlier treachery and ordering them to receive back their exiles. When the Pharsalians refused to admit him, he laid siege to their city. [4] However, since he proved unable to take the city by storm, and the Pharsalians held out for a long time under siege, for the moment he abandoned his designs on Thessaly and returned to Athens.[336] This was how Myronides, by performing a series of notable deeds in a short space of time, gained so widely bruited a reputation among his fellow citizens.

Such, then, were the events of this year.

84. When Kallias was archon in Athens [456/5], the Eleians held the 81st Olympiad, in which Polymnastos the Kyrenean won the *stadion;* and in Rome, Servius Sulpicius and Publius Volumnius Amentinus succeeded to the consulship.[337] [2] During their term, Tolmides, who was in command of [Athens'] naval forces and was Myronides' rival for both valor and reputation, was eager to accomplish some noteworthy achievement.[338] [3] Now at that time no one to date had ever ravaged Laconia: he therefore urged that the *demos* [vote to] raid the territory of the Spartans, guaranteeing that, with 1,000 hoplites aboard his triremes, he and they would lay waste Laconia and

---

ter the recent end of their revolt against Sparta; and that thus Tolmides' *periplous* and capture of Naupaktos (below, 11.84.6–8 with notes 340–343) were already being planned in Athens.

[336] Cf. Thucydides (1.111.1), who associates the attack on Thessaly with an attempt to restore one Orestes, son of Echekratidas, described as a "king" of the Thessalians, perhaps an elected *tagos,* but this is quite uncertain: Gomme 1945, 324, shows how little is really known about the details of Thessalian government. Herodotos (5.63.3, 7.6.2) also speaks of Thessalian "kings," including the Aleuadai, whom Haillet (2001, 180 n. 4) plausibly suggests that Athens hoped to re-establish with a view to alliance. Diodorus is generally supposed to have gotten the date of this attack several years too early: Badian (1993, 102) places it in 455/4, Hornblower (1991, 178) tentatively in 454/3. But the only reason for such downdating is that Thucydides (1.111.1) reports it immediately after the collapse of Athens' Egyptian expedition; and if the latter is dated in 457/6 rather than 454, there is no reason, even for Thucydidean fundamentalists, to query a date for the Thessalian incursion in the spring of 456, perhaps terminating in a withdrawal from Pharsalos about midsummer, on the assumption that the campaign against Lokris and Phokis took until the end of the 457 campaigning season.

[337] The consuls (actually for 461) were P. Volumnius Amintinus Gallus and Ser. Sulpicius Camerinus Cornutus (Broughton 1951, 36).

[338] Tolmides was general again in 447/6, and fell in battle at Koroneia: see below, 12.6.2, with further refs. Pausanias (1.27.5) saw his statue, together with that of his official seer Theainetos, during the expedition here described, on the Akropolis: an interesting, and surely significant, equation of values. His *periplous* is correctly dated by Diodorus: cf. Reece 1962, 114.

diminish Spartan prestige. [4] The Athenians approved his proposition. Now he secretly wanted to take a larger hoplite force with him, and therefore employed the following subterfuge. The citizens supposed he would draft for his expedition those young men who were in their prime and at the peak of their physical strength. Tolmides, however, was determined to take on campaign with him considerably more than the 1,000 men he had been allotted. He therefore approached every youth of exceptional physical strength, with the information that he was going to draft him. But, he said, it would look better for him to join as a volunteer, rather than appear to be serving under compulsion because of the draft. [5] By employing this argument, he persuaded over 3,000 to sign up as volunteers. When he saw that there were no more taking any interest, he then drafted 1,000 agreed upon from those who were left.[339] [6] As soon as all other preparations for the expedition were complete, he put to sea with fifty triremes and 4,000 hoplites. He made [his initial] landfall at Methana in Laconia and captured this stronghold. When the Lacedaemonians came to recover it, he withdrew again, and coasted round [the Peloponnese] to Gytheion, a Lacedaemonian seaport. This city, too, he reduced, setting fire to the Lacedaemonians' dockyards and laying waste the countryside around.[340] [7] From here he put out to sea, and sailed to Zakynthos from [a base on] Kephallenia.[341] He took this island, having done which

---

[339] Polyaenus (3.3) reports the same anecdote (Plut. *Per.* 18.2 has Tolmides getting volunteers the same way in 447/6). He also agrees with Diodorus' total of fifty ships and 4,000 troops. It would be interesting to know how many of the ships were troop carriers, and how many triremes (a question no one seems hitherto to have asked). The maximum load for the former would seem to be about 200, calling for some twenty vessels to accommodate them, and leaving a strike force of thirty triremes. Schol. Aeschin. 2.75 confirms the date (archonship of Kallias).

[340] Tolmides' clockwise circumnavigation (*periplous*) of the Peloponnese is best studied in conjunction with the map (Map 1, and cf. *BA* 58). His first strike cannot have been at Methone, which is not in Laconia but on the southwestern coast of Messenia (and has thus sparked quite unnecessary speculation about Tolmides' mysteriously doubling back on his tracks). Where he landed was in fact Methana (modern Aghios Andreas), at the southern end of the much-contested Thyreatic plain (*BA* 58 D3), now held by Sparta, and Diodorus' text should be emended accordingly. Since the rival claimant to the plain was Athens' ally Argos, this raid also had diplomatic value. Next came the attack on Gytheion, Sparta's port in the Lakonian Gulf, and the burning of the dockyards there (cf. Thuc. 1.108.5, schol. Aeschin. 2.75, Aristodem. 15.1), together with the capture of the nearby island of Kythera, and the town of Boiai facing it on the mainland near C. Malea (Paus. 1.27.5, schol. Aeschin. 2.75).

[341] Reading ἔπλευσεν ἐκ τῆς Κεφαλληνίας εἰς Ζάκυνθον: cf. 16.6.5, 9.4, where Diodorus uses virtually the same phrase. The alternative is to read τῆς Κεφαλληνίας as indicating that Zakynthos was either subject to Kephallenia (an awkward and unconvincing

he won over all the cities on Kephallenia itself, and then sailed on up to the mainland opposite and put in at Naupaktos.[342] This city, too, he took straight off, and settled with those Messenians of note who had been freed under truce by the Lacedaemonians. [8] It was only now that the Lacedaemonians had finally, after a prolonged war, overcome both the Messenians and the Helots: the Messenians, as stated above, they let depart from Ithome under truce, but those of the Helots who had been responsible for the revolt they punished, and the rest they enslaved.[343]

85. When Sosistratos was archon in Athens [455/4], the Romans elected as consuls Publius Valerius Publicola and Gaius Clodius Regillus.[344] During their term, Tolmides was occupied in Boiotia,[345] and the Athenians elected as general Perikles son of Xanthippos, a man of good family,[346] and sent him out

---

construction), or else merely in its general neighborhood. But the winning over of Kephallenia's cities suggests collaboration. Both islands formed part of the Ionian group off the western coast of Greece, immediately facing the Gulf of Corinth (see Map 1).

[342] Naupaktos is a port on the northern side of the Gulf of Corinth, at the westernmost end of the territory occupied by the Ozolian Lokrians (see Map 1, and cf. *BA* 55 D-C 4). On his way there, Tolmides also secured Chalkis (modern Misolonghi: Thuc. 1.108.5).

[343] Cf. above, 11.63–64 passim with notes. §8 looks like an additional note inserted as a gloss on the resettling of the Messenians: to implement the various terms of this particular truce could well have taken a year or more. If the Messenian War in fact ended in 458/7, as seems cumulatively probable, and Tolmides in 456/5 was responsible for the capture of Naupaktos, then there was a short period between the Messenians' departure from Ithome and their relocation in Naupaktos. Where, we may ask, did they spend the interim? Elis or Achaia would seem the likeliest choices, but certainty—both on this and on the close chronology—remains impossible. V. Parker (1993, 136) sees the problem, but makes unnecessary difficulties out of it.

Tolmides completed his *periplous* by raiding the territory of Sikyon, on the northern coast of the Peloponnese, immediately west of Corinth (Thuc. 1.108.5, Paus. 1.27.5: see Map 1, and cf. *BA* 58 D-E 1–2), after which he probably put in at Megara's port of Pegai (cf. 11.79.2 with note 313 above). A permanent flotilla, now that Chalkis, Naupaktos, and Pegai were under Athenian control, would from this point on patrol the gulf (cf. 11.85.1–2 below).

[344] The consuls (actually for 460) were P. Valerius Volusi Poplicola and C. Claudius [Crassus?] Inrigillensis Sabinus (Broughton 1951, 37).

[345] This activity seems to have formed part of the Second Sacred War. The Phokians, deprived of the Delphic Oracle and the Krisaian Plain in the First Sacred War (c. 590), had seized both c. 457, and the Boiotians were attempting to oust them. Details are obscure, but Athens made an alliance with the Phokians, and Perikles—perhaps calling in at Itea on his voyage to Akarnania (Plut. *Per.* 21)—confirmed them in possession. Cf. schol. Aristoph. *Birds* 556; *Suda* s.v. *hieros polemos;* and Schreiner 1997, 90.

[346] Perikles' father Xanthippos, a distinguished Persian War politician and general (above, 11.27.1, 3; 34.1; 37.1, 5; 42.2, with notes) was married to Agariste, niece of the Alk-

to attack the Peloponnese with fifty triremes and 1,000 hoplites. [2] After laying waste much of the Peloponnese, he sailed across to Akarnania and brought over [to Athens] all the cities there except for[347] Oiniadai.[348] Thus in the course of this year the Athenians won control of a great number of cities and acquired a high reputation for manly courage and strategic skill.[349]

86. When Ariston was archon in Athens [454/3], the Romans elected as consuls Quintus Fabius Vibulanus and Lucius Cornelius [C]uritinus.[350] During their term, Kimon of Athens negotiated a five-year truce between the Athenians and the Peloponnesians.[351]

---

maionid reformer Kleisthenes. Perikles himself first emerges as *choregos* (financial producer) for Aeschylus' play *The Persians* in 472; he prosecuted Kimon in 463/2, and the following year was associated with Ephialtes in the attack on the Areopagos (11.77.6 and note 306 above).

[347] Accepting (as do Vogel [1890], Oldfather [1946], and Haillet [2001]) Dindorf's emendation (supported by Thuc. 1.111.3) of πλὴν for the πλησίον of the MSS.

[348] Cf. Thuc. 1.111.2–3 and Plut. *Per.* 19.2–4, which confirm Diodorus' account. Perikles sailed from Pegai and ravaged the coast. He then crossed to Akarnania (see Map 1, and cf. *BA* 54 D 4–5) and sailed up the Acheloös River, devastating much Akarnanian territory, but failed in his attempt to capture Oiniadai. As Hornblower (1991, 178) emphasizes, "Strategically, Oiniadai was an important asset for control of the western end of the Corinthian gulf." The real problem is whether the second expedition reported under 453/2 is a doublet of this one (and if so, why), and how far the extra information in Thucydides and Plutarch can be used to resolve the question. See 11.88.1–2 with note 362 below.

[349] This is no exaggeration. By 455/4 (Haillet 2001, 182 n. 3) Athens controlled Doris and Phokis as well as Boiotia in central Greece, and had become virtual master of the Gulf of Corinth, as well as the Saronic Gulf, through its alliance with Megara and reduction of Aigina. The construction of the Long Walls linking Athens and Piraeus had been completed (Thuc. 1.108.3). Athens' powerful fleet, meanwhile—not significantly weakened by the setback in Egypt, be it noted—had used the Delian League (and its tribute) to turn the Aegean into a forerunner of Rome's *mare nostrum,* an economically profitable private lake.

[350] The consuls (actually for 459) were Q. Fabius Vibulanus and L. Cornelius Maluginensis Uritinus (Broughton 1951, 38).

[351] For this truce, cf. Thuc. 1.112.1; Theopomp. *FGrH* 115 F 88 (confirming the 454/3 date); Plut. *Cim.* 18.1, *Per.* 10.3–4 (dating Kimon's recall to 457 after Tanagra, cf. 11.80.6 with note 323, and Nep. *Cim.* 3.3). The problem (leaving aside the presence, and if so the status, of Kimon) is its date. Thucydides places this truce three years after Perikles' raid, either that described above, or its successor of 453/2 (see below, 11.88.2 with note 362). Most scholars assume this to mean 451 (though it could be 452), and therefore dismiss Diodorus' 454/3 dating, even though it is the sole item cited for that particular archon-year and presumably was vouched for by Diodorus' source. The error, if error it be, is hard to explain. A truce concluded in 453 would have expired in 448 rather than the usually accepted 446, and so there would be two open years before it was replaced by the Thirty Years' Peace (cf. 12.7 with note 33 below): while not impossible, this seems unlikely. It is just possible

[2] In Sicily,[352] the Egestans and the Lilybaians went to war <against the Selinountines> over the territory adjacent to the Mazaros River. A fierce battle took place between them, with heavy casualties on both sides, but this did not diminish their rivalry.[353] [3] Now after the admissions to citizenship that had taken place in so many communities, together with the reallotment of land, it followed—since many had been added to the citizen rolls in a disorganized and random fashion—that the cities' condition was less than healthy, so that they were once more lapsing into civil strife and anarchy.[354] It was above all in Syracuse that this evil had taken hold. [4] The responsibility lay with one Tyndarides, a fellow brimful of effrontery and presumption, who began by acquiring numerous followers from among the poor. These he armed and drilled, and thus created a personal bodyguard for himself, ready to set up a tyranny. At this point, however, now it was plain that he was reaching out af-

---

that an *unofficial* truce was negotiated by the still technically ostracized Kimon in 454/3, to be ratified officially in 451 on the completion of his ten-year sentence and his restoration to civic privileges; but this must remain highly speculative. It is worth noting that 454/3 is also the first year of the Athenian tribute-lists, with their tithe (ἀπαρχή) to Athena: the two events were surely related, but just how is uncertain. The public accounting implied by such an administrative move suggests a growing need for public accountability; how far this was dictated by the collapse of the Egyptian venture, unrest among the subject-allies, or even concessions to persistent criticism by the conservative opposition of unaudited use of League funds, cannot now be determined.

    [352] Diodorus here resumes the narrative left at 11.76.8 (with a brief addition at 11.78.5).

    [353] See Map 3, and cf. *BA* 47 A-B 3, where the topographical realities are clearly laid out. The long-standing puzzlement over this passage (see e.g., Freeman 1891, 338–342, 549–557), on the grounds that Lilybaion was only founded as a city in 397 (to replace Motya, sacked and destroyed by Dionysios I, 14.51–52), depends on the assumption that Egesta and Lilybaion were *fighting each other*, rather than, as would be far more natural, allies against attack. But this makes no sense. The promontory of Lilybaion, with its excellent water-supply, had always had a small Elymite and Phoenician population, but it constituted no possible kind of threat to Egesta, and would, indeed, have been equally vulnerable to Greek encroachment. As a glance at the map makes instantly clear, the Mazaros River forms a contested frontier not with Motya (as Haillet [2001, 182–183 n. 6] supposes), but with Selinous; and the bitter rivalry between Selinous and Egesta over, precisely, the Mazaros area near Lilybaion, went back over a century (cf. D.S. 5.9.2, dated to 580–576 B.C.E.). Of the various solutions proposed (Haillet 2001, 182–183 n. 6 lists several), the neatest and most satisfying is that of Wentker (1956, 59–60: not mentioned by Haillet), who supplies <πρὸς Σελινουντίους> after ἐνέστη πόλεμος of the MSS, and I have adopted it in my translation.

    [354] Cf. 11.76.2 and 6 with notes 291 and 299 above. As Haillet says (2001, 183 n. 1), the "common accord" (κοινὸν δόγμα) that had been responsible for these changes in 461/0 had been made over-hastily and without sufficient thought.

ter supreme power, he was brought to trial and condemned to death. [5] But while he was being escorted to prison, the followers for whom he had done so much charged in a body and laid violent hands on those escorting him. The city was in an uproar, but at this point the most responsible citizens got together, seized the revolutionaries, and did away with them, together with Tyndarides.[355] Now since such occurrences were now frequent, and many bold fellows had their minds set on a tyranny,[356] the [Syracusan] *demos* was induced to copy the Athenians, and to pass a law very like that which the latter had established in regard to ostracism.[357]

87. Among the Athenians, each citizen had to inscribe a potsherd (*ostrakon*) with the name of the person he considered best able to set up a tyranny over his fellow citizens.[358] Among the Syracusans, however, the name of the most powerful citizen had to be written on an olive leaf (*petalon*), and when the leaves were counted, whoever got the largest number went into exile for a five-year period. [2] In this way, they supposed they would humble the arrogance of the most powerful men in their respective cities, since the general objective they sought was not to punish them for breaking any law, but rather to curb such men's influence and self-aggrandizement. The Athenians called this type of legislation "ostracism" from its mode of implementation, while the Syracusan name for it was "petalism." [3] This law remained on the books in Athens for a long time;[359] but in Syracuse it was very soon repealed, for the

---

[355] On this episode, cf. Freeman 1891, 330–332; Berger 1989 and 1992; and, most recently, Consolo Langher 1997, 56–61. Diodorus' conservative sympathies are plain here. The "most responsible" (χαριέστατοι) citizens are clearly the landowners and merchants, successors of the Gamoroi, who objected to a reallocation of land that would include the lower orders, τῶν πενήτων (11.76.2 and note 291 above). It was from these last that Tyndarides drew his support, and they clearly wanted more substantial rights. If Diodorus is right that this was not an isolated instance, the social crisis was acute. As to the suppression of the attempt to rescue Tyndarides, Freeman (1891, 331 n. 4) rightly observes that "this sounds more like lynching than any legal process."

[356] Cf. Thuc. 6.38.2–3. What with Sicel nationalists, an angry populace in pursuit of better civic rights, and thousands of unemployed mercenaries on the loose, the situation was highly volatile, and any plausible charismatic leader will have had no difficulty in finding himself supporters.

[357] Above, 11.55.1–2 with note 206.

[358] An overly specific definition when one reflects that candidates included the pious and respectable Nikias!

[359] For about seventy years (488–417/6), counting from its first known use, or for just under a century if we date it back to Kleisthenes' legislation between 508 and 500 (Arist.

following reasons. [4] With those at the top being exiled, the most responsible citizens—men who by reason of their personal uprightness were in a position to bring about many constitutional reforms—were no longer involving themselves in public affairs, through their fear of this law: instead they led strictly private lives, busy with the improvement of their personal fortunes, and inclining toward luxury. It was, by contrast, the most unprincipled and presumptuous citizens who were now devoting themselves to public affairs, and turning the masses toward anarchy and revolution. [5] As a result, with civil strife once more on the rise, and the commons beginning to air grievances, the city relapsed into a state of acute and virtually continuous anarchy. A whole crowd of demagogues and informers was springing up, while the young were all busy practicing the clever tricks of public speaking: in a word, people were, in large numbers, discarding their traditional serious upbringing in favor of mean and trivial pursuits. Prolonged peace was promoting private wealth, but there was scant concern for concord or principled behavior. For these reasons, the Syracusans changed their minds and repealed the petalism law after using it for only a short period.[360]

Such, then, was the course of affairs in Sicily at this time.

88. When Lysikrates was archon in Athens [453/2], in Rome there were elected as consuls Gaius Nautius Rutilus and Lucius Minucius †Carutianus†.[361] During their term, Perikles, the Athenian general, went ashore in the Peloponnese and laid waste the territory of the Sikyonians. [2] The Sikyonians thereupon sallied out against him in full force, and a battle took place. Perikles was victorious, killed many fugitives, and chased the rest into their city, which he then besieged. He made assaults on the walls, but was unable to take the city; and when, on top of this, the Lacedaemonians sent help to the besieged, he withdrew from Sikyon and made landfall in Akarnania. Here he overran the Oiniadaians' territory, picked up a mass of booty, and then left

---

*Ath. Pol.* 22). Its discontinuation is associated with the removal of Hyperbolos, its last victim (Thuc. 8.73, Plut. *Nic.* 11.3–4).

[360] Whatever we may think of ostracism, it seems clear from this account that petalism came to be employed by the poor and their radical leaders as an instrument for systematically getting rid of the office-holders and landowners who stood in their way, and that the latter, realizing this, united to get it off the books. Cf. Hesych. s.v. *petalismos*; Pollux 8.19; Wentker 1956, 56–58; Consolo Langher 1997, 57.

[361] Consuls (actually for 458) were C. Nautius Rutilus and (as *suffectus* according to Fast. Cap., replacing ———— Carve[tus]) L. Minucius Esquilinus Augurinus (Broughton 1951, 39; cf. Samuel 1972, 257). It is possible that Diodorus' source conflated these last two.

Akarnania, again by sea.[362] [3] Next he proceeded to the [Thracian] Chersonese, and shared out this territory in settlers' allotments between 1,000 [Athe-
nian] citizens. Simultaneously with these events, Tolmides, the other general,[363] crossed over into Euboia, parceling out both it and the territory of the
Naxians among a second group of 1,000 citizens.[364]

---

[362] Inevitably, this episode has been dismissed as a doublet of the similar expedition reported at 11.85.1–2; see, e.g., Badian 1993, 214 n. 54. In 455 Perikles is shown ravaging the
coast of the Peloponnese and winning over all the towns of Akarnania except Oiniadai.
Here he goes ashore and besieges Sikyon, but is forced to withdraw by the Spartans, and
ravages Oiniadai's territory, but, again, without reducing the city itself. Haillet (2001, 184
n. 3) argues that these are separate expeditions. Thucydides (1.111.2–3) confirms the attack
on Sikyon, notes that Perikles took Achaian allies to Akarnania, and reports his failure to
capture Oiniadai by siege. Plutarch (*Per.* 19.2–4) agrees on his ravaging the Peloponnese,
defeating the Sikyonians in battle, using Achaian troops, overrunning Akarnania, besieging Oiniadai, and laying waste its territory. If there were two raids, the combined evidence
suggests that Thucydides and Plutarch were both describing the second: it is worth noting
that at 11.85.1, Perikles is allocated fifty triremes, whereas Plutarch (*Per.* 19.2) gives him 100,
a plausible increase after the earlier failure to reduce Oiniadai. The evidence suggests, on
balance, that Haillet is right to accept both episodes. If we disagree, we have to assume that
Diodorus found two chronologically conflicting accounts of the same raid, but (for whatever reason, death during final revision being the likeliest, see above, Introduction) failed
to reconcile or choose between them.

[363] Diodorus is very specific: ὁ ἕτερος στρατηγός. There were, of course, *ten* generals
elected in Athens annually. Oldfather (1946, 351 n. 2) explains Diodorus' statement as referring to the only two currently on active service, and this is the likeliest solution. However, Prof. Rubincam suggests to me, *per litt.,* that Diodorus might, alternatively, here and
elsewhere, "have been unconsciously influenced by the different structure of the Roman
chief magistracy of two consuls," an undeniably attractive theory.

[364] Cf. Paus. 1.27.5; Plut. *Per.* 11.5, 19.1–2; Andoc. 3.9. The "settlers' allotments" that
Diodorus mentions here are, as his Greek reveals, what were known as "cleruchies" (κλη-
ρουχίαι), that is, settlements where the occupants retained their Athenian citizenship and
privileges, acting in effect as imperial colonists. As Plutarch (*Per.* 11.5) makes clear, they po-
liced danger spots and discouraged rebellion among other neighboring subject-allies; at the
same time, they were drawn from Athens' poorer citizens, "thus relieving the city of a mass
of lazy and idle mischief-makers." For the Thracian Chersonese (the modern Gallipoli peninsula), see Map 2, and cf. *BA* 51 G-H 3–4. Its fertility and strategic importance had long
been recognized by Athens; Miltiades had secured it in 525/4, and Perikles (Plut. *Per.* 19.1–
2) now also fortified its neck against incursions from Thrace.
   Once again there is debate over the chronology. Cleruchs were themselves, by definition, not subject to tribute (*ATL* 3 : 285–286). However, it has become a scholarly article of
faith that since mass confiscation of land for cleruchs reduced a state's ability to pay, any
such imposition resulted in the lowering of that state's tribute assessment—a charitable
view, it might be thought, of Athens' attitude as a nascent imperial taskmaster. The best

[4] In Sicily, since Tyrrhenian [Etruscan] pirates were active at sea, the Syracusans chose Phayllos as admiral and sent him to Tyrrhenia. He sailed at first to the island called Aithaleia [Elba] and laid it waste, but then secretly took money from the Tyrrhenians and sailed back to Sicily without having accomplished anything worthy of note. [5] The Syracusans condemned him as a traitor and exiled him;[365] they then picked another commander, Apelles, and dispatched him against the Tyrrhenians with sixty triremes. He overran the Tyrrhenian coastal area, and then crossed over to Kyrnos [Corsica], which the Tyrrhenians at this time held. After ravaging the greater part of the island and reducing Aithaleia, he returned to Syracuse with a large number of captives and no small amount of other booty.[366] [6] After this, Ducetius, the Sicel leader, united all those cities that were of the same [i.e., Sicel] ethnic origin, Hybla excepted, into a single common federation. He was a man of action, and as such always in search of [politically] innovative activities: this was how

---

(indeed, it might be argued, the only) support for this theory is Andros, listed (Plut. *Per.* 11.5) as receiving 250 cleruchs from Perikles. Andros in 450 paid 12 talents; from 449 this rate is cut by half. Therefore (it is argued: see, e.g., Meiggs 1972, 120–123) the cleruchy was imposed in 450. This is a possible, but far from certain, deduction (*ATL* 3:298; Gomme 1945, 380). The rich island of Naxos, for which no tribute record before 447 survives, is then assessed at only 6⅔ talents: here, too, it is argued, the reduction proves a prior imposition of cleruchs. Maybe; but when? The further assumption that all these cleruchies were sent out more or less simultaneously is pure speculation, and improbable at that; Meiggs' unexplained assertion (1972, 122) that "the quota lists make a date for the cleruchy in the Chersonese earlier than 448 virtually impossible" is uncharacteristic nonsense. Perikles and Tolmides may even have both (Plut. *Per.* 11.5) unloaded 500 settlers on Naxos at different times (though conventional wisdom again naturally assumes a doublet here): after the island's earlier rebellion (Thuc. 1.98.4, 137.2), so cavalier an attitude should not surprise us (cf. Haillet 2001, 184 n. 1 ad fin.). Thus there is no reason why Tolmides' and Perikles' cleruchies should not have been sent out when Diodorus says they were, in 453/2: this will not preclude further settlements at a later date.

[365] This action "showed that the spirit of the days of petalism had not wholly died out," Freeman 1891, 336–337.

[366] In 474/3 Hieron had won a great sea battle over the Tyrrhenians [Etruscans]: see 11.51.1–2 with note 192. Since then Etruscan "piracy" (some of it commercial and naval dominance under another name) had reasserted itself. The Syracusans appear to have had an outpost on Pithekoussai (modern Ischia: see Map 4, and *BA* 44 E4). Aithaleia was the ancient name for Elba: the island was renowned in antiquity for its iron mines, and Diodorus has a detailed portrait of it at 5.13.1–2. Phayllos and Apelles are otherwise unknown. "Kyrnos" is Corsica: again, Diodorus offers a full account of it at 5.13.3–5. A monetary series figuring a sea beast (*ketos*) probably commemorates Apelles' success: Consolo Langher 1997, pl. vi, nos. 17–18. If Elba passed under Syracusan control now, it can only have been for a very brief period.

he came to muster a sizable army from the Sicel federation and remove Menae, his native city, [from its site,] relocating it in the plain. Also near the precinct of the so-called Palici he founded a notable city, which he named Palike after these deities.[367]

89. Since we have made mention of these gods, we should not fail to put on record both the antiquity and the incredible nature of their shrine and, generally speaking, the uniqueness as a phenomenon of "The Craters," as they are called. According to mythic tradition, this precinct surpasses all others in antiquity and the degree to which it inspires reverence, and tradition records numerous marvels associated with it.[368] [2] To begin with, the actual craters are not at all imposing in size, yet they hurl skyward extraordinary jets of water from untold depths, much as cauldrons heated from below by a banked-up fire throw up boiling water. [3] The water thus thrown up has the appearance of being boiling hot, but this is not known for certain, since no one dares

---

[367] On these events, cf. Freeman 1891, 365–368; Adamasteanu 1962, 174–181; Galvagno 1991, 114–116; Rizzo 1970, 110–124; Haillet 2001, 185 n. 3. The undoubted Hellenization of Ducetius enabled him to use Greek methods against the Greeks, but Rizzo's notion (1970, 111) of an idealized "genuine Greco-Sicel *koine*" is improbable, as is his argument (115) for a Sicel national army blessedly free of mercenaries. Ducetius wanted genuine Sicel independence and was in no position to refuse any help he could get. As Galvagno says (1991, 113), he aimed to unite the Sicel communities in a way that put them on an equal footing, politically and militarily, with the Hellenic colonial powers. In this scheme, the foundation of cities formed a key element, as did the readiness to pay federal taxes (Consolo Langher 1997, 66: Hybla refused) and to serve in a centralized federal army while retaining civic autonomy. For Menai/Menaenum and its imposing site, see 11.78.5 and note 311 above. Palike (see Map 3, cf. *BA* 47 F4) was on the hill of Rocchicella, some 300 yards east of the volcanic lake associated with the Palici: Adamasteanu 1962, 175–176. The location of Hybla remains uncertain (Manganaro 1974–75, 16).

[368] On the Palici and their shrine, see D.S. 36.3.3, 7.1; Strab. 6.2.9, C275; Dio Cass. 11.89.8; Macrob. *Sat.* 5.19.15–31; Steph. Byz. s.v. *Palike*; Manni 1963, 173ff. They were twin indigenous Sicel deities, similar to the Dioskouroi and the Kabeiroi, associated with two (now merged) volcanic pools, about 18 miles west of Leontinoi, and probably in some sense identified with the two gas-driven waterspouts that at times jetted skyward from their waters and gave the area its numinous reputation. This pool today is known as the Laghetto di Naftia (though efforts have been made to reattach it to the Palici). The (Hellenized) legend was that a local nymph, Thalia, impregnated by Zeus, prayed to be swallowed up by the earth to escape Hera's wrath. This was done, and the twins she bore made their way up to the surface via the volcanic jets of the lake (known as the Delloi or Deilloi), acquiring the name Palici (Παλικοί) from the supposed etymology πάλιν ἱκέσθαι, "to return." Their shrine has been identified in a grotto immediately below Rocchicella, near Palagonia. Cf. Haillet 2001, 186 n. 1.

to touch it; for the awe engendered by these gushers is so great that the phenomenon is thought to be due to some divine compulsion. [4] For the water smells overpoweringly of sulphur, while the chasm emits a loud and terrifying roar; and more amazing still, the water neither spills over nor subsides, but maintains a power and energy in its jet that raises it to a quite astonishing height. [5] Since this precinct is pervaded by so numinous an atmosphere, the most binding of oaths are sworn to there, and divine retribution instantly overtakes any who perjure themselves: some, indeed, have been bereft of their sight before they passed out of the precinct. [6] Moreover, the sense of divine awe is so great here that when litigants are under pressure from some person of greater influence, they seek adjudication on the basis of preliminary depositions sworn to in the name of these deities. This precinct has also for some while now been regarded as a sanctuary, and has brought great succor to slaves unlucky enough to have fallen into the clutches of uncivilized masters; [7] for their masters have no authority to forcibly remove those who have sought refuge at the shrine, and they remain there, safe from harm, until the owners win their consent through guarantees of humane treatment, backed up with oaths. Only then can they take them away.[369] [8] Nor is there any record of anyone who had furnished their menials such a guarantee ever breaking it, so strongly does the awe felt for these deities keep those who have sworn the oath in good faith with their slaves. The precinct itself is located on level ground fitting for a god, and has been adorned with an adequate number of colonnades and every other kind of recreational facility. On this topic, then, let what has been set down here suffice, and we shall now resume our narrative at the point where we left it.

90. When Ducetius had founded Palike and walled it strongly around, he shared out the nearby territory in allotments.[370] On account of the richness of the soil and the large number of settlers, it came about that this city achieved a rapid growth. [2] However, after a brief period of prosperity, it was torn down, and has remained uninhabited to this day: concerning which matter we shall provide a detailed account under the appropriate year.[371]

---

[369] The shrine was used as a sanctuary at the time of the second Sicilian slave revolt in 104: see D.S. 36.3.3 and 7.1. The moral comments are most probably Diodorus' own, and based on autopsy, rather than merely transcribed from Timaios.

[370] The first, and characteristic, activity of a Hellenic city-founder ($\kappa\tau\iota\sigma\tau\eta\varsigma$): cf. 11.78.5 for Menai/Menaenum, and 12.8 with Galvagno 1991, 115 n. 52 for Kale Akte.

[371] There is no further reference to Palike as such in Diodorus' surviving text and fragments. However, it is extremely unlikely that the Syracusans in particular would have allowed so symbolically potent a city to remain intact for long after the exile (11.92.1–4) or

[3] Affairs in Sicily, then, were such as we have described.

In Italy, fifty-eight years after the destruction of Sybaris by the Kroto-niates,[372] a certain Thessalian collected the surviving Sybarites and refounded their city on its site between two rivers, the Sybaris and the Krathis; [4] and since they had rich farmland, they quickly built up their fortunes. But when they had possessed the city for six[373] years, they were once again driven out of Sybaris, concerning which matter we shall attempt a detailed account in the following book [12.9ff.].

[The year 452/1 = Ol. 82.1 is missing in all surviving manuscripts.]

---

death (12.29.1) of its nationalist founder. Further, not a few scholars (e.g., Beloch 1912–27, 2.1: 136 n. 4; Wentker 1956, 77; Meister 1967, 51–52; and above all Galvagno 1991, 116–118) argue that Trinakie—the otherwise unknown city with a Masada-like defense that was ut-terly destroyed by Syracuse in 440, as graphically described by Diodorus at 12.29.1–4—is, in fact, to be identified with Palike. This is highly plausible (cf. Manganaro 1974–75, 17). In the Table of Contents for Book 12, the manuscript tradition describes the episode as be-ing conducted "against the Picenians" (ἐπὶ Πικήνους), which makes no sense; Beloch emended this to read "against the men of Palici" (ἐπὶ Π<αλ>ικήνους). "Trinakie" is iden-tical with "Thrinakie" and "Trinakria," both ancient indigenous names for Sicily: the na-tionalist implications are obvious. Galvagno (1991, 116) suggests that this may have been the name of Palike's acropolis, much as Thebes' acropolis was called the Kadmeia. An al-ternative possibility is that Palike was renamed Trinakie in order to give the Sicel move-ment more national appeal, and that this was the city's name as recorded in Diodorus' source for 12.29. The expansion of Ducetius' activities into western Sicily (below, 11.91.1 with notes 375–376) would be an appropriate moment for the change.

[372] I.e., in 510 B.C.E.: see 12.9–10 and note 43.

[373] ἕξ read by MF, as against ὀλίγα (PS), the latter being the preferred reading of Vogel [1890], Oldfather [1946], and Haillet [2001]. But the specific figure was almost certainly emended to the vague "a few" by a scribe who thought Diodorus had miscounted the years. But did he? I suspect that 11.90.3 is in fact a surviving, and misaligned, section from the otherwise lost year 452/1, with the final clause of 90.4 an addition by a later editor or scribe: this would explain much of the problem, and incidentally relieve us of Vogel's need to excise valid chronological information wholesale from 12.10.2. Fifty-eight years from 510/9 gives us a date of 452/1 (not, as previously calculated, 453/2), and a further six years takes us, precisely, to 446/5. The only error then will be Diodorus' five years rather than six at 12.10.2, easily accounted for by an external count from 451 rather than 452. At the same time, we should never forget that (as Prof. Rubincam reminds me, per litt.) "ancient chronographers were not always careful about the difference between inclusive and exclu-sive counting of years," and did not always (any more than we do today) make a clear dis-tinction between cardinal and ordinal numbers—a major bugbear for establishing accu-rate Greek or Roman dates. "In the eighth year" is more than seven, less than eight, years later. These ambiguities may well account for a good many of the one-year discrepancies that plague modern historians.

91. When Antidotos was archon in Athens [451/0], the Romans elected as consuls Lucius Postumius and Marcus Horatius.[374] During their term, Ducetius, who had the leadership of the Sicels, captured the city of Aitna after treacherously murdering its leader.[375] He then marched with his army into Akragantine territory and besieged Motyon, which was garrisoned from Akragas. When the Akragantines and Syracusans came to the city's aid, Ducetius brought them to battle, defeated them both, and chased them out of their camps.[376] [2] With winter now coming on, they returned each to their

---

[374] There has been serious confusion on Diodorus' part here, some of it caused, as so often, by a misreading of his Roman consular sources. He has the correct Athenian archon for 451/0, Antidotos, but he omits altogether the archon for 452/1, Chairephanes, together with any entry for that year. The consuls who provide the nearest match (not a very accurate one) for Diodorus' Lucius Postumius and Marcus Horatius are C. (or M.) Horatius Pulvillus and Q. Minucius Esquilinus, consuls for 457. This would mark a change in the hitherto consistent six-year chronological gap between Diodorus' (correct) Athenian archons and his (misdated) Roman consuls, which now increases from six years to seven. The extra year would be accounted for by the omission of the 452/1 archon-year. Now under 450/49 (12.3.1) Diodorus notes as consuls Lucius Quinctius Cincinnatus and Marcus Fabius Vibulanus, neither of whom is anywhere else recorded as holding consular office at that time. But Q. (not M.) Fabius Vibulanus was consul in 459 (noted by Diodorus in 11.86.1, under 454/3) and also both legate and city prefect in 458, the same year in which L. Quinctius Cincinnatus assumed the dictatorship, and an A. Postumius Albus Regillensis also served as an ambassador (Broughton 1951, 39–40). If Diodorus misread the first two as consuls now, and the third in the previous year, rather than as part of an interregnum, it would partially solve the problem; but even so, what induced him to compound the error by dropping an archon-year, unless this was a mistake he inherited, and the consular confusion was the result of an attempt to find the missing year? For 450/49 and subsequent years, Diodorus gives the Athenian archon correctly (though he calls Euthynos, the archon for 450/49, Euthydemos).

[375] Cf. Rizzo 1970, 125–132. See 11.76.3 and note 293 for Sicel/Syracusan cooperation in dislodging Hieron's Aitnaian settlers from Katana (461/0) and their occupation of Aitna/Inessa. Presumably the "leader" (unnamed) had refused overtures to join the now-expanding Sicel federation (συντέλεια), and Ducetius had calculated—rightly—that his removal would bring the city round. In any case, assassination came a great deal cheaper than siege warfare.

[376] This move into western Sicily marked a radical departure from Ducetius' previous activities, which had all been concentrated on creating and consolidating a federation of the Sicel communities located in the mountainous region northwest of Syracuse and centered on the Simaithos valley (see Map 3, and cf. *BA* 47 E-F 3–4). This area extended west only as far as Enna and the Heraian Mountains, and Syracuse had hitherto been inclined to leave it alone. But an attack on Motyon—identified by Adamasteanu (1962, 185–186 with earlier refs.) as the stronghold of Vassallaggi, some 20 miles northeast of Akragas, on the upper Salso River—signaled pan-Sicilian aspirations: the existing power-base now began to look like a springboard for ultimate Sicel control of the whole island, and both Syra-

own homes. The Syracusans arraigned their general Bolkon—who was responsible for the defeat, and indeed incurred suspicion of having secretly made a deal with Ducetius—found him guilty of treason, and put him to death.[377] At the beginning of summer [450] they appointed a replacement, assigning him a strong force, with a commission to eliminate Ducetius. [3] He thereupon set out with his army, and overtook Ducetius when he was encamped near Nomai.[378] A major pitched battle took place, with a high death toll on both sides, and the Syracusans barely succeeded in overcoming the Sicels. But then they put them to flight, and slew many of them as they fled. The bulk of the survivors reached safety in the various strongholds of the Sicels, but a few chose rather to share the hopes of Ducetius. [4] At the same time as these events, the Akragantines stormed the stronghold of Motyon, which was held by the Sicels remaining with Ducetius. They then joined forces with the already victorious Syracusans, and the two groups now set up camp together. Ducetius had been totally crushed by this defeat: some of his soldiers were defecting, others actively plotting against him, and he was in utter despair.

92. Finally, seeing that his remaining friends were going to lay hands on him, he stole a march on them by slipping away and riding to Syracuse at night.[379] While it was still dark, he came into the Syracusan marketplace, seated himself at the altars, and became a suppliant of the city, surrendering both his person and the territory of which he was master to the Syracusans. [2] His unlooked-for appearance brought the populace streaming into the marketplace, and the magistrates summoned [a meeting of] the assembly and put before them the question of what action should be taken concerning Ducetius. [3] Some of those who were in the habit of flattering the populace

---

cuse and Akragas reacted accordingly. Cf. Rizzo 1970, 132–136; Consolo Langher 1997, 68; Sjöqvist 1973, 52. Freeman 1891, 369–370, still has useful observations.

[377] Cf. 11.88.4–5 for the similar removal of Phayllos: Ducetius' cause seems to have attracted unexpectedly widespread sympathy outside his own Sicel community (Rizzo 1970, 136–141; Freeman 1891, 370–371).

[378] The site of Nomai is unknown, but Adamasteanu (1962, 186–190) has advanced good arguments for putting it on the northeastern inland route from Akragas, perhaps near Mt. Navone. With so much uncertain, emendation (e.g., to Menai, by Dindorf, accepted by Haillet [2001, 187 n. 4]) is unjustified.

[379] A glance at the map makes it clear that at least several days must have elapsed between Ducetius' escape from Motyon and his nocturnal ride into Syracuse, for which the departure point cannot have been more distant than Menai (one reason, though not a compelling one, for Dindorf's emendation of Nomai), and may well have been nearer.

argued that he should be punished as an enemy and suffer the appropriate penalty for his misdeeds. The older and more responsible [citizens], however, came forward and insisted that they needs must safeguard a suppliant, thus paying due heed both to Fortune and to [the risk of] divine retribution. They had to consider not what punishment Ducetius deserved, but rather what action it was fitting for the Syracusans to take, since to kill one who had fallen out of Fortune's favor was improper, whereas to maintain a pious attitude toward both gods and suppliants was a proof of public magnanimity. [4] At this, the *demos* cried out as with one voice that they should spare the suppliant. The Syracusans accordingly freed Ducetius from [any liability for] punishment, and sent him away to Corinth, ordering him to remain there permanently, and furnishing him with an adequate living allowance.[380]

[5] Since we have arrived at the year before the Athenian expedition to Cyprus under Kimon's leadership, we now, in accordance with the plan outlined at the beginning of this book, bring it to a close.[381]

---

[380] After making every allowance for religious piety in the matter of suppliants, we are left with some lingering political questions regarding this extraordinary story of Ducetius' surrender and exile (cf. Rizzo 1970, 147–153). Most significant is the fact that, if Diodorus' narrative can be trusted, it was not the radicals who pressed for clemency (indeed, they apparently were all in favor of the death penalty), but the landed conservatives, those Diodorus refers to as the "responsible citizens" (χαριέστατοι). What was more, the Sicel ex-leader not only rated as a privileged exile in Syracuse's mother-city of Corinth, but was provided with a living allowance. It is hard to resist the inference that the landowners still hoped to use the Sicels in their complicated game of Sicilian power-politics, especially against Syracuse's constant rival, Akragas. Yet equally clearly (as the execution of Bolkon and the reduction of Motyon showed), others were just as determined to avoid any Sicel expansion beyond traditional limits. For Ducetius' return to Sicily, foundation of Kale Akte, and death, see 12.8.1–13 and 12.29.1, with notes.

[381] Diodorus' omission of 452/1, and his use of 451/0 for detailed treatment of Ducetius, might suggest extensive neglect of the Greek mainland during this period; but in fact, not much of note is vouched for by our other sources that can be safely assigned to these years. The only really notable events (both of 451/0) are the Thirty Years' Peace between Argos and Sparta (Thuc. 5.14.4, 28.2), of which Diodorus shows knowledge at 12.42.4, and Perikles' citizenship law (Arist. *Ath. Pol.* 26.4) restricting the franchise to those of Athenian parentage on both sides.

# BOOK 12.1.1–12.37.1: 450–431 B.C.E.

1. One might well feel at a loss when pausing to consider the anomaly inherent in human existence: namely, that of those things deemed good, not one is found bestowed on mankind in its entirety, while among evils there is none so absolute that it lacks some advantageous element. We can find demonstrations [of this principle] by considering past events, especially those of major importance.[1] [2] For example, the expedition made against Hellas by Xerxes, the Great King of Persia, occasioned the greatest fear among the Greeks on account of the vastness of his forces, since it was for the issue of freedom or slavery that they would be fighting; and since the Greek cities of Asia [Minor] had already been enslaved, it was universally assumed that those of [mainland] Greece would suffer a like fate. [3] But—against all expectation—the war came to a wholly unforeseen end, so that not only were the inhabitants of Hellas freed from the dangers they had faced, but also won themselves high fame; and every Hellenic city was filled with such abundance of wealth that all men were amazed at this total reversal of fortune. [4] From this time forward for the next fifty years, indeed, Greece made huge advances in prosperity. During this period, financial plenty meant that the arts flourished as never before, and the record indicates that it was then that the greatest artists lived, including the sculptor Pheidias.[2] There were likewise great ad-

---

[1] As Casevitz remarks (1972, 93), this preamble reads as though it was designed as a preface to both Books 11 and 12, and it is possible that originally Book 11 did have such a preface, which is here partially recapitulated. The general moral tone is in line with that promoted by Diodorus in his general introduction (1.2.2). The various attempts to identify dominant influences, let alone direct sources, for the ideas expressed here range from Ephoros (inevitably) to Posidonios and the Stoics, are purely speculative, and can safely be ignored. Its quality is universally attacked (even by Sacks [1990, 19], who says that "no one should want to claim credit" for it), but mostly on the basis of Diodorus' seeming chronological ignorance at 12.1.5, on which see note 3 below.

[2] Pheidias son of Charmides (fl. c. 470 to c. 425) was the most famous and influential Athenian sculptor of his generation. He was best known for a series of gigantic statues—

vances in education: philosophy and oratory were prized throughout Greece, but above all by the Athenians. [5] {This was because the philosophers included Sokrates, Plato, and Aristotle, with their schools, while Perikles, as well as Isokrates and his students, were numbered among the orators.[3]} There were, too, men who have become famous as generals: Miltiades, Themistokles, Aristeides, Kimon, Myronides, and more besides, concerning whom it would take too long to write.[4]

2. The Athenians in particular had risen so high in prowess and renown that their name had become familiar throughout almost the whole of the inhabited world. To such a degree did they consolidate their supremacy that alone, with no help from the Lacedaemonians or [others in] the Peloponnese, they outfought vast Persian forces both on land and at sea, humbling the far-famed Persian leadership to such an extent that they compelled them, by treaty, to liberate all the cities of Asia.[5] [2] But concerning these matters we

---

the 40-foot chryselephantine Athena in the Parthenon; the bronze Athena Promachos, her spear tip supposedly visible from Sounion; an even more colossal Zeus at Olympia—but he also, if we can trust Plutarch (Per. 13), served as director-general of Perikles' building projects on the Akropolis, in particular the thematic development of the Parthenon's running friezes. Prosecuted in 438 for alleged embezzlement of gold and ivory, Pheidias fled to Olympia, where his workshop has been found. He was apparently put to death by the Eleans after completing his statue of Zeus.

[3] The inclusion here, in a period supposedly restricted to the Pentekontaetia (479–431 B.C.E.), of figures from the late fifth and even fourth centuries, has normally been ascribed either to chronological ignorance or to mere vague generalization on Diodorus' part (e.g., by Casevitz [1972, 93], who tiptoes around the problem by remarking merely that these names "accentuent l'impression de généralité mal accordée chronologiquement au sujet qui sera peu après circonscrit"). But two points may be noted here. (a) Diodorus in fact is well aware of the correct dates for those incorrectly listed: Sokrates (14.37.7), Plato (15.7.1), Isokrates and Aristotle (15.76.4). (b) He reveals a striking distaste, precisely, for philosophers (2.29.5–6, 9.9, 10.7.2–3) and for rhetoricians or orators (1.76, 9.26.3, 20.1–2.2). It is therefore at least plausible that the first sentence in §5 is an interpolation by some ancient Gelehrte who resented Diodorus' brevity in this regard. See, for the likelihood of interpolations in Diodorus, Vogel 1890, 1:xx.

[4] Here, as Casevitz (1972, 94) correctly notes, the generals noted all in effect belong to Book 11 rather than to Book 12: see 11.82.4; cf. 10.19.6, 27.3, 30.1, 31.1 (Miltiades); 11.2.5, 12.4–6, 15.4–16.1, 17.1–2, 17.4–19.6, 27.3, 39.4–40.4, 41.1–43.3, 54.2–5, 55.1–56.8, 57.1–59.4 (Themistokles); 11.29.4, 30.3–6, 33.1, 42.1–3, 44.2, 44.6, 46.4–5, 47.1–3 (Aristeides); 11.60.1–62.1, 82.4, 86.1, but also 12.4.2–6 (Kimon); 11.79.3–4, 81.4–82.5, 83.1–4 (Myronides). The list, interestingly, does not include Tolmides (11.84.1–8, 85.1, 88.3, and cf. 12.6.1–2).

[5] See 11.60–61, and 12.4.1–6 below, with notes.

have given a fuller and more particular account in two books, this and the preceding one: we shall turn now to immediate events, after first determining the chronological limits appropriate for this section. [3] In the previous book, starting from Xerxes' campaign, we dealt with the affairs of nations down to the year preceding the Athenians' expedition to Cyprus under Kimon's command; in the present one we shall begin with this Athenian campaign against Cyprus, and continue as far as the war that the Athenians voted to conduct against the Syracusans.[6]

3. When Euthydemos was archon in Athens [450/49], the Romans elected as consuls Lucius Quinctius Cincinnatus and Marcus Fabius Vibulanus.[7] During their term, the Athenians—who had been fighting the Persians on behalf of the Egyptians, and had lost their entire flotilla at the island known as Prosopitis[8]—after a brief interval once more decided to go to war with the Persians, [this time] on behalf of the Greeks in Asia Minor. They fitted out a fleet of 200 triremes and chose as their general Kimon son of Miltiades, with orders to sail to Cyprus and campaign against the Persians.[9] [2] Kimon took the fleet, which had been provided with first-class crews and ample supplies, and sailed for Cyprus.[10] At that point, the generals in command of the Persian

---

[6] I.e., the Sicilian Expedition of 415. This edition concludes at 12.37.1, on the eve of the Peloponnesian War; a subsequent volume will cover the war itself.

[7] The archon's name was in fact Euthynos: *IG* I³ 21.61, cf. HMA 292–293, 398: this variation occurs elsewhere. Diodorus' consuls as recorded here are nonexistent in the *Fasti*. For a possible explanation, see above, Book 11, note 374: at this point the chronological gap between archons (correctly dated) and consuls is seven years.

[8] Cf. 11.77.2–3 above, with notes 302–303.

[9] Other sources for this campaign are Thuc. 1.112.1–4; Plut. *Cim.* 18–19, cf. *Per.* 10.7; Aristodem. 13 (= HMA 21; Fornara 1983, no. 95, p. 100); Nep. *Cim.* 3.4; Isokr. 8.86 (?); Ael. *VH* 5.10 (?); *Suda* s.v. Kimon. I should make clear at this point that I do not accept any of the arguments—e.g., Schreiner 1997, 50–59; Barnes 1979, 163–176—that regard either this campaign or its predecessor a decade earlier (cf. 11.71.5 with notes 274–275, 74.3–4, 75, 77) as in any sense a doublet. Cyprus and Egypt seemed to offer a solution to several crucial problems (see below), the urgency of which was even greater in 450/49 than in 462/1.

[10] Diodorus dates the entire expedition within the archon-years 450/49 and 449/8, and despite scholarly arguments for an earlier date, well summed up by Meiggs (1972, 124–126), this seems to me (as it does to Badian [1993, 58–60, 103]) perfectly feasible. The preparations for the expedition probably took place in the latter half of 451/0; it may well have set out in the spring of 450 (i.e., in the archon-year 451/0); but I see no reason to discount Diodorus' very specific evidence further. Parker (1976, 32–34) lists as motives for this expedition (a) occupation of Cyprus to deny Persia a vital advance base in the eastern

forces were Artabazos and Megabyzos.[11] Artabazos, the commander-in-chief, was based in Cyprus, with 300 triremes, while Megabyzos was encamped in Cilicia at the head of a land army numbering 300,000. [3] Kimon now reached Cyprus and established control of the sea: he laid siege to Kition and Marion and reduced them both, treating the vanquished with humane consideration.[12] After this, when triremes from Cilicia and Phoenicia were on course for the island, Kimon put out to sea, forced an engagement, sank many of these ships, captured a hundred along with their crews, and chased the rest all the way to Phoenicia. [4] Those Persians with ships that had survived fled

---

Mediterranean, (b) acquisition of good harbors, fresh water, grain, timber, metals, etc., (c) use of Cyprus as a base to raid the Levantine coast, intercept Phoenician shipping, and encourage revolts against Persia, and (d) reduction of the Persian fleet through the removal of its sizable Cypriot component. Parker does not emphasize (b), which—especially as regards Athens' desperate search for grain and timber—I would see as the prime reason for action so far afield, and the only one justifying the huge outlay involved; it also more than explains the collateral interest in Egypt, then as later one of the great natural breadbaskets of the Mediterranean. Diodorus does not mention the fact, vouched for by Thucydides (1.112.3) and Plutarch (*Cim.* 18.4), that a flotilla sixty strong was detached from the main force to aid Amyrtaios, the rebel Egyptian leader in the western marshes, just as the earlier expedition had supported Amyrtaios' predecessor Inaros.

[11] For Artabazos, see above, 11.31.3ff., 44.4, 74.6 with note 288, 75.1–2, and 77.4; cf. Thuc. 1.129.1; Hdt. 7.66, 8.126, 9.66, 89–90; Briant 2002, 339. Megabyzos (or more correctly Megabyxos), Xerxes' son-in-law and satrap of Syria: 11.74.6 with note 288, 75.2, 77.4; cf. Hdt. 3.160, 7.82; Thuc. 1.109; Ctes. §§33–34, 41; cf. Briant 2002, index s.v. Megabyzus².

[12] Marion and Kition were both key harbors, the first on Chrysochou Bay on the northwestern side of the island, the second, the modern Larnaka, in the bay of that name on the southeastern coast (see Map 2, and *BA* 72, A2 and D3). If Kimon sailed in from the west, Marion would be his first obvious target. Over Kition, Diodorus is in disagreement with our other sources, most of which claim, with some unanimity, that (a) it was during the siege of this port that Kimon died, and (b) the siege was unsuccessful: Thuc. 1.112.4, Plut. *Cim.* 19.1, Nep. *Cim.* 3.4, *Suda* s.v. Kimon. If they are right, and this seems very likely, then Diodorus, in epitomizing, will have wrongly bracketed Kition with Marion as a successful siege. That it was an early one, however, does not necessarily mean that it did not drag on, in this case until after the great sea battle (see below): this is the point on which Thucydides (who kills off Kimon before the battle he elsewhere is credited with winning) seems to have misinterpreted his source. The geography of Cyprus suggests that Marion was used as a base for subsequent attacks on Kition and Salamis (the latter at the eastern end of the island, in Famagusta Bay; see Map 2, and *BA* 72, D2).

The lack of enthusiasm shown by Cypriot cities for supporting Kimon is hardly surprising. As Miller says (1997, 21), "They had already been 'liberated' and deserted once (478), only to be taken over by the Phoenicians again, and had already seen the Greeks start and give up a campaign when better opportunity arose." Modern parallels suggest themselves.

to the coastal area, where Megabyzos was encamped with the land forces, and went ashore there.[13] The Athenians sailed in, disembarked their troops, and joined battle. During this engagement, Anaxikrates, the deputy commander, after a brilliant fight, ended his life heroically. The rest gained the upper hand in the battle and, after killing large numbers, returned to the ships. The Athenians thereupon sailed back to Cyprus.[14]

Such were the events in the first year of this war.

4. When Pedieus was archon in Athens [449/8], the Romans elected as consuls Marcus Valerius Lactucus and Spurius Verginius Tricostus.[15] During their term, the Athenian general Kimon, who now enjoyed supremacy at sea, set about subduing the cities of Cyprus.[16] Since Salamis was garrisoned by a large Persian guard, and packed with every kind of weapon and missile, as well as grain and all other essential supplies, he came to the conclusion that his most advantageous course would be to reduce it by siege. [2] This, he figured, was the easiest way for him to become master of the entire island, and also to put the Persians at a complete loss: they would be unable, with Athens con-

---

[13] Since it is a good 100 miles from Salamis to either Cilicia or the Phoenician coast, this action perhaps extended over several weeks, and certainly was not limited to a single engagement: the ancient weakness for telescoping events into one crucial occasion is apparent here. Beloch (1912–27, 2.1:343–344 n. 4) argues for heavy Athenian casualties, though the losses can hardly have amounted to the 150 ships claimed by Isokrates (8.86) and Aelian (*VH* 5.10), which would have wiped out the "famous victory" altogether.

[14] This engagement, which effectively broke the back of Persian naval dominance in the eastern Mediterranean and was largely responsible for the subsequent diplomatic stand-off (below, 12.4.4–6 with notes 18–24), took place on 16 Mounichion in the spring of 449 (Badian and Buckler 1975, 226ff.), thus establishing the sequence of events described by Diodorus (the sole testimony with a specific chronological framework) within the archon-years 450/49 and 449/8. Cf. Plutarch (18.5), who, like Diodorus, follows up the victory with further activity around Cyprus and on the Egyptian front. The (Simonidean?) epitaph cited by Diodorus in the context of the Eurymedon (above, 11.62.3 with note 233), but probably in fact composed for this victory off Cyprus, agrees on the 100 enemy vessels captured. Thucydides (1.112.4) locates the engagement off Salamis, and confirms the subsequent land battle with Cilician-based troops. It seems clear from this that Kimon advanced systematically eastward from his Marion base, setting up the siege of Kition first, then meeting and defeating the Persian fleet based on Salamis and commanded by Artabazos, a necessary preliminary to besieging Salamis itself.

[15] The archon-year is correct; the consuls (M. Valerius Maximus Lactucinus and Sp. Verginius Tricostus Caeliomontanus) were those of 456 (Broughton 1951, 41–42). Diodorus is thus seven years out of agreement with the *Fasti* at this point.

[16] Cf. Plut. *Cim.* 18.5–6, Nep. *Cim.* 3.4.

trolling the seas, to relieve the Salaminians, and this abandonment of an ally would make them the target of scorn. In brief, were all Cyprus to be forcibly reduced, the [issue of the] entire war would be decided. This, indeed, is exactly what happened. [3] The Athenians set about the siege of Salamis, and launched daily assaults on its walls; but the troops in the city, being well supplied with missiles and other gear, easily stood them off.[17]

[4] Nevertheless, King Artaxerxes, after learning of the various setbacks on Cyprus, took counsel with his friends concerning the war, and judged it advantageous[18] to make peace with the Greeks.[19] He therefore furnished both

---

[17] For this siege in 449, Diodorus is our only source: it is, however, strategically plausible (see above). Diodorus' account leads straight into the subsequent (much-debated) peace negotiations, and places the Athenian naval and military withdrawal from the island *after* the peace settlement. *Pace* Badian (1993, 49), this makes complete sense: why give up your best bargaining chip before play begins? Plutarch (*Cim.* 19.1), citing Phanodemos (= *FGrH* 325 F 23), indicates that the Athenians withdrew from Kition a month after Kimon's death, but does not (as is sometimes assumed) show them returning home at once. Thuc. 1.112.4 is so brief that it seems to imply a withdrawal—that included the Egyptian squadron—*immediately after* the great Salamis victory, but this is intrinsically implausible (again, why win a victory if you then do nothing with it?). The likeliest scenario is that during the summer of 449, the Athenians, having secured control of the sea, systematically set about the reduction of the main cities, including Kition and Salamis; that during these operations Kimon died; that his death, and the difficulties encountered—tough resistance at Salamis, a famine at Kition (Thuc. 1.112.4) due to lack of cooperation from the local Cypriot Greeks, possible resurgence of Persian naval activity (Aristodem. 13)—predisposed Athens, no less than Artaxerxes, to look favorably on a settlement (cf. Badian 1993, 5). Diodorus will then be right in stating (12.4.6) that Athens only evacuated Cyprus (and withdrew its Egyptian squadron) after the peace had been ratified.

[18] It is seldom pointed out just how advantageous the eventual terms were to Persia: the Great King resumed de facto control of Cyprus, and the threat to Egypt was likewise removed. "By the Peace of Callias," as Meiggs says (1972, 483), "Athens renounced her military ambitions in the eastern Mediterranean and Cyprus was left to fend for herself." That Thucydides should tactfully pass over this *démarche,* and Herodotos, when mentioning Kallias' mission to Sousa in the mid-460s, should remain discreetly vague as to its purpose (7.151)—especially if his negotiations were unsuccessful—is not really surprising. Whether the peace looked glorious or not in the hindsight of the fourth century, to many contemporary Athenians it must have seemed a sad comedown from the triumphs of 480/79. Cf. Badian 1993, 11–12. It is perhaps in this context that we should consider Demosthenes' claim (19.273) that Kallias was fined fifty talents at his scrutiny on a charge of taking bribes during his diplomatic mission. Shooting the messenger was always a popular Athenian sport.

[19] The Peace of Kallias is one of the most hotly debated problems in all Greek history, and continues to generate an enormous bibliography. Basically, the question is this: Was such a formal peace ever in fact concluded, and, if it was, did it take place (a) c. 466, under Xerxes, with a renewal in 449 (cf. *Suda* s.v. Kallias), after—as I would argue—an ini-

his satraps and the commanders on Cyprus with the conditions, in writing, on which they could come to terms.[20] [5] As a result, Artabazos and Megabyzos sent ambassadors to Athens to discuss a settlement. The Athenians listened favorably to their proposals, and responded by dispatching ambassadors plenipotentiary, under Kallias son of Hipponikos.[21] A peace treaty was then

---

tial rejection by Artaxerxes on his accession, probably in 464/3 (cf. 11.61.1 and 71.2 with notes 227 and 273 above), or (b) in 449 for the first time? Those wanting a convenient conspectus of the evidence (also in HMA 344, trans. Fornara 1983, no. 95, pp. 97–103), a masterly summary of the problem as such, the history of its scholarship, and the arguments favoring (b), should consult Meiggs 1972, 129–151, 487–495 (cf. D. M Lewis in *CAH* v, 121–127). The case for (a)—with which I am in substantial agreement, not least on account of vigorous Athenian activity in areas under the Great King's jurisdiction throughout the decade immediately following—has been argued, with exemplary common sense, by Badian (1993, 1–72). Though there are still some dissentient voices, the *existence* of the treaty is now generally accepted. The main reason advanced against it was always the silence of Thucydides; and this can be explained (see above) as part of the general fifth-century embarrassment as to its implications. Theopompos (*FGrH* 115 F 154), because it was recorded in Ionic lettering (but then, it was mainly for Ionic consumption!), said it was a forgery; Theopompos was rabidly anti-Athenian, and also claimed that the renewal of the treaty with Artaxerxes' successor Darius in 424/3 (Andoc. 3.29) was directed *against the Greeks* (πρὸς Ἕλληνας), a phrase with clear reference to Athens' treatment of its subject-allies when relieved of the direct threat from Persia, against which its naval league had originally been constituted. Cf. below, note 22.

[20] Badian (1993, 42ff.) well emphasizes the delicate diplomatic protocol needed when dealing with the Achaimenid King of Kings, the theoretically omnipotent avatar of Ahura-Mazda: Artaxerxes may authorize terms, but he cannot be required to swear to anything himself, much less personally cede authority over the Greek cities. Thus the treaty was actually struck between Athens and the western satraps, primarily Megabyzos and Artabazos. This may well have been another factor causing doubt about the treaty's existence: for most Greeks, "the Barbarian" and the Great King were synonymous. See, e.g., Plut. *Cim.* 13.5, where Kallisthenes is cited as denying that "the Barbarian" made such an agreement, though in effect he observed its terms: this could be technically true, since the agreement Plutarch saw in Krateros' collection would have been between Athens and the satraps, even if Artaxerxes approved it.

[21] On Kallias (c. 520–c. 440 B.C.E.), see *APF* 258–262; *PA* 1: 519–520, no. 7825. He belonged to an immensely wealthy aristocratic family, a branch of the Kerykes clan, whose members held hereditary office as priests and torchbearers in the Eleusinian Mysteries. The wealth probably derived in great part from shrewd exploitation of the Laurion mines (his nickname was "Lakkoploutos," i.e., "Pit-rich"). He married (but probably later divorced) Kimon's sister Elpinike. The tradition that he won three Olympic chariot victories is hard (but not absolutely impossible) to reconcile with the surviving Olympic records. A seasoned diplomat, he turns up at Sousa leading a delegation to the Great King about 464 (Hdt. 7.151), and as a negotiator of the Thirty Years' Peace with Sparta (below, 12.7). In 449/8 he almost certainly returned to Sousa to negotiate, though the actual treaty was concluded with the local satraps.

concluded between the Athenians (and their allies) and the Persians, the main terms of which are as follows:[22] "All the Greek cities in Asia [Minor] are to be subject to their own laws. No Persian satrap is to come nearer than a three days' journey to the coast. No Persian warship is to enter the waters between Phaselis and Kyaneai. Provided the Great King's[23] generals observe these conditions, the Athenians shall not move troops into any territory under the king's jurisdiction."[24] [6] Once the treaty had been solemnized, the Athenians—after winning a brilliant victory, and securing most notable peace terms—withdrew their forces from Cyprus. However, as ill luck would have it, Kimon succumbed to an illness while still stationed on the island.[25]

---

[22]Other sources for the terms of the treaty are: Isokr. 4.118, 7.80, 12.59; Dem. 19.273; Lycurg. *In Leocr.* 73; Plut. *Cim.* 13.4; Ael. Arist. *Panath.* 153; Aristodem. 13; *Suda* s.v. Kimon; Livy 33.20.2. The clause relating to the Greek cities is cited by Diodorus alone. The distance the satraps were to keep from the coast varies between a three-day journey and a one-day journey (by horse, some specify). Of the points beyond which Persian warships were not to sail further west, Phaselis is a port on the western coast of the Gulf of Pamphylia, and Kyaneai is a town at the southern extremity of the Lycian promontory (though some argue that Diodorus and others meant the Kyanean Isles at the Bosporan entry to the Black Sea, which is possible: see below). This is also the location of the third limit specified, the Chelidonian Isles, at the southeastern corner of the same promontory. See Map 2, and cf. *BA* 65 E4 (Phaselis), C5 (Kyaneai), D5 (Chelidonian Isles).

[23]The MSS read: ταῦτα δὲ τοὺς βασιλέως {καὶ} τῶν στρατηγῶν ἐπιτελούντων. As we have seen, the Great King could not be a signatory to the treaty, even if he authorized it. I suspect that this was known to Diodorus' source, and probably to Diodorus himself, and that the clause originally had no καί in it (producing the sense translated here). The intrusive link will have been added by a scribe who, knowing the Great King to be an absolute autocrat, could not imagine a treaty leaving him, as it were, out of the loop, and thus assumed a καί had dropped out.

[24]This clause covered the general withdrawal of Athens from the eastern Mediterranean (even though, as Badian [1993] stresses, there were no balancing limitations set on Athenian naval movements), and the final abandonment of a Kimonian policy, the chief aim of which was to secure Cyprus and Egypt as friendly and reliable sources of grain and timber. The policy had been ruinously expensive in every sense, and in the end had failed to deliver the goods on a long-term basis. From now on Athens began to look elsewhere for its supplies: first to the Black Sea and southern Russia (hence, possibly, the limit on Persian fleets operating there, if the treaty specified the Kyanean Isles at the eastern Black Sea mouth of the Bosporos), then to Sicily and the West. By 445 Attica was suffering a grain famine (schol. Aristoph. *Wasps* 718; cf. *IG* i³ 30; HMA 10.22); this was relieved by a massive shipment from Amyrtaios' successor in the western Egyptian marshes, who either was called or called himself Psammetichos (Psamtek), the name of two Twenty-sixth Dynasty pharaohs. If this was a bid to secure the return of an Athenian expeditionary force to Egypt (cf. Plut. *Per.* 20.3; Busolt 1897, 500), it failed.

[25]Kimon almost certainly died in the late summer of 449, and this date used to be generally accepted (see, e.g., PA 1.563). I am not persuaded by Meiggs' backdating of his death

5. When Philiskos was archon in Athens [448/7], the Romans elected as consuls Titus Romilius Vaticanus and Gaius Veturius Cichorius, and the Eleians held the 83d Olympiad, in which Krison of Himera won the *stadion*.[26] [2] During their term, the Megarians revolted from the Athenians, sent ambassadors to the Lacedaemonians, and made an alliance with them. In annoyance at this, the Athenians sent into Megarian territory troops, who plundered the holdings and carried off much booty. When [the Megarians] emerged from Megara to defend their territory, a battle took place. The Athenians were victorious, and pursued the Megarians back within their fortifications.[27]

---

(and the campaign) to 451 (1972, 124−128), favored by Hornblower (1991, 179). His body was brought back to Athens and buried in the family vault (Plut. *Cim.* 19.4); there was also a cenotaph recorded at Kition. From 448 there was, for some thirty years (Eddy 1973, 341), "a kind of cold war between the two powers, a situation of vague menace, of raids, of small successes, of counter moves, of embassies and threats."

[26] T. Romilius Vaticanus and C. Veturius Cicurinus were consuls in 455 (Broughton 1951, 42).

[27] This episode is prior to, and quite distinct from, the coordinated revolt against Athens by Euboia, Sparta, and Megara of 446 (Thuc. 1.114: Diodorus' account below, ch. 7 with note, is brief and omits Megara's role) with which it is too often identified (e.g., by HMA 344). It is, clearly, one symptom of a general anti-Athenian movement, triggered in part by the Peace of Kallias (which was regarded, rightly or wrongly, as nullifying the chief raison d'être—defense against Persia—of the Delian League). For the general unrest thus generated throughout what was already a de facto Athenian empire, see Meiggs 1972, ch. 9, "The Crisis of the Forties," 152−174, cf. 176. It is true, as Meiggs reminds us (152), that the "alliance" (συμμαχίς) becomes "the cities that Athens controls," αἱ πόλεις ὅσων Ἀθηναῖοι κρατοῦσι. Athens' attitude toward its "subject-allies" undoubtedly toughened now, and setbacks abroad made it tougher still. It was only ten years or so since the Athenians had been Megara's staunch supporters (11.79.3−4 with note 314 above); now Sparta, Corinth, and the Peloponnesians generally began to look far more attractive as allies to Megara, not least after the collapse of Athens' land empire (below, 12.6.2, with note 29).

It may be worth speculating briefly on the underlying cause for this general tightening up by Athens, on its "subject-allies" of the former Delian League in particular. There was resentment at the apparent conversion of the League into an Athenian empire, and it has been well argued (*ATL* 3:277−279; Fornara 1983, 95M, 100−102 with earlier refs. and the epigraphical texts in translation) that the result was a remission of tribute for 449/8 or, more probably, 448/7. This is significant. Concessions and exploitation both focused on cash (cf. *IG* i³ 34 = Meiggs-Lewis no. 46, Fornara 1983, no. 98, the Kleinias Decree). As James Carville famously said, "It's the economy, stupid." The "tightening-up" was, first and foremost, as is generally agreed, an increasingly ruthless extraction of tribute. This suggests an urgent need for increased income on Athens' part. It is less often asked what, at this precise point, generated such a need. The collapse of Athens' Kimonian Cypro-Egyptian policy, combined with the grain famine of 445 (cf. below, note 52), suggest one answer. Until an alternative safe source not only of grain, but also of the timber crucial for Athens' imperial fleet was found and secured, these commodities had to be sought on the

6. When Timarchides was archon in Athens [447/6], the Romans elected as consuls Spurius Tarpeius and Aulus †Asterius† Fontinius.[28] During their term, the Lacedaemonians invaded Attica and laid waste a considerable amount of territory: then, after besieging certain of the fortresses, they returned to the Peloponnese. Meanwhile Tolmides, the Athenian general, took Chaironeia. [2] But the Boiotians regrouped their forces and ambushed Tolmides' troops, and a hard-fought battle took place at Koroneia, during which Tolmides fell fighting, and of the other Athenians, those who were not cut down were taken alive.[29] This major disaster meant that the Athenians (if they hoped to recover their prisoners) were forced to let all the cities of Boiotia choose their own forms of government.[30]

7. When Kallimachos was archon in Athens [446/5], the Romans chose as consuls Sextus Quinctius <. . .> Trigeminus.[31] During their term, since the

---

open market (e.g., southern Russia, where gold was the preferred mode of payment), and came very expensive. Athens' increased interest in the West, culminating in the ill-fated Sicilian Expedition of 415/3, can be seen as a logical consequence of this dilemma.

[28] The consuls (in fact for 454) were Sp. Tarpeius Montanus Capitolinus and A. Aternius Varus Fontinalis. Note that Diodorus (or more probably a later editor or scribe) has once again mangled a (roughly similar) Roman name, Aternius, into a Greek form with recognizable meaning, Ἀστέριος, i.e., "starry" (Perotti 1984, 169).

[29] See Thuc. 1.113.1–4; cf. 3.63.5, 3.67.3, 4.92.6; Plut. *Per.* 18.2–3; Paus. 1.27.5, 1.29.14. The decisive battle of Koroneia took place in spring 446, and casualties among upper-class Athenians were heavy, including Alkibiades' father Kleinias (thus leaving the boy as a ward of Perikles). Athens' occupation of Boiotia after Myronides' victory a decade earlier (11.83.1 with note 334 above) had been unobtrusive, but its policy of splitting up the Theban confederacy and encouraging independent city-states (Meiggs 1972, 176) had created a strong body of oligarchic exiles, who now staged a comeback. French (1971, 66–67 n. 127) points out that Athens, with its citizen-army, normally relied on the *threat* of intervention rather than the thing itself. Now, after taking Chaironeia (Thuc. 1.113.1) and selling its inhabitants into slavery (ἀνδραποδίσαντες), Tolmides put in a garrison. This kind of strongarming not only used up troops that could ill be spared, but risked their loss in the event of revolt. On this occasion, Athens was lucky to negotiate the evacuation of Boiotia after its defeat (Thuc. 1.113.3–4). A year later, the occupying force in Megara was not so fortunate: it was massacred (Thuc. 1.114.1).

[30] In one sense, of course, and strictly for its own ends, this was what Athens had actually been encouraging (see above, and Meiggs 1972, 176); and Boiotian Plataia remained Athens' ally (cf. D.S. 12.41–42). What Diodorus is implying here, however, is the resurrection of the Boiotian League headed by Thebes, and the return of a powerful united Boiotian army.

[31] The consuls (actually for 453) were Sex. Quinctilius and P. Curiatius Fistus Trigeminus (Broughton 1951, 43–44). Vogel (1890) rightly identified a small lacuna here in the manuscript tradition.

Athenians had lost prestige throughout Greece because of the defeat they suffered at Koroneia in Boiotia, numerous cities now defected from them. Since
the inhabitants of Euboia were leading figures in this revolt, Perikles (who had
been elected general) led a sizable expeditionary force against Euboia. He
stormed the city of Histiaia and deported its citizen body; the other cities he
frightened back into submission to Athenian authority.[32]

A thirty-year treaty was made [between Athens and Sparta], negotiated and
confirmed by Kallias and Chares.[33]

8. In Sicily, a war broke out between Syracuse and Akragas for the following reasons. The Syracusans had overcome Ducetius, the Sicel leader, and

---

[32] Diodorus' epitomizing here is particularly ruthless just where we would hope for detail. The main conflict to which he alludes (cf. Thuc. 1.114, Plut. *Per.* 22.1–2) is that involving the carefully coordinated revolts of Megara and Euboia (where the immediate
cause was probably an overly dictatorial Athenian cleruchy: Hornblower 1991, 184), immediately followed by (and probably planned with) a Spartan expeditionary force into Attica under King Pleistoanax: Diodorus mentions only the Euboia campaign. This was broken off by Perikles on news of the Megarian uprising, which he came back in haste to
suppress (Meiggs-Lewis no. 51 = Fornara 1983, no. 101 commemorates a Megarian guide
who led three Athenian tribal companies from Pegai to safety), probably also bribing Pleistoanax to go home (Plut. *Per.* 23.1, schol. Aristoph. *Clouds* 859 = Fornara 1983, no. 104)
before he returned to Euboia (Thuc. 1.114.3). The Histiaians were made an example of because they had killed the crew of a captured Athenian trireme: for the subsequent imposition of a cleruchy there, see below, 12.22.2. We have the peace terms imposed on Eretria
and Chalkis (*IG* i³ 39–40 = Fornara 1983, nos. 102–103) and the scare tactics are in evidence, including a requirement of denunciation to Athens of seditious behavior (ἐὰν ἀφι-
στεῖ τις κατερῶ Ἀθεναίοισι). Cf. Meiggs (1972, 176–181), who argues, persuasively, that
the Spartans invaded in May, and that the Euboian revolt was finally crushed by the end
of July 446.

[33] Cf. below, 12.26.2, 28.4; Thuc. 1.87.6, 115, 2.2.1 (the peace in fact lasted only fourteen
years), 4.21.3 (Athens' need for peace in 446 was great); Plut. *Per.* 24.1; other sources in
HMA 345. The five-year truce of 451(?) (above, 11.86.1 with note 351) had run out, and Athens badly needed relief from external, in particular Peloponnesian, pressure. The degree of
need can be gauged from the fact that Athens ceded (Thuc. 1.115.1) not only Troizen and
Achaia (which, as Meiggs says [1972, 182], will not have disturbed it unduly), but, far more
important, Pegai and Nisaia, Megara's ports on the Corinthian and Saronic Gulfs. It may
have been true (Meiggs 1972, 177) that the long walls Athens had built linking Nisaia to
Megara would help to block the road to a Spartan invasion of Attica; but they also formed
part of an alternative Isthmus crossing to that dominated by Corinth (cf. 11.79.2, with note
313), which explains why regaining control of Megara became increasingly important to
Athens in the decades that followed, emerging as a major *casus belli* by 431. In addition to
Kallias and Chares (otherwise unrecorded), Athens' negotiating team for the Peace had
eight other members, including Andocides (Andoc. 3.6).

when he became a suppliant absolved him from all charges, designating Corinth henceforth as his place of residence.[34] [2] But after a short stay in Corinth,[35] he broke the agreement, and—his excuse being that he had been instructed, by a divine oracle, to settle the Sicilian site of Kale Akte[36]—sailed
back to the island[37] with a group of colonists.[38] (Some of the Sicels were also
involved, among whom was Archonidas, the ruler of Herbita.[39]) [3] So it

[34] See above, 11.92.2–4, with note 380.

[35] How short? The general—and plausible—opinion (see, e.g., Wentker 1956, 74; Rizzo
1970, 153; Maddoli 1977–78, 151) is that Ducetius' return to Sicily, and the foundation of Kale
Akte, took place during 448 and 447, which would give him about two years in Corinth.

[36] Kale Akte ("The Fair Shore"), later known to Romans as Calacte or Calacta, was on
the northern (Tyrrhenian) coast of Sicily, about midway between Himera and Tyndaris,
and some 10 miles east of Halaesa (see Map 3, and cf. BA 47 E2), possibly on the site of
modern Caronia Marina. The coastal strip, though narrow, was fertile (Kale Akte earned
its name; cf. Freeman 1891, 378–379) and heavily wooded (Dunbabin 1948, 392); it had attracted interest as early as 494 (Hdt. 6.22–23). The city's orthogonal grid (Casevitz 1991,
97) suggests a connection with the Panhellenic (but largely Periklean) foundation of Thourioi a year or two later, which Hippodamos of Miletos, an early exponent of the rectangu-
lar or "gridiron" city plan, is known to have designed.

[37] Though the conditions of Ducetius' exile were generous, suggesting prior collusion of
some kind, for whatever purpose, between him and the Syracusans (11.92.4, with note 380
above), it was also to be permanent ($\kappa\alpha\tau\alpha\beta\iota o\hat{u}\nu$). Like most students of the period, I find
it impossible to believe that he was unsupervised to the point of being able to raise such
an expedition without at least the tacit approval of the Corinthians; nor that such approval
would have been given except on the authorization of Syracuse (possibly thinking of a
friendly Kale Akte as a handy outlet to the Tyrrhenian Sea, Rizzo 1970, 166). Maddoli (1977–
78, 151ff.) argues that Ducetius was still aiming at an anti-Syracusan Sicel national movement. This is quite likely: he and the Syracusans had been using each other for their own purposes from the start (cf. 11.76.3, 78.5 with note 311 above), and almost certainly still were.

[38] It would be helpful if we knew who, and from where, these—presumably Peloponnesian—colonists were: Rizzo's guess (1970, 156–157, 162–163) that they were Dorians,
even Corinthians, with links to Syracuse, and an agenda of blocking any expansion northward by Akragas in central Sicily (something of which Phalaris and Theron had dreamed),
has much to commend it.

[39] The site of Herbita is uncertain, though almost certainly in the northern end of the
island and within easy reach of Kale Akte. The traditional identification is with Nikosia or
nearby Sperlinga, about 10 miles northwest of Agyrion (see Map 3 and cf. BA 47 E3);
Boehringer (1981, 95ff.) opts for Gangi, a few miles further northwest on the southwestern
spur of the Nebrodes massif. Archonidas we also know from Thucydides (7.1.4), where his
recent death (c. 415/4) is noted, as well as the interesting fact that he (like his homonymous
son, IG ii² 32, cf. D.S. 14.16.1–2) was a "friend of Athens" ($\tau o\hat{\iota}\varsigma$ $\mathcal{A}\theta\eta\nu\alpha\acute{\iota}o\iota\varsigma$ $\phi\acute{\iota}\lambda o\varsigma$). That
Athens now (for good reasons: cf. above, note 24) was becoming increasingly interested in
the West is well known (cf. below, 12.9–10 for Thourioi, and Meiggs-Lewis nos. 63–64,
pp. 171–176 = Fornara 1983, nos. 124–125, for treaties with Rhegion and Leontinoi probably first made about this time: Kagan [1969, 154–155 nn. 2–3] is properly cautious re-

came about that the Akragantines—partly out of envy of the Syracusans, and partly because (they charged) the Syracusans had freed Ducetius, their common enemy, without consulting them—declared war on Syracuse.[40] [4] The cities of Greek Sicily were divided, some lining up with Syracuse, others with Akragas: thus both sides put sizable armies into the field. Great rivalry was evident between the various cities when they encamped facing one another on either side of the Himera River.[41] A pitched battle was fought, in which the Syracusans were victorious and killed over 1,000 Akragantines. After the battle, the Akragantines sent an embassy to negotiate terms, and the Syracusans made peace with them.

9. Events in Sicily, then, were as described above. In Italy, the foundation of the city of Thourioi came about, in the following circumstances.[42] When at an earlier period the Greeks had founded Sybaris as an Italian city, because of the richness of the soil it had achieved rapid growth. [2] Since it lay between two rivers, the Krathis and the Sybaris (from which it got its name), its inhabitants, by exploiting this extensive and richly productive region, acquired very considerable wealth. Further, their practice of granting citizenship to numerous [applicants] swelled their numbers to such an extent that they were reputed to be the largest city in Italy:[43] their population so outstripped the rest that they had 300,000 citizens.

---

garding conclusions drawn from these fragmentary and badly worn inscriptions). That Athens also may have made contact with Ducetius is an interesting (and by no means impossible) suggestion of Maddoli's (1977–78, 154–156): it would not be the first time that the Sicel leader had played both ends against the middle. If the Athenians did take note of Kale Akte, the reason for their interest is obvious: immediate access, for shipbuilding timber, to the vast forest of the hinterland, the modern Bosco di Caronia, still covering over 50 square miles as late as the nineteenth century (Dunbabin 1948, 392).

[40] Even if the Syracusans were not in collusion with Ducetius (and in fact, such collusion is virtually certain), Akragas certainly believed they were; and their "envy" (φθονοῦν-τες) can only refer to what they saw as a Dorian-backed deal to bring a vital stretch of the northern Sicilian coast into Syracuse's orbit: a direct threat to their own plans, and those of the Ionian/Chalcidic Sicilian Greeks generally. Seen thus, the declaration of war should come as no surprise.

[41] Near Himera itself (see Map 3, and cf. BA 47 D3), and thus substantially further west than Kale Akte, implying a 40-mile advance along the coast by Syracusan (and presumably also Sicel) forces.

[42] Chs. 9–19 form a lengthy excursus on the foundation of Thourioi, and the code of laws allegedly drafted for that city by Charondas, together with a note (chs. 20–21) on another southern Italian lawgiver, Zaleukos of Epizephyrian Lokroi.

[43] Sybaris was traditionally founded by Achaians and Troizenians (Arist. Pol. 5.2.10, 1303a30–35; Strabo 6.1.13, C.263; cf. D.S. 8.17) around 719/8 (the chronology is based on

There now [510/09] emerged among them a popular leader called Telys, who, by bringing charges against the most important men in the city, persuaded the Sybarites to exile 500 of their richest citizens, and to impound their property for public use.[44] [3] These exiles went straight to Kroton, where they sought sanctuary at the altars in the marketplace. Telys then sent ambassadors to the Krotoniates, with the message that they should either surrender the exiles or prepare themselves for war. [4] An assembly was thereupon convened, with the agenda of discussing whether to hand over their suppliants to the Sybarites or face a war with a more powerful opponent. Neither council nor *demos* could decide this issue. At first, because of [the threat of] war, public opinion inclined toward surrendering the suppliants. Subsequently, however, when Pythagoras the philosopher advised them to ensure the suppliants' safety, they reversed their opinion, and prepared to face war on those grounds.[45] [5] The Sybarites thereupon marched against them with 300,000

---

Diodorus' statement at 11.90.3 [see note 373 above] that the attempt to refound it in 252/1[?] took place fifty-eight years after its destruction by Kroton, i.e., 510/09, and the statement of [Skymnos] 360 [cf. Dunbabin 1948, 24] that its original foundation took place 210 years before that). For its location near the coast (some 5 miles east-northeast of Cozzo Michelicchio) on the Gulf of Taras (mod. Táranto), see Map 4, and cf. *BA* 46 D-E 2. Diodorus' description is accurate. The city lay on a great alluvial plain, one of the largest and most fertile in all of Italy, about 35 miles south of Siris, and 70 miles north of its great rival Kroton, between the Krathis [modern Crati] and Sybaris [modern Coscile] rivers. Its wealth in grain, vineyards, cattle, fisheries, and fowling was proverbial (Varro *RR* 1.44.2, Athen. 12.519d, Timaios *FGrH* 566 F 9, Ael. *VH* 12.24). This gave its inhabitants a reputation for profligate luxury (Hdt. 6.127.1; D.S. 8.18–20; Strab. 6.113, C.263; Ael. *VH* 1.19, 9.24, 12.24; Athen. 6.273b–c, 12.511c, 518c–f, 523c, 526b, and elsewhere), leading to moral explanations for their downfall; more realistic was the shock and horror expressed by their wealthy trading partner Miletos (Hdt. 6.21.1; Athen. 12.518c–519d, 521b–d). The pass from the plain to the western coast of Italy facilitated the establishment by Sybaris during the sixth century of outposts at Laos, Skidros, and Poseidonia (later Paestum). The essential fact to bear in mind is Sybaris' vast natural wealth, which made it a prize worth anyone's time and trouble. Strabo (6.113, C.263), who reports the city's circumference as over 6 miles (50 *stadia*), confirms the (certainly exaggerated) figure of 300,000 inhabitants: Casevitz (1972, 98) suggests that this may be an overall figure for its local "empire" (four tribes and twenty-five subject-cities), but the evidence is highly suspect.

[44] Hdt. 5.44 refers to Telys as "king" (from the Sybarite viewpoint) and "tyrant" (as seen by the Krotoniates). For Diodorus he was a "popular leader" (δημαγωγός) and thus, clearly, a classic late-sixth-century τύραννος, attacking and displacing an entrenched aristocratic/plutocratic oligarchy, represented by the 500 exiled citizens (cf. Casevitz 1972, 98).

[45] Pythagoras left his native island (Samos) for Kroton to escape the tyranny of Polykrates (Diog. Laert. 8.3): this must have been before 522, when Polykrates was executed by the Persians (Hdt. 3.124–125). In 510/09 he was about seventy (Diog. Laert. 8.44) and had another decade still to live. He is credited with drafting a constitution for Kroton, and the government of the city was apparently an oligarchy controlled by his followers (Diog.

men, against whom the Krotoniates mustered 100,000[46] under the command
of Milo the athlete, who through his unrivaled physical strength was the first
to rout those ranged against him. [6] This man, a six-time Olympic cham-
pion, whose courage matched his bodily power, is said to have gone into battle
wearing his Olympic wreaths, and rigged out in the manner of Herakles with
lion skin and club. He was, indeed, responsible for [Kroton's] victory, and
earned the wondering admiration of his fellow citizens in consequence.[47]

10. The Krotoniates in their fury refused to take any prisoners, but killed
all who fell into their hands during the rout, so that the larger part of the Sybarites perished. They then sacked the city itself, and reduced it to a mere
wasteland.[48] [2] Fifty-eight years later [452/1], Thessalians helped refound the
city, but a little while later, in the Athenian archonship of Kallimachos [446/5],

---

Laert. 8.3); this will have inclined them in favor of the oligarchic exiles from Sybaris. Athe-
naeus (12.521d–e) cites Phylarchos for the Sybarites having murdered thirty envoys from
Kroton: if this is true (and not merely moralists' invented proof of Sybarite overblown arrogance, pride going before a celebrated fall), they will presumably have been the ambassadors who brought news of Kroton's refusal to surrender. It would also explain the Krotoniates' subsequent furious refusal to take prisoners (12.10.1).

[46] These figures (shared by Strabo 6.113, C.263) are, even more certainly than those
given for the population (which they duplicate), much exaggerated: in all likelihood they
are part of a general tendency to maximize Sybarite excess in every area (cf. some of Herodotos' figures for Xerxes' invading army). We should never forget, either, when studying
the motives for war in such a case as this, that the natural resources of Sybaris—and, to a
lesser extent, those of Kroton, itself occupying a fertile (Strab. 6.1.12, C.262) and well-
watered plain on the eastern side of the Bruttian peninsula (see Map 4, and cf. *BA* 46 F3)—
offered a constant economic temptation. The circuit of Kroton's walls was no less than
12 miles (Livy 24.3), almost double that of Sybaris; as the head of the Italiote League, Kroton exercised considerable regional power.

[47] For Milo, the famous wrestler, multiple Olympic victor, and friend of Pythagoras, see
also Strab. 6.1.12, C.263; D.S. 9.14.1; Paus. 6.14.5–8; Ael. *VH* 2.24; Philostr. *VA* 4.28; Aul.
Gell. 15.16; *Suda* s.v. Milon. He was said, among other feats, to have carried a heifer the
length of the Olympic stadium, and afterward to have eaten it in a single day, which suggests that not all the excess was Sybarite. Timaios (reported by Athen. 12.522a) relates that
after their great victory, the Krotoniates, too, lapsed into luxury.

[48] According to Strabo (6.1.13, C.263), either two months or nine days (text uncertain)
elapsed between battle and sack. It must have been on learning of the defeat that the Sybarites (according to Herakleides Ponticus, cited by Athen. 12.521–522) stripped Telys of
power and executed both him and his supporters. Strabo also notes that the victorious Kro-
tonians diverted the Krathis River (cf. Hdt. 5.44) to help in the city's destruction. It is seldom asked just why this prime piece of real estate (see the excellent photograph in von
Matt 1961, pl. 168) should have been treated in such a fashion, or how long, in fact, the city
remained a wasteland—certainly not until 452/1, as is too often supposed, since in the
mid-470s we find Kroton *besieging* Sybaris (D.S. 11.48.4 with note 184), a clear indication

they were driven out by Krotoniates, in the period now under discussion, five years after the second foundation.[49] [3] Shortly thereafter, the city was transferred to a new site and given a new name. Its founders were Lampon and Xenokritos, and the circumstances were as follows.

The Sybarites, thus evicted for the second time from their homeland, sent ambassadors to Greece, to the Lacedaemonians and Athenians, asking for their help in getting back, and inviting them to participate in the settlement.[50] [4] The Lacedaemonians ignored them, but the Athenians agreed to take part in the venture. They therefore manned ten ships and dispatched them to the Sybarites under the command of Lampon and Xenokritos;[51] they also sent a proclamation around the cities of the Peloponnese, throwing open this colonizing enterprise to anyone who cared to participate in it.[52] [5] Volunteers

---

(confirmed by numismatic evidence) that not only the city, but also its walls, had already been rebuilt to the point where they were defendable.

[49] Cf. 11.90.3, with note 373. Diodorus there attributes the city's rapid resurgence to its "rich farmland." Strabo's highly compressed account (6.1.13, C.263) records the brief refoundation, but omits Kroton's action, moving straight on to the subsequent colonization of the site.

[50] As Kagan (1969, 156) sensibly points out, this joint application must have postdated the Thirty Years' Peace (early spring 445); it is highly unlikely to have been made while Athens and Sparta were at war with one another, but once peace had been established "it was natural to apply for help to the two hegemonal states of Greece."

[51] It is important to distinguish the initial Athenian response to the Sybarite appeal (the dispatch of ten ships) from the subsequent international (Panhellenic) venture represented by the name change to "Thourioi." It is equally necessary to bear in mind that recent archaeological evidence—see the articles of Guzzo (1973) and Rainey (1969); and cf. Vallet 1976, 1024–1025 n. 16, 1032 n. 42; Sensi Sestito 1976, 249–254; Kagan 1969, 157–158—places Thourioi not at a distance from Sybaris, but on the southern area of the original site, so that there is virtually no difference between them: this, among other things, explains the Sybarites' continued claims to "first-comer" preferential treatment. Nor is there any reason why the original Athenian party, with its leaders, should not have remained *in situ* throughout. Lampon and Xenokritos were both seers: Aristoph. *Birds* 521 with schol., 988; schol. Aristoph. *Clouds* 332; Plut. *Per.* 6.2–3, *Mor.* 812d; Phot., Hesych., and *Suda* s.v. Thouriomanteis; *Vit. Anon. Thuc.* 7. So was Hieron, the religious adviser of Nikias, cited as a co-leader by Plutarch (*Nic.* 5.2). This emphatically religious leadership is suggestive: see below.

[52] This declaredly "Panhellenic" foundation, however we interpret its motivation, was Athenian in origin, and to a great extent in constitution (Ehrenberg 1948, 165–170; Graham 1964, 36). To what extent it was, as Ehrenberg believed, a Periklean imperial venture is another matter. That Perikles was behind it there seems no doubt. But why? It is worth remembering, at this point, (a) the collapse of Kimon's Cypro-Egyptian policy; (b) the exactly contemporary 445 B.C.E. famine in Attica, relieved only by a shipment of grain from the rebel pharaoh in the western marshes, Psammetichos (above, note 24); and (c) the mass

were numerous.⁵³ An oracular response was received from Apollo, telling them to found a city in the place where they would be

Drinking water in measure, but eating bread without measure.

So they sailed for Italy, and when they reached Sybaris proceeded to search for the place in which the god had commanded them to settle. [6] Not far from Sybaris they found a spring called Thouria, fitted with a bronze water-pipe of the sort known to locals as a *medimnos*. Convinced that this must be the spot indicated by the god, they walled it around, founded their city there, and named it Thourion after the spring.⁵⁴ [7] They divided the city lengthwise into four with avenues named respectively Herakleia, Aphrodisia, Olympias,

---

of colonies/cleruchies being sent out to Imbros, Chalkis, Eretria, Erythrai, Kolophon, the Chersonese, and elsewhere (*ATL* 3:299–300), a clear indication (Kagan 1969, 157; and cf. Plut. *Per.* 11.5) of "the need to rid Athens of excess population." It is hard to believe that the motives for this reaching out to one of the naturally richest sites in the West did *not* include the chance of securing desperately needed grain and timber. Apollo was right (below): "Eating bread without measure" (ἀμετρὶ δὲ μᾶζαν ἔδοντες) was what it was all about.

⁵³ Strabo (6.1.13, C.263) makes it clear that there was an initial period in which the Athenians simply joined the Sybarites as colonists in response to the original appeal (cf. Sensi Sestito 1976, 249–250). It looks very much as though this caused concern in Sparta: the Spartans, cautious as ever regarding overseas commitments, had rejected the Sybarite appeal, and would not have looked kindly on what must have seemed to them, coming immediately after the Thirty Years' Peace, to be a flagrant resumption of Athenian imperial expansionism. At this time of crisis, Perikles could not afford a resumption of hostilities with Sparta. Turning the whole thing into a Panhellenic venture, open to all comers, and renaming the site, however slight the move ("Sybaris" had unfortunate associations), was one way of countering their fears. But the concession (see below) was to carry a heavy price-tag. Rutter (1973, 166–167) queries the idea of the Athenians as a driving force in Thourioi because of their less than adequate showing as the new city developed; but had Perikles taken firm action, the whole concept of a Panhellenic venture would have been exposed as a patent sham. The Athenians were spiked by their own propaganda.

⁵⁴ Though this oracle has been generally condemned as spurious (e.g., by Parke-Wormell 1956, 1:50ff.; Fontenrose 1978, 156, 329; Rutter 1973, 162), it would surely have not taxed Delphi overmuch in the circumstances: this was an easy one, to which a general skepticism regarding foundation oracles does not necessarily apply. Clearly the oracle was sought (one late tradition, Zenob. 5.19, says by the Sybarites) after dissension had arisen between the Sybarites and the new colonists (in the summer of 445: see below); whether by Sybaris itself or by Athens (as part of the Panhellenic move) is uncertain. The latter is perhaps more likely, and can be linked to a subsequent second contingent of colonists (with Diodorus' account here, cf. Plut. *Mor.* 835c–d, dating it to 444/3, the archonship of Praxiteles) that included Protagoras, Herodotos, the town-planner Hippodamos, and Lysias the orator. The naming and walling formed the normal initial ritual phase of a foundation (Casevitz 1972, 100).

and Dionysias; breadthwise they divided it by means of three avenues, naming these Heroa, Thouria, and Thourina.[55] <. . .> When these narrow alleys were filled up, it was evident that, as regards housing, the city had been admirably planned.[56]

11. However, the Thourians lived peaceably together for a short time only,[57] after which acute civil dissension broke out between them—and not without reason. The former Sybarites were assigning the most prestigious offices to themselves, and the unimportant ones to those who had been enrolled as citizens later. They were also of the opinion that, among women citizens, their wives should take precedence when sacrifices were made to the gods, while later arrivals should yield place to them.[58] What was more, the

[55] For the orthogonal plan of Thourioi, cf. Martin 1974, 40–41. This is generally taken to have been the work of Hippodamos of Miletos (on whom see Arist. *Pol.* 2.5.1, 1267b, cf. 7.10.4, 1330b) from the fact of his early participation in the colonizing venture; that most of his activity in this area took place several decades later (Rutter 1973, 165, with earlier refs.) does not necessarily rule out his having been the designer here. As the following sentence makes clear, these main avenues were spaced well apart, and between them a large number of minor streets and alleys developed.

[56] Diodorus has a textual crux here. The two main readings are (a) ὑπὸ δὲ τούτων [PMF, Casevitz], (b) τούτων δὲ [P² S, Vogel, Oldfather], both readings being followed (in all MSS) by τῶν στενωπῶν πεπληρωμένων τὰς οἰκίας: Wesseling and Reiske emended the last two words to ταῖς οἰκίαις, in which all subsequent editors have followed them—unnecessarily, I would argue. None of the various emendations and readings proposed (e.g., by Kontis, Castagnoli 1971, and Casevitz 1972, admirably summarized by Vallet 1976, 1023–1032) meets the requirements either of syntax or of common sense, and need not be discussed here. No one to my knowledge has hitherto suggested the obvious solution: that what we have is a lacuna. We need neither to match blocks with nationalities, nor to explain how avenues have suddenly shrunk into alleys, a reference to which (possibly as surviving from the old, or at least rebuilt, site) must have dropped out of the text. The descriptive sequence is clear, and if the site did overlap with that of old Sybaris, the new planners' activities will have resembled those of Baron Haussmann when he set out to modernize Paris with avenues and boulevards. I therefore posit a lacuna, read (b), and retain τὰς οἰκίας as an accusative of respect.

[57] If Diodorus is right, no longer than the summer of 445 (below, 12.22.1): this would place their slaughter, and the expulsion of the survivors, *before* the second wave of colonizers arrived in 444/3, and explain the apparent discrepancy between Diodorus and Strabo (6.1.13, C.263), who clearly makes this clash antedate the "removal" to Thourioi.

[58] They did this on the old traditional basis: as the original colonists (ἄποικοι), they held themselves privileged by definition over any later arrivals (ἔποικοι), and this despite the fact that, as their appeal (and the city's prior history) had shown, they were manifestly incapable of preserving Sybaris against hostile incursions unaided (Moggi 1987, 68–72). Hence the clash with the Athenian group, which planned to put the new foundation in a position to maintain and defend itself, something that called for the kind of collective

land adjacent to the city they were parceling out into holdings for themselves, while the outlying tracts went to the newcomers.[59] [2] When dissension arose for these causes as stated, the citizens who had been added to the rolls later, being both more numerous and more powerful, massacred virtually all of the original Sybarites, and settled the city by themselves.[60] Since their territory was extensive as well as fertile, they brought in numerous settlers from Greece, assigning them their own part of the city and allotting them land-holdings on an equal basis. [3] Those who stayed on soon acquired great wealth. They established friendly relationships with the Krotoniates, and in general practiced good government. Under the democratic system that they set up, they divided the citizens into ten tribes, giving each one a name from the various peoples that composed them. Three consisted of people from the Peloponnese: these tribes they named the Arcadian, the Achaian, and the Eleian. A like number, formed from racially linked groups dwelling outside [the Peloponnese], they named the Boiotian, the Amphictyonian, and the Dorian; while the remaining four, made up from other peoples, became the Ionian, the Athenian, the Euboian, and the Nesiotic tribes.[61] They also chose as their lawgiver the

---

equality and goodwill (ὁμόνοια) envisaged by Plato and Aristotle (cf. Plat. *Laws* 5.745c–d; Arist. *Pol.* 7.9.7–8, 1330a14–25; with Moggi 1987, 75ff. and n. 35) and suggested by Diodorus (§2 ad fin.). That such defense would be necessary is amply proved by Thourioi's numerous subsequent conflicts with neighbors such as Taras, Terina, and the Lucani, as well as Kroton: D.S. 23.2; Strab. 6.1.14, C.264; Polyaen. 2.10.1–2, 4; cf. Moggi 1987, 74 n. 30 with further refs.

[59] Moggi's acute analysis (1987, 72ff.) renders obsolete all previous discussion (which he summarizes) on the reasons for this attempt at preferential land-distribution. The inner territory was not by definition richer or more fertile, any more than the outer lands necessarily had poorer soil or were fit only for grazing or hunting. Their proximity to the city center facilitated not only the transport of goods for market distribution, but also involvement in civic politics. Most important of all, however, in a city open to constant attack, it was the frontiersmen of the outer territories who both bore the brunt of all raids and were called upon to defend (Moggi [1987, 74] speaks of "una sorta di cintura protettiva") the more privileged central holdings. The Athenians, who understood all this very well, had no intention of being treated as second-class citizens by the losers they had come to help.

[60] Strabo (6.114, C.264; cf. Arist. *Pol.* 5.2.10, 1303a32–34) says they "felt contempt for them" (καταφρονήσαντες δὲ αὐτῶν), and it was this that led to the Sybarites' violent removal. This seems very plausible. For the fate of those Sybarites who escaped, see below, 12.22.1 with note 92.

[61] If Diodorus' account of Thourioi's new social system is correct (and there is no reason to doubt it), it would seem that the Kleisthenic ten-tribe system established in Athens was here refurbished on a genuinely Panhellenic basis. Cf. Kagan 1969, 162–163. Egalitarian in principle, this also contained the ethnic seeds of its own later divisive *stasis:* see below, 12.35.1–3, with note 188. It is interesting, not least when we bear in mind the markedly religious affiliation of the founders (above, note 51), that one tribe was "amphicty-

best of all citizens that were highly esteemed for learning: Charondas.[62]
[4] This was the man who, after making a study of all legislations, picked out
the best elements in them, which he then embodied in his own laws. But
he also worked out and formulated many ideas of his own,[63] and these it

---

onic," i.e., not regional, but drawn from a league of cities linked to a sanctuary (in this case
almost certainly Delphi). The Nesiotic tribe was drawn from the Aegean islands—thus for
the most part from Athens' subject-allies.

[62] The Ionian Charondas of Katana (on the coast of Sicily southeast of Mt. Etna) and
the Achaian Zaleukos of Epizephyrian Lokroi (on whom see 12.20–21, with notes) were
the earliest known Greek lawgivers (on the shadowy Dorian Diokles, see D.S. 13.35.3, and
Freeman 1892, 722–727). It is no accident (Bonner and Smith 1970, 1:69–70) that legal
codification should have begun in the colonial West. Different conditions required different solutions, which overrode traditional conservatism. Often, too (as in the case of Thourioi), colonists came from a number of cities, with divergent laws. Charondas made laws
not only for Katana, but for other Chalcidic cities on the coasts of Sicily and southern Italy
(Plat. *Rep.* 10.599E; Arist. *Pol.* 2.9.5, 1274b23ff.). His *floruit*, like that of Zaleukos, was most
probably in the seventh century B.C.E., and in any case he was dead by the end of the sixth.
Thus (Niese 1899, 2181) he cannot have legislated directly for Thourioi; nor indeed (though
this is most often assumed) does Diodorus specifically claim that he did. Diogenes Laertius (9.50) cites Herakleides Ponticus' treatise *On Laws* for Protagoras (one of Thourioi's
early colonists) having been the city's lawgiver, and this is highly plausible. Others (Athen.
11.508a, *Suda* s.v. Zaleukos) attribute Thourioi's laws to Zaleukos, and since he supposedly
made them for Sybaris, this, too, is likely. If we say that Protagoras largely used Charondas, but also borrowed items from Zaleukos for what seemed best suited to a Panhellenic
colony, we will probably be not too far from the truth.

[63] Charondas was of the middle class (Arist. *Pol.* 4.9.10, 1296a19–22), actively involved
in the politics of Katana and, when exiled from there, those of Rhegion (Ael. *VH* 3.17). Aristotle (*Pol.* 2.9.5, 1274a24–32) quotes, but only to challenge, the (perhaps inevitable) tradition that he studied under Zaleukos. Aristotle also claims (*Pol.* 2.9.8, 1274b6–8) that the
one original item in Charondas' code was the procedure of initial denunciation and intention to prosecute (ἐπίσκηψις) in cases of perjury (ψευδομαρτυρία). This incidentally
proves his early date, since ἐπίσκηψις was established in Athens long before the foundation
of Thourioi: Harrison 1968–71, 2:192–193; Gagarin 1986, 74. Aristotle also comments
(*Pol.* 2.9.8, 1274b6–8) on the subtle precision of Charondas' legal draftsmanship (parodied
by Herodas, 2.46ff.), which compared well (he claims) with that of Aristotle's own contemporaries. Aristotle mentions two of his laws: (a) higher fines for the rich than for the
poor in a case of refusal to serve on a jury (*Pol* 4.10.6, 1297a23–24; cf. Gagarin 1986, 109–
110); and (b) a four-year limit on service as general (*Pol.* 5.6.8, 1307b7ff.). Elsewhere we
learn that Charondas legislated against the extension of credit, insisting on immediate
payment (Theophrastos in Stob. 4.2.20; Gagarin 1986, 65–66 with n. 161); that he believed
in the *lex talionis* ("an eye for an eye": below, 12.17.4–5); and that his legislation probably
included family law (Arist. *Pol.* 1.1.6, 1252b14). It is interesting, but perhaps not significant,
that—with one doubtful exception—none of these cases is mentioned in Diodorus' account that follows, and, conversely, that none of the laws Diodorus does describe is referred

will not be irrelevant to put on record here, for the better instruction of our readers.[64]

12. First, there is the decree he instituted regarding such men as brought in a stepmother to be in charge of their existing children:[65] these he banned from serving as counselors for their fatherland, in the belief that anyone who planned so ill with regard to his own children would be an equally poor counselor to the state.[66] His argument was that those whose first marriages had been successful should remain content with their good fortune, whereas those who had made unfortunate marriages, and then repeated their mistake, must be regarded as lacking in plain sense. [2] Those found guilty of *sykophantia*, he decreed, should, when they went out, wear a tamarisk wreath, so as to make clear to all their fellow citizens that they had won first prize for base conduct.[67] In consequence, certain persons who had been condemned on this

---

to in connection with Charondas elsewhere. Freeman 1891, 451–457, though in parts outdated, still remains a useful summary.

[64] How far, if at all, the various "laws" that follow reflect early colonial legislation, and how far any genuine matter in them has been overlaid with later anecdotage and moralizing apothegms, is impossible, for lack of evidence, to disentangle. That, of course, has not stopped scholars from trying. Though Charondas and Zaleukos have a Pythagorean flavor (Dunbabin 1948, 73), and later Pythagoreans may well have adapted and edited the original codes, the tradition (below, 12.20.1 with note 84) that both were pupils of Pythagoras is (on chronological grounds alone) manifestly false. For a well-documented, if ultra-skeptical, survey, see Hölkeskamp 1999, 137–144; cf. Adcock 1927, 95ff.; Dunbabin 1948, 68–75. I am grateful to my former colleague Professor Michael Gagarin for drawing my attention to Hölkeskamp's exhaustive monograph.

[65] The unkindness of stepmothers ($\mu\eta\tau\rho\upsilon\iota\alpha\acute{\iota}$) was proverbial: Hdt. 4.154; Hes. *WD* 825; Plat. *Menex.* 237B; Isaios 12.5; Plut. *Mor.* 201e, 237b. Literary precedent (e.g., the case of Phaidra) is no proof of the spuriousness of this law: the topos derived from an observable social fact. Cf. 12.14.1–2 below for the popularity of the notion in antiquity.

[66] The term Diodorus uses for "counselors" is $\sigma\acute{\upsilon}\mu\beta\upsilon\lambda\upsilon\iota$. In discussing the four-year limit on service as a general at Thourioi (above), Aristotle specifically claims (*Pol.* 5.6.8, 1307b14–15) that those Thourian magistrates responsible for the maintenance of the laws were so described. It thus seems clear that this example of Diodorus' did, in fact, belong in the Thourian code. Hölkeskamp (1999, 142 n. 84) challenges the interpretation of $\sigma\acute{\upsilon}\mu$-$\beta\upsilon\lambda\upsilon\iota$ here in this sense, but without argument and, it would seem, simply to diminish the likelihood of the provision having any archaic basis.

[67] There is no one adequate English translation of *sykophantia* ($\sigma\upsilon\kappa\upsilon\phi\alpha\nu\tau\acute{\iota}\alpha$)—least of all "sycophancy," which carries a very different meaning from the ancient Greek (and particularly Athenian) activity, about which, as it happens, we know a good deal: see detailed accounts in Bonner and Smith 1970, 2:39–74; McDowell 1978, 62–66. It has been variously identified as "irresponsible or malicious prosecution," "criminal libel or blackmail"

charge, unable to bear such great humiliation, voluntarily removed themselves from the company of the living. When this happened, all who had regularly practiced *sykophantia* were [scared into] fleeing the city; and the government, rid of this plague, thenceforth enjoyed a happy existence.[68]

[3] Charondas also wrote an unparalleled law on the keeping of bad company, something that all other lawgivers had overlooked. His assumption was that good men, through friendship and habitual intercourse with those of base character, sometimes have their own morals corrupted: that badness, like some pestilent disease, invades the life of mankind, infecting the souls even of the best. This [he concluded] was why many men of average character become ensnared by factitious pleasures, and end up stuck with really abominable habits. Wanting, therefore, to banish this source of corruption, the lawgiver banned all friendship and intimate association with base persons, drafted laws against the keeping of bad company, and by means of stringent penalties discouraged those about to commit such errors.[69] [4] He also framed another law

---

(Harrison 1968–71, 2:61), and as including "calumny and conspiracy, false accusation, malicious prosecution, threats of legal proceedings to extort money" (Kennedy, cited by Bonner and Smith 1970, 2:42–43). All these attributes can, in various cases, be shown to be true. The most notorious function of the *sykophantes* was as an informer, the equivalent of the later Roman *delator;* but ancient descriptions are equally varied, a list of attributes rather than definitions: Aeschin. 2.145 (repeated slander), Dem. 57.34 (false prosecutions), Lys. 25.3, Isokr. 15.24 (blackmail). Even the meaning of the word itself has been in dispute since antiquity. Yet the barrage of abuse (above all in the plays of Aristophanes: Bonner and Smith 1970, 2:43–47; McDowell 1978, 63–65) sometimes obscures the fact that both acting as an informer and prosecuting as an individual, far from being illegal, formed the cornerstone of the Athenian legal system, where the role of the public prosecutor was unknown. The fact that it was possible to prosecute a *sykophantes* (Bonner and Smith 1970, 2:63; McDowell 1978, 65) shows that *sykophantia* had to involve *abuse* of the system: in an ultra-litigious society that habitually used the courts as an extension of political in-fighting, the frequency of such abuse should not occasion surprise.

[68] Hölkeskamp (1999, 141) challenges both the age and the authenticity of this provision, seeing its moralizing quality as wholly alien to the nature of any early legislation known to us. The likeliest explanation is that it was inserted in the Thourioi code by Protagoras, who knew the habits of Athenian *sykophantai* at first hand (and was later to become their target: Diog. Laert. 9.54, 55; Philostr. 1.10.4).

[69] Though this is a fine example of Hölkeskamp's "moralisierend-belehrende Tendenz" (1999, 141), it is interesting that it bears a remarkable resemblance to Theognis' advice to Kyrnos (27–38), including the recommendation to stay clear of low company (31–32: κακοῖσι δὲ μὴ προσομίλει / ἀνδράσιν. Since Theognis was certainly as early as the sixth century, and may even have been as early as the seventh (West in *OCD* 1503), this gives the recommendation cited by Diodorus sufficient antiquity to be genuine, even if its legal nature remains dubious. Cf. 12.14.1 below.

of greater merit even than this one, and similarly overlooked by previous law-givers. This laid down that all the sons of citizens should learn to read and write, and that the state should be responsible for paying teachers' salaries. His assumption here was that the indigent, who could not afford such fees from their own resources, would [otherwise] be deprived of the best and highest pursuits.[70]

13. Indeed, this lawgiver ranked literacy above every other kind of learning, and was right to do so: for this is what enables the bulk—and the most valu-able part—of human affairs to be carried out: voting, letter-writing, the en-grossment of laws and covenants, and all other things that most contribute to the proper regulation of life. [2] Who could sufficiently praise the acquisition of letters? It is by this alone that the dead survive in the memory of the living, or that people in places widely separated one from the other communicate, even with those at the greatest distance from them, by means of the written word, just as though they were close by. Also, as regards wartime treaties be-tween peoples or monarchs, the firmest guarantee that such agreements will hold good is provided by the specificity of a written text. In sum, this is what alone preserves the most satisfying pronouncements of wise men and the or-

---

[70] This, the most interesting of the regulations recorded by Diodorus, has also met with more than its fair share of skepticism (e.g., Thomas 1992, 1321 n. 11; Hölkeskamp 1999, 142; Harris 1989, 98). It is true that the association of culture with literacy on which Diodorus expatiates in ch. 13 is reckoned to be more characteristic of the Hellenistic and Greco-Roman periods than of the classical, let alone the archaic, Greek world (Thomas 1992, 130–131), and indeed that early Greece regarded writing with some suspicion (Hartog 1988, 277–281); but earlier moves in the direction of universal education, and remarks on the advantages to the *polis* of writing—often very similar to Diodorus'; cf. Arist. *Pol.* 8.2.6, 1338a15–17—are by no means rare in the early fourth and even in the fifth century: Gor-gias *Palamedes* fr. 11a, 30; Eur. *Suppl.* 433; Plat. *Laws* 7.804c–e, 809e–810b; Arist. *Pol.* 2.6.16, 1270b28, 8.1.3, 1337a33ff., 8.2.3, 1337b24ff., cf. 1.5.12, 1260b17–21 (female education). There is also the economic question: in the classical era, education had to be paid for, and was expensive, so that only the wealthiest, οἱ πλουσιώτατοι, could afford it: Plat. *Protag.* 326C, Xen. *Mem.* 2.2.6, Dem. 18.265, cited by Harris (1989, 101), who remarks that "for cases of subsidized elementary education in Greek cities we have to wait for the Hellenis-tic age." Yet Harris himself rightly points out elsewhere (1989, 138–139) that the proximity of non-Greek native populations (Lucanians, Oenotriae) may have sharpened the need of Greek colonists to preserve their Hellenic identity—for which, of course, the ability to read and write Greek would be crucial. Colonists, as we have seen (Bonner and Smith 1970, 1:69), had special needs. It is more than possible, then, that Charondas did legislate for state-sponsored education. Even if he did not, it is highly probable that Protagoras would have insisted on such a provision for Thourioi.

acles of the gods, not to mention philosophy and all educational knowledge, and is forever handing them on to generation after generation down the ages. [3] Thus, while we must acknowledge that nature is the cause of life, we must also agree that the *good* life is brought about by an upbringing grounded in literacy. It was, then, to right the wrong done the illiterate (in thus depriving them of certain enormous benefits) that [Charondas] by his legislation judged them deserving of public concern and expenditure; [4] and whereas earlier legislators had decreed that private individuals, when sick, should enjoy medical services at the expense of the state, he went far beyond what they did, since they [merely] thought bodies worth healing, while he offered care to souls burdened through lack of education. Indeed, while we must pray that we never stand in need of those [other] physicians, we most heartily desire that all our time may be spent among such teachers of knowledge.

14. Both of the earlier laws here mentioned have received witness from many poets in verse: that on keeping bad company as follows:

> The man who loves the company of the base
> I never question, well aware that he
> is just like those whose comradeship he seeks.[71]

while the law regarding stepmothers produced this:

> The lawgiver Charondas, men say, in one
> of his decrees, among much else, declares:
> The man who on his children foists a stepmother
> should rank as naught and share in no debate
> among his fellows, having himself dragged in
> this foreign plague to damn his own affairs.
> If you were lucky the first time you wed
> (he says), don't press your luck; and if you weren't,
> trying a second time proves you insane.[72]

It is certainly true that anyone who makes the same mistake twice may justly be regarded as a fool. [2] Philemon, too, the comic playwright, writing about habitual seafarers, says:

---

[71] Euripides *Phoenix* fr. 812 Nauck. The passage is quoted at considerably greater length by Aeschines in his speech against Timarchos (1.152). The lines immediately preceding those given by Diodorus declare: "So I, like any man of common wisdom, / figure the truth by looking into a man's / nature, the character of his daily life."

[72] Fragment of an unidentified late comic poet: fr. adesp. 110 Kock.

> That law stirs wonder in me—not when a man
> sets out by sea the first time, but the second.[73]

In the same way, one might assert that one is not amazed by a man's marrying, but only if he marries twice: for it is preferable to expose oneself twice to the sea than to a woman. [3] The greatest and most terrible domestic dissensions are those that pit children against their fathers because of a stepmother, something that occasions the portrayal on the tragic stage of countless such lawless acts.

15. Charondas wrote yet another law that deserves our endorsement: the one dealing with the guardianship of orphans. On the surface this law would appear, when first examined, to have no exceptional or particularly praiseworthy feature; but when looked at again, and subjected to close scrutiny, it reveals zealous study and high merit. [2] Now what he wrote was that the property of orphans should be managed by the next of kin on the father's side, but that the orphans themselves should be brought up by their relatives on the mother's side.[74] Now at first sight this law reveals no wise or exceptional content; but on examining it more deeply, one finds it justly worthy of praise. For when one looks for the reason why he entrusted the property of orphans to one group, but their upbringing to another, the lawgiver's outstanding ingenuity becomes apparent: [3] for the relatives on the mother's side, having no claim on the distribution of the orphans' inheritance, will not make plots against them; while the close kin on the father's side are in no position to hatch such plots, since they are not entrusted with their physical protection.

---

[73] Philemon, c. 365–?262 B.C.E. (D.S. 23.6.1), from Syracuse (or possibly Soloi in Cilicia), was a poet of the New Comedy and Menander's main rival: he obtained Athenian citizenship not later than 307/6. Living to be about a hundred, with faculties unimpaired until the end, he is credited with ninety-seven comedies: his first victory at the Dionysia was in 327 B.C.E. His fragments reveal a strong, if plodding, weakness (as here) for moralistic aphorisms. Cf. W. G. Arnott in *OCD* 1159.

[74] For no reason given, Hölkeskamp (1999, 143) concedes that this law might be grounded in fact: possibly because (n. 89) it matches a virtually identical clause in the Gortyn Code on Crete. There is nothing similar in the various provisions for orphans in Athenian law (McDowell 1978, 93–98). The purpose of the law, Hölkeskamp suggests, was to prevent abuse (up to and including murder) of an underage orphan heir by the deceased father's male relatives (who nevertheless still handled the property), whereas the relatives of the mother (possibly still living: the loss of a father alone produced orphan status), having no chance of inheriting, were less likely to mistreat him (or her). Possibly (this explanation is largely a précis of Diodorus); but it could have been a matter of simple humane consideration for an adolescent's well-being.

Moreover, since, if the orphans die of an illness or some other accidental hazard, the estate reverts to them, they will manage that estate with more than usual care, since they treat as [already] their own expectations in fact dependent upon the whims of fortune.

16. He also drafted a law aimed at those who deserted their post in wartime, or flatly refused to take up arms at all in defense of their fatherland.[75] Whereas other legislators had stipulated death as the punishment for such men, Charondas decreed that they should sit in the marketplace for three days dressed as women. [2] Now this law is both more humane than its equivalent elsewhere, and also, because of the extreme humiliation it inflicts, tends subconsciously to deter those similarly inclined from cowardly behavior; for death is preferable to suffering so great an indignity in one's native city. At the same time, he did not do away with the offenders, but saved them for the state's military needs, his belief being that the punishment meted out for their disgraceful offense would make them determined to vindicate themselves, and by fresh deeds of valor wipe out their past shame.

[3] It was through the stringency of the laws he enacted that this lawgiver ensured their maintenance. For instance, he prescribed obedience to the law

---

[75] Desertion (λιποταξία)—which included the chargeable subcategories of cowardice (δειλία) and throwing away one's shield (ῥιψασπία)—was, like the avoidance of military service (ἀστρατεία), regarded with contempt and severely punished in a society where warfare was a way of life, and defense of the *polis* by its citizens crucial. We know (as so often) more about Athens than about other states when it comes to military discipline, but this is one area where it is safe to say that the same, or similar, rules applied generally. Lysias (14.4–9) makes it clear (cf. Pritchett 1974, 234) that such serious cases could be tried by military court-martial; but interestingly, the penalty, despite Diodorus' assertion, was seldom death: exile, loss of civic rights (ἀτιμία), or both, were far more frequent. Though in the fifth century, Athenian generals (στρατηγοί) had the right to inflict the death penalty, they used it sparingly, and by Aristotle's day (*Ath. Pol.* 61.2) seem to have lost the right altogether. Also, though the exact punishment is not known elsewhere, the *spirit* of this supposed law of Charondas is very much in evidence, and not only at Athens: not surprisingly, when public shame was always so powerful a deterrent (as the fate of the two Spartan survivors of Thermopylai shows, Hdt. 7.231–232). The Spartan regent Pausanias made offenders stand all day with an iron anchor on their shoulders (Plut. *Arist.* 23.2). A similar Spartan punishment for indiscipline (ἀταξία) was, again, to stand in public holding up one's shield (Xen. *Hell.* 3.1.9). Officers were cashiered with ignominy (Lys. 3.45, Arist. *Ath. Pol.* 61.2). The death penalty was, on occasion, enforced (D.S. 12.62.5 on shield-dropping; cf. Front. *Strat.* 4.1.17, Xen. *Hell.* 1.1.15), but in general "unmanly conduct was restrained by the odium attached to it" (Pritchett 1974, 245: his entire ch. 12, "Greek Military Discipline," 232–245, is the *locus classicus* on the subject. Cf. also McDowell 1978, 159–161; Bonner and Smith 1970, 2:55, 61, 261–264; Harrison 1968–71, 2:32).

whatever the circumstances, even if it had been fundamentally ill-drafted; at the same time, he allowed for redrafting should the need arise. [4] His argument was this: to be overruled by a lawgiver was reasonable, but [to be overruled] by a private citizen was wholly out of place, even should this be to one's advantage. He [had in mind] those who serve up in court the excuses and devious tricks of lawbreakers rather than the actual letter of the law; and it was above all by this means that he stopped them from using their innovative quibbles to undermine the laws' paramount authority.[76] [5] This was why, when one of those who had advanced such arguments was haranguing the jurors about the [proper] way to punish lawbreakers, he told them they must save either the law or the man.

17. However, what has been described as the most improbable legislation by Charondas is that to do with his revision of the legal code. Remarking that in most cities the sheer number of efforts to revise the laws both debased established legislation and encouraged civil dissension in the masses, he drafted a decree that was both personal and quite extraordinary. [2] His ruling was that anyone wishing to amend a law should put his neck in a noose when advancing his proposed revision, and so remain until the *demos* returned a verdict on it. If the assembly accepted the amendment, the proposer would be released; but if his proposal was voted down, he was to be hanged on the spot.[77] [3] With such legislation in force regarding revision of the laws, subsequent lawmakers were held back by fear, and not one of them dared to utter a word on the subject. Indeed, from that day to this, only three men in Thourioi are related as having, on account of certain compelling circumstances, presented themselves before the council in charge of revision.[78]

---

[76] For Greek reluctance to alter existing laws, see Bonner and Smith 1970, 1:75. McDowell (1978, 48–49), discussing Athenian legislation by "lawgivers" (νομοθέται), remarks that this concern was much more acute in the fourth century than in the fifth. Diodorus' report (§4) of objections to overruling "by a private citizen" (ὑπὸ ἰδιώτου) reveal an antidemotic bias in his source: at Athens, in the last resort, the assembly (ἐκκλησία) had final authority over any lawgiver.

[77] An identical law is described by Demosthenes (24.139–141, cf. Polyb. 12.16.9ff.) but attributed to Epizephyrian Lokroi, i.e., in all likelihood regarded as the work of Zaleukos rather than of Charondas. What we seem to have here is not so much an error on Diodorus' part (so, most recently, Hölkeskamp 1999, 139) as one of the eclectic measures adopted for Thourioi by Protagoras.

[78] Demosthenes, similarly, claimed that only one such change was made in 200 years (cf. Bonner and Smith 1970, 1:75). The text of the final clause is uncertain. The MSS (emendations noted) read: παρὰ τοῖς Θουρίοις τρεῖς οἱ πάντες εἰσηγοῦνται [ἱστοροῦνται Wurm, λέγονται Madvig] διορθωθῆναι [διορθωταί Reiske] διὰ <τό> [Oldfather] τινας

[4] In the first case, there was a law that if a man put someone's eye out, he himself should lose an eye by way of reprisal.[79] Now a certain one-eyed man had had that eye destroyed, and thereby lost his sight entirely. He therefore argued that the offender, by forfeiting one eye only in return, had paid less than a fair penalty, since he who blinded a fellow citizen, and paid only the penalty prescribed by law, would not have suffered a comparable loss. To be fair, and make the punishment equitable, anyone who robbed a one-eyed man of sight should have *both* his eyes put out.[80] [5] Thus the one-eyed man, who had become extremely embittered, had the courage to raise in the assembly the matter of his personal loss, and while lamenting to his fellow citizens

---

ἀναγκαίας περιστάσεις ἐπὶ τὴν ὑπὲρ τῆς διορθώσεως συμβουλίαν παραγενέσθαι. Oldfather (accepting both Wurm and Reiske, and using his added τό to make διά govern the entire clause through παραγενέσθαι) translates: "History records but three men who proposed revision among the Thourians, and these appeared because circumstances arose which rendered proposals of revision imperative." This does not translate the Greek, even as amended. Casevitz accepts Wurm, retains διορθωθῆναι (thus making construal impossible), keeps Oldfather's τό, and translates: "On ne mentionne en tout et pour tout à Thourioi que trois réformateurs qui furent amenés par les circonstances à proposer une révision." This does not translate the amended Greek either. The first thing to recognize is that διορθωθῆναι can *only* apply in the passive to the laws revised or corrected: the implication then is that τρεῖς οἱ πάντες refers to laws, not men. This is clearly how Vogel (1890) took the Greek: we could then translate: "Among the Thourians three laws only are reported as having been so revised, because of certain compelling circumstances." However, this then makes syntactical nonsense of the rest of the sentence, ἐπὶ . . . παραγενέσθαι, which Vogel then blandly got rid of by bracketing it in its entirety as an interpolation. Unless we are to assume a lacuna (which I still suspect may be the case) between mention of the laws themselves and their three courageous revisers, we have to get rid of διορθωθῆναι as an intrusive gloss, drop Oldfather's τό, and revise our thinking about the object of διά (*only* the "compelling circumstances"), the subject of παραγενέσθαι (the would-be revisers, not their corrections), and, equally important, the meaning of συμβουλίαν ("council," not "advice"). The Greek can then be translated, as above. (Though the emendations for εἰσηγοῦνται improve the Greek, they are not strictly necessary.)

[79] The notion of retaliation (the *lex talionis* in Roman law) is one of the oldest and most widespread notions in European and Near Eastern history: cf. Exodus 21.23, "Life for life, eye for eye, tooth for tooth, hand for hand, foot for foot," etc., and *Lex XII Tab.* 8.2–4: "si membrum rupsit . . . talio esto." Demosthenes (see below) associates such a law with Epizephyrian Lokroi, i.e., with Zaleukos, but there is no reason why so basic a notion should not have been understood by both. To assume borrowing is unnecessary. Gagarin (1986, 62) appositely cites G. R. Driver and J. C. Miles, *The Babylonian Laws* (Oxford, 1952), 408: "Once it is realized that the natural remedy for an assault is retaliation, and that talion was a fundamental principle of early law . . . a similar treatment of similar offences may be expected amongst different peoples in similar stages of civilization."

[80] An identical story is recounted by Demosthenes (24.139–141) but attributed to the Lokrians. Cf. Arist. *Rhet.* 1365b17, Ael. *VH* 13.24 (specifically attributed to Zaleukos).

over the mishap he had suffered, also proposed to the commons a revision of the law, winding up by putting his neck in a noose. He got his proposal carried, had the law as it stood revoked and the amendment confirmed, and also escaped death by hanging.

18. The second law to be revised was one giving a wife the right to divorce her husband and [thereafter] marry whomsoever she pleased. A husband who was well advanced in years had a younger wife who had left him. This man proposed before the Thourians a rider amending the law, to the effect that a woman who left her husband might indeed marry whomsoever she pleased— provided that he was no younger than his predecessor; and similarly, that if a man put away his wife, he could not then marry a woman younger than the wife he had divorced. [2] This petitioner likewise had his proposal carried, got the earlier law set aside, and escaped the risk of being hanged; while his wife, thus prevented from moving in with a younger man, remarried the husband she had left.[81]

[3] The third law to be revised, one that also features in Solon's legislation, was the one concerning heiresses. Charondas decreed that the next of kin be legally required to marry an heiress, and that an heiress similarly be required to marry her closest relative, who then had either to marry her or, in the case of an indigent heiress, to pay 500 drachmas into an account for her dowry.[82]
[4] A certain orphaned heiress, of good family but wholly without means of

---

[81] Hölkeskamp (1999, 139–140) dismisses this law as spurious and "historically worthless," on the grounds (a) that it bears no relation to any other divorce law known in Greece, and, a corollary of this, (b) that it in no way concerns itself with the practical details of property, children, and succession. This has not stopped others from accepting it (e.g., Bonner and Smith 1970, 1:79; Niese 1899, 2182; others cited by Hölkeskamp 1999, 139–140 n. 64). While its flavor certainly comes over as more Hellenistic than archaic, it is perhaps over-confident to dismiss it out of hand.

[82] Cf. Plut. Sol. 20.2–3; Harrison 1968–71, 1:10–12; McDowell 1978, 95–98. The term "heiress" for *epikleros* is unavoidable but misleading: the property did not come to her absolutely (or, indeed, to the man she married), but was simply held by her in trust until her son was of an age to inherit. As the Solonian law insisted, the husband of an *epikleros* was obliged to have intercourse with her at least three times a month: the overriding object of the legislation (McDowell 1978, 96) "was to get a male heir in direct descent from her father." The alternative (of a payment toward the dowry) is confirmed by Demosthenes (43.54) and Isaios (1.39, where the rate is adjusted to the Athenian property class: 500 drachmas for the highest [*Pentekosiomedimnoi*], 300 for the Knights [*Hippeis*], 150 for the Yeomen [*Zeugitai*]). The original relationship between western Greek and Solonian (or post-Solonian) legislation is impossible to determine with any certainty (Hölkeskamp 1999, 140–141 is characteristically dismissive of all of Diodorus' evidence). Once again, the eclecticism of Protagoras may underlie much of the surviving tradition.

support, and because of her poverty unable to marry, sought remedy from the *demos,* weeping as she laid before them the hopeless and despised nature of her position. She then went on to describe her proposed amendment to the law, that instead of the 500 drachmas payment, it should state that the next of kin *must* marry the heiress assigned to him by law. The *demos* out of pity voted for the amendment; and thus while the orphan escaped hanging, the next of kin (who was wealthy) was compelled to marry a penniless heiress who brought him no dowry.

19. It remains for us to speak of Charondas' death, concerning which a most peculiar and unlooked-for accident befell him. When he left town for the country, he had armed himself with a dagger as a defense against highwaymen. On his return he found the assembly in session and the populace greatly upset, and being curious as to the cause of dissension, he went in. [2] Now he had once passed a law that no one should enter the assembly carrying a weapon, and it had slipped his mind on this occasion that he himself had a dirk strapped to his waist. He thus offered certain of his enemies a fine opportunity to bring a charge against him. But when one of them said, "You've revoked your own law," he replied, "No, by God, I shall maintain it," and with that drew his dirk and killed himself. Certain writers, however, attribute this act to Diokles, the lawgiver of the Syracusans.[83]

[3] Now that we have expatiated at sufficient length on matters concerning Charondas the lawgiver, we would like to add a brief discussion of another lawgiver, Zaleukos, since these men chose very similar ways of life, and were in fact born in neighboring cities.

20. Zaleukos[84] was by birth a Lokrian from Italy, a man of good family and much esteemed for his education, having been a student of Pythagoras the

---

[83] On Diokles, see above, note 62, as well as 13.33.2, 13.35.1–5. The same anecdote is repeated by Diodorus at 13.33.2–3, where it is associated solely with Diokles, and Charondas is not mentioned. Whether it is true of either of them—its anecdotal quality generally earns it a scornful dismissal, most recently by Hölkeskamp (1999, 138)—cannot be confidently determined: that a moral tale is *ben trovato* does not automatically disprove it.

[84] For Zaleukos, see von Fritz 1967; Dunbabin 1948, 68–73; Gagarin 1986, 58–62. Much of Diodorus' account is clearly based on a late, Pythagorean-inspired, and hagiolatric tradition shared by Diogenes Laertius (8.1.15–16) and Iamblichos (*Vit. Pyth.* 23, 104, 130, 172; cf. von Fritz 1967, 2299; Dunbabin 1948, 70) that both improves his social standing and (against all chronological evidence) makes him, inevitably, a student of Pythagoras (c. 550–c. 500 B.C.E.). Lokroi was traditionally founded in 673, and Eusebius further (*Chron.* 2.86–87) gives the date of Zaleukos' legislation as 663 or 661: early but not impossible. Aristotle (*Pol.* 4.9.10, 1296a18–22) lists Zaleukos, like Charondas, as middle-class.

philosopher. Since he enjoyed a high reputation in his native city, he was chosen as lawmaker, and proceeded to hand down, from scratch, a completely
new code of laws,[85] beginning with the heavenly deities. [2] For right at the
beginning, in the general preamble to his legislation,[86] he stated that the city's
inhabitants must, first and foremost, by reason as by faith, believe that the
gods do indeed exist; that intelligent contemplation of the heavens, and the
ordering and pattern thereof, should leave them with the conviction that these
creations are the result neither of chance nor of human labor; that they should
[therefore] revere the gods as the cause of all that is fine and good in human
existence; and that they should keep the soul clean of all evil, on the grounds

---

He also states (fr. 548 Rose = schol. Pind. *Ol.* 11.17) that Zaleukos' appointment as lawgiver (νομοθέτης) came at a time of intense political upheaval (πολλῆς ταραχῆς). He thus
can be seen as yet another example (like Solon in Athens or Pittakos in Mytilene) of an
emergency arbitrator between a predominantly aristocratic/conservative government and
the newly emergent *demos*. The tradition recorded by schol. Pind. *Ol.* 11.17 that he was a
shepherd (ποιμήν) may well derive from his being known in populist circles as a λαοῦ
ποιμήν, "shepherd of the people" (Dunbabin 1948, 69). As Gagarin says (1986, 59–60),
these men were political outsiders, called in to legislate for hopelessly embroiled partisans.

[85] We know very little about the Zaleukan code, and much of the evidence is dubious.
Probably our best witness is Ephoros, cited by Strabo (6.1.8, C.260 = *FGrH* 70 F 139), who
states (a) that it was written down, (b) that it was derived from the Spartan, Cretan, and
Athenian Areopagite codes, (c) that the laws on contracts (περὶ τῶν συμβολαίων) were
drafted in simpler language, and (d) that whereas previously penalties for various crimes
had been left to the discretion of the judges, they were now, in the interest of equal justice,
specified and put on record. Apart from (b), which looks like guesswork, these supposedly
being the oldest and most venerable codes, the rest can be accepted, and (d) is of great importance as marking the transition to statute law, which could be invoked on appeal. The
Pindar scholiast (above) also informs us that Zaleukos claimed to derive his laws from
Athena, as the Cretans did theirs from Minos and Rhadamanthys, to lend them divine authority (Plat. *Laws* 624A–625A; Gagarin 1986, 60 n. 36). We hear of a law—for the breaking of which the penalty was death—against drinking unmixed wine without a doctor's
prescription (Athen. 10.429A, Ael. *VH* 2.37). Polybius (12.16.4) tells us that those from
whom seizure was made were entitled to retain the disputed property prior to trial. Otherwise our evidence is limited to the *lex talionis* and the neck-in-noose provision we have
already noted. Cf. Dunbabin 1948, 70.

[86] This preamble (προοίμιον) is also mentioned by Cicero (*Leg.* 2.7.8–10) and Stobaeus
(IV, p. 123H, cited by Casevitz 1972, 102). Plato (*Laws* 722E) has the Athenian Stranger
claim that no one had yet prefaced a city's laws (νόμους πολιτικούς) with such a preamble,
and on this basis Dunbabin (1948, 70–71) and others proclaim the preamble mentioned
here a forgery. It may not be as simple as that. Plato is discussing (719Cff.) the need for
such prefatory statements, and at 722E–723B goes on to say that existing laws in fact often
include such statements, though they tend not to be recognized as such. At the same time
it is quite possible that what Cicero and the rest had access to was, in effect, a Pythagorean
rewrite.

that the gods take no joy in the sacrifices or costly outlay of the wicked, but rather in the just and decent practices of good men.[87] [3] After thus in his preamble summoning the citizen body to follow piety and justice, he tacked on a further requirement, that they should treat none of their fellows as an irreconcilable enemy, but should assume, when enmity came between them, that matters would come back eventually to resolution and a renewal of friendship; and that anyone who acted otherwise should be regarded by his fellows as being of a wild and uncivilized temperament.[88] He also exhorted the officers of state not to be aggressive or over-proud, and not to make judgments on the basis of friendship or enmity. Further, among his various ordinances were many that he himself formulated, with outstanding wisdom.

21. For instance, where all other societies imposed financial penalties on erring wives, he found a most artful device whereby to curb their licentiousness, through the following laws that he drafted. A free woman could not be escorted abroad by more than one female attendant—unless she was drunk. Nor could she leave the city at night—except to commit adultery; nor could she wear gold jewelry or a purple-bordered dress—unless she was a courtesan. A husband, similarly, could not wear a gilded ring or an outer garment in the Milesian style—unless set on whoring or adultery.[89] [2] As a result, by

---

[87] The similarity of these ideas to Stoic thought has often been noted; but Casevitz (1972, 102) correctly points out that Plato (again in the *Laws,* 886A) offers a very similar proof of divinity. Here as elsewhere, Plato can be seen as reworking Pythagorean concepts. For Pythagoreanism in Plato, see Burkert 1972, 83–96.

[88] This clause, too, smacks of (Platonic) Pythagoreanism: cf. Plat. *Gorg.* 507E: "The wise men tell us that heaven and earth, gods and men are bound together by kinship and love and orderliness and temperance and justice." Cf. Guthrie 1962, 200ff.; and for Pythagorean notions of friendship, Konstan 1997, 82, 114–115.

[89] This kind of sumptuary legislation, in particular laws curbing the alleged extravagance and license of women, was a common feature of early Greek legislation (Bonner and Smith 1970, 1:82): see, e.g., Plut. *Sol.* 21.4 on that of Solon. In colonial society, where a mercantile *tiers état* was rapidly expanding, traditional class distinctions were in flux, and fortunes could be made without reference to blood or land, an urgent need will have been felt both to control public morals and to prevent the kind of ostentatious behavior that led to *stasis* (Brugnone 1992, 5–24). Similar sanctions are reported from Syracuse (Phylarchos *FGrH* 81 F 45 = Athen. 12.521b–c). In the examples cited here (whether genuine or not), we once again see the use of public opinion to shame individuals into acceptable conduct. Since none of these provisions was easily enforced, it was left to alert citizens to draw the (unflattering) inference when they saw the law being flouted. If a woman with multiple attendants was *by legal definition* drunk, or a richly dressed and beringed husband *by legal definition* an adulterer, this (it was probably thought) would be a more effective restraint than any number of roving inspectors (such as the Athenian γυναικονόμοι, Arist. *Pol.* 1299b23–24).

imposing a sense of shame in lieu of the old penalties, he had no trouble in steering [citizens] away from damaging luxury and licentious practices; for no one wanted to become a laughing-stock among the other citizens by openly admitting to such shameful and self-indulgent habits. [3] He wrote excellent laws on many other vexed aspects of life, including contracts;[90] but it would take too long to recount these, and they are not germane to the plan of this history. We shall therefore resume our narrative at the point where we left it.

22. When Lysimachides was archon in Athens [445/4], the Romans elected as consuls Titus Menenius and Publius Sestius Capitolinus.[91] During their term, the Sybarites, fleeing from the perils of civil dissension, settled on the Traïs River. They remained there for some while, but later were driven out by the Bruttii and done away with.[92] [2] In Greece, the Athenians, having recovered Euboia and expropriated the Histiaians from their city, now sent out to it a colony of their own, consisting of 1,000 citizens, under Perikles' command, parceling out both city and surrounding countryside into settlers' holdings.[93]

23. When Praxiteles was archon in Athens [444/3], the 84th Olympiad was held, in which Krison of Himera won the *stadion;* and in Rome ten men were elected as legislators: Publius Clodius Regillanus, Titus Minucius, Spurius Veturius, Gaius Julius, Gaius Sulpicius, Publius Sestius, Romulus, and Spurius Postumius Calvinius. These were the men who tabulated the laws.[94] [2] Dur-

---

[90] Cf. above, note 85.

[91] The consuls (actually for 452) were T. Menenius Lanatus and P. Sestius Capitolinus Vaticanus (Broughton 1951, 44).

[92] These were the Sybarites who escaped the slaughter described at 12.11.2. The Traïs (modern Trionto) is about 25 miles southeast, down the coast from the original site, and the escapees settled on the eastern side of it (*BA* 46 E2; cf. Turano 1975, 84). The date for their final expulsion and massacre will have been after 356/5 (cf. D.S. 16.15.1–2; Strab. 6.1.4, C.255; Just. 23.1.2–6, 10–14), since it was then that the Bruttii (or Brettii: *bruttii,* the Lucanian term for runaway slaves, may have been a nickname) revolted from their Lucanian masters and established their own state.

[93] Cf. above, 12.7 and note 32. Diodorus' text there agrees with Thuc. 1.114.3 and Plut. *Per.* 23.2 in making the actual expropriation of the Histiaians take place in 446, *before* the Thirty Years' Peace: what he says here, with its carefully emphasized aorist participles (ἀνακτησάμενοι, ἐκβαλόντες), does not, as is sometimes carelessly assumed, contradict that dating. Theopompos *FGrH* 115 F 387 (= Strab. 10.1.3, C.445) gives the number of settlers as 2,000; but 1,000 seems to have been the more common figure for such ventures (Meiggs 1972, 122, 178 n. 4).

[94] This first appointment of the Decemviri took place in 451. It was the result of a tribune's proposal in 462—either to form a commission to publish the laws, or to legislate

ing their term, the Thourians and the Tarantines were continually at war, raiding and laying waste each other's territory by land and sea. Though they engaged in numerous minor battles and skirmishes, they achieved no action worthy of note.[95]

24. When Lysanias was archon in Athens [443/2], the Romans again chose ten men as legislators: Appius Clodius <Claudius>, Marcus Cornelius, Lucius Minucius, Gaius Sergius, Quintus Publius, Manius Rabuleius, and Spurius Veturius.[96] [2] These men proved unable to complete their appointed task.[97]

---

to curb the authority of the consuls, or both—followed, inevitably, by a decade of inconclusive wrangling. (What it almost certainly was *not*, though some had reason to promote the notion—see, e.g., Livy 3.31.7–8, Dion. Hal. *AR* 10.58.4—was a permanent replacement for existing forms of government.) The Varronian chronology (followed by Diodorus) seems (on the evidence of chs. 23–26.1) to have allowed two years only (451–450) for the Decemvirate, as opposed to the three in Livy and Dionysios, but it may, nevertheless, be correct: cf. A. Drummond in *CAH* vii.2, 625 n. 1. Though Diodorus (correctly) speaks of ten names, only eight appear here (A. Manlius Vulso and P. Curiatius [or possibly Horatius] are missing), and the fault is probably that of careless scribes confronted with a long list lacking any semantic coherence. The eight that appear are, more correctly, Ap. Claudius Crassus Inrigillensis Sabinus, T. Genucius [or Minucius?] Augurinus (both listed also as consuls in *Fast. Cap.,* though not by Diodorus), Sp. Veturius Crassus Cicurinus, C. Iulius Iullus, Ser. Sulpicius Camerinus, P. Sestius Capito Vaticanus, T. Romilius Rocus Vaticanus, Sp. Postumius Albus Regillensis. Cf. Broughton 1951, 45–46. For the full list, see Livy 3.33.1–36.2, Dion. Hal. *AR* 10.56.1–2; further sources in Broughton 1951. For details as to Decemvirate legislation, and the validity or otherwise of Diodorus' account, see notes 97–98, 102, and 107 below.
  [95] Cf. below, 12.36.4 and note 193. Thourioi and Taras were natural opponents, on opposite sides of the Gulf of Taras (mod. Táranto; see Map 4), the one in Lucanian, the other in Calabrian territory. In addition to control of the sea approaches, they also fought for domination of the long intervening coastal strip round the head of the gulf, and in particular for agriculturally rich Siris. The Thourians had the exiled Spartan Kleandridas as their general. A brief attempt at joint colonization failed (Strab. 6.1.14, C.263); in 433/2 Taras got sole control of Siris and colonized it under the new name of Herakleia.
  [96] Again, Diodorus' list comes up short: only seven names appear on it. Missing (Livy 3.36.3–37.8, Dion. Hal. *AR* 10.59.1–60.6) are: Q. Fabius Vibulanus, T. Antonius Merenda, K. Duillius [Longus?]. Sp. Veturius (listed for the 451 panel) does not appear elsewhere among those chosen in 450 and seems to replace Sp. Oppius Cornicen. Q. Publius is actually Q. Poetelius Libo Visolus. The rest are: Ap. Claudius Crassus Inregillensis Sabinus, M. Cornelius, L. Minucius Esquilinus Augurinus, M.[?] Sergius Esquilinus, M. Rabuleius. Cf. Broughton 1951, 46–47; Perotti 1984, 170.
  [97] This task was the compilation and setting down of the first Roman written legal code, the so-called Law of the Twelve Tables (*Lex XII Tabularum:* for a convenient survey of the surviving fragments, see E. H. Warmington, *Remains of Old Latin*, vol. 3, rev. ed. [London, 1967], 424–515, and for a good recent analysis, Cornell 1995, 278–292). There is general agreement that the first ten of these *tabulae* were drafted by the 451 committee. Over the

One of them,[98] out of lust[99] for a maiden who was of good character, but penniless, at first tried to seduce her by bribery, and then, when she would not submit to his advances, sent a public informer[100] round to her house, with orders to bring about her enslavement. [3] When the informer declared that she was indeed his slave, and brought her before the magistrate,[101] the latter then

---

last, there are two differing opinions. Cicero (*Rep.* 2.63) attributes them to the Decemviri of 450, whereas Diodorus (12.26.1) has them added by the consuls of 449, L. Valerius Potitus and M. Horatius Barbatus (a view supported by Oldfather [1946, 420–421 n. 2, citing Beloch], and perhaps attributable to confusion caused by the discrepancy in length of competing accounts of the Decemvirate). This is by no means the only way in which Diodorus' account diverges from the more standard version offered by Livy and Dionysios (Livy 3.9–64, Dion. Hal. *AR* 10.1–11.50). See below, 12.25.2–26.1, with notes 108, 110, 112.

[98] Appius Claudius: what follows here is one of the most famous stories in early Roman history, also narrated at length by Livy (3.44–48) and Dionysios (*AR* 11.28–40): the sacrifice of Verginia, leading to the Second Secession of the Plebs to the Aventine. Though clearly overlaid with much secondary elaboration, and perhaps the subject of a traditional ballad (as typological parallels with the story of Lucretia would suggest), it may well have a basis in fact rather than being a mere late invention (see Cornell's sensible remarks: 1995, 275). For the circumstances, see the excellent short accounts by Drummond in *CAH* vii.2, 227–235, and Cornell 1995, 272–276. Our sources agree that the second Decemvirate attempted to prolong its absolute (emergency) powers by refusing to stand down, and thus imposing a kind of ad hoc dictatorship without reference to senate or people. Attacks by the Sabines and the Aequi brought on a military crisis. Horatius and Valerius, the consuls-to-be of 449, spoke out against the Decemviral regime; but it was the armies mobilized to defend Rome that brought matters to a head by, in effect, mutinying over Appius Claudius' attempted enslavement of Verginia. The Decemviri—one of whose two additional *tabulae* (if in fact theirs) banned intermarriage between patricians and plebeians—now resigned (probably early in 449, which would explain some of the chronological variations), and a slew of consular legislation, the so-called Valerio-Horatian Laws, followed (449). As Cornell says (1995, 273), "Modern scholars have attacked the traditional narrative from every point of view." Only the essential points will be treated here. What is important (as Cornell also stresses, 276) is the *result:* the Twelve Tables and their implementation.

[99] Dionysios (*AR* 11.28.3) suggests that in fact he wanted to marry her, but could not because (a) she was already formally betrothed to L. Icilius, and (b) he himself was already married.

[100] This was one M. Claudius, a *cliens* of Appius Claudius: Livy 3.44.5, Dion. Hal. *AR* 11.28.5. Diodorus, as the reader will note, names no names throughout his narrative of the episode: Ogilvie (1965, 477) deduced from this not only that Diodorus' version depended on an early source, which is quite likely, but also that "the very name Verginia was simply a hypostatization of *virgo* and that the identity of her father as Verginius and the names of the remaining characters were all gradual embellishments," which is not.

[101] The Greek MSS read: καὶ πρὸς τὸν ἄρχοντα καταστήσαντος †δουλαγωγεῖν†. Vogel (1890) bracketed the last word as an intrusive marginal gloss on ἄγειν εἰς δουλείαν; Wurm and Oldfather amended it to δουλαγωγουμένην, referring to the girl; Casevitz followed Vogel in bracketing it, but also emended καταστήσαντος, quite unnecessarily, to καταν-

formally entered the charge against her of being a slave. After hearing the accuser's case, he handed over the girl, at which point the informer took possession of "his slave" and carried her off.[102] [4] The girl's father, who had been present,[103] and took it very hard that no one would listen to him, happened to pass by a butcher's shop, where he grabbed the cleaver left lying on the block and proceeded—in his determination that she should not suffer ravishment—to strike his daughter a blow with it that killed her,[104] after which he hurried out of the city to the military encampment that was then located on Mt. Algidus. [5] There he made an appeal to the troops, weeping as he reported the calamity that had befallen him, and aroused their pity and strong sympathy. They sallied forth in a body to bring aid to the unfortunate, and charged into Rome at night, fully armed, occupying the hill known as the Aventine.[105]

25. When dawn broke, and the soldiers' hatred of the crime that had been committed became manifest, the ten legislators, in support of their fellow

---

τήσαντος, which he then mistranslated as "en la denonçant comme esclave." His concern (1972, 104) was that the verb lacked αὐτήν as an object, whereas in fact it simply picks up ἰδίαν . . . δούλην from the previous clause and parallels φήσαντος there. Vogel's solution is the simplest and most sensible, and I have adopted it in my translation.

[102] Oldfather (1946, 421), understandably misled by the lack of identifying labels, makes the magistrate a third party and Appius the prosecutor. Casevitz's version hedges its bets (unless we take "notre magistrat" as something more than a sly hint). But both Livy (3.44.9ff.) and Dionysios (AR 11.28.6ff.) state specifically that Appius himself was the presiding magistrate on the tribunal, and that (as we would expect) it was the client, M. Claudius, who brought the charge. In fact, Diodorus' Greek (though more than usually elliptic and pronominal) can sustain this meaning (see my translation): nevertheless, his failure to identify the decemvir as the magistrate is certainly confusing. In Livy and Dionysios, the departure of the client is preceded by considerable argument from the girl's supporters, including her uncle (or great-uncle) Numitorius and her fiancé L. Icilius.

[103] Identified by Livy (3.44.2) and Dionysios (AR 11.28.1) as a plebeian centurion, L. Verginius, then serving in the army against the Aequi, and thus not present during this initial attempt on his daughter's honor and status, but as having to secure leave and return to Rome in a hurry from his station on Mt. Algidus (immediately southeast of the Alban Mount: see BA 43 D3).

[104] Cf. Livy 3.48.4–6, Dion. Hal. AR 11.37.4–6. Diodorus, whether relying on an earlier, simpler version of the story, or because of his declared distaste for rhetoricians (1.76, 9.26.3), spares us the endless pages of high-minded attitudinizing that we have to slog through in our two main sources for the Verginia episode before arriving at this point.

[105] Cf. Livy 3.50.12ff., Dion. Hal. AR 11.43.5ff., Sall. Jug. 31.17. This act became known as the Second Secession of the Plebs: see Ogilvie 1965, 489–490. For the earlier secession (also to the Aventine), see Livy 2.32.3.

magistrate,[106] mustered a strong body of young men, intending to settle the issue by armed combat. The intense contention thus aroused led the more responsible citizens (who foresaw just how dangerous this situation might become) to broker an agreement between the two sides,[107] earnestly begging them to give over their dissension and not to risk overwhelming their fatherland with so serious a crisis. [2] All were finally persuaded, and they reached an agreement with one another. Ten tribunes were to be elected, with the greatest authority among all the officers of state, and these were to act as guardians of civic freedom.[108] Of the annually elected consuls, one should be chosen from the patricians, and one, invariably, from the plebeians, the people being empowered to appoint both from the plebeians [should they so desire].[109] [3] They did this in their determination to lessen the overall supe-

---

[106] Oldfather (1946, 422 n. 1) suggests that this "is probably a defective translation of *decemuiri collegae auxilium ferentes*," but does not indicate where he feels the (not at once obvious) defect may lie. In any case, the notion of a solution by armed combat does not feature in Livy's account. (That of Dionysios unfortunately has a massive lacuna at this point [*AR* 11.44.5−6], resuming only with the Valerio-Horatian laws of 449.)

[107] The main agents were the future consuls of 449, L. Valerius Potitus and M. Horatius Barbatus (Livy 3.51.12−13, 53−54), who reconciled the orders "as friends of both the plebeians and the patricians" (Broughton 1951, 47). The Decemviri finally stepped down; Appius Claudius and Sp. Oppius committed suicide (Livy 3.58.6−9, Dion. Hal. *AR* 11.46.3−4), the remaining eight went into exile (Broughton 1951, 48 with refs.). The terms of the agreement have been in dispute since antiquity; Diodorus' account differs in several respects from that reported by Livy. It is interesting, given Diodorus' context of southern Italian and Sicilian Greek legislation, that he does not mention the alleged journey in 454 by a Roman commission to Athens and other Greek cities to study the laws (those of Solon in particular): Livy 3.31.8, Dion. Hal. *AR* 10.51, 54. The commission itself may be fictional, but Greek influence on the Twelve Tables (probably by way of Lokroi, Thourioi, and Syracuse rather than mainland Greece) is clear: Cornell 1995, 275.

[108] The office of tribune in fact went back some way: Diodorus himself (11.68.8 with note 263) records the appointment of four in 471/0. Oldfather (1946, 422−423 n. 2) claims, commenting on this passage, that Diodorus "had forgotten that he had already acknowledged the existence of tribunes." But it is not the *existence* of tribunes that is at issue here but their increasing *number*. The date for the total to be brought up to ten is contested. For Diodorus it is 450/49 (Varro [*LL* 5.81, cf. Drummond in *CAH* vii.2, 228] seems to suggest 449 as the date for the inception of the tribunate as such, but this is improbable in the extreme). Dionysios (*AR* 10.30.6) gives the date as 457, as does Livy (3.30.7); Valerius Maximus (6.3.2) has it as 486[?]; while Livy elsewhere (2.44.6) apparently puts it as early as 493.

[109] Though the old belief that plebeians were at first debarred by law from the consulship may well be untrue (Derow in *OCD* 384), nevertheless Diodorus anticipates the reservation of one consulship to the plebeians by almost a century: the proposal of the tribunes C. Licinius and L. Sextius (367/6, Livy 6.42) was ratified by a plebiscite, and only became regular in 342.

riority of the patricians, since these men, because of their blue blood and the prestige conferred on them by their ancestry, were virtual masters of the city. The agreement also contained a clause stating that when the tribunes had served their year in office, they must ensure that a like number were appointed in their place: failure to do so would mean their being burned alive.[110] Further, if the tribunes could not reach agreement among themselves, they were responsible for ensuring that the mediator between them was free to act without let or hindrance. This, then, was the resolution of the civil strife in Rome.

26. When Diphilos was archon in Athens [442/1], the Romans elected as consuls †Kankon† Horatius and Lucius Valerius †Turpinus†.[111] During their term, in Rome, since the codification of the laws was still unfinished on account of civil strife, the consuls completed it. Now of the so-called Twelve Tables, ten had been finished, and the consuls drafted the remaining two.[112] With the legislation they had embarked on now complete, the consuls engraved it upon twelve bronze plaques, which they nailed to the rostra then located in front of the senate house.[113] The brief and concise manner in which

---

[110] Livy (3.55.14) reports a similar proposal, brought by the tribune M. Duillius, but with a penalty of scourging followed by decapitation. In general, the purpose of the legislation brought about by the Second Secession (after the mythic accretions have been stripped away) was probably (Drummond in *CAH* vii.2, 230) "intended to reassert the role of the tribunate in the face of attempts in the Twelve Tables to restrict its activity, and recognition or reaffirmation of its right to fulfil its basic function." It is also true, and important, that what we have here is not, in the last resort, a truly radical movement. There was no attempt to fundamentally change the sociopolitical structure, let alone redistribute property or land. What we see rather is that (Drummond, 242) "the primary interest of the plebeian leaders lay in the removal of barriers to their personal advancement within the existing framework."

[111] The consuls (actually for 449) were L. Valerius Potitus and M. Horatius Barbatus, the men primarily responsible for the abrogation of the Decemvirate and the reconciliation of the patrician and plebeian orders (see above). Cf. Broughton 1951, 47–48, 49–50; Perotti 1984, 170–171. "Kankon" is clearly a corruption of "Markon"; "Turpinus" suggests "Turrinus," which may have been the cognomen of Horatius, transferred to Valerius by a careless scribe.

[112] For the authorship of *tabulae* XI and XII, see note 107 above: it may well be that they were roughed out by the Decemvirs and completed by the consuls as part of the Valerio-Horatian laws. On the latter, see the convenient summary provided by Cornell (1995, 276–278). They included a measure recognizing, and safeguarding, the status of plebeian offices; a prohibition on the creation of magistracies immune from appeal; and the legalization of binding plebiscites (Livy 3.53.3), of which there were over thirty between 449 and 287 B.C.E.

[113] Cf. Livy 3.57.10, Dion. Hal. *AR* 10.57.7. The rostra were removed by Caesar in 45 (see above, Introduction, p. 5). The phrase "then located" (τότε κειμένους) is one of the few chronological guides we possess to the date of composition for any part of the *Bibliotheke*.

this legislation was drafted has continued to excite admiration down to our own times.[114]

[2] During the period covered by these events, the majority of nations in the inhabited world remained quiet, since just about all of them were at peace.[115] The Persians had two treaties with the Greeks, the first being with the Athenians and their allies. By this treaty the Greek cities of Asia [Minor] were to be subject to their own laws.[116] They also concluded a later pact with the Lacedaemonians, and this contained a clause stating the exact opposite, that is, that the Greek cities of Asia [Minor] were to be subject to the Persians.[117] There was likewise peace between the various Greek states, now that the Athenians and the Lacedaemonians had agreed on a thirty-year truce.[118] [3] In Sicily, too, peace prevailed, since the Carthaginians had made a treaty with Gelon, the Sicilian Greek cities had of their own volition ceded the hegemony to Syracuse, and the Akragantines, after their defeat at the Himera River, had come to terms with the Syracusans.[119] [4] Things were quiet among

---

[114] This admiration (if real) has not been shared by modern scholars. Even allowing for the fact that what we know of the Tables has to be pieced together from fragmentary citations in later writers, the language is both archaic and obscure, the matter consists chiefly of ultra-laconic injunctions and prohibitions, the grammar presents numerous ambiguities (ill-defined pronouns, switches of subject), and Cornell (1995, 279) notes "a marked inability to generalise or express abstractions." Main concerns include: family law (marriage, divorce, inheritance and property, including slaves); injury (assault, damage to property); debt and credit; and both judicial and religious procedural law. The striking omission is any surviving reference to public or constitutional law.

[115] It is interesting, and has often been noted (see, e.g., Casevitz 1972, 105), that a precisely similar gap, between the evacuation of Euboia (446/5) and the outbreak of the Samian Revolt (441/0), is recorded by Thucydides in his account of the Pentekontaetia (1.115.1–2). The natural explanation, so often doubted, is surely that Diodorus knew and read at least the relevant parts of Thucydides' *History*. Cf. Lévy 2001, 336ff., and above, Introduction.

[116] For this nonaggression pact, the so-called Peace of Kallias, see above, 12.4.4–6, with notes.

[117] The Spartans made several unsuccessful bids for Persian alliance, notably at the outset of the Peloponnesian War: cf. D.S. 12.41.1, and Thuc. 2.7.1, 67.1; but the first actually to be concluded was made in 412 (Thuc. 8.37), and that referred to here is clearly its successor in 411 (Thuc. 8.58), which contains a clause (§2) matching that recorded by Diodorus: "All the King's territory in Asia shall be [treated as] the King's; and with regard to his own territory the King shall dispose as he sees fit." The suspicion arises that this second treaty was included by Diodorus simply because of its neatly chiastic contrast with the first.

[118] For the Atheno-Spartan Thirty Years' Peace, see above, ch. 7, with note 33.

[119] For the Carthaginian treaty with Gelon, in 480/79, see 11.26.1–3 with notes 105–106. Gelon died in 478 (11.38.7). For the prosperity and peace of Syracuse, cf. above, 11.72.1–2 with note 276. Peace on the island, as should by now be apparent, was neither so

the Italian and Celtic peoples, as well as in Iberia, and throughout just about all the rest of the inhabited world. Consequently, during this period no military action worthy of mention took place, and universal peace prevailed; while festivals, games, sacrificial feast-days in honor of the gods, and all other elements that go to make a happy life flourished everywhere.

27. When Timokles was archon in Athens [441/0], the Romans elected as consuls Lar[inu]s Herminius and Titus †Stertinius Structor†.[120] During their term, the Samians went to war with Miletos over a dispute concerning Priene.[121] Perceiving that the Athenians were inclining favorably toward Miletos,[122] they revolted from Athens.[123] The Athenians, who had elected Perikles as general, thereupon dispatched him with forty triremes against the Samians. [2] He made landfall on Samos, forced his way into the city, and took it over. He then set up a democracy, fined the Samians eighty talents, and took the same number of young men as hostages. Having thus taken care of everything in a few days, he returned to Athens.[124]

---

general nor so durable as Diodorus here suggests. For the defeat of Akragas at the Himera River in 446/5, see above, 12.8.1–4 with note 41.

[120] The consuls (actually for 448) were Lars (or Spurius) Herminius Coritinesanus and T. Verginius Tricostus Caeliomontanus (Broughton 1951, 50). Perotti (1984, 171) suggests a possible way for the corruptions to have occurred in uncial script.

[121] Main sources: Thuc. 1.115.2–117; Plut. *Per.* 24.1–2, 25–28; Aristoph. *Wasps* 281–284 with schol. None of these spells out the nature of the quarrel, but it can be deduced with a fair degree of certainty: cf. Meiggs 1972, 188–189; Kagan 1969, 170–171. Samos had always been one of the few genuinely independent members of the Delian League, contributing ships rather than protection money: it was now controlled by an oligarchy. Miletos—to begin with also oligarchic—had twice revolted, in 450/49 and 446(?); after the second outbreak had been put down, Athens imposed a democracy: Meiggs 1972, 561–565; Kagan 1969, 100–101.

[122] Samos clearly was after territorial expansion in the *peraia* at the expense of a weakened Miletos: Stadter 1989, 242–243 with refs. As Kagan (1969, 100–101) rightly says, the Athenians could not allow their strong "subject-allies" to become even stronger (and hence more independent) at the expense of those whose defenses Athens had itself eviscerated. The political motive for supporting Miletos is clear. At the same time, it was inevitable that Perikles' enemies would accuse him of favoring Miletos because his mistress Aspasia was a Milesian: Plut. *Per.* 24.1; Athen. 13.589d; *Suda* and Harpokrat. s.v. Aspasia. Cf. Stadter 1989, 233–234. Canard this may be, but the relationship can only have encouraged the decision he took on other grounds.

[123] They did this after refusing a request to submit to Athenian arbitration: Plut. *Per.* 25.1. The war may well have begun before the end of the 442/1 archon-year, and the funds allotted to Perikles to deal with the situation may have likewise been authorized before the change of magistrates in early July.

[124] In late July 441. The cost of the operation so far—if we take the first payment

[3] However, Samos was [soon] split by civil dissension, with one group backing the democracy and another in favor of aristocratic rule, so that the city was in utter disorder. Those who opposed the democracy crossed over to Asia and traveled up to Sardis, to seek help from the Persian satrap, Pissuthnes. Pissuthnes gave them 700 soldiers, hoping thus to gain control of the island.[125] The Samians sailed back home at night, taking the troops that had been given them, and—through the assistance of certain citizens—got into the city unobserved. They made themselves masters of Samos without any difficulty, and deported from the city all who opposed them. Next they went to Lemnos and surreptitiously rescued the hostages.[126] Then, after taking every precaution to safeguard Samos, they openly declared themselves enemies of the Athenians.[127] [4] The Athenians again chose Perikles as general and sent

---

recorded in *IG* i³ 363.5 as referring to Samos rather than Byzantion, convincingly argued by Fornara (1979, 9–12) against Meritt (1932) and Lewis (1952)—was 128 talents. The chronology of the Samian revolt has been the subject of wildly variant and arbitrary interpretations, well summarized by Fornara (1979, 7). For the most part I follow Fornara's own schema (7–14), which I find historically well-argued and by far the most convincing. Thucydides (1.115.3) adds that a garrison was left behind, and Plutarch (*Per.* 25.1–2) stresses Perikles' refusal of various supposed bribes offered him (on which see Stadter 1989, 244–245). Their accounts largely agree with Diodorus', except that both put the fine at fifty talents, and the number of hostages likewise at fifty. Neither the acrophonic nor the alphabetic system of counting offers the likelihood of confusion between fifty and eighty (represented in the latter by ν and π respectively). We do not know the source of Diodorus' information (the usual knee-jerk guess of Ephoros offers no help): either pro-Samian testimony exaggerated the figure, or pro-Athenian witnesses minimized it. If I incline toward the latter explanation, it is because fifty is a conventional round figure, whereas eighty is not. This Athenian reaction, in both its high-handed imperial arrogance and its dangerous underestimation of potential violent resistance, vividly illustrates the new post-449 Periklean policy, well summarized by Briant (2002, 680–681) as the abandonment of major Kimonian-style anti-Persian expeditions (particularly in the eastern Mediterranean) and their replacement by ever-increasing pressure on Athens' subject-allies.

[125] Pissuthnes, the satrap of Lydia, was here pursuing "a conscious policy of disruption," Stadter 1989, 245. According to Plutarch (*Per.* 25.3), it was Pissuthnes who not only supplied the Samian rebels, but rescued the Lemnian hostages on their behalf.

[126] These events will have taken place during the late summer and fall of 441. We do not need, with Fornara (1979, 12–14), to place them all in the early months of 440. The declaration of hostility to Athens will surely have been held back, not merely while Samos' defenses were secured, but until the end of the sailing season, i.e., late October or early November of 441, when the Athenian fleet would be dry-docked.

[127] Thuc. 1.115.4–5, Plut. *Per.* 25.3. These accounts basically agree with Diodorus': Thucydides adds that the Samian oligarchs, after regaining power, promptly mounted another expedition against Miletos, and—more importantly—that Byzantion joined the revolt, which suggests some international coordination as well as widespread discontent (Meiggs 1972, 189–190). We do not know *when* Byzantion joined: Fornara (1979, 14) suggests that

him off against the Samians with sixty ships.[128] He promptly fought a sea battle against seventy Samian triremes and beat them.[129] Then, after calling up twenty-five vessels as reinforcements from Chios and Mytilene,[130] he and they laid joint siege to Samos.[131] After a few days, however, Perikles, leaving part of his force for the siege, put out to sea to intercept the Phoenician squadron that the Persians had sent to relieve Samos.[132]

---

it was as a result of the Samian fourteen-day success in 440, which is plausible; in any case, Athens seems to have had no real problem in dealing with the Byzantine rising. As Kagan (1969, 172) says of the Samians, "The defeat did not cow them; it infuriated them." They were now (Plut. *Per.* 25.3) "firmly resolved to vie with Athens for mastery of the sea," πάνυ προθύμως ἐγνωκότας ἀντιλαμβάνεσθαι τῆς θαλάττης, a determination that put a new and most dangerous Aegean-wide complexion on their rebellion. Cf. Stadter 1989, 243: "The successful defection of such a power would almost certainly have meant the rapid end of Athenian domination of the Aegean."

[128] The matter was urgent: he will have sailed as early as possible in the season, i.e., not later than early April 440 (Fornara 1979, 143).

[129] Thuc. 1.116.1; Plut. *Per.* 25.3. The battle was fought, probably in late April 440, off the island of Tragia (modern Agathonisi: see Map 2, and cf. *BA* 61 D3), some twelve miles south of Samos and sixteen miles due west of Miletos. Sixteen of Perikles' sixty ships had been detached, some to solicit support from Chios and Mytilene, others southward to watch for the possible intervention of a Persian (i.e., Phoenician) fleet. The Samian fleet (twenty of its vessels being transports) was on its way back from Miletos.

[130] Kagan (1969, 175–176) plausibly connects the fact that Chios and Lesbos not only abstained from revolt but actively supported Athens' repressive measures with the diplomatic activities there of the famous and well-connected Athenian playwright Sophokles (Athen. 13.603d–604b), elected general for 441/0 (it was said) as a tribute to his play *Antigone,* rather than for any military skill, and shrewdly posted to the two other great naval islands of the eastern Aegean by Perikles. As Kagan says, "No envoy from Athens could be more certain of a friendly welcome and a thorough hearing from the upper classes in the empire. This could be very useful for Athens at a time when there was good reason to expect restlessness and possible treachery from these very people." For other possibilities (self-interest, divisive racial considerations), cf. Hornblower 1991, 190–191.

[131] Thuc. 1.116.2, Plut. *Per.* 26.1, which give both stages of this move: the seizure of the harbor (though Aristotle, cited by Plutarch [*Per.* 26.3], also reports an engagement in which Perikles was defeated), followed by a victory over Samian troops, and a land-based blockade, begun in early May. Thucydides alone reports the arrival at this point, in addition to the twenty-five ships from Lesbos and Chios, of a forty-vessel Athenian squadron quite distinct from the later reinforcements mentioned by all three sources. This brought the overall Athenian total up to 100: the revolt was being taken very seriously indeed.

[132] Thuc. 1.116.3, Plut. *Per.* 26.1. Perikles took sixty triremes on this mission of interception (late May or the beginning of June?), making for Kaunos in Caria (see Map 2, and cf. *BA* 65 A4), aiming to meet and engage the Phoenicians as far from Samos as possible, with luck before they even entered the Aegean. Thucydides reports that a small Samian squadron had slipped out and sailed south to solicit naval help. The involvement of Persia in the Samian affair (with both Pissuthnes and the fleet intervening) at once made it more

28. The Samians, convinced that Perikles' departure had given them an ideal opportunity to attack the ships that remained, sailed out against them, won the engagement, and were very full of themselves in consequence.[133] [2] However, when Perikles heard about the defeat of his forces, he at once turned back and assembled a powerful fleet, being determined to crush the enemy squadrons once and for all. The Athenians hastened to send him sixty triremes,[134] and the Chians and Mytilenaeans thirty. With this enlarged armament, Perikles resumed the siege by both land and sea, making continuous assaults.[135] [3] He also utilized siege engines, being the first to employ so-

---

alarming from Athens' viewpoint; as Stadter emphasizes (1989, 247), "Because of Pissouthnes, the Athenians had a real fear of a Persian attempt to take advantage of the revolt of Samos to weaken their control of the Aegean."

[133] Thuc. 1.117.1, Plut. *Per.* 26.2–4. The Samian admiral was Melissos son of Ithagenes, a distinguished Eleatic philosopher. The Athenian camp was not properly protected (ἀφάρκτῳ); its guard-ships were destroyed, and the Athenian squadron that faced this Samian sally was defeated with heavy losses. "For about fourteen days," Thucydides says, "they had mastery of the sea in their region, bringing in and carrying out whatever they had a mind to." This "mastery of the sea," brief though it was, Athens never forgot: in 411 it was recalled (Thuc. 8.76.4) that Samos "had come within a hair's breadth, during the war between them, of taking from Athens her mastery of the sea (τὸ Ἀθηναίων κράτος τῆς θαλάσσης)." The Samians tattooed their numerous prisoners on the forehead with the *samaina*, a Samian symbol representing a special local type of ship (Plut. *Per.* 26.3–4), in return for a similar Athenian practice of tattooing Samian prisoners with the Athenian owl (Ael. *VH* 2.9; Photius and *Suda* s.v. Σαμίων ὁ δῆμος: Plutarch has the symbols reversed). Runaway or obstreperous slaves were tattooed: Stadter 1989, 249–250 offers an interesting general note on the practice.

[134] Thucydides (1.117.2) names the commanders (στρατηγοί) involved (see below), and this is a good chronological marker, since none of them features in Androtion's list (*FGrH* 324 F 38 = HMA 13) of "the ten generals at Samos," which includes Perikles and Sophokles, and thus clearly is the Board of Generals for 441/0, while Thucydides' names belong to their successors (the Board of 440/39). This also agrees with schol. Aristoph. *Wasps* 283 ad fin. (HMA 29), dating the Samian revolt to the two archon-years of Timokles and Morychides (441/0 and 440/39). The treasurers of 441/0 paid out 368 talents on the campaign to date.

[135] Thuc. 1.117.2–3, Plut. *Per.* 27.1. The resumption of the siege was preceded by a naval defeat of Melissos. The phrase "continuous assaults" (συνεχεῖς προσβολάς) probably refers to Perikles' splitting his force into eight divisions, and assaulting the walls with each in rotation (Plut. *Per.* 27.2). The Athenian contingent was under five commanders: Tlepolemos, Antikles, Hagnon, Phormio, and Thucydides. About the first two we have no certain knowledge. Hagnon, son of Nikias and father of Theramenes, was in 437/6 to reestablish the colony of Ennea Hodoi (Nine Ways) as Amphipolis: cf. 12.32.3 with note 164. Phormio emerged as a distinguished naval commander during the Peloponnesian War (*OCD* 1174). This Thucydides can be neither Perikles' conservative opponent, the son of Melesias (ostracized c. 443, during the period when, according to both Diodorus [26.2] and Thucydides [1.115.1–2], nothing of note was happening), nor the historian (too old, if that Thucydides only came of age at the outbreak of war [Thuc. 5.26.5, with Hornblower

called rams and tortoises, which Artemon of Klazomenai built for him.[136] Thus by prosecuting the siege energetically, and [finally] breaching the walls with his siege engines, he became master of Samos.[137] After punishing those responsible [for the revolt],[138] he dunned the Samians for the cost of the siege, assessing the figure at <1,>200 talents. [4] He also impounded their fleet and demolished their city-walls.[139] This done, he returned to Athens.

---

1991, 191]). He may have been the son of Pantainetos claimed by Theopompos (schol. Aristoph. *Wasps* 947, cf. *PA* 1:473, no. 7272) as a political opponent of Perikles; but this is quite uncertain, and the name was not uncommon.

[136] Plut. *Per.* 27.3–4 also mentions the tradition of Perikles having been one of the first Greeks to utilize siege equipment, citing Ephoros (*FGrH* 70 F 194), who was clearly on this occasion Diodorus' source also. As Stadter points out (1989, 253), Ephoros took great interest in inventions. "Rams" are self-explanatory. "Tortoises" (χελῶναι, *testudines*) were siege-sheds, used to begin with as mobile protection for rams (Marsden 1969, 50, 101, 109). Artemon of Klazomenai is also mentioned as the inventor of the "tortoise" by the elder Pliny (*NH* 7.202, cf. Vitruv. 10.2.9). For his confusion with an earlier man of the same name (recorded by Plutarch *Per.* 27.3–4), see Stadter 1989, 253–254. Marsden (1969, 50 n. 7) is unduly skeptical of the Periklean association.

[137] The siege lasted over eight months (Thuc. 1.117.3, Plut. *Per.* 28.1). Fornara (1979, 13, cf. 9) ingeniously works out, from the naval payments involved, that this period was calculated from the initial blockade in May 440, not from Perikles' resumption of it on his return from Kaunos. Thus the final capitulation came in December 440 or January 439. Diodorus' source, in all likelihood, gave a date for the beginning of the revolt, but left the subsequent chronology vague.

[138] Apart from the tattooing, which seems to have included the rank-and-file, we have to consider the punishment handed out to the senior officers and ringleaders. Douris of Samos, reported at Plut. *Per.* 28.1–3 = *FGrH* 76 F 67, claimed that the trierarchs and marines were taken to Miletos, and there shackled by the wrists and ankles to posts or boards in the marketplace, with iron collars round their necks (not crucified, a misleading translation), as the Persian Arktaÿktes had been at the end of the 479 campaign (Hdt. 9.120). This procedure was known as *Apotympanismos* (Keramopoullos 1923; Bonner and Smith 1970, 2:279–287). It was the equivalent of being hanged in chains, as practiced in Tudor England (Robert Aske, the leader of the Pilgrimage of Grace, was so executed). Its particular cruelty lay in its being long and lingering: the Samian victims were still alive after ten days. At this point Perikles ordered their heads beaten in with clubs. Needless to say, this report has provoked much incredulity (Plutarch reports it only to dismiss it; cf. most recently Karavites 1985, 48–53; and K. Latte, in *RE* suppl. vol. 7, 1940, cols. 1606–1607). But Athens had had a bad scare, as well as losing a great deal of money (see below): a deterrent example will have been regarded as essential. Meiggs (1972, 191–192) accepts the report, as does Stadter (1989, 258–259). Meiggs pertinently observes: "The Athenian purpose was to show that they were fighting Samos to protect the new Milesian democracy from Samian oligarchs"—of whom many, no doubt, as wealthy trierarchs, will have been dying a slow death, exposed to jeers, and worse, in the agora of Miletos.

[139] The treasurers for 440/39 paid out 908 talents for the cost of operations at Samos, bringing the total to a minimum of 1,404. It is unfortunate that of the literary sources men-

The thirty-year truce between the Athenians and the Lacedaemonians was still firmly in place up to this point.[140]

Such were the events that took place during this year.

29. When Morychides was archon in Athens [440/39], the Romans elected as consuls Lucius Julius and Marcus Geganius, and the Eleians held the 85th Olympiad, in which Krison of Himera won the *stadion* for the second time.[141] During their term, in Sicily, Ducetius, the former leader of the Sicel cities, established the city [Kale Akte] of the Calactians, and while settling numerous colonists there, [once more] made a bid for the Sicel leadership; but in the midst of this endeavor his life was cut short by illness.[142] [2] Since Trinakie was the only Sicel city that the Syracusans had failed to make subject to them,

---

tioning a figure, only Nepos (*Timoth.* 1.2) clearly states the sum—1,200 talents—generally agreed to have been regarded as the total in antiquity. Neither Thucydides (1.117.3) nor Plutarch (*Per.* 28.1) states a figure at all. Both Isokrates (15.111, ἀπὸ διακοσίων [νεῶν] καὶ χιλίων ταλάντων]) and Diodorus here (ταλάντων <χιλίων> διακοσίων) require emendation, however plausible, to produce the right sum. It is just possible that the 200-talent assessment mentioned by Diodorus represents the agreed *annual* payment: we know from both Thucydides and Plutarch that the indemnity was to be paid by installments, κατὰ χρόνους. They also confirm the demolition of the walls and the impounding of the fleet, and add that hostages were taken to ensure regular payment. For the treaty and oath of loyalty subsequently imposed on the Samians, see *IG* i³ 48 = Meiggs-Lewis no. 56 (pp. 151–154); Fornara no. 115 (pp. 129–130); cf. Fornara 1979, 14–18; and Prandi 1978, 58ff.

[140] As the Corinthians later reminded the Athenians (Thuc. 1.40.5), Athens' action against Samos (not surprisingly) provoked strong reactions from Sparta and other members of the Peloponnesian League. It was the Corinthians who then argued—being at the time on reasonably good terms with Athens, cf. Hornblower 1991, 83–84—that each side should be free to punish its own allies as it saw fit (φανερῶς δὲ ἀντείπομεν τοὺς προσήκοντας ξυμμάχους αὐτόν τινα κολάζειν), a proposal that appears to have carried the day.

[141] Like Casevitz, I emend the archon's name to Μωρυχίδου from the Μυρισχίδου or Μυριχίδου of the MSS. The consuls (actually for 447) were M. Geganius Macerinus and C. Iulius(?) Iullus. At 12.49.1, Diodorus has the latter, correctly, as Gaius (Broughton 1951, 50–51). Krison of Himera had in fact already won the *stadion* twice on Diodorus' reckoning: see above, 12.5.1 and 12.23.1. For a runner, this eight-year stretch was a remarkable achievement, beaten only by the legendary Leonidas of Rhodes, victorious in *four* successive Olympiads (those of 164, 160, 156, and 152). Plato twice (*Protag.* 335E, *Laws* 8.840E) praises Krison for his rigorous training regimen (Casevitz 1972, 30 n.1).

[142] On Ducetius' settlement of Kale Akte, see above, 12.8.2 with notes 35–39; and cf. Galvagno 1991, 99ff. Casevitz (1972, 30 n. 2) suggests that the shift to Sicily may have been dictated to Diodorus by a reading of Thucydides, who moves on directly (1.118.1) to the incidents involving Corcyra and Potidaea "a few years later" (μετὰ ταῦτα δὲ ἤδη . . . οὐ πολλοῖς ἔτεσιν ὕστερον).

they decided to launch an expedition against it;[143] they also had a strong suspicion that the Trinakians, as being of the same race, might lay claim to the leadership of the Sicels. This was a city that had in it many distinguished men, since it had always taken first place among the cities of the Sicels, being full of commanders who prided themselves on their warrior spirit. [3] So the Syracusans mustered all their forces, both from Syracuse itself and from the cities allied with them, and marched against Trinakie. The Trinakians had no allies, all the other [Sicel] cities being subject to the Syracusans, but nevertheless they mounted a courageous defense, holding out passionately against great odds. They slew great numbers themselves, and all died fighting heroically. [4] In like fashion, most of the older men took their own lives rather than face the humiliation to which they would be exposed after the city fell. The Syracusans, after so signally defeating men hitherto unconquered [by anyone], sold the rest of the population into slavery and completely demolished their city, sending the pick of the booty to Delphi as a thank-offering to the god.

30. When Glaukinos was archon in Athens [439/8], the Romans elected as consuls Titus Quinctius and Agrippa Furius.[144] During their term, the Syracusans, on account of the successes described above, laid down 100 new triremes and doubled the number of their cavalry; they also paid attention to their infantry arm, and raised extra revenue in advance by imposing heavier tribute on the Sicels who had been made subject to them.[145] These actions they took with the intention of gradually subjugating all Sicily.

[2] At the same time as these events,[146] in Greece, the so-called Corinthian

---

[143] For the probable identification of Trinakie as the Sicel stronghold of Palike, see above, Book 11, note 371.

[144] The consuls (actually for 446) were T. Quinctius Capitolinus Barbatus and Agrippa Furius Fusus (Broughton 1951, 51). Diodorus' MSS have the archon as Glaukides, but see HMA 398 for evidence supporting Glaukinos (correctly read by Casevitz).

[145] I.e., not only the reduction of Trinakie/Palike, with the resultant increase of tribute from the Sicel communities Diodorus mentions, but also the earlier defeat at the Himera River of Akragas (12.8.1, 3–4 with notes 40–41, 12.26.3), which ceased from then to be a major force in Sicilian affairs. See Consolo Langher (1997, 72), who rightly emphasizes the return in Syracuse to government by the old Gamoroi, i.e., the great landowners and *latifondisti*, plus the emergent hoplite class, who now form Diodorus' χαριέστατοι.

[146] During the Corcyraean and Potidaean episodes, until 432/1 (12.37.1)—when, with the arrival of Phormio in Chalcidice, he returns to the generally accepted dateline—Diodorus follows a chronological schema two years higher than that deducible from the rest of our surviving evidence: e.g., he has the sea battle at 12.31.2 in 437 rather than in 435, and the engagement off Sybota in 435 rather than in 433. Internally, he agrees with the Thucydidean sequence, including a close chronological link (Thuc. 1.57.1) between the two epi-

War had its beginning for the following reasons.[147] The Epidamnians, who live on the Adriatic coast and are colonists of the Corcyraeans and Corinthians, split into warring factions, and the prevailing group exiled a large number of their opponents.[148] However, these exiles united together, brought in the Illyrians on their side, and with them sailed against Epidamnos. [3] Now the barbarians had fielded a large force, with which they first laid waste the countryside, and then proceeded to besiege the city. The Epidamnians, who by themselves were no match for them in battle, sent ambassadors to Corcyra, asking the Corcyraeans, as their kinsmen, to render them aid. When Corcyra ignored this request,[149] they dispatched an embassy to Corinth in pursuit of

---

sodes. The discrepancy becomes most obvious at the end of ch. 34, where he abandons the Potidaian narrative for two whole archon-years (434/3 and 433/2, filling these with notes on Thourioi and Meton's calendar), only resuming it at ch. 37 in the archon-year 432/1. From Thuc. 1.64.1–3 it is evident that Phormio's arrival, to replace the deceased Kallias, followed no more than a month or two after the battle. For the further chronological problems involved, see note 195 below. Diodorus' source (whether Ephoros or another) for the earlier events here described seems to have known, and followed, a chronology two years behind that assumed by Thucydides (Gomme [1945, 52] wants to put all the blame on Diodorus, but this is unconvincing). Such a dating scheme may be wrong; but it is surprising, as we shall see, how fragile much of the hitherto unquestioned evidence (including that for the key date of Sybota) turns out to be.

It also may not be coincidental that we are now at the beginning of what Hornblower (2002, 103–107) aptly characterizes as the Great Gap in Thucydides: that is, the omission or playing-down of various significant episodes falling roughly between 439 and 434 B.C.E. These include (a) the Athenian alliance with Akarnania (438), an encroachment on Corinth's sphere of interest; (b) the (re-)founding of Amphipolis by Hagnon in 437/6; (c) Perikles' Black Sea expedition of 437/6(?) (Plut. *Per.* 20; *IG* i³ 1180); and (d) a number of activities in the West, including the foundation of Thourioi (446/5) and alliances (443, renewed c. 433) with Rhegion and Leontinoi (Meiggs-Lewis nos. 63 and 64 = Fornara nos. 124 and 125). Of these, Diodorus mentions (b) the re-founding of Amphipolis at 12.32.3, and from (d), the foundation of Thourioi at 12.9–11.

[147] Diodorus here basically follows Thucydides' account, 1.24–26. For Epidamnos, later renamed Dyrrhachium, the modern Durazzo (and more recently Durrës) on the Albanian coast, see Map 4, and cf. *BA* 49 B2. The Illyrian hinterland was occupied by a native tribe, the Taulantii (described by Thuc. 24.2 as well as by Diodorus §3 as βάρβαροι).

[148] While it is true that the Epidamnians were colonists from Corcyra, the Corcyraeans were themselves colonists from Corinth (Thuc. 24.2). Thucydides (24.5) tells us that the successful faction was "the people" (ὁ δῆμος) and that those they expelled en masse were "the powerful" (τοὺς δυνατούς), i.e., the aristocrats and landowners.

[149] Why did they? As Kagan (1969, 208) says, "One would think that the Corcyraeans would be glad of a chance to increase their influence in Epidamnus." He rightly discounts any specific action on the basis of known class alignment, and suggests rather an attitude of isolationist indifference, tempered by a cynical readiness to let both sides exhaust themselves, and then cash in on the resultant weakness.

an alliance, declaring Corinth to be their one true mother-city, and at the same time soliciting colonists.[150] [4] The Corinthians, out of pity for the Epidamnians—but also because they detested the Corcyraeans, since of all their colonists only these did not send the customary sacrificial beasts to their mother-city—decided to respond to this request.[151] They therefore sent Epidamnos colonists, and also enough troops to garrison the city.[152] [5] The Corcyraeans, in annoyance at this action, dispatched fifty triremes under one of their generals, who sailed to Epidamnos and ordered the inhabitants to take back their exiles.[153] They also sent ambassadors to the Corinthians, requesting that the status of the colony be determined in court, not by an act of war.[154] When the Corinthians would not agree to their proposals,[155] both sides decided to go to war, and began fitting out substantial naval forces and

---

[150]Thucydides (25.1) adds the crucial information that, before approaching Corinth, the Epidamnians consulted the Delphic Oracle, asking not only whether they should appeal to Corinth, but also whether they should *make over their city to the Corinthians as its founders,* presumably on the grounds (Thuc. 24.2) that "some Corinthians" had taken part in the original foundation—and that the oracle had endorsed the proposal, recommending that they make the Corinthians their "leaders" (ἡγεμόνας). This not only highlights the political, no less than religious, issues that a religious oracle could still be called on to handle in the fifth century, but also is a reminder of Delphi's still undiminished prestige after the Persian Wars. Dodona was, after all, both an older shrine and closer to Epidamnos; but for a life-and-death matter, the Epidamnians chose Delphi. See Hornblower 1991, 69.

[151]Thuc. 1.25.3–4, a passage that confirms the (very genuine) religious bone of contention, often underestimated, but also adds the important fact that one major reason for this cavalier behavior on the part of the Corcyraeans was their great wealth and naval power (120 triremes). In other words, they could afford to emulate those other naval imperialists, the Athenians. This, too, will have helped dictate the Corinthian response to Epidamnos.

[152]Thuc. 26.1–2. The garrison troops included detachments from Ambrakia and the island of Leukas (see Map 4). They went overland to avoid Corcyraean naval interception, by way of Corinth's colony of Apollonia, twenty miles south of Epidamnos.

[153]Thuc. 1.26.3. The Corcyraeans apparently made two approaches to Epidamnos, the first with twenty-five vessels, the second "with another squadron" (ἑτέρῳ στόλῳ); whether this was in addition to, or a replacement for, the first is not clear. In any case, the squadron established a blockade. This resulted in the organization by Corinth of a major colonizing expedition, to be accompanied by thirty Corinthian ships and 3,000 hoplites.

[154]Diodorus' MSS read: ἐπὶ δὲ τοὺς φρουροὺς [or φρουροῦντας] Κορινθίους πρέσβεις ἀπέστειλαν. . . . That ambassadors should have been sent to a garrison is improbable enough in itself; from Thuc. 1.28.1–5 we learn that this embassy went, as we might expect, to Corinth. What Diodorus wrote was "to the Corinthians" (ἐπὶ δὲ τοὺς Κορινθίους); φρουροὺς is clearly an intrusive gloss. This Corcyraean approach was prompted by Corinth's preparations (above).

[155]Thuc. 1.29.1.

rounding up allies. Thus the Corinthian War, so-called, broke out for the above-mentioned reasons.

[6] Meanwhile [156] the Romans were at war with the Volscians: to begin with they met only in skirmishes and minor engagements, but later [the Romans] won a major pitched battle, and massacred most of their opponents.

31. When Theodoros was archon in Athens [438/7], the Romans elected as consuls Marcus Genucius and Agrippa Curtius †Chilo†. [157] During their term, in Italy, the nation of the Campani came into existence, acquiring its name from the rich soil of the plain nearby. [158]

In Asia, the kings of the Kimmerian Bosporos, the dynasty known as the Archaianaktidai, [had] ruled for forty-two years; and the successor to the kingdom was Spartakos, who had a seven-year reign. [159]

[2] In Greece, the Corinthians were still at war with the Corcyraeans. When both had readied their naval forces, they moved them into position for a sea battle. The Corinthians bore down on the enemy with seventy well-equipped vessels; but the Corcyraeans met them with eighty, and defeated them. They then reduced Epidamnos, putting to death all prisoners they took bar the Corinthians, whom they chained and jailed. [160] [3] After this sea battle

---

[156] Actually in 446 (see note 144 above). For the defense by the consuls against Volscian and Aequian attacks, see Livy 3.66.1–70.15, Front. *Strat.* 2.8.2. On these incursions in general, see Cornell 1995, 304–309, and in *CAH* vii.2, 292–294.

[157] The consuls (actually for 445: Broughton 1951, 52) were M. Genucius Augurinus and C. (or Agripp.) Curtius Philo (Chilo? by Greek transposition of $\Phi$ into $X$).

[158] What happened here was that after initial peaceful infiltration, Oscan-speaking Samnite immigrants, during the mid-fifth century, took over the principal Campanian cities, including Capua (Livy 4.37.1), and proclaimed themselves a new Italic nation, the Campani. See Frederiksen 1984, 134–157; Cornell 1995, 305–306. E. H. Bunbury (*DGRG* 1:490) observes that "originally the name of Campania appears to have been applied solely to the inhabitants of the great plain," so the explanation of the name that Diodorus gives may well be correct.

[159] See D. C. Braund in *OCD* 1434. The Archaianaktidai ruled from 480 to 438 B.C.E.; the Spartokid dynasty survived until c. 110 B.C.E., when Mithradates VI Eupator took over the Bosporan kingdom. Spartokos (less correctly Spartakos) I ruled 438 (as "archon" rather than king) until 433/2: cf. below, 12.36.1. He will have been one of the "kings and dynasts" with whom Perikles made contact during his tour of the Black Sea, probably a year later, presumably in search of reliable sources of grain (cf. Stadter 1989, 217): it is significant that immediately afterward, Plutarch notes (*Per.* 20.2) that he was not tempted to make another expedition to Egypt, which was clearly thought of as having a similar purpose to his Black Sea cruise.

[160] Thuc. 1.29.1–5: the Corinthians are here reported as having seventy-five ships and 2,000 hoplites, but the Corcyraeans' total of eighty vessels agrees with Diodorus' figure

the Corinthians withdrew, in considerable disarray, to the Peloponnese, while the Corcyraeans, who were now supreme at sea in those parts, kept raiding the Corinthians' allies and laying waste their land.[161]

32. When this year was over, the [new] archon in Athens was Euthymenes [437/6], while in Rome, in lieu of consuls, three military tribunes were elected: Aulus Sempronius, Lucius Atilius, and Titus Quinctius.[162] During their term, the Corinthians, after being thus worsted at sea, decided to build up a more substantial fleet. [2] So, after amassing large quantities of timber and hiring shipwrights from various cities, they began with zealous enthusiasm to make ready not only triremes, but also every kind of weapon and missile, and, in a word, to stockpile all the gear they needed for the war. Regarding the triremes, some they laid down new, some worn-out ones they rebuilt, and others they requisitioned from their allies. [3] Since the Corcyraeans were doing much the same thing, and were no whit less determined about it, it was clear that the war was going to intensify very considerably.[163]

While these events were in progress, the Athenians also founded a colony

---

(the remaining forty out of 120 were busy blockading Epidamnos). The Corcyraean victory destroyed fifteen Corinthian ships. Thucydides puts the reduction of Epidamnos on the same day as the victory at sea; he agrees on the treatment of the Corinthian prisoners, but claims that the others (i.e., the Leukadians and Ambrakiots, 12.26.1) were sold as slaves (ἀποδόσθαι) rather than executed.

[161] Thuc. 1.30.2–4 presents a rather different scene, according to which for the rest of the season the two sides faced one another in a virtual stand-off, the Corinthians encamped at Aktion (*not* the well-known Actium, far away to the southeast) near the promontory of Cheimerion, the Corcyraeans at Cape Leukimne (or Leukimma), on the southeastern coast of Corcyra, immediately opposite (see the map in Gomme 1945, facing p. 196). The location of Cape Leukimne is certain; those of Aktion and Cheimerion remain highly speculative.

[162] The military tribunes (actually for 444) were A. Sempronius Atratinus, L. Atilius Luscus, and T. Cloelius. They abdicated after three months due to "flaws in the auspices at their election" (Broughton 1951, 53; cf. Livy 4.7.2–3). T. Quinctius Barbatus was in fact the interrex appointed as a result (Livy 4.7.10).

[163] Thuc. 1.31.1. Thucydides specifically states that these activities took up τὸν . . . ἐνιαυτὸν πάντα τὸν μετὰ τὴν ναυμαχίαν καὶ τὸν ὕστερον. This does not, as is sometimes thought, mean the rest of that year and the whole of the year following, but (Gomme 1945, 166 ad loc.) *two twelve-month periods* following the battle. If we date this battle in the spring or summer of 435, we reach early 433 for the appeal to Athens and the subsequent battle of Sybota in the summer. Diodorus' schema places both events in 435, in the archonship of Lysimachos. Thucydides' ambiguity here may well have helped to confuse the later chronological tradition. See below, note 166.

at Amphipolis, taking some of the settlers from among their own citizens, and others from garrisons in the area.[164]

33. When Lysimachos was archon in Athens [436/5], the Romans elected as consuls Titus Quinctius and Marcus Geganius Macerinus, and the Eleians held the 86th Olympiad, that in which Theopompos of Thessaly won the *stadion*.[165] During their term, the Corcyraeans, on discovering the magnitude of the forces being assembled against them, sent ambassadors to the Athenians soliciting their support.[166] [2] Since the Corinthians had done the same thing,

---

[164] Diodorus gives a fuller account of the various foundations on or near this key site (see Map 1, and cf. *BA* 51 B3) at 12.68.1–2, cf. schol. Aeschin. 2.31 = HMA 3; see also above, 11.70.5 and note 271, for the earlier ill-fated venture in 464/3 terminated at Drabeskos. The successful colonization of 437/6 under Hagnon (above, note 135) is described by Thucydides at 4.102.3. Amphipolis lay in a bend of the Strymon, with river access to the ship timber of Macedonia, and on the line of the east-west land route afterward developed as the Via Egnatia; the gold and silver mines of Mt. Pangaios were in its immediate hinterland. Both economically and strategically it was of immense value, and its loss in 424 by the historian Thucydides to Brasidas proved irreparable.

[165] The consuls (actually for 443) were M. Geganius Macerinus and T. Quinctius Capitolinus Barbatus (Broughton 1951, 53).

[166] There would be fewer problems regarding Diodorus' chronology of τὰ Κερκυραῖα were it not for *IG* i³ 364 (Meiggs-Lewis no. 61, pp. 167–168 = Fornara no. 126, p. 143), an account of the expenses of the Athenian squadrons sent to Corcyra. Why should the approach to Athens not have been first made in 435? Because the payments must fall within the same archon-year as the actions to which they relate, and ever since the discovery of *IG* i³ 364, it has been accepted that the eponymous archon mentioned in it was Apseudes (433/2). On that basis, the battle of Sybota is dated to the high summer (August?) of 433, and the entire sequence readjusted accordingly. Diodorus' schema is, as usual, dismissed without argument (for the usual scathing remarks, see Gomme 1945, 198, and in general 51–54). Yet even Gomme (53) concedes, without seeing how illogical this is, that the date Diodorus has for Hagnon's foundation of Amphipolis (437/6), *though in the same sequence*, is correct. Let us look at the inscription. All we have of the archon's name is the first letter, A-, near the end of a line. Lewis supplements in the next line [φσεύδος ἄρχο]ντος. The inscription is recorded as stoichedon (33–35 letters average per line), but with syllabic division observed. This is clearly the basis on which Apseudes was selected: the name makes a good fit. But had Thucydides rather than Diodorus provided the chronology that was dumped without hesitation on the basis of this supplement, I suspect that more notice might have been taken of the archon for 435/4, Antiochides, whose name (alone among archons within range) also begins with A-. It will be objected that the name is too long for a strict stoichedon fit. But is it? Even on the accepted count, there is room for one more letter on line 1. The restoration Ἀ[ν-/τιοχίδος ἄρχο]ντος is only one letter longer than that using Apseudes, in a name with two iotas in it. This does not seem to me beyond the bounds of possibility.

an assembly was convened, at which the *demos,* after listening to the ambassadors [of both sides], voted to make an alliance with Corcyra.[167] Having done so, they at once sent them ten fully equipped triremes,[168] with a promise to send more later if they should have need of them.[169] [3] The Corinthians, having failed to obtain an alliance with Athens, commissioned ninety triremes themselves, and got sixty more from their allies. With the 150 fully equipped warships that this gave them, and after appointing to the command their most highly regarded generals, they set sail for Corcyra, having decided

---

[167] Thuc. 1.31.2–44.3, including lengthy speeches attributed to the rival Corinthian and Corcyraean delegates in Athens. It is fairly clear why Corcyra would wish to enlist Athens' support, and Corinth to prevent this: the Athenian navy was by far the most powerful in the Aegean. It should be emphasized that the role of Corinth as Sparta's major partner in the Peloponnesian League was essentially preventive, and Kagan (1969, 205–221) is right to discount economic theories about Corinthian interests in Illyria and the West. It was *Athens'* new, and increasing, imperial interest in Magna Graecia and Sicily, coupled with its high-handed treatment of Samos, that was causing League members alarm, and hinting at a collision course between the two rival Aegean coalitions. But why—a much debated point—should the Athenians want to involve themselves in this affair at all? The answer (which I have always thought obvious) has perhaps become easier to understand since the activities of OPEC and the Gulf Wars.

That Athens' interests were in large part economic there can be little doubt. Kimon's expeditions to Cyprus and Egypt, the famine of 445, Perikles' cruise into the Black Sea, the establishment of Amphipolis and Thourioi, the treaties with Rhegion and Leontinoi, the eventual expeditions to Sicily: all carry a subtext involving the pursuit of grain, timber, and precious metals. An empire without bread starves. A naval empire without ship timber rapidly becomes a contradiction in terms. From a strategic viewpoint, Plutarch (*Per.* 29.1.9; cf. Thuc. 1.44.2) understands the Corcyraean debate very well. With war already a distinct possibility, Athens' chance to acquire as an ally an island with the next most powerful fleet after its own made excellent sense. As both Thucydides (1.44.3) and Diodorus (12.54.3) emphasize, Corcyra was also a key point on the coastal voyage to Sicily. To control a trade route was no less important than controlling the source of the essential import that traveled it.

[168] Thucydides (1.45.1–3) makes clear that Athenian policy was to avoid a direct confrontation with Corinth—and thus an infraction of the Thirty Years' Peace—if this was possible. For the same reason, the squadron was very small, and directed to take action only if the Corinthians were to attempt a landing at Corcyra or in Corcyraean territory, in which case they were to "hinder them as much as they could" ($\kappa\omega\lambda\acute{\upsilon}\epsilon\iota\nu$ $\kappa\alpha\tau\grave{\alpha}$ $\delta\acute{\upsilon}\nu\alpha\mu\iota\nu$). I am reminded of Lytton Strachey's response when asked, during his interview as a would-be conscientious objector during World War I, what he would do if he came upon a German soldier raping his sister. "I should attempt to interpose myself between them." One of the commanders was Kimon's son Lakedaimonios: Plutarch (*Per.* 29.2–3) attributes this to Perikles' desire to snub and belittle Kimon's heirs, whereas in fact it would seem to have been part of a rather ham-fisted attempt to conciliate the Spartans.

[169] Thucydides (1.44.3) makes no mention of this promise, which does not necessarily mean that it was not given.

to force an immediate sea battle.[170] [4] When the Corcyraeans learned that the enemy fleet was not far off, they put out against them with 120 triremes, including those provided by Athens. A hard-fought engagement took place, in which to begin with the Corinthians prevailed; but later the Athenians showed up with twenty more ships, furnished in accordance with their second agreement,[171] and this tipped the balance in favor of a Corcyraean victory.[172] The next day, when the Corcyraeans put out in full strength against them, the Corinthians did not leave harbor.[173]

34. When Antiochides was archon in Athens [435/4], the Romans elected as consuls Marcus Fabius and Postumus Aebutius †Ulecus†.[174] During their term,[175] the Corinthians were highly annoyed with the Athenians, since the

---

[170] Thucydides (1.46–51, 54) presents a detailed account of this sea battle, fought off the Sybota Islands (see Map 1, and cf. BA 54 B 3). The numbers given on either side agree with Diodorus', except that Thucydides (1.46.1) gets his 150 Corinthian total from 90 Corinthian + 50 allied vessels, an arithmetical slip that if made by Diodorus would have aroused comment; Hornblower (1991) ignores it, while Gomme (1945, 190–194), in a confused and unusually irritable attack on Beloch for having the presumption to challenge Thucydides' figures for this engagement generally, also makes no direct comment on it.

[171] Thucydides only introduces the twenty additional triremes at 1.50.5, toward the end of the engagement, commenting that "the Athenians had dispatched them later as a back-up for the ten, in fear that (as actually happened) the Corcyraeans would be defeated, and their own ten ships would be too few to support them." This does not sound like non-involvement. Hornblower (2002, 109–110) posits a third (cf. Thuc. 1.44.1) Athenian assembly for this decision, increasingly bellicose in mood, which Thucydides casually plays down to minimize its aggression. Diodorus' "second agreement" (τῇ δευτέρᾳ συμμαχίᾳ) may refer to this, but sounds more like a formally revised treaty.

[172] See Thuc. 1.50–51, which makes clear that what happened was rather an indecisive stand-off, and may explain why, later, both sides claimed the victory (Thuc. 1.54.2).

[173] Thuc. 1.52.1–3. The Corinthians were concerned about getting home, fearing the Athenians would regard the treaty as broken and block their passage. In fact (Thuc. 53.4), the Athenians, reverting to their initial stance of a defensive-only alliance with Corcyra, gave them free passage.

[174] The consuls (actually for 442) were M. Fabius Vibulanus and Post. Aebutius Helva Cornicen (Broughton 1951, 54). Oldfather (1946, 443 n. 2, followed, diffidently, by Perotti 1984, 172) supposes "Ulecus" to be "a corruption of Alba or Elba," but this seems unlikely.

[175] In 433/2, according to the consensus of modern scholars, working from an August/September date for Sybota; Diodorus' 435/4 depends on his dating of the Corcyra episode (above), and *could* have been due in part to his, or his source's, misunderstanding of Thuc. 1.31.1 (note 163 above). Gomme (1945, 222) calls this "a purely mechanical dating where [Diodorus] had no express authority"; but it is at least as likely that Diodorus read Thuc. 1.57.1, and noted that this placed the beginning of the Potidaea affair "immediately after the Corcyra sea battle" (εὐθὺς μετὰ τὴν ἐν Κερκύρᾳ ναυμαχίαν). As we have seen, it is also possible that a combination of Diodorus' schema with Thuc. 1.31.1 would yield a date of

latter had not only fought side by side with the Corcyraeans, but had been responsible for their victory in the sea battle.[176] [2] So, being determined to pay the Athenians back, they got one of their own colonies, the city of Potidaia, to revolt from Athens.[177] In like fashion, Perdikkas, the king of Macedon, who also had his differences with the Athenians, persuaded those Chalcidians who had broken with Athens to abandon their coastal cities and all settle in Olynthos.[178] [3] When the Athenians heard about the defection of Potidaia, they sent out thirty ships with instructions to lay waste these rebels' territory and to sack their city.[179] Those thus dispatched made landfall in Macedonia

---

spring 434, which in this context is more likely. Internally, Diodorus and Thucydides are in substantial agreement.

[176] Thuc. 1.56.2, cf. Plut. *Per.* 29.4. At this point, very soon after Sybota, the Athenians required the Potidaians to (a) dismantle their defense wall on the Pallene isthmus; (b) furnish hostages; and (c) dismiss the Corinthian magistrates (ἐπιδημιούργους) that they had until then received annually. The tribute lists are interesting here. In 434 Potidaia is still paying the regular six talents noted as far back as 444, and probably assessed in 446. After that, the evidence is lost until 431, when Potidaia is, not surprisingly, absent from the Pallene/Chalcidic group. The bounce from six to fifteen talents assumed in 434/3 and on the lost 432/1 *tabula*—presumably to lend epigraphic support to the accepted date of the revolt—depends on a wholly implausible, indeed bizarre, guess by the editors of *ATL* that *for several years,* and without correction, a stone-cutter reversed the assessments for Potidaia and Skione: *ATL* 3:64–65, 321, surprisingly accepted by Lewis at *IG* i³ 278.5. Only Kagan (1969, 275 n. 8) rightly rejects it out of hand. The fifteen-talent raise is a chimaera, and should be eradicated from the evidence. Potidaia, as far as the tribute lists go, could have revolted at any point from 434 onward.

[177] Potidaia lay on the narrow neck of the Pallene peninsula in Chalcidice (see Map 1, and cf. *BA* 51 A4; Gomme 1945, maps facing pp. 220, 222). The urgings both of the Corinthians and of Perdikkas (see below) became known to Athens before Potidaia actually revolted: Thuc. 1.56.2.

[178] Perdikkas II of Macedon (c. 452–413/2 B.C.E.) was an astute and shifty opportunist who survived by switching sides again and again before and during the Peloponnesian War (Hammond in *OCD* 1137–1138; Hammond and Griffith 1979, 115–136; Badian 1993, 172–174). Allied with Athens until the establishment of Amphipolis in 437/6, he thereupon set out to stir up as much trouble for Athens as he could: Thucydides (1.57.2–5) explains his approach to the Chalcidic cities as a way of winning neighbors as supporters in a general revolt led by Potidaia, and adds that he was pressing Corinth to the same end. But his immediate complaint was that Athens, seeing him as a lost cause, had promptly made an agreement with his brother Philip and Derdas I, prince of the Macedonian highland outkingdom of Elimia.

[179] Thucydides (1.58.1–59.1) states that the Athenian thirty-ship squadron, which also included 1,000 hoplites, (a) was already being sent out to deal with Perdikkas, and (b) was given additional orders—though these seem not to have received any priority: overconfidence again—to implement the requirements placed on Potidaia (above). These orders were issued when the Athenians heard rumors of, and were determined to *forestall* (προκαταλαμβάνειν), the planned revolt. This coincided with a Potidaian embassy to Ath-

according to their instructions from the *demos,* and at once laid siege to Potidaia.[180] [4] When the Corinthians sent a contingent of 2,000 troops to relieve the besieged, the Athenian *demos* countered with 2,000 of its own.[181] A battle took place on the isthmus near Pallene, which the Athenians won, killing more than 300 of the enemy.[182] Potidaia was now completely invested.[183]

---

ens (which didn't work out) and another to Sparta (which did: the Spartans promised—a promise unfulfilled—to invade Attica if Athens moved against Potidaia). Not surprisingly, when the Athenian squadron reached the Thracian coast, it found the general revolt already in full swing. Neither the timing nor the instructions in Diodorus (the Athenians react to a fait accompli; the instructions—slash-and-burn, sack—are more stringent) agree with those in Thucydides. Diodorus, who as we have seen clearly read Thucydides, here preferred an alternative source (whatever it may have been: Ephoros is merely a guess). Presumably he felt Thucydides was airbrushing Athenian brutality, which on occasion he does indeed seem to have done. Diodorus' version also, interestingly, suggests that the Athenians were not expecting serious resistance, let alone a long siege: precisely the same expensive mistake they had made over Samos.

[180] Thuc. 1.59.2 states, on the contrary, that far from immediately besieging Potidaia, they joined Philip and Derdas and began campaigning in Macedonia, where they captured Therme and besieged Pydna (see Map 1, and cf. *BA* 50 C3–4). Diodorus, or his source, omits the Macedonian *démarche* altogether.

[181] Thuc. 1.60–61 passim. The 2,000 Corinthian troops under Aristeus reached Thrace forty days after the revolt broke out (i.e., June at the earliest, and probably around July or August of 433). They seem to have moved directly toward Potidaia, which in fact, if Thucydides is right, had not yet been put under siege at all. The initial Athenian expedition was scarcely large enough to divide its forces. The second Athenian contingent of 2,000 men and forty ships, under Kallias son of Kalliades and four other generals, made for Macedonia and joined in the siege of Pydna. News of Aristeus' march on Potidaia finally jolted them out of their complacency. They patched up a rapid peace with Perdikkas, after which the whole force—3,000 hoplites plus 600 Macedonian cavalry and various other allies—moved southeast into the Chalcidic peninsula, with the now-seventy-strong flotilla following them along the coast. Even now they do not seem to have been in any great hurry. They encamped at Gigonos, on the coast of the Thermaic Gulf, about midway between Therme and Potidaea.

[182] Thuc. 1.62–63 describes this battle. Aristeus and the Corinthians set up their defense on the northern side of Potidaia, stationing the Chalcidic allies and 200 Macedonian cavalry at Olynthos, between seven and eight miles distant. (Perdikkas of Macedon, having already once again switched sides, had come in as their cavalry commander, so that Macedonian horsemen were now fighting on both sides.) Kallias, the Athenian general, blocked off any flank attack from Olynthos and, despite a successful charge by Aristeus, won the battle, dying (like Epaminondas) in the moment of victory. Aristeus fought his way back into Potidaia through the water of the harbor. In addition to Kallias, Athenian losses were about 150. Both Sokrates and Alkibiades fought in this engagement: Plat. *Symp.* 219–220 passim.

[183] Again, Thucydides (1.64.1) tells a slightly different story. After their victory, the Athenians blocked off the northern front of Potidaia, but the southern side of the city, fac-

[5] Simultaneously with these events, the Athenians founded that city in the Propontis known as †Letanon†.[184]

In Italy, the Romans sent settlers to Ardea and divided up the [adjacent] territory into land-holdings.[185]

35. When Krates was archon in Athens [434/3], the Romans elected as consuls Quintus Furius Fusus and Manius Papirius Crassus.[186] During their term,[187] in Italy, the inhabitants of Thourioi, who had been assembled from numerous cities, split into hostile factions over two problems: from which city should the Thourians be said to have come as settlers, and what man should properly be called their founder? [2] The Athenians asserted their right to the first privilege, since the bulk of the colony's settlers had come from Athens; but the cities of the Peloponnese, which likewise had contributed not a few of their citizens to the founding of Thourioi, maintained that the entitlement of the colony should be ascribed to them. [3] Similarly with the second point: since many highly qualified men had shared in the process of colonization, and had performed numerous essential services, there was much discussion about this, since each one of them was eager to have the honor. In the end,

---

ing the Pallene peninsula, remained unguarded, since the Athenians felt they were not strong enough to divide their forces and complete the blockade without risking a Potidaian attack. The Pallene side was only blocked off later—Thucydides (1.64.2) does not, frustratingly, say how much later, though it can only have been a matter of months at the outside—by a relieving force under Phormio. See below, note 195.

[184] Identity quite uncertain. Cobet suggested Δρέπανον, a site about which virtually nothing is known (identified by BA 52 F3 with the later Helenopolis, on the Mysian shore of the Gulf of Astakos). Niese proposed Ἀστακός itself, the coastal town south of Nikopolis at the head of the gulf of the same name; this was adopted by the editors of ATL (1: 471–472, 603; 4:151 col. 1 s.v. Ἀστακός) and by Oldfather (1946). However, unless we really stretch the meaning of Diodorus' ἔκτισαν to "took over" (i.e., with a cleruchy) or "colonized," it is hard to see how a city already assessed for tribute in 450 could be founded in 435/4.

[185] Ardea was on the coast of Latium, between Ostia and Antium. For its colonization (actually in 442), see Livy 4.11.5–7; Dion. Hal.11.62.4; and cf. Cornell 1995, 302–303.

[186] The consuls (actually for 441) were C. Furius Pacilus Fusus and M' (or M.) Papirius Crassus (Broughton 1951, 54).

[187] It is at this point that Diodorus breaks off his narrative of the Potidaian campaign, returning to it at 12.37.1, after a two-year break marked only by two unrelated items, the dispute over Thourioi's foundation and Meton's reform of the Athenian calendar, both clearly fillers of a gap between two incompatible chronologies, the later of these, which Diodorus adopts from 432/1 on, being based, ultimately, on Thucydides' dating (2.2.1) for the Theban attack on Plataia in spring 431. For difficulties with this latter passage, see below, note 195.

the Thourians sent to Delphi to find out just whom they should name as their city's founder. The god's oracular response was that he himself should be regarded as the founder. Once the dispute had been settled in this manner, they declared Apollo the founder of Thourioi, after which the citizen body, thus freed from civil dissension, returned to their previous state of concord.[188]

[4] In Greece, King Archidamos of the Lacedaemonians died[189] after a forty-two-year reign, and Agis succeeded him, to remain king for twenty-seven years.

36. When Apseudes was archon in Athens [433/2], the Romans elected as consuls Titus Menenius and Proclus Geganius Macerinus.[190] During their term, Spartakos, king of the Bosporos, died, after seven years on the throne, and was succeeded by Satyros, who reigned for forty years.[191]

[2] In Athens, Meton son of Pausanias, who had won a high reputation as an astronomer, published what is known as his nineteen-year cycle, which he set to begin on the thirteenth day of the Athenian month Skirophorion. By the end of these nineteen years, the stars [sic] return to the positions from which they started, thus completing what we may term the circuit of a Great Year, called by some in consequence Meton's Year.[192] [3] This man would

---

[188] This nice example of diplomatic arbitration by a theodicy also hints at Delphi's support for Panhellenism. See Graham 1964, 26. On Thourioi in general, see above, chs. 10–11, with notes. The emphasis on religious leadership is very much in line with the appeal to Delphic Apollo here (cf. Fontenrose 1978, 156–157, 329).

[189] King Archidamos II actually died in 427/6, as Diodorus (who noted his activities during the first phase of the Peloponnesian War; see, e.g., 12.42.6) knew perfectly well. For a possible explanation of the error, see above, Book 11, note 182; and cf. Casevitz 1972, 109–110. Archidamos' son and successor, Agis II, played a leading role in the war, then in 413 was cuckolded by Alkibiades, who formed a liaison with his wife Timaia. Agis died in 400.

[190] The consuls (actually for 440) were Proculus Geganius Macerinus and T. Menenius Agripp. Lanatus (Broughton 1951, 55). We should note, during this year, Athens' renewal of treaties with Rhegion and Leontinoi, probably linked to Athenian pressure at Delphi for acknowledgment as founding city of Thourioi, and evidence of its steadily increasing interest in the West. See Meiggs-Lewis nos. 63–64, pp. 171–176 = Fornara 141–143, nos. 124–125.

[191] See above, note 159, and D.S. 14.93.1, under the archon-year 393/2, where Satyros is correctly named (the MSS here read Σέλευκος), but the length of his reign is given as forty-four years: Vogel (1890) there deletes τέτταρα after τετταράκοντα as a case of dittography, in my view correctly.

[192] On Meton, see Meritt 1928, 88, and 1961, 216; Pritchett 1964, 235–236; Bickermann 1968, 29; Woodhead 1981, 115–118 (for an excellent short introduction to the complexities of the Athenian calendar); and, for a brief but authoritative general survey, G. J. Toomey in OCD 969–970; a full astronomical analysis in Evans 1998, 185–186. What Meton and

seem to have been quite extraordinarily accurate in his prediction and written forecast, since the stars do indeed accomplish their cycle, and produce the consequent effects of this, in accordance with his written calculations. As a result, from that day to this, most Greeks go by the nineteen-year cycle, and are not cheated of the truth in so doing.

[4] In Italy, the Tarantines expropriated the inhabitants of Siris from their native city, added a number of settlers from among their own citizens, and founded the city known as Herakleia.[193]

37. When Pythodoros was archon in Athens [432/1], the Romans elected as consuls Titus Quinctius and †Nittus† Menenius, and the Eleians held the 87th Olympiad, in which the *stadion* was won by Sophron the Ambrakiot. During their term, in Rome, Spurius Maelius was done away with while aiming for tyrannical power.[194] The Athenians, after scoring a brilliant victory at Potidaia, sent out Phormio as general to replace Kallias, who had fallen in the line of battle.[195] Phormio took over command of the army and dug in for the

---

Euktemon did, in the first instance in 432, was to observe the summer solstice (the beginning of the solar year) as part of an attempt to measure the length of the year more accurately. Philochoros *FGrH* 326 F 120 = schol. Aristoph. *Birds* 997 says this was done by setting up a sundial (ἡλιοτρόπιον) on the wall of the Pnyx. Aristophanes turns Meton's researches into a joke; the cycle was not adopted as an official regulatory device, despite being fine-tuned in 330 by Kallippos and c. 125 by Hipparchos. Skirophorion, the last month of the Athenian lunar calendar, was roughly equivalent to June; Diodorus' date has epigraphical confirmation. The point of the nineteen-year cycle was to adjust the lunar year by intercalation, made necessary by the fact that a tropical year is longer than twelve synodic months by 0.3683 month. Search for a whole number led to $19 \times 0.3693 = 6.9977$. Intercalation of an extra month in seven of nineteen months produces, in nineteen calendar years, 235 lunar months, or an average of 12.3684 months per annum, an excellent fit with the solar 12.3683. Diodorus, who speaks of "stars" (ἄστρα) rather than planets, was clearly no astronomer (Oldfather 1946, 448 n. 1).

[193] Cf. 12.23.2 and note 95. On Herakleia, see also Strab. 6.1.14, C.264; it was slightly north of Siris, near modern Policoro: see Map 4, and cf. *BA* 46 E1.

[194] The consuls (actually for 439) were Agrippa (Livy 4.13.6: for "Nittus," see Perotti 1984, 172) Menenius Lanatus and T. Quinctius Capitolinus Barbatus (Broughton 1951, 56). Sp. Maelius was an equestrian who, at a time of near-famine, bought up grain wholesale from Etruria and sold it to the plebs at giveaway prices, thus assuring himself a populist power-base. It was to deal with Maelius' supposed attempt "to make himself king" that L. Quinctius Cincinnatus was "called from the plough" (Cic. *Sen.* 56) a second time. Maelius was killed by a patrician, C. Servilius Ahala. The whole episode is shrouded in myth and propaganda. Main sources: Livy 4.13.12–16.1, Dion. Hal. 12.1–4; cf. Cornell 1995, 268, 451; Broughton 1951, 56.

[195] Thuc. 1.64.1–2. It is clear from Thucydides that the action Diodorus resumes here from 12.34.4, under the archon-year 435/4, was in fact more or less continuous, and thus to

siege; but though he made endless assaults on the city, its defenders stood him off valiantly, and the siege became a lengthy business.[196]

---

be located near the end of 433/2. "Afterward" (χρόνῳ ὕστερον), on learning of these events, the Athenians send out Phormio: say late July or August. This agrees well with the largely persuasive general arguments laid out in Gomme 1945, 421–425, where the Potidaia battle is dated to June 432. However, Gomme (like all students of the chronology of this period) has also to take into account Thucydides' specific, and very unusual, effort to date the beginning of the Peloponnesian War, at 2.2.1. Since this passage pinpoints the attack on Plataia to a specific month, and *inter alia* backdates from there to the battle of Potidaia, it should solve the whole problem. Unfortunately, since one of its key readings is a contradiction in terms, and the other virtually impossible, it merely adds to the confusion, leaving us with nothing better than the choice of several dubious emendations.

First, we have his statement that the archon for 432/1, Pythodoros, still had two months to serve (ἔτι δύο μῆνας ἄρχοντος) at the time of the Theban attack on Plataia, the end of that archon-year being c. 4 July (Meritt 1932, 176). This puts us at the beginning of May. But he also says it was at the beginning of spring (ἅμα ἦρι ἀρχομένῳ), and in the Thucydidean dating system (Gomme 1956b, 707–710), this means the first week in March. Hence the first emendation: the two months left for Pythodoros become four (Kruger, arguing that the alphabetic numeral δ [4] was misread as δύο). But Thucydides also equates the beginning of spring with the *sixth month* (μηνὶ ἕκτῳ) after the battle of Potidaia, which would give us a date in October 432. This not only crowds subsequent events to an almost impossible degree, but also goes against the cumulative weight of our other evidence (Gomme 1945, 424–425). It is not impossible, but highly unlikely. Therefore emendation has again been proposed, this time for ἕκτῳ: the most plausible suggestion is δεκάτῳ (Lipsius, followed by Hude), though ἐνάτῳ is also possible. This would give us a date for the battle of Potidaia of May or June 432. We can then place Phormio's activities (establishing his base at Aphytis on the Pallene peninsula, a leisurely raiding progression northward to Potidaia, the building of the Pallene wall) in the high summer and fall of 432. It is not an absolutely certain schema, but on balance it remains more probable than not.

[196] Diodorus makes no mention during 432/1 (any more than does Thucydides) of the Megarian complaint about being excluded from Athenian ports and harbors, though this was to form one of the leading reasons for the declaration of hostilities. However, he does discuss the decree and its impact retrospectively at 12.39.4–5. Cf. Thuc. 1.67.4, 139.1–2; Plut. *Per.* 29 and 30.2–3, with Stadter 1989, 269, 274–276.

# APPENDIX A: THE TERMINAL DATE
# OF THE *BIBLIOTHEKE*

What has often been picked on as the most striking discrepancy in Diodorus' chronology, that to do with the terminal date of his work, is in fact also the most revealing. In the introductory proem, while discussing the plan and structure of the *Bibliotheke*,[1] Diodorus makes a very specific chronological statement (1.4.7). The final twenty-three books (Books 18–40) cover the period from the death of Alexander (323 B.C.E.) to the beginning of Caesar's Gallic Wars. Diodorus correctly dates the latter to "the first year of the 180th Olympiad,"[2] that is, 60/59 B.C.E. In the very next paragraph—following, as he tells us, the *Chronology* of Apollodoros, who used the Eratosthenic estimate of 1184 to date the Trojan War—he reckons 80 years to the Return of the Herakleidai (1104), 328 years from then to the 1st Olympiad (776/5, the canonical date), and 730 more years εἰς τὴν ἀρχὴν τοῦ Κελτικοῦ πολέμου, his terminal point. He correctly reckons the total span as 1,138 years. But when we calculate the terminal point on this basis, we arrive, not at 60/59, but at 46/5. What, everyone asks, has been going on here? That Diodorus' actual terminal point was 60/59 is virtually proven by the surviving fragments of Book 40: these go back at least as far as 69 (40.1a–b), and the latest datable passage alludes to the Catilinarian conspiracy of 63 (40.5). Since the later books (21–39) average at most twelve years apiece, it is hard to believe that the narrative of

---

[1] Rubincam (1987, particularly 317ff.) has demonstrated, largely by an exemplary analysis of Diodorus' surprisingly accurate use of cross-references (on which see also the earlier work of R. Starr, *AJPh* 102 [1981]: 431–437), how carefully and economically the overall structure of the *Bibliotheke* was organized, with "relative compactness in proportion to its huge scope" (314): Polybios and Poseidonios needed as much or more space to cover a mere 120 and 85 years respectively.

[2] 1.4.7 ad fin.: τούτου [sc. the Gallic campaign] δ᾽ αἱ πρῶται πράξεις ἐπετελέσθησαν Ὀλυμπιάδος τῆς ἑκατοστῆς καὶ ὀγδοηκοστῆς κατὰ τὸ πρῶτον ἔτος. For the correctness of 60/59 as the opening year of the Gallic campaign, see, e.g., M. Gelzer, *Caesar: Politician and Statesman* (Cambridge, Mass., 1968), 84–85; and Sacks 1990, 177 n. 78.

Book 40 went far beyond 60 B.C.E., and out of the question that it extended to 46/5.

How, then, are we to explain the discrepancy? For skeptical traditionalists, the answer is all too predictable: Diodorus simply used a chronography with the wrong date for the Gallic campaign, and copied its conclusions in his usual mindless way.[3] Alternatively, a copyist's error is invoked.[4] But as Sacks has demonstrated, neither explanation makes sense.[5] The text cannot be corrupt, since Diodorus repeats his overall chronological calculation twice in succession (1.4.6–7; 1.5.1), reaching the same conclusion both times. Nor will blind stupidity, based on a false date, account for the error, since in the first passage we find the correct date given (the first year of the 180th Olympiad = 60/59). Skeptics may doubt Sacks' reasonable assertion that "no matter how sloppy Diodorus might at times be, it is unthinkable that he could make such a gross error involving a contemporary event":[6] but the evidence, fortunately, speaks for itself.

At several points in the early books,[7] Diodorus promises to discuss Caesar's campaign in Britain "at the appropriate point," ἐν τοῖς οἰκείοις χρόνοις, a regular phrase of his throughout the *Bibliotheke*. Rubincam's claim that he is normally punctilious about fulfilling such anticipatory promises has too many exceptions to carry much weight; more persuasive is Diodorus' clear knowledge of Britain, and of Caesar's activities there.[8] The manifest conclusion, admirably argued by Rubincam and Sacks,[9] is that, as an impassioned admirer of the lately divinized Dictator,[10] Diodorus did indeed originally plan

---

[3] See, e.g., Schwartz 1903, col. 665: "Ich weiss keine andere Erklärung, als daß die von Diodor benützte chronologische Tabelle bis 46/5 reichte und er deren Schlußsumme einfach abgeschrieben hat." A similar explanation is to be found in Burton 1972, 40–42.

[4] This used to be the favored solution. Emendations by Scaliger and others are listed in Wesseling and Eyring 1793–1807, 1:303–306. Sacks (1990, 170 n. 47) also cites Wachsmuth 1892, 1:5.

[5] Sacks 1990, 169–172.

[6] Sacks 1990, 170.

[7] See, e.g., besides 1.4.7, 3.38.2–3, 5.21.2, 5.22.1; and cf. Perl 1957, 4–7.

[8] Rubincam 1989, 39–61, esp. 41 n. 7 and 50 n. 23. For other unfulfilled promises in the *Bibliotheke*, see, e.g., 4.23.3, 4.29.6, 5.6.4, 11.90.1, 12.16.1–2, 19.10.3. For Britain and its conquest in the *Bibliotheke*, see in particular 40.7.1–2, cf. 3.38.2–3, 5.21.1–23.4, 32.3, 38.5.

[9] Rubincam 1987, 327–328; Sacks 1990, 169–172.

[10] Zecchini 1978, 13–20; Rubincam 1987, 327; Sacks 1990, 170–172. Diodorus regularly refers, with formulaic phraseology (προαγορευθεὶς θεός, (ἐπ)ονομασθεὶς θεός, κληθεὶς θεός), to Caesar as already divinized: 1.4.7, 4.19.2, 5.21.2, 5.25.4, 32.27.1, 3. Since Caesar was being talked of as a god from the moment of his funeral in 44 B.C.E., and his cult was formally consecrated on 1 January 42 (App. *BC* 2.148, Dio Cass. 47.18.3–6; cf. D. Weinstock, *Divus Julius* [Oxford, 1971], 386, cited by Sacks 1990, 171 n. 55), we have a *terminus ante*

to cover Caesar's life to within two years of the (not then anticipated) Ides of March, leaving off at a point (46/5) when, after victories at Pharsalos, Thapsos, and Munda, followed by a quadruple triumph and appointment as *Dictator perpetuo,* he had reached the pinnacle of his career. If, as Rubincam convincingly argues,[11] Diodorus originally planned his work in seven hexads, Books 41 and 42 would, precisely, have covered the period 60–46. What happened, clearly, was that the historian, despite his obsession with Caesar, and to the detriment of his work's overall symmetry,[12] changed his mind at the last moment, subsequently forgetting—or not living long enough—to rework his chronological figures and eliminate references to Caesar's campaigns.[13] What made him do so?

One theory, that of Oldfather,[14] can be dismissed out of hand: according to him, "as Diodorus grew old, and perhaps a little tired, he gave up his original plan." Now while it may well be true that the sheer "magnitude of the undertaking" ($\tau\grave{o}$ $\mu\acute{e}\gamma\epsilon\theta o\varsigma$ $\tau\hat{\eta}\varsigma$ $\acute{v}\pi o\theta\acute{e}\sigma\epsilon\omega\varsigma$, 1.3.4) wore him down over the years,[15] it takes more than weariness to persuade a writer to abandon, right at the end, a complex structural scheme on which he has set his heart. Far more plausible is the explanation advanced by Rubincam and (in great detail) by Sacks:[16] that political conditions during, and immediately after, the civil wars that destroyed the Republic made any extended treatment of Caesar, from the Second Triumvirate onward, risky in the extreme. The *Bibliotheke,* as we have seen (above, pp. 6–7), shows no knowledge of Actium, or of Octavian's subsequent annexation of Egypt. Diodorus, like so many others, would still, right up to the end, have been hedging his bets between Octavian and Antony, though there were good personal reasons (p. 7) for him to be less than sympathetic to Octavian, or indeed to Roman colonial habits generally.

---

*quem* for at least the editing of these books. (At 3.38.2 the title is missing, which suggests earlier composition.) Diodorus regarded Caesar, like Alexander, as a key historical figure and chronological marker (Sacks 1990, 172 n. 59).

[11] Rubincam 1998b, 231–232.

[12] Rubincam (1998b, 233) asks the obvious question: Why did Diodorus not in his general proem (say at 1.4.6) "spell out the details of the original organizational scheme . . . ? . . . The answer must be that by the time he wrote the final version of that general preface he had realized that the changed terminal point spoiled the perfection of the hexadic scheme. He preferred, therefore, to de-emphasize that aspect of the organization of the *Bibliotheca.*"

[13] Cf. Sacks 1990, 170–171.

[14] Oldfather 1946, xix.

[15] So argued also by Rubincam (1987, 326), citing Diodorus' own complaint about "a task that seemed impossible," $\tau\grave{o}$ $\deltao\kappao\hat{v}\nu$ $\check{a}\pi o\rho o\nu$ $\epsilon\hat{i}\nu\alpha\iota$ (1.4.2).

[16] Rubincam 1987, 327–328; Sacks 1990, ch. 6, "Diodorus in the World of Caesar and Octavian," 160–203.

In Rome, Diodorus—unlike almost every other intellectual Greek émigré—reveals no connections whatsoever with Roman patrons, and no apparent interest in the rhetorical circles established by the émigrés themselves. The contrast with those other Sicilians whom we know to have been domiciled in Rome—Caecilius of Kale Akte and Sextus Clodius—is striking. Both of these were rhetoricians, enjoyed Roman favor, and belonged to well-known intellectual circles.[17] Diodorus gives no sign of any such affiliations. Indeed, he reveals a certain uncommon distaste for his rhetorical and philosophical contemporaries.[18] As Sacks reminds us, "Such attitudes would not endear him to the intellectual class at Rome, or to its patrons."[19] They also suggest that Diodorus was not dependent on teaching for his livelihood, and thus probably possessed a fairly substantial private income. If this was true, it may explain his apparent isolation; and if he was isolated, he will certainly have lacked a network of friends and patrons to help him in times of trouble.

Times of trouble, indeed, spanned the entire period that Diodorus finally decided to omit from his *Bibliotheke,* and after Caesar's death in 44 the situation got even worse. The Sicilians had welcomed Pompey's beneficent rule as governor in 82/1—Diodorus gives him a ringing endorsement,[20] particularly, and predictably, because of his ἀρετή, his incorruptibility, and his sober lifestyle—and they offered similar enthusiastic allegiance to his son Sextus, who confirmed Antony's offer of full citizenship.[21] The contrast with Octavian's later vindictive treatment of Sicily during the mid-30s (above, pp. 6–7) scarcely needs emphasizing. Strabo (6.2.6, C.272–3) records that the island's central plain was virtually depopulated. Diodorus, who saw Alexander and Caesar, correctly, as the two benchmark agents of historical change, has one reference only (cast in studiedly neutral terms) to Octavian, and that concerns his retaliatory action against Tauromenium (16.7.1).[22] Thus it is not hard to

---

[17] Sacks 1990, 188–189 with refs.

[18] Orators: 1.76.1–3, 12.53.4 (and cf. 9.26.3); philosophers: 2.29.5–6, 9.9, 10.7.23. At 20.1–2.2 Diodorus castigates the rhetorical excesses of other historians.

[19] Sacks 1990, 189.

[20] Diod. 38/39.20 (cf. 9): οὕτως εὐστόχως καὶ ἀδωροδοκήτως ἐποιεῖτο τὰς ἀποφάσεις . . . οὕτως αὐστήρως καὶ σωφρόνως ἐποιήσατο τὴν ἐπιδημίαν. Cicero, too, praised his conduct in office: 2 *Verr.* 16.42; *Leg. Man.* 9.30, 20.61; Plut. *Pomp.* 10.2.

[21] Sacks 1990, app. I ("Sicilian Enfranchisement"), 207–210.

[22] That one of Octavian's aims was to free Rome from possible grain shortages and the recurrent fear of piracy will have made little if any impression on the islanders. In any case, revenge for their desperate, and highly inconvenient, resistance was clearly the dominant motive behind his ruthless reaction. For famine in Rome and the control of Sardinia, Corsica, and northern Africa, as well as Sicily, by Sextus Pompeius, see App. *BC* 5.67, 74.

see where Diodorus' sympathies will have lain when, about 35 B.C.E., Greek intellectuals "were forced to choose, not between Rome and its enemies, but between two Roman leaders"—indeed, between East and West.[23]

At the same time, the final outcome of that struggle was very much still in the air. Without backers or powerful friends in Rome, without the confidence—or perhaps even the inclination—to switch sides as events dictated,[24] Diodorus surely had an overpoweringly strong motive to play it safe, to round off his work at the first hint of Rome's lethal civil conflict.[25] Whether this was enough to prevent him becoming a marked man as Octavian consolidated his power, whether his repeated call for compassion ($\phi\iota\lambda\alpha\nu\theta\rho\omega\pi\iota\alpha$) and moderation ($\epsilon\pi\iota\epsilon\iota\kappa\epsilon\iota\alpha$)—surely a plea on behalf of his own savagely war-torn country—fell on deaf ears, personally no less than politically, we shall never know. But his ambivalent attitude to Rome and Roman imperialism is unmistakable. He has praise for the Senate (30.9); he emphasizes that Rome's wars were just (28.3). Yet careful reading reveals that he draws a very clear line between past and present. While Rome had leaders like Aemilius Paullus, he stresses (30.23.2), all was well; but since the Social Wars in particular (which he characterizes, significantly if with aberrant judgment, as the most important in recorded history, 37.1.1–6), Romans have suffered a catastrophic moral decline into greed, vice, and self-indulgence.[26] He praises Caesar; he praises Pompey (38/39.9, 20); he is virtually silent, as we have seen, about Octavian. Did he, one wonders, ever, prior to Actium, express an (almost certainly favorable) opinion, however guardedly, on Mark Antony? Octavian, whose career reveals a more than usually sharp ability to read between the lines of even the most cautious political statement, would not have missed it if he did.

---

[23] Sacks 1990, 190.

[24] For instances of those who did, see R. Syme, *The Roman Revolution* (Oxford, 1939), 262; G. W. Bowersock, *Augustus and the Greek World* (Oxford, 1965), 35–36, 135; Sacks 1990, 190.

[25] Ambaglio (1995, 16) airily assures us that Diodorus "would have had little trouble in not offending the susceptibilities of the Dictator's political heirs," and that the idea of his exercising "a prudent reticence regarding the fall of the Republic" is about as fantastic as the theory that he stopped short in order to avoid competing with Asinius Pollio. This argument suggests a less than adequate familiarity with the brutal political ambiguities prevailing during a violent civil war, the outcome of which was wholly unpredictable.

[26] 31.26.2, 37.3.2–6: by now, admittedly, a platitude, and one he may well have picked up from Polybios: see Polyb. 31.25–29 passim; and B. Shimron, "Polybius on Rome: A Reconsideration of the Evidence," *SCI* 5 (1979/80): 94–117, esp. 101–103. It was the crucial period after 60/59 where the real danger lay.

# APPENDIX B: ATHENIAN LOSSES
# IN THE EGYPTIAN CAMPAIGN

The Athenian losses recorded in the Egyptian campaign (cf. II.77.5) by all our major sources are staggering. Thucydides (1.110.1) says "the majority of them perished." Ctesias (§34, 40b15) puts the figure of those who surrendered at "over 6,000." Since they had to trek westward across desert, in the height of summer, to reach safety at Cyrene, we should not be surprised to learn that "few out of many" made it home (Thuc. 1.110.1). But what were the expedition's overall losses? The fourth-century rhetorician Isokrates (8.86), in a passage citing Athens' various heavy losses, puts the total at 200 triremes, with their crews, in Egypt, and another 150 off Cyprus. He is copied by Aelian (*VH* 5.10). These figures are incredible. The number of triremes is more than Athens' total fleet; the manpower, at 70,000 (350 × 200), is over twice the city's able-bodied free male population.[1] We can dismiss the Cypriot figure as a false inference drawn from the relief squadron of fifty ships sent out in ignorance of the defeat (Thuc. 1.110.4), on the assumption that this last was detached from another fleet of 200 (on which see below) that was likewise lost. But that still leaves us with an impossible loss of 200 triremes and 40,000 men. Even if we write off one-third of the figure as allied rather than Athenian casualties,[2] the total still defies belief. Similar casualties in Sicily (413 B.C.E.) severely crippled Athens and brought it to ultimate defeat at Aigospotamoi (404); yet a year or two after Egypt, Athens has no shortage of manpower, and a sizable fleet scoring successes in Phoenicia and elsewhere. How are we to explain this?

The figure of 200 ultimately must derive from Thucydides (1.104.2), and the defense, against all reason, of enormous casualties stems from a determination to treat Thucydides as the *vox Dei*.[3] But what does Thucydides in fact

---

[1] Holladay 1989, 179 n. 12.

[2] Holladay 1989, 178.

[3] See, e.g., Meiggs 1972, 101–108, 439–441, 473–477. The complex numerical calculations of Bigwood (1976, 10–15), which suffer from the same weakness, make heavy weather of the evidence and finally confuse rather than enlighten.

say? That a fleet this size was (like others both earlier and later) on its way to Cyprus. That the Athenians left Cyprus (with how many ships is unstated), went to Egypt, sailed up the Nile, secured Memphis, and laid siege to the White Fort. Even if all 200 ships went to Egypt (and that is doubtful, though Diodorus at 11.74.3 confirms it), the idea of the whole fleet then navigating the Nile makes no kind of strategic sense. What *does* make sense is a fleet of about 150 patrolling Cyprus, the mouths of the Nile, Phoenicia, and the eastern Mediterranean in general, while a smaller detachment went upriver to support Inaros and occupy the head of the Delta. Over a long period, the occupying force would be regularly relieved. This is precisely the scenario that our other evidence confirms.

When in 450 Kimon launched another expedition to Cyprus and Egypt, he had a fleet of 200 triremes, and he detached sixty of these for campaigning in Egypt (Plut. *Cim.* 18.2–4). Ctesias (§32, 40a30) similarly specifies a flotilla of forty triremes sent upriver to Inaros at his request. The flotilla of fifty that was surprised and defeated in 457 (Thuc. 1.110.4) had come as a (probably annual) *relief* squadron (διάδοχοι). This is confirmed by Justin, who reports that Athenian forces were depleted at the time through sending a fleet to Egypt, but that subsequently "*the return of their men* brought up their naval and military strength once more."[4] Even so, the minimum losses[5] would have been bad enough: sixty-five Athenian triremes and thirty from Samos, Chios, and Lesbos (even with up to 40 percent alien rowers) meant 8,000–9,000 Athenian citizens, 4,000–5,000 mercenaries, 6,000 island crews. Ctesias' figure of 6,000 for those who started the trek to Cyrene suggests how many had already died in combat. This was generally a period of heavy losses (probably sustainable, *inter alia,* because of a mid-century population explosion). Aristotle (*Ath. Pol.* 26.1) gives a figure of 2,000–3,000 casualties per expedition; this agrees well with an inscription of 459/8[6] that lists 180 names from *one only* of the ten Athenian tribes, in a year (459/8: cf. 11.78.2 and note 309) when there was successive fighting in the areas of Cyprus, Egypt, Phoenicia, Halieis, Aigina, and the Megarid. Even in these terms, the Egyptian casualty lists were heavy enough. But though they sustained combat losses, the major patrolling fleets clearly made it home.

---

[4] Just. 3.6.6–7: "post reditum suorum aucti et classe et militum robore."
[5] Holladay 1989, 179.
[6] *IG* i² 929 = Meiggs-Lewis no. 33.

*Map 1. Mainland Greece*

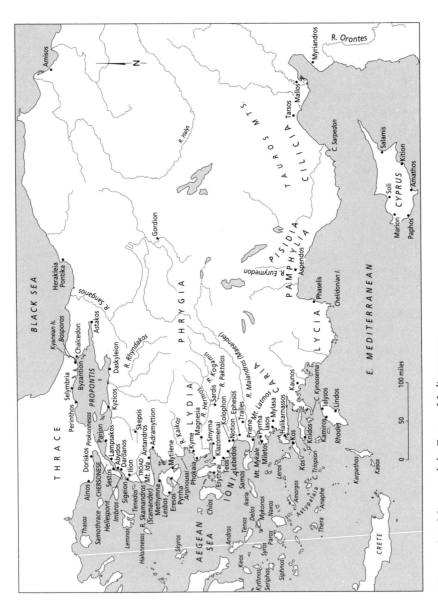

Map 2. Asia Minor and the Eastern Mediterranean

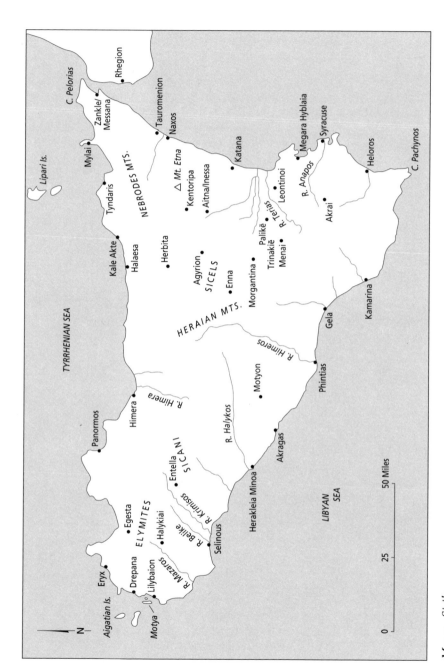

*Map 3. Sicily*

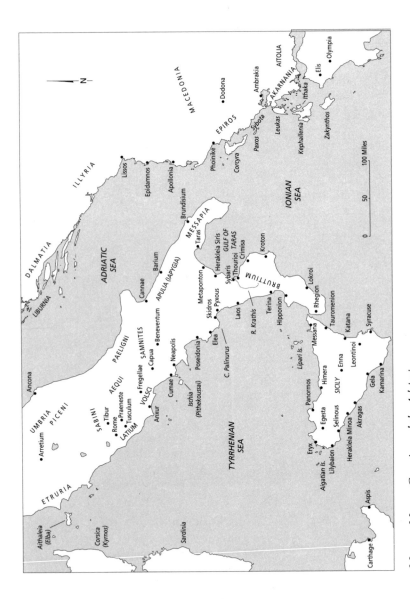

Map 4. *Magna Graecia and the Adriatic*

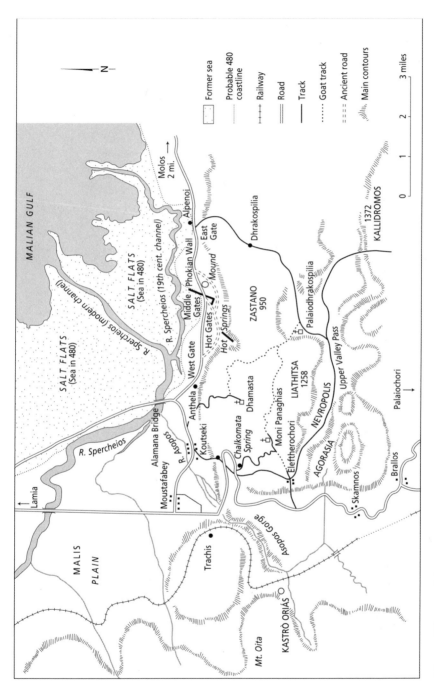

Map 5. *Thermopylai*

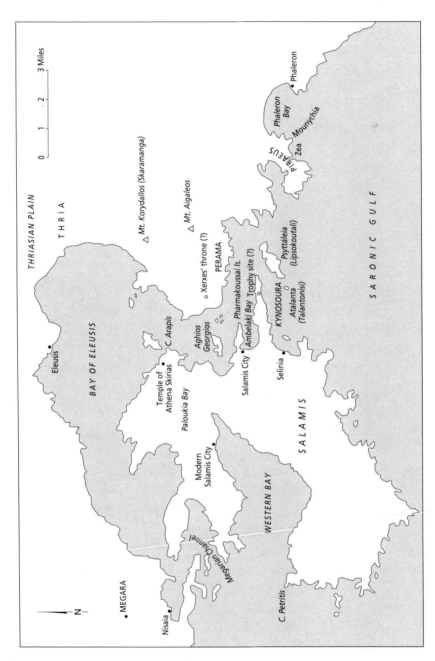

Map 6. *Salamis and the Bay of Eleusis*

THRIASIAN PLAIN

T H R I A

△ *Mt. Korydallos (Skaramanga)*

BAY OF ELEUSIS

Eleusis

△ *Mt. Aigaleos*

○ Xerxes' throne (?)

PERAMA

C. Arapis

*Aghios Georgios*

Temple of Athena Skiràs

Paloukia Bay

*Pharmakoussai Is.*

Salamis City

*Ambelaki Bay* Trophy site (?)

KYNOSOURA

*Psyttáleia (Lipsokoutáli)*

*Atalanta (Talantonisi)*

Selinia

Modern Salamis City

S A L A M I S

WESTERN BAY

Megarian Channel

C. Petritis

MEGARA

Nisaia

N

PIRAEUS

Zea

Mounychia

Phaleron Bay

Phaleron

S A R O N I C   G U L F

0   1   .   2   3 Miles

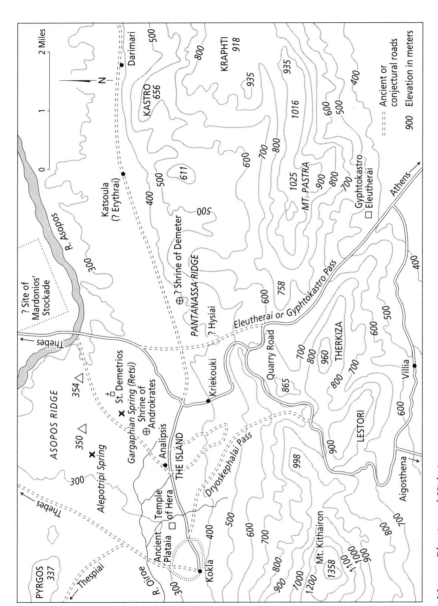

*Map 7. Plataia and Kithairon*

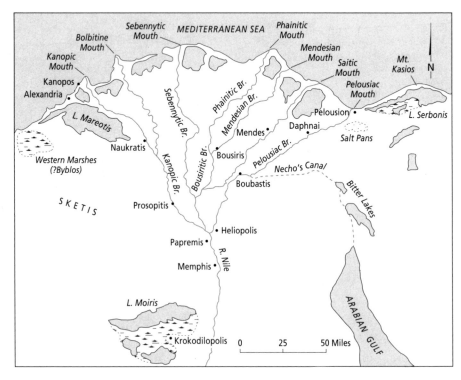

*Map 8. The Egyptian Delta*

# CHRONOLOGICAL TABLE

Seriously disputed dates are marked with an asterisk (*) and a reference to the point in the text and/or notes where they are discussed. From 484 to 451 B.C.E., references are to Book 11, and from 450 to 431 to Book 12, unless otherwise indicated.

| Date, Archon | Mainland Greece | Aegean, Asia, Africa | Sicily & the West |
|---|---|---|---|
| 484 | Xanthippos ostracized | Xerxes begins preparations for invasion of Greece | ?Carthaginian alliance with Persia* (11.1.4, note) |
| June | | | Carthage arming |
| July Leostratos 484 | | | |
| 483 June | Rich strike in Laurion silver mines | Persia recovers control of Egypt | |
| July Nikodemos | | Persian supply depots created | Gelon arming |
| | | | Depopulation of Gela and Kamarina |
| | | Work begun on Athos canal | Terillos expelled from |
| 483 | | | Himera by Theron |
| 482 | ?Aristeides ostracized | ?Revolt in Babylonia | Pythian victory of Hieron in horse race |
| June | Themistokles' decree to build new fleet | | |

| Date, Archon | Mainland Greece | Aegean, Asia, Africa | Sicily & the West |
|---|---|---|---|
| July Unknown 482 | | | |
| 481 June | | | |
| July Hypsichides ... 481 | Greek League convened at Sparta (Oct.)<br><br>Athens concludes peace with Aigina | Xerxes' forces reach Sardis: envoys sent to Greek states<br><br>Greek spies sent to observe Persians | Greek mission to Gelon<br><br>Gelon's demand for share of command rejected |
| 480 June | | Persian forces crossing into Europe: roll call at Doriskos | |
| July Kalliades ... 480 | Artemision-Thermopylai line established<br><br>Persians in Pieria<br><br>?Birth of Euripides<br><br>Defeat of Leonidas at Thermopylai<br><br>Artemision evacuated<br><br>Final evacuation of Athens<br><br>Xerxes sacks Athens, takes Akropolis<br><br>Battle of Salamis<br><br>Retreat of main Persian fleet and army<br><br>Special force under Mardonios withdraws to Thebes | Storms destroy part of Persian fleet<br><br>Naval engagements inconclusive<br><br>Xerxes' forces return to Asia | Anaxilas of Rhegion and Terillos of Himera side with Carthage against Syracuse<br><br>Invasion of Sicily by Hamilcar and Carthaginians<br><br>Battle of Himera |

| Date, Archon | Mainland Greece | Aegean, Asia, Africa | Sicily & the West |
|---|---|---|---|
| 479 | Mardonios in Thessaly: approach to Athens | | |
| | Second evacuation of Athens | | |
| June | Mardonios invades Attica, burns Athens | | |
| July Xanthippos | ?Oath of Plataia | Persian defeat at Mykale | |
| | Battle of Plataia: final defeat of Persians | Ionians join Greek league | |
| | Dedication of Serpent Column at Olympia | Athenian siege of Sestos | |
| 479 | ?Initial moves toward "Delian league" at Athens | Persia loses Sestos and the Hellespont | |
| 478 | Athens rebuilding city walls | Pausanias frees Cyprus, captures Byzantion | Treaty between Gelon and Carthage |
| | Themistokles' mission to Sparta; arrest of Spartan envoys in Athens | | Syracusan sumptuary laws |
| | | | Death of Gelon; Hieron's accession |
| June | | | Polyzelos governor of Gela |
| July Timosthenes | | ?Pausanias approaches Themistokles* (11.54.5, note) | Polyzelos dedicates Bronze Charioteer at Delphi, weds Gelon's widow Damarete |
| 478 | | | Polyzelos seeks refuge with Theron of Akragas |

| Date, Archon | Mainland Greece | Aegean, Asia, Africa | Sicily & the West |
| --- | --- | --- | --- |
| 477 | Themistokles building walls of Piraeus harbor | Pausanias returns to Byzantion | War between Hieron and Theron |
| | Trireme-building program in Athens (20 per year) | | Rome defeated by Veii at battle of Cremera |
| June | Recall, trial, and acquittal of Pausanias | | |
| July Adeimantos 477 | Themistokles star attraction at Olympic Games | | Revolt against Thrasydaios, governor of Himera |
| 476 | Themistokles produces Phrynichos' *Phoenician Women* | | Theron and Hieron conclude peace |
| | | | Hieron resettles Naxos and Katana/Aitna |
| | Olympic victories of Hieron and Theron | | Theron resettles |
| June | | | Himera |
| July Phaidon | Leotychidas II of Sparta exiled | | Aeschylus' first visit to Sicily |
| | Accession [as regent until 469/8?] of Archidamos II | | Sybaris besieged by Kroton |
| | | | Death of Anaxilas of Rhegion; succeeded |
| 476 | | | by Mikythos |
| 475 June | | | Eruption of Etna |
| July Dromokleides | Loss of Spartan supremacy at sea, consideration of war against Athens* | | |
| 475 | (11.50.1–5, note) | | |

| Date, Archon | Mainland Greece | Aegean, Asia, Africa | Sicily & the West |
| --- | --- | --- | --- |
| 474 June | | | |
| July Akestorides 474 | | | Hieron and Cumaeans defeat Tyrrhenians off Ischia |
| 473 June | | | |
| July Menon 473 | | | War between Taras and Iapygia |
| 472 June | Aeschylus' *Persians* Themistokles acquitted at 1st trial (or ostracism) | | Death of Theron; succeeded by Thrasydaios |
| July Chares 472 | | | Hieron defeats Thrasydaios Thrasydaios flees country |
| 471 June | | ?Kimon expels Pausanias from Byzantion | |
| July Praxiergos 471 | *Synoikismos* of Elis ?Death of Pausanias* (II.55.1) | | Thrasydaios executed in Megara Akragas sets up oligarchy of "The Thousand" Mikythos founds Pyxous ?4 tribunes appointed in Rome |

| Date, Archon | Mainland Greece | Aegean, Asia, Africa | Sicily & the West |
|---|---|---|---|
| 470 | ?Ostracism of Themis-tokles*: he takes up residence in Argos (spring: 11.55.1, note) | ?Persian recovery of Cyprus | |
| June | ?Birth of Sokrates | | |
| July Demotion | | ?Kimon takes Eion & Skyros, brings back "bones of Theseus"* (11.60.1–5, note) | |
| 470 | | ?Subjugation of Karystos | |
| 469 | Kimon & fellow generals as judges in theater | Revolt of Naxos | |
| | ?Second indictment of Themistokles*: he leaves Argos, flees to Corcyra (early summer: | | |
| June | 11.36.1, note) | | |
| July Apsephion (?Phaion) 469 | ?Themistokles moves from Corcyra as suppliant of Admetos* (fall) | | |
| 468 | Sophokles' 1st production | ?Kimon sails to Caria and Lycia* (early spring: 11.60.3–5, note) | |
| | Archidamos II leading resistance to Helot Revolt | ?Themistokles leaves Epiros,* travels across northern Greece & Aegean to Asia Minor (spring/early summer) | |
| | | ?Themistokles with Lysitheides* (11.56.5–8, | |
| June | | notes) | |

| Date, Archon | Mainland Greece | Aegean, Asia, Africa | Sicily & the West |
|---|---|---|---|
| July Theagenides | ?Kimon's 1st expedition against Helots* (11.63.1, 64.2?, notes) | Kimon's naval victory off Cyprus* (11.60.5–7, note) | |
| | Argos fighting Mycenae | ?Themistokles to Xerxes* (late summer/ fall: 11.56.5–8, notes) | |
| | Mycenae under siege | | |
| 468 | | Hostility to Themistokles at Persian court: he withdraws for a year to learn Persian* (fall) | |
| 467 June | Fall of Mycenae; city destroyed | | |
| July Lysistratos | Forces of Tiryns (and Sparta) defeated by Argos at Oinoë; Tiryns destroyed | ?Themistokles returns to the Achaimenid court* (early fall); his status in Persia confirmed with honors (11.57.5–7, notes); ?he leaves for Magnesia (fall)* | Restoration of democracy in Akragas; peace settlement with Hieron |
| | | | Mikythos abdicates as ruler of Rhegion |
| 467 | | | Death of Hieron; his brother Thrasyboulos succeeds him in Syracuse |
| 466 June | | ?Kimon's victory at the Eurymedon* (11.61, with note) | Civil war in Syracuse |
| July Lysanios | Kimon finances southern bastion of Akropolis from Eurymedon booty | | Thrasyboulos defeated, withdraws to Lokroi; end of Deinomenid dynasty |
| | | | Syracuse grants subject-cities independence |
| 466 | | | Eleutheria festival established in Syracuse |

| Date, Archon | Mainland Greece | Aegean, Asia, Africa | Sicily & the West |
|---|---|---|---|
| 465<br><br>June | | Revolt of Thasos begins<br>Kimon besieges Thasos | Aliens, mercenaries excluded from office in Syracuse* (11.72.1 note) |
| July<br>Lysitheos<br><br><br><br><br><br><br><br><br>465 | Appeal by Thasos to Sparta | Assassination of Xerxes (Aug.)<br><br>?Artabanos briefly usurps throne* (11.69.1, note)<br><br>?Egypt begins preparations for revolt* (11.69.1, note)<br><br>?Artaxerxes succeeds (Dec.) | |
| 464<br><br><br><br>June | ?Trouble between Athens and Aigina* (11.70.2, note)<br><br>Athens' colonizing expedition to Ennea Hodoi | ?Themistokles renegotiates with Artaxerxes* (11.56.4)<br><br>?Argive, Athenian embassies to Sousa* (11.71.2, note) | |
| July<br>Archidemides<br>464 | ?2nd major earthquake in Sparta region* (11.63.1, note) | ?Final Egyptian decision to revolt* (11.71.4, note) | |
| 463<br><br>June | | Athenian subject-allies considering revolt* (11.70.3–4, note)<br><br>Surrender of Thasos | |

| Date, Archon | Mainland Greece | Aegean, Asia, Africa | Sicily & the West |
|---|---|---|---|
| July Tlepolemos | Spartan expedition against Mt. Ithome | Artaxerxes purges satraps, reorganizes government | Mercenaries' revolt in Syracuse |
| | Kimon's expedition in response to appeal by Sparta | Egyptian removal of Persian tribute-collectors* (11.71.4, note) | |
| | Sparta rejects Kimon's force | | |
| 463 | | Inaros proclaimed pharaoh, recruits mercenaries | |
| 462 | Appeal to Athens by Inaros | Kimon and Athenian fleet en route to Cyprus | Mercenaries still holding out in Syracuse |
| | ?Sparta promises Thebes aid in return for Thebes attacking Athens | ?Transfer of League treasury from Delos to Athens* (11.64.3, 77.2, notes) | |
| June | | Artaxerxes preparing for Egyptian expedition | |
| July Konon | | Achaimenes appointed commander of Egyptian expedition | |
| | | Persian force encamps by Nile | |
| | | Athenian squadron diverted to Egypt | |
| 462 | | Athenians & Egyptians defeat Persians, besiege them in White Fort (Memphis) | |

| Date, Archon | Mainland Greece | Aegean, Asia, Africa | Sicily & the West |
|---|---|---|---|
| 461 | Megabazos' mission to Sparta<br><br>Ostracism of Kimon<br><br>Ephialtes strips Areopagos of major powers | Artaxerxes raises 2nd Egyptian expedition under Artabazos & Megabyzos | Syracusan assaults on Achradine & Ortygia |
| June | | | |
| July<br>Euthippos | Athenian alliance with Argos & Thessaly, de facto break with Sparta | Artabazos & Megabyzos march to Phoenicia and Cilicia<br><br>Athenians fail to storm White Fort, continue siege<br><br>Artabazos & Megabyzos reach Phoenicia and Cilicia (Sept.)<br><br>Persians commissioning ships, organizing supplies | Mercenaries still holding out in Syracuse |
| 461 | | | |
| 460 | ?Assassination of Ephialtes* (11.77.6, note)<br><br>?Athenian regulation of Eleusinian Mysteries | Persian fleet assembled<br><br>Persian amphibious advance on Egypt* (75.4, note)<br><br>Siege of White Fort continues | Syracusans finally defeat mercenaries<br><br>Syracusans and Ducetius defeat Hieron's settlers in Katana<br><br>"Common accord" established in Sicily |
| June | | | |
| July<br>Phrasikleides | ?Sicilian mercenaries aid Sparta to fight Helot Revolt* (11.76.5, note) | Persian fleet & army reach Memphis, break siege of White Fort<br><br>Persians adopt defensive strategy | Katanians resettle in Aitna/Inessa<br><br>Expropriated citizens return to Gela, Akragas, Himera, Rhegion, Zankle |
| 460 | | | |

| Date, Archon | Mainland Greece | Aegean, Asia, Africa | Sicily & the West |
|---|---|---|---|
| 459<br><br>June | Final defeat of Helot Revolt | ?Themistokles' refusal to lead Persian forces against Athenians* (11.58.3. note) | |
| July<br>Philokles<br><br><br><br><br><br><br><br>459 | Megara seeks Athenian alliance, defense force<br><br>Outbreak of 1st Pelop. War<br><br>Spartans seize Halieis<br><br>Athens & Aigina at war<br><br>?Spartan attack on Argos defeated at Oinoë* (11.78.2, note) | ?Death of Themistokles<br><br>Athens campaigning on Cyprus<br><br>?Beginning of Prosopitis siege (Oct.)* (11.77.2, note) | |
| 458<br><br><br><br><br><br><br><br><br><br><br><br><br>June | ?Corinth invades Megarid* (11.79.3 note)<br><br>Athenian expedition against Aigina<br><br>Battles of Halieis and Kekryphaleia<br><br>Athenian naval defeat of Aigina; city under siege<br><br>Final surrender of Aigina (?Oct.)* (11.78.4 note)<br><br>Athens building Long Walls | ?Athenians raid Phoenicia | Ducetius founds Menaenum, campaigns against Morgantina |
| July<br>Habron<br><br>458 | ?End of Messenian War<br><br>Myronides'* (11.79.3 note) victories in Megara<br><br>Phokian attack on Doris | | |

| Date, Archon | Mainland Greece | Aegean, Asia, Africa | Sicily & the West |
|---|---|---|---|
| 457 | Spartan-enforced peace between Phokis & Doris | ?April-May: end of siege of Prosopitis* (11.77.2, note) | |
| | Athenian archonship opened to *zeugitai;* institution of pay for jurors | ?Final reduction of Athenian forces in Egypt* (11.77.2 note) | |
| | Athenians occupy passes of Mt. Geraneia | | |
| | ?Sparta forces Boiotian cities to submit to Theban rule* (11.81.3, note) | | |
| | Thessalians defect from Athens to Sparta | | |
| | Battle(s) of Tanagra | | |
| June | Spartan withdrawal, 4-month truce | | |
| July Mnesitheides | ?Recall of Kimon* (11.80.6 note) | | |
| | Surrender of Aigina (?Aug.)* (11.78.5, note) | | |
| | ?Battle of Oinophyta* (11.82.5, 83.1, notes) | | |
| 457 | Myronides demolishes walls of Tanagra, overruns Boiotia | | |
| 456 | Myronides marches against Opountian Lokrians | | Death of Aeschylus in Gela |
| | Myronides overpowers Phokians | | |
| June | Myronides' abortive siege of Pharsalos, return to Athens | | |

| Date, Archon | Mainland Greece | Aegean, Asia, Africa | Sicily & the West |
|---|---|---|---|
| July Kallias | Tolmides' *periplous:* he raids Methana | | |
| | Tolmides fires dock-yards at Gytheion | | |
| | Tolmides on Kephallonia, captures Zakynthos | | |
| 456 | Tolmides resettles Messenians at Naupaktos | | |
| 455 June | Tolmides raids Sikyon | | |
| July Sosistratos | Tolmides in Boiotia | | |
| | 2nd Sacred War | | |
| 455 | Perikles' (?1st ) expedition to Akarnania & Peloponnese | | |
| 454 | ?Completion of Long Walls | | |
| June | ?Roman commission in Greece to study laws* (11.25.1, note) | | |
| July Ariston | ?Unofficial truce negotiated between Athens & Sparta by Kimon* (11.86.1, note) | | Tyndarides attempts to seize power in Syracuse, is lynched |
| 454 | | | ?Egesta & Lilybaion fighting Selinous |
| 453 June | | | Brief establishment of petalism in Syracuse |
| July 453 | | | |

| Date, Archon | Mainland Greece | Aegean, Asia, Africa | Sicily & the West |
|---|---|---|---|
| 452 | Perikles takes cleruchies to Chersonese | Destruction of Athenian colony at Drabeskos* (11.70.5, note) | Ducetius creates Sicel federation |
|  | Tolmides takes cleruchies to Euboia* (11.88.3, note) & Naxos |  | Foundation of Palike [?= Trinakie* (11.90.2, note)] |
| June |  |  | Ducetius distributes land allotments |
| July Chairephanes 452 |  | ?Betrayal and execution of Inaros* (11.77.3 note) | ?Sybaris refounded* (11.90.3–4, note) |
| 451 | ?Kimon's return | | Decemviri appointed in Rome |
|  | 5-year official Athens-Sparta truce |  |  |
| June | 30-year Argos-Sparta peace |  |  |
| July Antidotos | Perikles' citizenship law | | Ducetius captures Aitna |
|  | Preparations for Kimon's expedition to Cyprus |  | Ducetius besieges Motyon, defeats combined forces of Akragas & Syracuse |
| 451 |  |  | Syracuse executes Bolkon |
| 450 | Kimon's expedition to Cyprus sails | Megabyzos in Cilicia | Syracuse defeats Ducetius at ?Nomai |
|  |  | Artabazos with Persian fleet off Cyprus | Akragas storms Motyon |
|  |  | Cleruchies from Athens to Naxos, Andros, | |
| June |  | Lemnos | Ducetius rides to Syracuse as suppliant |

| Date, Archon | Mainland Greece | Aegean, Asia, Africa | Sicily & the West |
|---|---|---|---|
| July<br>Euthydemos | | Kimon reduces Marion<br><br>Athenian squadron detached to aid Amyrtaios (Egypt)<br><br>Kimon begins siege of Kition<br><br>Revolt of Miletos | Ducetius exiled to Corinth<br><br>Drafting of Twelve Tables in Rome<br><br>2nd Secession of Roman Plebs to Aventine |
| 450 | | | ?10 tribunes in Rome |
| 449<br><br><br><br><br><br><br><br><br><br>June | | Kimon's naval and military victory at Salamis (spring)<br><br>Kimon lays siege to Salamis<br><br>Artaxerxes supplies Artabazos with terms for treaty* (12.4.4, note) | ?Resignation of Decemviri* (12.25.2, note) |
| July<br>Pedieus<br><br><br><br><br><br><br><br><br><br><br>449 | Persian mission to Athens | Salamis, Kition holding out<br><br>Kimon dies at Kition<br><br>?Kallias concludes peace treaty with Persians* (12.4.5, note)<br><br>Athenian troops withdrawn from Cyprus & Egypt | Valerio-Horatian laws at Rome |
| 448<br><br><br><br><br>June | ?One-year remission of tribute by Athens* (12.5.2, note)<br><br>Megara revolts from Athens, makes alliance with Sparta | | |

| Date, Archon | Mainland Greece | Aegean, Asia, Africa | Sicily & the West |
|---|---|---|---|
| July Philiskos 448 | Athenian raid into Megarian territory, victory | | ?Now return of Ducetius to Sicily |
| 447 June | Work on the Parthenon begun | | Ducetius establishes Kale Akte |
| July Timarchides 447 | ?Spartans invade Attica, besiege fortresses, withdraw<br><br>Tolmides captures Chaironeia | Athenian cleruchies to Imbros and the Chersonese | |
| 446 June | Defeat of Tolmides at Koroneia, loss of Boiotia<br><br>Revolts of Megara and Euboia<br><br>Spartan invasion of Attica<br><br>Perikles buys off? Sparta, deals with Megara, returns to Euboia | Perikles to Euboia; returns | ?Akragas now declares war on Syracuse over, return of Ducetius<br><br>Romans at war with Volscians |
| July Kallimachos 446 | Final defeat of Euboian revolt, expropriation of Histiaia<br><br>Peace negotiations begun between Athens and Sparta | ?2nd revolt of Miletos<br><br>Miletos revolt suppressed, imposition of democracy<br><br>?Athenian regulations for Chalkis & Eretria | Syracuse defeats Akragas at battle on Himera River<br><br>Sybarites driven out by Krotonians |
| 445 June | 30-year peace between Athens and Sparta ratified<br><br>Athenian grain famine relieved by Psammetichos | ?Athenian colony of lowest property-classes to Brea | Athens joins (re-)foundation venture at Sybaris (10 ships)<br><br>"Panhellenic" colonization of Thourioi |

| Date, Archon | Mainland Greece | Aegean, Asia, Africa | Sicily & the West |
|---|---|---|---|
| July Lysimachides 445 | Athenian cleruchs to Histiaia | | Old Sybarites murdered or driven out of Thourioi, resettle by Traïs River |
| 444 June | | | |
| July Praxiteles 444 | | | 2nd wave of colonists to Thourioi (Herodotos, Hippodamos, Protagoras, et al.) Reorganization of Thourioi's tribes; legal code established Thourioi at war with Taras |
| 443 June | Ostracism of Thucydides s.o. Melesias | | ?Athenian treaties with Rhegion & Leontinoi ?Athenian fleet at Neapolis |
| July Lysanias 443 | | | |
| 442 June | Comedy added to Lenaia | | Rome sends settlers to Ardea |
| July Diphilos 442 | | | |
| 441 June | | | |

| Date, Archon | Mainland Greece | Aegean, Asia, Africa | Sicily & the West |
|---|---|---|---|
| July<br>Timokles<br><br><br><br><br><br><br><br><br><br>441 | | Samos at war with Miletos over Priene; revolts from Athens<br><br>Perikles' 1st expedition to Samos<br><br>*Stasis* on Samos, antidemocratic forces regain control with Pissuthnes' aid; Samian declaration of hostilities with Athens | |
| 440<br><br><br><br><br><br><br><br>June | | Perikles' 2nd Samian expedition: naval victory off Tragia (?April/May)<br><br>Samos under siege (May)<br><br>Perikles sails south to intercept Phoenician squadron | |
| July<br>Morychides<br><br><br><br><br><br><br><br>440 | Censorship of comedy imposed in Athens | Samians under Melissos win naval engagement<br><br>Return of Perikles to Samos: siege continues<br><br>Reduction of Samos (late fall?) | Syracuse back in hands of old landowners & supporters<br><br>Ducetius falls ill and dies while aiming for Sicel leadership<br><br>Syracusans besiege, capture & destroy Trinakie [?= Palike] |
| 439<br><br><br><br><br>June | Peloponnesian League hostile reactions to Athens' treatment of Samos: Corinth's laissez-faire policy adopted | | Rome: Sp. Maelius sells grain cheap to plebs, killed while supposedly aiming at tyranny |

| Date, Archon | Mainland Greece | Aegean, Asia, Africa | Sicily & the West |
|---|---|---|---|
| July<br>Glaukinos<br><br><br><br>439 | [D.'s dating-scheme for Corinthian-Corcyraean War begins; for preferred dating see under 437 et seq.] | | Syracuse building up naval and military armaments |
| 438<br><br>June | Euripides' *Alcestis*<br><br>Work begins on pediments of Parthenon | | |
| July<br>Theodoros<br><br><br><br><br><br>438 | Athens: statue of Athena Parthenos dedicated<br><br>Partial completion of Parthenon<br><br>?Prosecution of Pheidias | Spartokos becomes king in Kimmerian Bosporos | |
| 437<br>June | Work on Propylaia begun | | |
| July<br>Euthymenes<br><br><br><br><br>437 | Restrictions on comedy lifted<br><br>?Beginning of Corcyraean-Corinthian War* (12.30.2, note) | Hagnon (re-)founds Amphipolis<br><br>Perdikkas II of Macedon splits with Athens | |
| 436<br>June | ?Prosecution of Anaxagoras | ?Perikles' naval mission into the Black Sea | |
| July<br>Lysimachos<br>Myrrhinusios<br>436 | | | |

| Date, Archon | Mainland Greece | Aegean, Asia, Africa | Sicily & the West |
|---|---|---|---|
| 435<br><br>June | ?Battle of Leukimne between Corinth and Corcyra* (12.30.2, note; 31.2–3, note) | | |
| July<br>Antiochides<br><br>435 | Both Corinth and Corcyra building up naval and military forces | | |
| 434<br>June | | | |
| July<br>Krates<br><br>434 | | | Dissension in Thourioi over founder and founding city resolved by Delphic Oracle: Apollo the founder |
| 433<br><br>June | Athenian alliance with Corcyra<br><br>?Battle of Sybota | | |
| July<br>Apseudes<br><br><br><br><br><br><br><br><br><br><br><br>433 | Meton's 19-year cycle adjusting lunar calendar<br><br>?Megarian Decree<br><br>Corinth urges Potidaia to revolt<br><br>Perdikkas of Macedon stirring up Chalcidic cities<br><br>Athenian alliance with Philip and Derdas in Macedonia | Death of Spartokos king of Kimmerian Bosporos; succeeded by Satyros | Tarantines expropriate citizens of Siris, found Herakleia<br><br>?Renewal of Athenian treaties with Rhegion & Leontinoi |

| Date, Archon | Mainland Greece | Aegean, Asia, Africa | Sicily & the West |
|---|---|---|---|
| 432 | Revolt of Potidaia | | |
| | Athenian force en route to deal with Perdikkas; captures Therme, besieges Pydna | | |
| | Corinthian troops sent to Potidaia | | |
| | Athenian force to Chalcidice | | |
| June | ?Battle of Potidaia* (12.37.1, note) | | |
| July Pythodoros | ?Phormio sent to Potidaia* (12.37.1, note) | | |
| | Phormio builds Pallene wall, continues siege of Potidaia | | |
| | ?Prosecution of Aspasia | | |
| 432 | Megarian complaint of exclusion from Athenian ports, etc. | | |
| 431 | Euripides' *Medea* | | |
| | Theban attack on Plataia (March?) | | |
| June | Peloponnesian invasion of Attica (May) | | |
| July Euthynos 431 | | | |

# BIBLIOGRAPHY

TEXTS, TRANSLATIONS, AND COMMENTARIES

Bizière, F. 1975. *Diodore de Sicile: Bibliothèque Historique*. Book 19. Budé edition. Paris.

Bonnet, M., and E. R. Bennett. 1997. *Diodore de Sicile: Bibliothèque Historique*. Book 14. Budé edition. Paris.

Booth, G. 1721. *The Historical Library of Diodorus the Sicilian*. In 15 books [i.e., Books 1–15 only]. 2d ed. London. [First ed., 1700.]

Bowen, A. J. 1992. *Plutarch: The Malice of Herodotus*. Warminster.

Bowersock, G. W. 1968. *Pseudo-Xenophon: Constitution of the Athenians*. In *Xenophon*, vol. 7, *Scripta Minora*, 459–507. Cambridge, Mass.

Burton, A. 1972. *Diodorus Siculus. Book I: A Commentary*. Leiden.

Casevitz, M. 1972. *Diodore de Sicile: Bibliothèque Historique*. Book 12. Budé edition. Paris.

Chambry, E., and L. Thély-Chambry, trans. and ed. 1936. *Justin: Abrégé des Histoires Philippiques de Trogue Pompée et Prologues de Trogue Pompée*. 2 vols. Paris.

Chamoux, F., P. Bertrac, and Y. Vernière. 1993. *Diodore de Sicile: Bibliothèque Historique*. Book 1. Budé edition. Paris.

Eck, B. 2003. *Diodore de Sicile: Bibliothèque Historique*. Book 2. Budé edition. Paris.

Edelstein, L., and I. G. Kidd. 1989. *Posidonius*. Vol. 1, *The Fragments*. 2d ed. Cambridge. (Abbreviated Edelstein-Kidd.)

Fischer, C. T. 1906. *Diodori Bibliotheca Historica*. Vols. 4–5. Leipzig.

Goukowsky, P. 1976. *Diodore de Sicile: Bibliothèque Historique*. Book 17. Budé edition. Paris.

Haillet, J. 2001. *Diodore de Sicile: Bibliothèque Historique*. Book 11. Budé edition. Paris.

Henry, R. 1947. *Ctésias: La Perse, l'Inde, Les Sommaires de Photius*. Brussels.

Kidd, I. G. 1988. *Posidonius*. Vol. 2, *The Commentary (i) Testimonia and Fragments 1–149*. Cambridge.

———. 1999. *Posidonius*. Vol. 3, *The Translation of the Fragments*. Cambridge.

Labriola, I., P. Martino, and D. P. Orsi. 1988. *Diodoro Siculo, Biblioteca Storica, Libri XI–XV*. Palermo.

Macan, R. W. 1895. *Herodotus: The Fourth, Fifth, and Sixth Books*. 2 vols. London.

Mandes, M. 1901. *Commentaire historique et critique sur l'histoire grecque de Diodore* [in Russian]. Odessa.

McDougall, J. I. 1983. *Lexicon in Diodorum Siculum*. 2 vols. Hildesheim.

Micciche, C. 1992. *Diodoro Siculo, Biblioteca storica: Frammenti dei libri IX–X, Libri XI–XIII*. Milan.

Oldfather, C. H. 1946. *Diodorus of Sicily, Vol. IV: Books IX–XII.40.* Cambridge, Mass.

Stylianou, P. J. 1998. *A Historical Commentary on Diodorus Siculus, Book 15.* Oxford.

Terrasson, J. 1737–41. *Histoire universelle de Diodore de Sicile. Traduite en français par J. T.* 7 vols. Paris.

Veh, O., and W. Will. 1998. *Diodorus Siculus: Griechische Weltgeschichte, Buch XI–XIII.* Stuttgart.

Vial, C. 1977. *Diodore de Sicile, Bibliothèque Historique.* Book 15. Paris.

Vogel, F. 1888–93. *Diodori Bibliotheca Historica.* Vols. 1–3. Leipzig.

Walton, F. R. 1957. *Diodorus of Sicily.* Vol. 11, *Fragments of Books XXI–XXXII.* Cambridge, Mass.

———. 1967. *Diodorus of Sicily.* Vol. 12, *Fragments of Books XXXIII–XL.* General Index by R. Geer. Cambridge, Mass.

Wesseling, P., and J. N. Eyring, eds. 1793–1807. *Bibliothecae historicae libri qui supersunt e recensione Petri Wesselingi, cum interpretatione Latina Laur. Rhodomani atque annotationibus variorum integris indicibusque locupletissimis. Nova editio cum commentationibus III Chr. Gotte. Heynii et cum argumentis disputationibusque Ier. Nic. Eyringii.* 11 vols. Amsterdam.

Yardley, J. C., and R. Develin, trans. and ed. 1994. *Justin: Epitome of the Philippic History of Pompeius Trogus.* Atlanta.

GENERAL

Accame, S. 1955. "La fondazione di Turi." *RFIC* 33: 164–174.

Adamasteanu, D. 1962. "L'Ellenizzazione della Sicilia ed il momento di Ducezio." *Kokalos* 8: 167–198.

Adcock, F. E. 1927. "Literary Tradition and Early Greek Code-makers." *CHJ* 2: 95–109.

Adler, A., ed. 1928–38. Suidae Lexicon. 5 vols. Leipzig.

Africa, T. W. 1962. "Ephorus and Oxyrhynchus Papyrus 1610." *AJPh:* 86–89.

Alganza Roldán, M. 1986. "Diodoro y el arte adivinatorio: Apuntes sobre el tratamiento de la mántica en la Biblioteca." *EFG* 2: 113–122.

Alonso-Núñez, J. M. 1990. "The Emergence of Universal History from the 4th to the 2nd Centuries B.C." In *Purposes of History,* ed. V. Herman, G. Schepens, and E. de Keyser, 173–192. Leuven.

———. 1996. "Ctésias, historien grec du monde perse." In *Le IVᵉ siècle: Approches historiques,* ed. P. Carlier, 325–333. Paris.

Ambaglio, D. 1995. *La Biblioteca storica di Diodoro Siculo: Problemi e metodo.* Como.

Andrewes, A. 1985. "Diodorus and Ephorus: One Source of Misunderstanding." In *The Craft of the Ancient Historian: Essays in Honor of Chester G. Starr,* ed. J. W. Eadie and J. Obe), 189–197. Lanham, Md.

Appelbaum, S. 1979. *Jews and Greeks in Ancient Cyrene.* Leiden.

Asheri, D. 1980. "Rimpatrio di esuli e ridistribuzione di terre nelle città siciliote, ca. 466–461 x.C." In Φιλίας χάριν: *Miscellanea in onore di Eugenio Manni,* 145–158. Rome.

Badian, E. 1993. *From Plataea to Potidaea: Studies in the History and Historiography of the Pentecontaetia.* Baltimore.

Badian, E., and J. Buckler. 1975. "The Wrong Salamis?" *RhM* 113: 226–239.

Barber, G. L. 1979. *The Historian Ephorus.* New York. (Original ed., Cambridge 1935.)

Barnes, J. 1953–54. "Cimon and the First Athenian Expedition to Cyprus." *Hist.* 2: 163–176.

Barrett, J. F. 1977. "The Downfall of Themistokles." *GRByS* 18: 291–305.

Baynham, E. 1998. *Alexander the Great: The Unique History of Quintus Curtius.* Ann Arbor.

Bello, L. 1960. "Ricerche sui Palici." *Kokalos* 6: 71–97.

Beloch, K. J. 1912–27. *Griechische Geschichte.* 2d ed. 4 vols. in 8. Strasburg, Leipzig, and Berlin.

Bengtson, H. 1971. "Zur Vorgeschichte der Schlachte bei Salamis." *Chiron* 1: 89–94.

Benvenuti Falciai, P. 1982. "Diodoro 12.10.7 e la città ippodamea." *Prometheus* 8: 225–232.

Berger, S. 1989. "Democracy in the Greek West and the Athenian Example." *Hermes* 117: 303–314.

———. 1992. *Revolution and Society in Greek Sicily and Southern Italy.* Historia Einzelschriften 71. Stuttgart.

Bickerman, E. J. 1968. *Chronology of the Ancient World.* London.

Bicknell, P. J. 1986. "The Date of the Fall of the Emmenid Tyranny at Akragas." *CCC* 7: 29–35.

Bigwood, J. M. 1976. "Ctesias' Account of the Revolt of Inarus." *Phoenix* 30: 1–25.

———. 1978. "Ctesias as Historian of the Persian Wars." *Phoenix* 32: 19–41.

———. 1980. "Diodorus and Ctesias." *Phoenix* 34: 195–207.

Bloch, M. 1950. "Critique historique et critique des témoignages." *Annales* 5.1: 1–8.

Blösel, W. 2004. *Themistokles bei Herodot: Spiegel Athens im fünften Jahrhundert.* Stuttgart.

Boehringer, C. 1981. "Herbita." *Numismatica e Antichità* 10: 95–114.

Bonner, R. J., and G. Smith. 1970. *The Administration of Justice from Homer to Aristotle.* 2 vols. Reprint. New York. (Original ed., Chicago 1930.)

Bosworth, A. B. 2003. "Plus ça change . . . Ancient Historians and Their Sources." *CA* 22: 167–197.

Bravo, B. 1993. "Rappresentazioni di vicende di Sicilia e di Grecia degli anni 481– 480 a.C. presso storici antichi. Studio di racconti e discorsi storiografici," *Athenaeum* 81 (1993) 39–99, 441– 481.

Breebaart, A. 1996. "Weltgeschichte als Thema der antiken Geschichtsschreibung." *Act. Hist. Neerland.* 1: 1–21.

Briant, P. 1996. *Histoire de l'empire perse, de Cyrus à Alexandre.* Paris.

———. 2002. *From Cyrus to Alexander: A History of the Persian Empire.* Trans. P. T. Daniels. Winona Lake, Ind.

Brodersen, K. 1992. "Zur Überlieferung von Diodors Geschichtswerk." *ZPE* 94: 95–100.

Broughton, T. R. S. 1951. *The Magistrates of the Roman Republic.* Vol. 1, *509 B.C.–100 B.C.* New York.

Brown, T. S. 1952. "Timaeus and Diodorus' Eleventh Book." *AJPh* 73: 342–351.

———. 1958. *Timaeus of Tauromenium.* Los Angeles.

———. 1978. "Suggestions for a Vita of Ctesias of Cnidus." *Hist.* 27: 1–19.

Brugnone, A. 1992. "Le leggi suntuarie di Siracusa." *PP* 47: 5–24.

Buck, R. J. 1970. "The Athenian Domination of Boeotia." *CPh* 65: 217–227.

Büdinger, M. 1895. *Die Universalhistorie im Alterthume.* Vienna. (112–182 on Diodorus.)

Buonocore, M. 1980. "L'impostazione cronologica della pentecontaetia tucididea." *MGR:* 51–127.

Burde, P. 1974. "Untersuchungen zur antiken Universalgeschichts-schreibung." Diss., Munich.

Burkert, W. 1972. *Lore and Science in Ancient Pythagoreanism.* Cambridge, Mass.

Burn, A. R. 1977. "Thermopylae Revisited and Some Topographical Notes on Marathon and Plataiai." In *Greece and the Eastern Mediterranean in Ancient History and Prehistory,* ed. K. H. Kinzl, 89–105. Berlin.

———. 1984. *Persia and the Greeks: The Defence of the West, c. 546–478 B.C.* 2d ed. London.

Busolt, G. 1889. "Diodors Verhältniss zum Stoicismus." *JahrbCP* 140: 297–315.

———. 1897. *Griechische Geschichte bis zur Schlacht bei Chaeroneia.* Band III, Teil 1, *Die Pentekontaëtie.* Gotha.

Camacho Rojo, J. M. 1986a. "En torno a Diodoro de Sicilia y su concepción moralizante de la historia." *EFG* 2: 53–60.

———. 1986b. "El concepto de Tyche en Diodoro de Sicilia." *EFG* 2: 151–167.

———. 1986c. "Actitudes del hombre frente a la Tyche en la Biblioteca Histórica de Diodoro de Sicilia." *EFG* 2: 169–191.

———. 1992. "La noción de destino (πεπρωμένη) en Diodoro de Sicilia." *FlorIlib* 2: 83–100.

*Cambridge Ancient History.* 1988. 2d ed. Vol. 4, *Persia, Greece and the Western Mediterranean, c. 525–479 B.C.* Ed. J. Boardman et al. Cambridge. (Abbreviated *CAH* iv.)

———. 1989. 2d ed. Vol. 7, part 2, *The Rise of Rome to 220 B.C.* Ed. F. W. Walbank et al. Cambridge. (Abbreviated *CAH* vii.2.)

———. 1992. 2d ed. Vol. 5, *The Fifth Century B.C.* Ed. D. M. Lewis et al. Cambridge. (Abbreviated *CAH* v.)

———. 1994. 2d ed. Vol. 6, *The Fourth Century B.C.* Ed. D. M. Lewis et al. Cambridge. (Abbreviated *CAH* vi.)

Camp, J. M. 1986. *The Athenian Agora.* London.

Canfora, L. 1990. "Le but de l'historiographie selon Diodore." In *Purposes of History: Studies in Greek Historiography from the 4th to the 2nd Centuries B.C.,* ed. V. Herman, G. Schepens, and E. de Keyser, 313–322. Leuven.

Caratelli, G. P., ed. 1996. *The Western Greeks.* Milan.

Carawan, E. M. 1987. "*Eisangelia* and *Euthyna:* The Trials of Miltiades, Themistocles, and Cimon." *GRByS* 28: 167–208.

Casevitz, M. 1985. "La femme dans l'oeuvre de Diodore de Sicile." In *La Femme dans le monde méditerranéen,* vol. 1, *Antiquité,* 113–135. Lyon.

———. 1990. "Le vocabulaire politique de Diodore de Sicile: Politeia, politeuma et leur famille." *Ktéma* 15: 27–33.

———. 1991. *Naissance des dieux et des hommes.* Paris.

Cássola, F. 1982. "Diodoro e la storia romana." *ANRW* II, 30.1: 724–773.

Castagnoli, F. 1971. "Sull'urbanistica di Thurii." *PP* 139: 301–307.

Cawkwell, G. L. 1970. "The Fall of Themistocles." In *Auckland Classical Essays Presented to E. M. Blaiklock,* 39–58. Oxford.

Chamoux, F. 1990. "Un Historien mal-aimé: Diodore de Sicile." *BAGB:* 243–252.

Chisoli, A. 1993. "Diodoro e le vicende di Ducezio." *Aevum* 67: 21–29.

Cichorius, C. 1887. "De fastibus consularibus Cap. III, De fastibus Diodori." *Leipziger Stud. zur classischen Philologie* 9: 208–219.

Clarke, K. 1999a. *Between Geography and History: Hellenistic Constructs of the Roman World.* Oxford.

———. 1999b. "Universal Perspectives in Historiography." In *The Limits of Historiography: Genre and Narrative in Ancient Historical Texts,* ed. C. S. Kraus, 249–279. Leiden.

Connor, W. R. 1967. "History without Heroes: Theopompus' Treatment of Philip of Macedon." *GRByS* 8: 133–154.

Conomis, N. C. 1958. "Lycurgus against Leocrates 81." *PAA* 33: 111–127.

Consolo Langher, S. N. 1997. *Un Imperialismo tra Democrazia e Tirannide: Siracusa nei Secoli V e IV a.C.* Rome.

Cornell, T. J. 1995. *The Beginnings of Rome: Italy and Rome from the Bronze Age to the Punic Wars.* London.

Corsaro, M. 1998. "Ripensando Diodoro. Il problema della storia universale nel mondo antico." *Med. Ant.* 1: 405–436.

Cusumano, N. 1996. "Sul lessico politico di Diodoro: συντέλεια." *Kokalos* 42: 303–312.

Dalley, S. 2003. "Why Did Herodotus Not Mention the Hanging Gardens of Babylon?" In *Herodotus and His World,* ed. P. Derow and R. Parker, 171–189. Oxford.

Daskalakis, A. V. 1962. *Problèmes historiques autour de la bataille des Thermopyles.* Paris.

Davies, J. K. 1971. *Athenian Propertied Families, 600–300 B.C.* Oxford. (Abbreviated *APF.*)

Deane, P. 1972. *Thucydides' Dates, 465–431 B.C.* Don Mills, Ont.

Deman, A. 1985. "Présence des Égyptiens dans la seconde guerre médique (480–479 av. J.C.)." *CE* 60: 56–74.

Devillers, O. 1998. "Un portrait 'césarien' de Gélon de Sicile (XI, 20–26)." *AC* 67: 149–167.

Dinsmoor, W. B. 1950. *The Architecture of Ancient Greece: An Account of Its Historical Development.* 3d rev. ed. London.

Dodds, E. R. 1951. *The Greeks and the Irrational.* Berkeley.

Dorati, M. 1995. "Ctesia falsario?" *QS* 21: 35–52.

Dover, K. J. 1988. "Anecdotes, Gossip and Scandal." In *The Greeks and Their Legacy: Collected Papers,* 45–52. Oxford.

Drews, R. 1960. "Historiographical Objectives and Procedures of Diodorus Siculus." Diss., The Johns Hopkins University.

———. 1962. "Diodorus and His Sources." *AJPh* 83: 383–392.

———. 1963. "Ephoros and History Written κατὰ γένος." *AJPh* 84: 244–255.

———. 1965. "Assyria in Classical Universal Histories." *Hist.* 14: 129–142.

———. 1973. *The Greek Accounts of Eastern History.* Washington, D.C.

———. 1976. "Ephorus' κατὰ γένος History Revisited." *Hermes* 104: 497–498.

Drögemüller, H.-P. 1969. *Syrakus. Gymnasium,* Beiheft vi. Heidelberg.

Drummond, A. 1980. "Consular Tribunes in Livy and Diodorus." *Athenaeum* 58: 57–72.

Dunbabin, T. J. 1948. *The Western Greeks.* Oxford.

Ebert, J. 1982. "Zum Perser-Epigramm von Delphi (Diod. XI 14,4)." *ZPE* 47: 35–36.

Eck, B. 1990. "Sur la vie de Ctésias." *REG* 103: 409–434.

Eddy, S. K. 1970. "On the Peace of Callias." *CPh* 65: 8–14.

———. 1973. "The Cold War between Athens and Persia, c. 448–412 B.C." *CPh* 68: 241–258.

Ehrenberg, V. 1948. "The Foundation of Thurii." *AJPh* 69: 149–170.

Errington, R. M. 1967. "The Chronology of Polybius' Histories, Books I and II." *JRS* 57: 96–108.

Evans, J. 1998. *The History and Practice of Ancient Astronomy.* Oxford.

Fabricius, K. 1932. *Das Antike Syrakus. Klio,* Beiheft 32. Leipzig.

Farrington, B. 1936. *Diodorus Siculus, Universal Historian.* Swansea. (= *Head and Hand in Ancient Greece: Four Studies* [London, 1947], 55–87.)

Ferguson, J. 1975. *Utopias of the Classical World.* London.

Finkelstein, J. J., and P. Hulin, eds. 1964. *The Sultantepe Tablets.* Vol. 2. London.

Finley, M. I. 1975. "Utopianism Ancient and Modern." In *The Use and Abuse of History,* 178–192. London.

Flower, M. A. 1994. *Theopompus of Chios: History and Rhetoric in the Fourth Century B.C.* Oxford.

———. 1998. "Simonides, Ephorus, and Herodotus on the Battle of Thermopylae." *CQ* 48.2: 365–379.

Fontenrose, J. 1978. *The Delphic Oracle.* Berkeley.

Fornara, C. W. 1966. "Some Aspects of the Career of Pausanias of Sparta." *Hist.* 15: 257–271.

———. 1979. "On the Chronology of the Samian War." *JHS* 99: 7–18.

———, ed. 1983. *Translated Documents of Greece and Rome.* Vol. 1, *Archaic Times to the End of the Peloponnesian War.* 2d ed. Cambridge.

Fornara, C. W., and L. J. Samons II. 1991. *Athens from Cleisthenes to Pericles.* Berkeley.

Forrest, W. G. 1960. "Themistocles and Argos." *CQ* 10: 221–341.

Frederiksen, M. W. 1984. *Campania.* London.

Freeman, E. A. 1891. *The History of Sicily from the Earliest Times.* Vol. 2, *From the Beginning of Greek Settlement to the Beginning of Athenian Intervention,* Oxford.

———. 1892. *The History of Sicily from the Earliest Times.* Vol. 3, *The Athenian and Carthaginian Invasions.* Oxford.

Freeman, K. 1941. "Thourioi." *G&R* 10: 49–64.

French, A. 1964. *The Growth of the Athenian Economy.* London.

———. 1971. *The Athenian Half-Century, 478–431 B.C.: Thucydides I 89–118.* Sydney.

Frost, F. J. 1998. *Plutarch's Themistocles: A Historical Commentary.* Rev. ed. Chicago.

Frye, R. N. 1966. *The Heritage of Persia.* New York.

Gabba, E. 1979. "Eduard Schwartz e la storiografia greca." *ASNP* III.9: 1033–1049.

———. 1981. "True History and False History in Classical Antiquity." *JRS* 71: 50–62.

Gagarin, M. 1986. *Early Greek Law.* Berkeley.

Galvagno, E. 1991. "Ducezio 'eroe': Storia e retorica in Diodoro." In Galvagno and Molé Ventura 1991, 99–124.

Galvagno, E., and C. Molé Ventura, eds. 1991. *Mito, storia, tradizione: Diodoro Siculo e la storiografica classica.* Catania.

Garland, R. 1987. *The Piraeus: From the Fifth to the First Century B.C.* Ithaca, N.Y.

Gillis, D. 1979. *Collaboration with the Persians.* Wiesbaden.

Glotz, G. 1938. *Histoire Grecque.* Vol. 2. Paris.

Gomme, A. W. 1945. *A Historical Commentary on Thucydides.* Vol. 1. Oxford. (Corr. ed. 1959.)

———. 1956a. *A Historical Commentary on Thucydides.* Vol. 2. Oxford. (Corr. ed. 1962.)

———. 1956b. *A Historical Commentary on Thucydides.* Vol. 3. Oxford. (Corr. ed. 1962.)

Graf, D. 1984. "Medism: The Origin and Significance of the Term." *JHS* 104: 15–30.

Graham, A. J. 1964. *Colony and Mother City.* Manchester.

Green, P. 1971. *Armada from Athens.* London.

———. 1993. *Alexander to Actium.* Rev. ed. Berkeley.

———. 1996a. *The Greco-Persian Wars.* Rev. ed. Berkeley.

———. 1996b. "The Metamorphosis of the Barbarian: Athenian Panhellenism in a Changing World." In *Transitions to Empire,* ed. R. W. Wallace and E. M. Harris, 5–36. Norman, Okla.

———. 1997. "'These Fragments Have I Shored against My Ruins': Apollonios Rhodios and the Social Revalidation of Myth for a New Age." In *Hellenistic Constructs: Essays in Culture, History, and Historiography,* ed. P. Cartledge, P. Garnsey, and E. Gruen, 35–71. Berkeley.

Guido, M. 1963. *Syracuse: A Handbook to Its History and Principal Monuments.* 3d ed. London.

Guthrie, W. K. C. 1962. *A History of Greek Philosophy.* Vol. 1, *The Earlier Presocratics and the Pythagoreans.* Cambridge.

Guzzo, P. 1973. "Scavi a Sibari." *PP* 23: 278–314.

Hammond, N. G. L. 1956. "The Battle of Salamis." *JHS* 76: 32–54.

———. 1967. *Epirus.* Oxford.

———. 1973. *Studies in Greek History.* Oxford.

———. 1986. *A History of Greece to 322 B.C.* 3d ed. Oxford.

———. 1996. "Sparta at Thermopylae." *Hist.* 45: 1–20.

Hammond, N. G. L., and G. T. Griffith. 1979. *A History of Macedonia.* Vol. 2, *550–336 B.C.* Oxford.

Hammond, N. G. L., and L. J. Roseman. 1996. "The Construction of Xerxes' Bridge over the Hellespont." *JHS* 116: 88–107.

Harris, W. V. 1989. *Ancient Literacy.* Cambridge, Mass.

Harrison, A. R. W. 1968–71. *The Laws of Athens.* 2 vols. Oxford.

Harrison, T. 2000. *The Emptiness of Asia: Aeschylus and the History of the Fifth Century.* London.

Hartog, F. 1988. *The Mirror of Herodotus.* Berkeley.

Heichelheim, F. M. 1955. "The Toronto Epitome of a Sicilian Historian." *SO* 31: 88–95.

Hignett, C. 1963. *Xerxes' Invasion of Greece.* Oxford.

Hill, G. F. 1951. *Sources for Greek History between the Persian and the Peloponnesian Wars,* Rev. R. Meiggs and A. Andrewes. Oxford. (Abbreviated *HMA.*)

Hölkeskamp, K.-J. 1999. *Schiedsrichter, Gesetzgeber und Gesetzgebung im archaischen Griechenland. Historia* Einzelschriften 131. Stuttgart.

Holladay, A. J. 1989. "The Hellenic Disaster in Egypt." *JHS* 109: 176–182.

Hornblower, J. 1981. "Diodorus and Hieronymus." In Hornblower, *Hieronymus of Cardia,* ch. 2 (18–75), esp. 18–29. Oxford.

———. 1991. *A Commentary on Thucydides.* Vol. 1, *Books I–III.* Oxford.

———. 1996. *A Commentary on Thucydides.* Vol. 2, *Books IV–V.24.* Oxford.

———. 2002. *The Greek World, 479–323 B.C.* 3d ed. London.

Housman, A. E. 1905. *D. Iuniii Iuuenalis Saturae.* Cambridge.

How, W. W., and J. Wells. 1912. *A Commentary on Herodotus.* 2 vols. Oxford.

Jacoby, F. 1913. "Herodotos." *RE* S-B ii, cols. 205–520. Stuttgart.

———. 1922. "Ktesias." *RE* xi.2, cols. 2032–2073. Stuttgart.

———. 1949. *Atthis.* Oxford.

Jal, P. 1994. "Monographies historiques et ἱστορίαι κοιναί (κατοχικαί): Quelques remarques." *REL* 72: 56–78.

Kagan, D. 1969. *The Outbreak of the Peloponnesian War.* Ithaca, N.Y.

———. 1981. *The Peace of Nicias and the Sicilian Expedition.* Ithaca, N.Y.

Karavites, P. 1985. "Enduring Problems of the Samian Revolt." *RhM* 128: 40–56.

Keaveney, A. 2003. *The Life and Journey of Athenian Statesman Themistocles (524–460 B.C.?) as a Refugee in Persia.* Studies in Classics 23. Lewiston.

Keramopoullos, A. 1923. Ὁ ἀποτυμπανισμός. Athens 1923.

Kidd, I. G. 1998. "Posidonius as Philosopher-Historian." In *Philosophia Togata,* vol. 1, ed. J. Barnes and M. T. Griffin, 38–50. Oxford.

Kirchner, J. 1901–3. *Prosopographia Attica.* 2 vols. Berlin. (Abbreviated *PA.*)

Konstan, D. 1997. *Friendship in the Classical World.* Cambridge.

Kontis, J. D. 1956 [1959]. "Ἡ διαίρεσις τῶν Θουρίων." *AE:* 100–113, 216–217.

Kraay, C. M. 1958. "The Coinage of Sybaris after 510 B.C." *NC:* 13–37.

———. 1966. *Greek Coins.* London.

———. 1976. *Archaic and Classical Greek Coins.* Berkeley.

Kraft, J. C., G. Rapp, et al. 1987. "The Pass at Thermopylae, Greece." *Journ. Field Arch.* 14: 181–198.

Kuhrt, A. 1995. *The Ancient Near East, c. 3000–330 B.C.* Vol. 2. London.

Kukofka, D.-A. 1992. "Karthago, Gelon, und die Schlacht bei Himera." *WJbA* 18: 49–75.

Kunz, M. 1935. "Zur Beurteilung der Proömien in Diodors historischen Bibliothek." Diss., Zurich.

Laffranque, M. 1964. *Poseidonios d'Apamée: Essai de mise au point.* Paris.

La Genière, J. de. 2001. "Xenoi en Sicile dans la première moitié du Vᵉ siècle." *REG* 114: 24–36.

Lang, M. 1990. *Ostraka.* The Athenian Agora, vol. 25. Princeton.

Laqueur, R. 1911. "Ephoros." *Hermes* 46: 161–206, 321–354.

———. 1958. "Diodorea." *Hermes* 86: 257–290.

Lazenby, J. F. 1993. *The Defence of Greece, 490–479 B.C.* Warminster.

Lenardon, R. J. 1959. "The Chronology of Themistokles' Ostracism and Exile." *Hist.* 8: 23–48.

———. 1978. *The Saga of Themistocles.* London.

Lenfant, D. 1996. "Ctésias et Hérodote, ou les réécritures de l'histoire dans la Perse achéménide." *REG* 109: 348–380.

———. 1999. "Peut-on se fier aux 'fragments' d'historiens? L'exemple des citations d'Hérodote." *Ktéma* 214: 103–121.

Lens Tuero, J. 1986. "Sobre la naturaleza de la Biblioteca Histórica de Diodoro de Sicilia." *EFG* 2: 9–43.

———, ed. 1994. *Estudios sobre Diodoro de Sicilia.* Granada.

———. 1999. "El eufemismo en la 'Biblioteca Histórica' de Diodoro de Sicilia." In *Studi sull'eufemismo,* ed. F. de Martino and A. H. Sommerstein, 393–430. Bari.

Lévy, E. 2001. "Diodore de Sicile récrivant Thucydide (D.S. xii, 62.6–7 et 67, 3–5, versus Thuc. iv, 12.3 et 80)." *Ktéma* 26: 333–341.

Lewis, D. M. 1952. "Towards a Historian's Text of Thucydides." Diss., Princeton University.

Loomis, W. T. 1990. "Pausanias, Byzantion and the Formation of the Delian League: A Chronology." *Hist.* 39: 487–492.

Loraux, N. 1986. *The Invention of Athens: The Funeral Oration in the Classical City.* Trans. A. Sheridan. Cambridge, Mass.

Maddoli, G. 1977–78. "Ducezio e la fondazione di Calatte." *AFLPer* 15.1: 149–156.

Magno, P. 1983. "Le guerre tra Messapi e Tarentini." In *Monum. Apuliae et Iapigiae Pubbl. di Studi Pugliesi,* vol. 3, 7–14. Brindisi.

Manganaro, G. 1974–75. "La caduta dei Dinomenidi e il politikon nomisma in Sicilia nella prima metà del V sec. a.C." *AIIN* 21/22: 9–40.

Manni, E. 1963. *Sicilia Pagana.* Palermo.

———. 1971. "Diodoro e la storica italiota." *Kokalos* 17: 131–145.

———. 1981. *Geografia fisica e politica della Sicilia antica.* Rome.

Manuel, F. E., and F. P. Manuel. 1979. *Utopian Thought in the Western World.* Cambridge, Mass.

Marincola, J. 1997. *Authority and Tradition in Ancient Historiography.* Cambridge.

———. 1999. "Genre, Convention and Innovation in Greco-Roman Historiography." In *The Limits of Historiography: Genre and Narrative in Ancient Historical Texts,* ed. C. S. Kraus, 281–324. Leiden.

Marsden, E. W. 1969. *Greek and Roman Artillery: Historical Development.* Oxford.

Martin, R. 1974. *L'Urbanisme dans la Grèce antique.* 2d ed. Paris.

McDowell, D. M. 1978. *The Law in Classical Athens.* London.

Meiggs, R. 1972. *The Athenian Empire.* Oxford.

Meiggs, R., and D. Lewis. 1988. *A Selection of Greek Historical Inscriptions to the End of the Fifth Century B.C.* Rev. ed. Oxford.

Meister, K. 1967. "Die Sizilische Geschichte bei Diodor von den Anfängen bis zum Tod des Agathokles. Quellenuntersuchungen zu Buch IV–XVI." Diss., Munich.

———. 1970. "Das persisch-karthagische Bündnis von 481 v. Chr. (Bengtson, Staatsverträge II nr. 129)." *Hist.* 19: 607–612.

Meritt, B. D. 1928. *The Athenian Calendar in the Fifth Century B.C.* Cambridge, Mass.

———. 1932. *Athenian Financial Documents of the Fifth Century.* Ann Arbor.

———. 1961. *The Athenian Year.* Berkeley.

Meritt, B. D., H. T. Wade-Gery, and M. F. McGregor. *1939–53. The Athenian Tribute Lists.* Vols. 1–4. Vol. 1: Cambridge, Mass., 1939; vol. 2: Princeton, 1949; vol. 3: Princeton, 1950; vol. 4: Princeton, 1953. (Abbreviated *ATL*.)

Miller, M. C. 1997. *Athens and Persia in the Fifth Century B.C.: A Study in Cultural Receptivity.* Cambridge.

Milton, M. P. 1979. "The Date of Thucydides' Synchronism of the Siege of Naxos with Themistokles' Flight." *Hist.* 28: 257–275.

Moggi, M. 1977. "Autori grechi di Persika 2: Carone di Lampsaco." *ASNP* 7: 1–26.

———. 1987. "Organizzazione della *chora,* proprietà fondiaria e *homonoia:* Il caso di Turi." *ASNP* 17: 65–88.

Momigliano, A. 1969. "Tradizione e invenzione in Ctesia." In *Quarto Contributo alla storia degli studi classici e del mondo antico,* 181–212. Rome.

———. 1982. "The Origins of Universal History." *ASNP* 12: 533–560. (Reprinted in *Settimo Contributo* . . . [Rome, 1984], 77–103.)

Morrison, J. S., J. E. Coates, and N. B. Rankov. 2000. *The Athenian Trireme: The History and Reconstruction of an Ancient Greek Warship.* 2d ed. Cambridge.

Morrison, J. S., and R. Williams. 1968. *Greek Oared Ships.* Cambridge.

Müller, D. 1987. *Topographischer Bildkommentar zu den Historien Herodots: Griechenland.* Tübingen.

Murray, G. 1946. "Theopompus, or the Cynic as Historian." In *Greek Studies,* 149–170. Oxford.

Neubert, R. 1890. *Spuren selbstständiger Thätigkeit bei Diodor.* Bautzen.

Niese, B. 1899. "Charondas." *RE* II, cols. 2180–2182. Stuttgart.

Nikolaou, N. 1982. "La Bataille de Salamine d'après Diodore de Sicile." *REG* 95: 145–156.

Ogilvie, R. M. 1965. *A Commentary on Livy Books 1–5.* Oxford.

Olmstead, A. T. 1948. *A History of the Persian Empire.* Chicago.

Oost, S. I. 1976. "The Tyrant Kings of Syracuse." *CPh* 71: 224–236.

*The Oxford Classical Dictionary.* 1996. Ed. S. Hornblower and A. Spawforth. 3d ed. Oxford. (Abbreviated *OCD*.)

Page, D. L. 1941. *Select Papyri.* Vol. 3, *Literary Papyri, Poetry.* London. (Abbreviated Page *SP*3.)

Palm, J. 1955. "Über Sprache und Stil des Diodors von Sizilien. Ein Beitrag zur Beleuchtung der hellenistischen Prosa." Diss., Lund.

Pareti, L. 1914. "La battaglia di Imera." In *Studi siciliani ed italioti,* 113–172. Florence.

Parke, H. W., and D. E. Wormell. 1956. *The Delphic Oracle.* 2d ed. 2 vols. Oxford.

Parker, R. A., and W. H. Dubberstein. 1956. *Babylonian Chronology, 626 B.C.–A.D. 75.* Brown University Studies 19. Providence.

Parker, S. T. 1976. "The Objectives and Strategy of Cimon's Expedition to Cyprus." *AJPh* 97: 30–38.

Parker, V. 1993. "The Chronology of the Pentekontaetia from 465 to 456." *Athenaeum* 81: 129–147.

Paršikov, A. E. 1970. "On the Chronology of the Athenian Campaign in Egypt." *VDI* 111: 100–112. (Eng. résumé.)

Pavan, M. 1961. "La theoresi storica di Diodoro Siculo." *Rend. Accad. Linc.* 16: 19–52, 117–150.

———. 1987. "Osservazioni su Diodoro, Polibio, e la storiografia ellenistica." *Aevum* 61: 20–28.

Pearson, L. 1939. *Early Ionian Historians.* Oxford.

———. 1981. *The Local Historians of Attica.* Chico, Calif.

———. 1987. *The Greek Historians of the West: Timaeus and His Predecessors.* Atlanta.

Peek, W. 1978. "Die Perser in Delphi." *Philologus* 122: 2–5.

Pelekidis, C. S. 1974. "Συμβολὴ στὴν ἱστορία τῆς Πεντεκονταετίας." In Δωδώνη, vol. 3, 409–439. Ioannina.

Perl, G. 1957. *Kritische Untersuchungen zu Diodors Römischer Jahrzählung.* Deutsche Akademie der Wissenschaften zu Berlin: Schriften der Sektion für Altertumswissenschaft 9. Berlin.

Perotti, A. 1984. "De Romanorum magistratuum nominibus apud Diodorum." *Latinitas* 32: 161–176, 267–280.

Pfeiffer, R. 1968. *History of Classical Scholarship: From the Beginning to the Hellenistic Age.* Oxford.

Piccirilli, L. 1971. "La controversia fra Ierone e Polizelo in Diodoro, negli scholia vetera e nello scholion recens a Pindaro, Ol. ii.29." *ASNP* 1: 65–79.

———. 1975. "Charone di Lampsaco e Erodoto." *ASNP* 5: 1239–1254.

Pinsent, J. 1975. *Military Tribunes and Plebeian Consuls: The Fasti from 444 V to 342 V.* Historia Einzelschriften, Heft 34, ch. 8, 45–50, "Diodorus' Fasti of the Military Tribunate." Wiesbaden.

Pinzone, A. 1998. "Per un commento alla *Biblioteca storica* di Diodoro Siculo." *Med. Ant.* 1: 443–484.

Podlecki, A. J. 1975. *The Life of Themistocles.* Montreal.

———. 1976. "Themistocles and Pausanias." *RFIC* 104: 293–311.

Pownall, F. 2004. *Lessons from the Past: The Moral Use of History in Fourth-Century Prose.* Ann Arbor.

Prandi, I. L. 1978. "Il trattato fra Atene e Samo del 439/8 (IG² 50) e il problema della democrazia nell'isola dopo l'intervento ateniese." *Aevum* 52: 58–61.

Prestianni Giallombardo, A. M. 1998. "La tradizione manoscitta della 'Bibliotheke' di Diodoro: Riflessioni sulle edizioni critiche." *Med. Ant.* 1: 485–504.

Pritchett, W. K. 1964. "Athenian Calendar Problems." *TAPA* 95: 200–260.

———. 1974. *The Greek State at War.* Pt. 2. Berkeley.

Quinn, T. J. 1964. "Thucydides and the Unpopularity of the Athenian Empire." *Hist.* 13: 257–266.

Raccuia, C. 1978–79. "La tradizione sull'intervento ateniense in Egitto: Caratteri e problemi." *Helikon* 18/19: 210–227.

———. 1990. "Sul consiglio di Samo (479 a.C.): Considerazioni storiche e storiografiche." *Messana,* n.s. 1: 71–106.

Radt, S. L. 1993. "Textkritisches zu Diodor." *Mnemosyne* 46: 56–68.

Rainey, F. 1969. "The Location of Archaic Greek Sybaris." *AJA* 73: 261–273.

Raubitschek, A. E. 1966. "The Peace Policy of Pericles." *AJA* 70: 37–41.

Reece, D. W. 1962. "The Date of the Fall of Ithome." *JHS* 82: 111–120.

Reid, C. I. 1969. [Rubincam]. 1971. "Diodorus and His Sources." Diss., Harvard University. (Diss. abs. in *HSCP* 75 [1971]: 205–207.)

———. 1974. "Ephoros, Fragment 76, and Diodoros on the Cypriote War." *Phoenix* 28: 123–143.

———. 1976. "A Note on Oxyrhynchus Papyrus 1610." *Phoenix* 30: 357–361.

Reuss, F. 1886. "Timaios bei Plutarch, Diodor und Dionys von Halikarnass." *Philologus* 45: 245–277.

———. 1896a. "Diodor und Theopompos." *JahrbCP* 153: 317–326.

———. 1896b. "Die Chronologie Diodors." *JahrbCP* 153: 641–671.

Rhodes, P. J. 1970. "Thucydides on Pausanias and Themistocles." *Hist.* 19: 387–400.

———. 1985. *The Athenian Empire. Greece & Rome* New Surveys in the Classics, no. 17. Oxford.

Rizzo, F. P. 1970. *La repubblica di Siracusa e il momento di Ducezio.* Palermo. (Note rev. by K. Meister, *Gnomon* 47 [1975]: 772–777.)

Robert, L. 1938. *Études épigraphiques et philologiques.* Paris.

Robertson, N. 1980. "The True Nature of the 'Delian League,' 478–461 B.C," pt. 2. *AJAH* 5.2: 110–133.

Robinson, E. 2000. "Democracy in Syracuse, 466–412 B.C." *HSCPh* 100: 189–205.

Romm, J. S. 1992. *The Edges of the Earth in Ancient Thought.* Princeton.

Roux, G. 1974. "Éschyle, Hérodote, Diodore, Plutarque racontent la bataille de Salamine." *BCH* 98: 51–94.

Rubincam, C. I. R. 1987. "The Organization and Composition of Diodorus' *Bibliotheke.*" *EMC* 31: 313–328.

———. 1989. "Cross-References in the *Bibliotheke historike* of Diodoros." *Phoenix* 43: 39–61.

———. 1998a. "New Approaches to the Study of Diodoros Facilitated by Electronic Texts." *Med. Ant.* 1: 505–513.

———. 1998b. "How Many Books Did Diodorus Siculus Originally Intend to Write?" *CQ* 48: 229–233.

———. 1998c. "Did Diodorus Siculus Take Over Cross-References in His Sources?" *AJPh* 119: 67–87.

Rusconi, M. 1975. "Le notizie romane di Diodoro e gli Annales Maximi." *CISA* 3: 105–110.

Rutter, N. K. 1970. "Sybaris: Legend and Reality." *G&R* 17: 168–176.

———. 1973. "Diodorus and the Foundation of Thurii." *Hist.* 22: 155–176.

———. 1993. "The Myth of the 'Damareteion'." *Chiron* 23: 171–188.

Sacks, K. S. 1981. *Polybius on the Writing of History.* Berkeley.

———. 1982. "The Lesser Proemia of Diodorus Siculus." *Hermes* 110: 434–443.

———. 1990. *Diodorus Siculus and the First Century.* Princeton.

———. 1994. "Diodorus and His Sources: Conformity and Creativity." In *Greek Historiography,* ed. S. Hornblower, 213–232. Oxford.

———. 1998. "Dating Diodorus's *Bibliotheke.*" *Med. Ant.* 1: 437–442.

Salmon, J. B. 1984. *Wealthy Corinth: A History of the City to 338 B.C.* Oxford.

Samons, L. J., II. 2000. *Empire of the Owl: Athenian Imperial Finance.* Stuttgart.

Samuel, A. E. 1972. *Greek and Roman Chronology.* Munich.

Sancisi-Weerdenburg, H. 1987. "Decadence in the Empire or Decadence in the Sources? From Source to Synthesis: Ctesias." In *Achaemenid History,* vol. 1, *Sources, Structures, and Synthesis,* 33–45. Leiden.

Schepens, G. 1977. "Historiographical Problems in Ephorus." In *Historiographia Antiqua: Commentationes Lovanienses in honorem W. Peremans septuagenarii edita,* 95–118. Leuven.

Scherr, A. 1933. *Diodors XI. Buch, Kompositions- und Quellenstudien.* Tübingen.

Schreiner, J. H. 1976–77. "Anti-Thukydidean Studies in the Pentekontaetia." *SO* 51: 19–63, and 52: 19–38.

———. 1997. *Hellanikos, Thukydides and the Era of Kimon.* Aarhus.

Schumacher, L. 1987. "Themistokles und Pausanias." *Gymnasium* 94: 218–246.

Schwartz, E. 1903. "Diodoros (38)." In *RE* V.i, cols. 663–704. (= Schwartz 1959, 35–97.)

———. 1959. *Griechische Geschichtsschreiber.* 2d ed. Leipzig.

Scramuzza, V. M. 1937. "Roman Sicily." In *An Economic Survey of Ancient Rome,* ed. T. Frank, vol. 3, 225–377. Baltimore.

Sélincourt, A. de, trans. 2003. *Herodotus: The Histories.* Rev. J. Marincola. Harmondsworth.

Sensi Sestito, G. de. 1976. "La fondazione di Sibari-Thurii in Diodoro." *Rend. Ist. Lomb.* 110: 243–258.

———. 1991. "La storia italiota in Diodoro: Considerazioni sulle fonti per i libri vii–xii." In Galvagno and Molé Ventura 1991, 125–152.

Shrimpton, G. 1977. "Theopompus' Treatment of Philip in the *Philippica.*" *Phoenix* 31: 123–144.

Sinatra, D. 1992. "Xenoi, misthophoroi, idioi oikétores: Lotte interne ed equilibri politici a Siracusa dal 466 al 461." *Kokalos* 38: 347–363.

Sinclair, R. K. 1963. "Diodorus Siculus and the Writing of History." *PACA* 6: 36–45.

Sjöqvist, E. 1962. "I Greci a Morgantina." *Kokalos* 8: 52–68.

———. 1973. *Sicily and the Greeks: Studies in the Interrelationship between the Indigenous Populations and the Greek Colonists.* Ann Arbor.

Smart, J. D. 1967. "Kimon's Capture of Eion." *JHS* 87: 136–138.

Soltau, W. 1889. *Römische Chronologie.* Ch. 18, "Die Chronologie Diodor's," 367–386. Freiburg i.B.

Sordi, M. 1976. "Atene e Sparta dalle guerre persiane al 462–1 a.C." *Aevum* 50: 25–41.

Spoerri, W. 1959. *Späthellenistiche Berichte über Welt, Kultur, und Götter: Untersuchungen zu Diodor von Sizilien.* Basel.

———. 1991. "Diodorea." *MH* 48: 310–319.

Stadter, P. A. 1989. *A Commentary on Plutarch's Pericles.* Chapel Hill.

———. 1992. "Thinking about Historians." *AJPh* 113: 81–85.

Strogeckij, V. M. 1982. "Diodorus of Sicily and the Problem of Universal History." In *Concilium Eirene XVI*, 101–106. Prague.

Szegedy-Maszak, A. 1978. "Legends of the Greek Law-givers." *GRByS* 19: 199–209.

Talbert, R. J. A., ed. 2000. *Barrington Atlas of the Greek and Roman World*. Princeton. (Abbreviated *BA*.)

Tarn, W. W. 1948. *Alexander the Great*. Cambridge.

Thomas, R. 1992. *Literacy and Orality in Ancient Greece*. Cambridge.

Thomsen, R. 1972. *The Origin of Ostracism*. Copenhagen.

Tod, M. N. 1948. *A Selection of Greek Historical Inscriptions*. Vol. 2, *From 403 to 323 B.C.* Oxford.

Troilo, E. 1940–41. "Considerazioni su Diodoro Siculo e la sua storia universale." *Atti Ist. Ven.*: 17–42.

Turano, C. 1975. "Le conoscenze geografiche del Bruzio nell'antichità classica." *Klearchos* 17: 29–95.

Vallet, G. 1976. "Avenues, quartiers, et tribus à Thourioi, ou comment compter les cases d'un damier (à propos de Diod. xii, 10 et 11)." In *Mélanges offerts à Jacques Heurgon: L'Italie préromaine et la Rome Républicaine*, vol. 2, 1021–1032. Rome.

Vanderpool, E. N. 1973. "Ostracism at Athens." *Lectures in Memory of L. T. Semple* 2: 217–270.

Verdin, H., G. Schepens, and E. De Keyser, eds. 1990. *Purposes of History: Studies in Greek Historiography from the 4th to the 2nd Centuries B.C.* Leuven.

Vidal-Naquet, P. 1991. "Diodore et le Vieillard de Crète." In Casevitz 1991, ix–xxx.

Volquardsen, C. A. 1868. *Untersuchungen über die Quellen der griechischen und sicilischen Geschichten bei Diodor, Buch XI bis XVI*. Kiel.

von Fritz, K. 1967. "Zaleukos." *RE* IX A.2, cols. 2298–2301. Stuttgart.

von Matt, L. 1961. *Magna Graecia*. Explanatory text by U. Zanotti-Bianco. Trans. H. Hoffmann. New York.

Wachsmuth, C. 1892. *Über das Geschichtswerk des Sikelioten Diodors*. Leipzig.

———. 1895. *Einleitung in das Studium der alten Geschichte*. Leipzig.

Walbank, F. W. 1968–69. "The Historians of Greek Sicily." *Kokalos* 14/15: 476–498.

———. 1972. *Polybius*. Berkeley.

———. 1975. "*Symploke:* Its Role in Polybius' Histories." *YClS* 24: 197–212. (= Walbank 1985, 313–324.)

———. 1985. *Selected Papers: Studies in Greek and Roman History and Historiography*. Cambridge.

Walker, P. H. 1957. "The Purpose and Method of 'The Pentekontaetia' in Thucydides." *CQ* 51: 27–38.

Wallace, P. W. 1969. "Psyttaleia and the Trophies of the Battle of Salamis." *AJA* 73: 293–303, pls. 65–66.

Walters, K. R. 1978. "Diodorus 11.82–84 and the Second Battle of Tanagra." *AJAH* 3: 188–191.

Warmington, B. H. 1969. *Carthage*. 2d ed. London.

Wentker, H. 1956. *Sizilien und Athen: Die Begegnung der attischen Macht mit den Westgriechen*. Heidelberg.

White, M. E. 1964. "Some Agiad Dates: Pausanias and His Sons." *JHS* 84: 140–152.

Wickersham, J. 1994. *Hegemony and Greek Historians*. Lanham, Md.

Wiedemann, T. 1981. *Greek and Roman Slavery*. Baltimore.

Will, E. 1994. *Le Monde grec et l'Orient*. Vol. 1, *Le V$^e$ siècle (510–403)*. 5th ed. Paris.

Wilson, J. B. 1987. *Athens and Corcyra: Strategy and Tactics in the Peloponnesian War*. Bristol.

Woodhead, A. G. 1981. *The Study of Greek Inscriptions*. 2d ed. Cambridge.

Wycherley, R. E. 1978. *The Stones of Athens*. Princeton.

Zecchini, G. 1978. "L'atteggiamento di Diodoro verso Cesare e la composizione della Bibliotheca Historica." *Rend. Ist. Lomb.* 112: 13–20.

———. 1987. "La conoscenza di Diodoro nel tardantico." *Aevum* 61: 43–52.

# INDEX

All locators designate page numbers. Those in **bold** figures refer to the translation; a suffixed plain Roman n indicates that the topic is also mentioned in a footnote or footnotes on the corresponding page or pages.

Plain Roman locators with suffixed n indicate material mentioned in footnotes but not in the corresponding page of the translation.

Locators in *italics* refer to maps.

Arrangement of material within entries is predominantly chronological, though some material of a topical nature is alphabetically ordered.

and building of harbor at Piraeus, 100–101n
and inception of Delian League, 103–104n, 106–107n
ostracized, 253
Aristeus (Corinthian general), 231n
Ariston, tyrant of Athens, 22–23
aristocracies
Athenian, 115n, **152n**. *See also* Areopagos; Kimon
Delian League, 218n
Greek, and prestige of land victories, 63n
Roman patricians, 213–214n
Syracusan, 176n, 222n, 270
Aristodikos of Tanagra, 152n
Ariston (Athenian archon), **165, 265**
Aristophanes, 16n
Aristotle, 18, **178n**
armor, Persian and Greek styles of, **58**
Arnakes (Persian royal eunuch), 73n
Artabanos (Persian usurper), 119n, 120n, **137–138n**, 260
Artabazos (Persian satrap)
retreat after Plataia, **88, 89, 90n**
and Pausanias, 103n
campaigns in Cyprus and Egypt, 146n, **149–152n, 179–180n**, 262, 266
and Peace of Kallias, **182–183n**
Artaxerxes I, king of Persia
accession of, **138n**, 260
embassies from Greeks, 126n, 140n, 260
early reforms, **140n**, 261
and Egyptian revolt, **141–142n, 144–146n**
and Peace of Kallias, **182–184n**, 267
and Themistokles, **119n**, 260
Artaÿktes (Persian general), 95n
Artemision, *245*
amphibious Artemision-Thermopylai defense line, **54, 66n**, 254
battle of, 45, **64–65n**
Artemon of Klazomenai, 220n
Asopos River, **86, 87,** *245, 251*
Aspasia, 216n, 273
asphalt, Dead Sea, 4
assembly of Greeks. *See* congress, Greek
Astyages, 41

Astylos of Syracuse (Olympic victor), 10, **49n**
Athena, cult of
of the Brazen House (Poliachos), Sparta, **104–105n**
Parthenos, Athens; cult statue, 271
Athenaios of Naukratis, 12, 31n, 41
Athens, *245*
and battle of Salamis, 71n, 72n, 83n
Mardonios sacks, **84–85n**, 255
force at Plataia, **86, 87, 89, 90n**
commemoration of war dead, **91n**
rebuilding of walls, **97–99n, 106n**, 255
building of harbor at Piraeus and development of navy, **99–102n, 106n, 110–111n**, 256
famine (445), 184n, **185–186n, 192–193n, 228n**, 268
and Corinthian War, **227–228n, 229–230n**
and revolt of Potidaia, **230–231n, 234–235n**, 272–273
—Buildings and monuments, 178n, 271
Parthenon, 130n, 271
Pnyx, 234n
statues of Tolmides and Theainetos, 162n
*See also under* walls, defensive
—External relations
and grain and timber supplies, 103n, 184n, **185–186n, 189n, 192–193n, 225n, 227n, 228n, 240n**
naval power: rise in Persian War, **97–98, 100n, 106n, 165n**, 253; development after war, **99–102n, 106n, 110–111n**, 256; achieves supremacy, **110–111n**, 256; power after Eurymedon, **127–128**
regional supremacy, **178n**
and West, 184n, 186n, **188–189n, 228n, 233n**. *See also under* Leontinoi; Rhegion; Thourioi
*See also* colonization; Delian League; imperialism; *and under other states, particularly* Aigina; Argos; Boiotia; Corinth; Euboia; Megara; Persia; Sparta

Chalkis, Aitolia (Misolonghi), 164n, *245*
Chalkis, Euboia, 187n, 193n, *245*, 268
Chares (Athenian archon), **187**, 257
Charitimides (Athenian commander),
    145n, 150n
Charon of Lampsakos, 31, 40n, 41–42
Charondas (lawgiver, of Thourioi), 4, 39,
    195–206n, 207n
Chelidonian Isles, 184n, *246*
Chersonese, 169n, 193n, *246*, 266, 268
Chios, 54, 243, *246*
    and Samian revolt, 218n, **219**
Christian writers, 32–33, 34
chronology, 2
    achronic passages attached to particular
        years, 12
    Athenian archon lists, 2, 10, 11, 12, 18,
        23, 153n
    Christian writers and, 32
    dates of Diodorus' activities, 2, 4–6,
        7–8, 9, 238–239n
    Diodorus' system, 2, 10–12, 23, 32, 237–
        241; discrepancies between Greek
        and Roman, 49n, 83n, 99n, 107n,
        113–114n, 232n; supposed ignorance
        and 12.1.5, 34n, 178n
    Fasti as source of error, 10, 11, 23, 49n
    gaps in MSS, 12n, 173n
    Hellanikos', 18
    inclusive and exclusive counting of
        years, 173n
    of mythical history, 14
    official lists, 18
    Olympiads, 10, 11, 18, 21, 23, 237, 238
    Polybios', 21, 23
    terminal date of *Bibliotheke*, 34n, 237–
        241
    Thucydides', 10n, 129n, 150–151n
    Timaios', 10, 18, 21, 23
    years: 484/3, 253; 483/2, 253; 482/1, 254;
        481/0, 254; 480/79, 10, 11, **49–83**,
        254–255; 479/8, **83–96**, 255; 478/7,
        **96–99**, 255–256; 476/5, **107–109**,
        256; 475/4, **110–111**, 256–257; 474/3,
        **111**, 257; 473/2, **112**, 257; 472/1, **112**–
        **114**, 257; 471/0, **114–124**, 257–258;
        470/69, **124–128**, 258; 469/8, **128**–

**131**, 258; 468/7, **131–133**, 259; 467/6,
**133–134**, 259; 466/5, **134–137**, 259–
260; 465/4, **137–138**, 260; 464/3, **138**–
140, 260; 463/2, **140–144**, 261; 462/1,
**144–146**, 261–262; 461/0, **146–149**,
262; 460/59, **149–152**, 262–263;
459/8, **152–154**, 263; 458/7, **154–158**,
263–264; 457/6, **158–162**, 264; 456/5,
**162–164**, 265; 455/4, **164–165**, 265;
454/3, **165–168**, 265; 453/2, **168–173**,
265–266; 452/1, 173n, 266; 451/0,
**174–176**, 266; 450/49, **179–181**, 267;
449/8, **181–184**, 267; 448/7, **185**, 268;
447/6, **186**, 268; 446/5, **186–189**, 268;
445/4, **209**, 269; 444/3, **209–210**,
269; 443/2, **210–214**, 269; 442/1,
**214–215**, 269; 441/0, **216–221**, 270;
440/39, **221–222**, 270; 439/8, **222**–
**225**, 271; 438/7, **225–226**, 271; 437/6,
**226–227**, 271; 436/5, **227–229**, 271–
272; 435/4, **229–232**, 272; 434/3, **232**–
**233**, 272; 433/2, **233–234**, 272–273;
432/1, **234–235**, 273
Cilicia, *246*
    Persian forces pass through, 146n, 149n,
        180n, 262, 266
    ships in Persian navy, **51**, **54**, 71n, **72**, 125
Cincinnatus. See Quinctius Cincinnatus, L.
circulation of works, private, 9
citations of Diodorus by other writers, 12
citizenship
    Athenian law, 176n, 266
    Sicilians and Roman, 240
Civil Wars, Roman, 239–241
Claudius, M. (*cliens* of Ap. Claudius), 211n
cleruchies, Athenian, 169n. See also colo-
    nization: by Athens
Clodius, Sextus, 240
coinage
    Sicilian, 81n, 142n, 149n
    of Themistokles, at Magnesia on the
        Maiandros, 122n
colonization
    by Akragas, 109n, 256
    by Athens, 169n, 192–193n, 209n,
        266, 268, 269. See also Amphipolis;
        Histiaia; Skyros; Thourioi

foreign, in Sicily, 113n, 135n, 154n, 257; revolt in Syracuse, 137n, 143–144n, 147, 260, 261–262; settlement in Messenia, 148–149n, 262

Messana. *See* Zankle

Messenia, *245*

    revolt, 128–131n, 149n, 156n, 259–263 *passim;* end, 154n, 156n, 161–162n, 164n, 263

    mercenaries from Sicily settled in, 148–149n, 262

metals, precious, 139n, 183n, 227n, 228n, 253

Methana, 163n, *245,* 265

Methone (Messenia), 163n, *245*

metics, Athenian (resident aliens), 102n

Meton: and revision of Athenian calendar, 233–234n, 272

Mikythos, tyrant of Rhegion and Zankle, 107–108n, 133–134n, 256, 259

    founds Pyxous, 124n, 133n, 257

Miletos, *246*

    contingent at Mykale, 93–94n

    and Sybaris, 190n

    war with Samos, 216n, 220n, 270

    revolts, 267, 268

military service, law on, 202n

Milo of Kroton (Olympic victor), 191n

Miltiades, 178n

mines

    Laurion, 183n, 253

    Thracian, Mt. Pangaios, 139n, 227n

Mithridates (Persian court eunuch), 137–138n

Mnesitheides (Athenian archon), 158, 264

moderation (ἐπιείκεια), 7, 38, 241

Molossis, 118–119n, *245*

monarchy, Diodorus' admiration for, 38

morale of Greeks during Persian War, 69, 70n, 78, 92n

morality, modern historians' retrojection of own, xi, 38

moralizing, xi

    Christian writers and, 32

    Ephoros, 16

    Poseidonios of Apamea, 22

Theopompos of Chios, 16–17, 18, 20

Timaios, 18–19

    *See also under* Diodorus Siculus

Morgantina, 154n, *247,* 263

Morychides (Athenian archon), 219n, 221, 270

motivation, ad hominem, xi, 16, 23, 38

Motyon, 74n, 174n, 175, 176n, *247,* 266

Mycenae, 131–133n, *245,* 259

Mykale, *246*

    battle of, 45, 70n, 91–94n, 96, 255

Mylae, 7, *247*

Myous, 121n

myriarch/chiliarch theory on troop figures, 46–47, 74n

Myronides son of Kallias, 155n, 159–162n, 178n, 186n, 263, 264

Myrrhinusios (Athenian archon), 271

Mysia, 51

myth

    Alexander's conquests lead to reworking of, 19

    Diodorus and, 3, 8–9, 12, 13, 14, 38

    Ephoros and, 15, 16

    exempla from, 3, 13, 16

Mytilene, 218n, 219, *246*

Naupaktos, 164n, *245,* 265

Naxos, island of, 42, 119n, *246,* 258

    Athenian colonization, 169n, 170n, 266

Naxos, Sicily, 109n, *247,* 256

Neapolis, *248,* 269

Nemea, *245*

    Panhellenic games, 132

Nicolson, Harold, ix

Niebuhr, Barthold Georg, 33–34

Nikodemos (Athenian archon), 253

Nikogenes (Themistokles' host), 120n

Nikomedes son of Kleomenes, 156n

Nineveh, Diodorus' location of, 29n

Nisaia, 154n, 187n, *245*

Nock, A. D., 1

Nomai, 175n, 266

numbers, exaggeration of, 50n, 56n, 59n, 77n, 86n, 242–243

    chiliad-myriad confusion, 46–47, 74n

universal history, 13–15, 19–23, 32
urban grid planning, 80n, 188n, 193–194n
utopias, 4, 20, 23

Valca, Fossa di, 113–114n
Valerio-Horatian Laws, 211n, 214–215n, 267
Valerius Potitus, L. (*cos.* 449), 211n, 213n, 214–215n, 267
Veii, 113n, 256
vengeance, divine, 3
Verginia, 211–212n
Verginius, L., 212n
Verres, C., 6
Volquardsen, C. A., 24–25, 26
Volsci, 96n, 225n, *248,* 268
"vulgate tradition," x, xi, 31, 38, 39–42
    Ctesias as example, 42–47
    value, 36–37, 39–40, 42–47

walls, defensive
    Athens: city and Akropolis, 97–99n, 106n, 128n, 255; Long Walls to Piraeus, 157n, 165n, 263, 265
    Isthmus, 69, 85n
    Megara-Nisaia, 187n
    Pallene, 273
    Thebes, 159
    walling rituals in new cities, 193–194n
war-years, chronology using, 10n
Wesseling, Peter, 33

White Fort, Memphis, 145n, 146n, 149–152n, 261, 262
Wilamowitz-Moellendorff, Ulrich von, 1
wine, law on drinking unmixed, 207n
women, Diodorus' attitude to, 4, 38, 200–201

Xanthippos (Athenian archon), 255
Xanthippos son of Ariphron (Athenian general), 84, 91, 94, 95n, 100–101n, 253
Xenokritos (founder of Thourioi), 192n
Xenophanes of Kolophon, 134n
Xenophon of Corinth (Olympic victor), 138n
Xenophon son of Gryllus (historian), xii, 24–25
Xerxes, king of Persia
    expedition to Greece, 49–73, *250*
    and defeat at Mykale, 94
    and Pausanias, 102–103n
    assassination, 119n, 120n, 137–138n, 260
    reversal of fortune, 177

Zakynthos, 163n, *245, 248,* 265
Zaleukos (lawgiver of Epizephyrian Lokroi), 4, 39, 196n, 203n, 204n, 206–209n
Zankle (Messana), 107–108n, 148n, *247, 248,* 262